Gender Discrimination and Inequality in Contemporary India:
Dimensions and Voices of Protests

Gender Discrimination and Inequality in Contemporary India:
Dimensions and Voices of Protests

Ed.

Jaya Shrivastava

KALPAZ

First Published, 2018

Published by

Kalpaz Publications
C-30, Satyawati Nagar,
Delhi – 110052
E-mail: kalpaz@hotmail.com
Ph.: 9212142040

Printed at: G. Print Process, Delhi

Cataloging in Publication Data—DK
Courtesy: D.K. Agencies (P) Ltd. <docinfo@dkagencies.com>

Shrivastava, Jaya, Ed.
Gender discrimination and inequality in contemporary India : dimensions and voices of protests / Jaya Shrivastava.
pages cm
Includes bibliographical references.
ISBN 9789386397270 (HB)

1. Sex discrimination against women—India. 2. Women—India—Social conditions. 3. Women—India—Economic conditions. 4. Women—Government policy—India. 5. Protest movements—India. 6. Equality—India. I. Title.

LCC HQ1237.5.I4S57 2018 | DDC 305.420954 23

Contents

III. ECONOMIC DIMENSION

IV. DEVELOPMENT POLICIES AND PROGRAMMES

V. VOICES OF PROTESTS

Preface

This book is an outcome of a National Seminar on "Gender Discrimination and Inequalities in Contemporary India: Status, Causes and Solutions (GDICI-2014)" held on November 11-12, 2014 at the Department of Sociology of Babasaheb Bhimrao Ambedkar University (A Central University), Lucknow, India to discuss, address and analyze a range of issues related to the status and causes of gender discrimination and inequalities in India from interdisciplinary perspectives and to explore appropriate solutions to the age-old marginalisation of women. Gender discrimination and inequalities is the most challenging societal problem of the human society in general and the Indian society in particular. It concerns the half of the humanity, i.e. women who are the basis of human reproduction, nurture and survival. All humans are born free but women have remained enchained for ages in varying forms despite society passing from various successive phases of development. Women continue to be discriminated in multiple ways in many new ways, in addition to the age-old discriminatory ways, even in the current age of globalisation. It is true that women's status varies across social and physical spaces, but they all suffer from multi-fold discriminations - social, economic, political, cultural – which cut across caste, class, community and territorial boundaries.

Gender-based discrimination and inequalities in India have been structural in nature. Women have been discriminated in both the public and private spheres. They have been deprived of right to property; have dismal and ineffective representation in political domain and little say in decision making even at the family level; they are considered and treated as socially inferior to men. Their discrimination has been structural and is institutionalised. Their systemic discrimination has effaced their identity, autonomy, representation and voice. Gender discrimination is deeply ingrained in Indian culture which dialectically sustains gender-based structural inequalities in different spheres of life. India gained Independence in 1947 with the noble vision of transforming the society from being a highly gendered system which crushed women into a gender just system. Along with growth several special affirmative policies and measures have been adopted by the Indian state for creating a society free from gender based discriminations and inequalities. Women have also not remained a mute spectator. There have been women's movements of varied colours in India which put incessant pressure on the state, the civil society and in the private sphere to ameliorate the condition of Indian women.

As a result, the status of a small section of women has improved but even they are still treated as socially inferior and discriminated and dominated over in the public and private spaces. A large mass of women continues to be exploited, oppressed. Women are increasingly viewed as objects and commodities of consumption, as reflected in the rising incidents of crimes against women all over in the contemporary world, and more so in India. Such a situation shocks our conscience and makes it imperative to ponder over seriously and sincerely in an alternative way to understand the plight of women and visualise and strategise for the most appropriate action so that women become free from all types of discriminations and inequalities. Keeping this in mind, the theme of the book was conceptualised which focus on understanding exactly the status of women in contemporary India, knowing the basic causes of gender discrimination and inequalities, and the ways and strategies to establish a fully gender just society.

The present book includes selected papers presented at the seminar which have been revised and updated by the contributors for the purpose of publication. The volume is thematically divided into five sections besides the Introduction chapter. Introduction (chapter 1), first, briefly discusses the conceptual framework of gender discrimination and inequality drawing from the feminist literature on the subject and thereafter gives details about the chapters included in the volume.

Section I of the volume deals with the conceptual dimension of the theme of gender discrimination and inequality. It includes three chapters (chapters 2-4) which cover certain aspects of the conceptual discourse on gender in social science, including the issue of sexual minorities and also the philosophical issue of gender-based divisiveness of consciousness. Section II consists of four chapters (chapters 5-8) covering some of the important issues of gender discrimination and inequality in India in the social and cultural domains which deal with gender socialisation, female infanticide, marriage and divorce of Muslim women, legal profession, mental health issue of women in prison, and access to mobile phone. Section III includes four chapters (chapters 9-12) which focus on gender discrimination and inequality in economic domain pertaining to some important economic issues, viz., land ownership, work participation, wage and also impact of development-induced displacement which is common in the process of increasing industrialisation and urbanisation in the country. Section IV comprises six chapters (chapters 13-18) which discuss some of the state policies and programmes for ameliorating the status of women in India after Independence, viz., rights of women against sexual harassment at workplace, Tribal women SHGs, SHG-Bank linkage programme, MGNREGA, and utilisation of health services by women. Section V includes two chapters (chapters 19-20) in which it provides a brief analysis of mobilisations and movements by women and a glimpse of certain voices of protests against gender discrimination and inequality in literature.

I am grateful to Babasaheb Bhimrao Ambedkar University (A Central University) and Indian Council of Social Science Research (ICSSR) for providing financial support for organizing the seminar. I am thankful to all the delegates who presented their papers and actively participated and made the deliberations highly engaging and enriching in the seminar, especially Key-Note Speaker of the Inaugural Session of the Seminar Prof. Maitrayee Choudhuri (Professor of Sociology (JNU), who provided an extensive and critical overview of the Discourse of Gender within Sociological framework. Further, I am indeed grateful to Prof. Nandu Ram (JNU), Prof. Rajesh Gill (Punjab University), Prof. Abha Chauhan (University of Jammu, Jammu) and Dr. Indrani Mukherjee (CWDS, New Delhi) from the core of my heart for having given us a very enlightening and enriching understanding in the seminar. I extend my heartfelt thanks to Prof. A. K. Kaul (BHU, Varanasi), Prof. Jaikant Tiwary (BHU, Varanasi), Prof. Ajeet Pandey (BHU, Varanasi), Dr. Santosh K. Rai (BU, Jhansi), Prof. Nikhil Kumar (VKSU, Ara), Dr. Manoj K. Jena (JNU), Dr. Suresh Babau (JNU), Prof. B. N. Prasad (ANSISS, Patna), Prof. Nishi Pandey (L.U., Lucknow), Prof. Ranu Uniyal (L.U.), Prof. Preeti Saxena (BBAU, Lucknow), Prof. Vishwa Vallabh (XLRI, Jamshedpur), Prof. Sanjay Salunke (Dr. Babasaheb Ambedkar Marathwada University, Aurangabad) and Prof. N. M. P. Verma (BBAU, Lucknow) for sharing their insightful thoughts on the topic and to make the discussion stimulating. My gratitude is due to many friends and colleagues who helped me to organize the seminar. Among them, special mention must be made of Prof. Kameshwar Choudhary for his candid comments and suggestions on the volume, Prof. B. B. Malik, Prof. Manish K. Verma, Prof. B. N. Dubey, Dr. Brajesh Kumar and Dr. Rachana Gangwar. I extend my thanks to non-teaching staff Ajay Kumar, Swapnesh Mishra and Rajiv Ranjan Pandey who supported me during the seminar.

My vote of thanks could not be complete without mentioning the role of my parents, siblings, and my husband who have been a constant source of love, care, support and strength throughout the work. I am thankful to Mr. Mukul Srivastava, my husband for encouraging me to get it done. I am ever grateful to my mother Mrs. Savita Srivastava and my father Mr. S. N. P. Srivastava who encouraged me day and night to make it possible. I dedicate this work to my parents with love and respect.

Contributors

1. **Indrani Mazumdar**, Sr. Fellow & Associate Professor, Centre for Women's Development Studies, New Delhi.
2. **Vishwa Ballabh**, Professor of Economics, Chairperson-Entrepreneurship Development Centre and Coordinator- Centre for Rural Management at XLRI, Jamshedpur.
3. **G.S. Mehta**, Professor, Giri Institute of Development Studies, Lucknow.
4. **Sanatan Nayak**, Professor, Department of Economics, Babasaheb Bhimrao Ambedkar University (A Central University), Lucknow.
5. **Gopal Singh**, Professor, Department of Mass Communication & Journalism, Babasaheb Bhimrao Ambedkar University (A Central University), Lucknow.
6. **Preeti Misra,** Professor, Department of Human Rights, Babasaheb Bhimrao Ambedkar University (A Central University), Lucknow.
7. **Nikhil Kumar**, Professor, University Department of English, V. K. S. University, Arrah, Bihar.
8. **Lakkineni Mallaiah**, Associate Professor, Department of Economics, Babasaheb Bhimrao Ambedkar University (A Central University), Lucknow.
9. **Kailash Chandra Sharma**, Faculty Member, Bankers Institute of Rural Development. Lucknow.
10. **Jaya Shrivastava,** Associate Professor, Department of Sociology, Babasaheb Bhimrao Ambedkar University (A Central University), Lucknow.
11. **Shiv Kumar Yadav**, Associate Professor, Department of English, College of Commerce, Patna.
12. **Niharranjan Mishra,** Associate Professor, Department of Humanities and Social Sciences, NIT Rourkela, Odisha.
13. **Anuja**, Assistant Professor, Centre for the Study of Discrimination and Exclusion, School of Social Sciences, Jawaharlal Nehru University (JNU), New Delhi.

14. **Rajeev K. Kumar,** Assistant Professor, Division of Sociology and Social Anthropology, A. N. Sinha Institute of Social Studies, Patna.
15. **Ginni Braj,** Assistant Professor, Department of Political Science, National P.G. College, Lucknow.
16. **Vandana Singh**, Associate Professor (History), Dr. Ram Manohar Lohiya, National Law University, Lucknow.
17. **Asif Akhtar Khan**, Assistant Professor, Department of Management Studies, CIPET, Ministry of Chemicals and Fertilizers, Lucknow.
18. **Mukesh Bharti,** Research Scholar, Department of Human Rights, School for Legal Studies, Babasaheb Bhimrao Ambedkar University (A Central University), Lucknow.
19. **Ritu Agarwal,** Assistant Professor, Amity University, Lucknow Campus.
20. **Faisal Akhtar,** Research Scholar, Department of Business Administration, DDU Gorakhpur University, Gorakhpur.
21. **Malti Singh**, Research Scholar, Department of Economics, Babasaheb Bhimrao Ambedkar University (A Central University), Lucknow.
22. **Shivani Tiwari,** Research Scholar, Department of Economics, Babasaheb Bhimrao Ambedkar University (A Central University), Lucknow.
23. **Dinabandhu Sahoo**, Research Scholar, Department of Humanities and Social Sciences, NIT, Rourkela, Odisha.
24. **Bhavna Suman**, Guest Faculty, Department of Political Science, Babasaheb bhimrao Ambedkar (Central) University, Lucknow.
25. **Md. Taique Anwer,** Project Fellow, Centre of Advanced Study, Department of History, Aligarh Muslim University, Aligarh.
26. **Neelu Sharma,** Research Scholar, Department of Mass Communication & Journalism, Babasaheb Bhimrao Ambedkar University (A Central University), Lucknow.
27. **Pooja Batra,** Fellow in Management, IIM Indore. Prior to joining IIM Indore as fellow she was Research Associate, Working on issues related to rural deprivation, health and leadership development at XLRI School of Management, Jamshedpur.

List of Table

List of Figures

1

Introduction

— ***Jaya Shrivastava***

Gender discrimination and inequalities are prevalent in society, operational and visible in daily life at the level of the individual, family, community and society at large and reflected institutionally as well as in social and cultural norms. In a society like India where stereotypical gender roles and norms are strongly enforced/ ascribed to/institutionalised, women are systematically discriminated in multiple ways which obliterated their identity, autonomy, representation and voice. In fact, gender-based discrimination and inequalities have been imperative features of Indian society and structural in nature for centuries covering the socio-cultural, economic and political domains of life. The status of women in India differs along, class, caste, and community lines; hence the nature and magnitude of discrimination, inequalities and violence also vary. Social hierarchy, class structure, cultural variations and distribution of power and privileges make the situation complex. It is widely observed that women belonging to different social classes, races, ethnic and age groups are more vulnerable than their male counterparts of the same social class/ group. They have been discriminated in both the public and private spheres. In the past, they were deprived of right to property; they were not permitted to have representation in political sphere and decision making even at the local level; they were not supposed to have access to education; they were considered and treated as socially inferior to men. Even in contemporary society, women have less ownership of assets and property and they earn less - they are paid less than men for equal work. Also women are less skilled and have fewer opportunities to develop skills and have fewer decision making possibilities within the family and in public sphere. They face greater risk of sexual abuse, domestic and other forms of violence and are often dominated by male members in the family. Gender discrimination is institutionalised and deeply ingrained in Indian culture which dialectically sustains gender-based structural inequalities in different spheres of life viz social, political, economic, cultural etc.

This chapter provides a theoretical framework of issues related to gender discrimination and inequality in order to develop a clear understanding of the issue under discussion. Gender discrimination refers to inequality or difference in the access to resources by gender. Several reports [Blackden and Bhanu (1999); International Labour Organisation (1995)] claim that in many countries women face difficulty in accessing human capital, land and financial or other assets. Gender inequality can be conceptualised and assessed from various perspectives. According to Vina Mazumdar (n.d.), "Gender inequality is just part of a more pervasive inequality among the various sections of the population…the task of redressing inequality is enormous, and the job of establishing gender equality is formidable…". Like many other societies the Indian society has been highly inegalitarian in many ways like caste and class based inequalities and patriarchal domination reflected in multi-fold gender based inequalities – social, cultural, economic, political, educational. Gender is an all-encompassing form of inequality, as it operates across all classes, castes and communities. Derez and Sen (2013: p. 214) affirm that economic and social factors such as class, gender or race, that contribute to inequalities, do not function in isolation but are interlinked and the 'mutual reinforcement of inequalities' get further strengthened with addition of every new dimension of inequality. Sen (1992:125) has conceptualised gender inequality from a capability perspective. He states that "the question of gender inequality…can be understood much better by comparing those things that intrinsically matter (such as functionings and capabilities), rather than just the means (to achieve them) like…resources".

Various studies have defined multidimensional gender inequality indices which measure inequality in capabilities like Sen. For the conceptualisation of gender inequality in post-industrialised western as well as developing societies, Ingrid Robeyns (2003; 71-72) has proposed a list of capabilities after comparing the lists proposed by Sabina Alkire (2002); Alkire and Black (1997), Martha Nussbaum (1995, 2000) and Swedish approach to the quality of life measurement (Robert Erikson 1992). This list includes Life and Physical health, Mental Well-being, Bodily integrity and safety, social relations, political empowerment, education and knowledge, domestic work and nonmarket care, paid work and other projects, shelter and environment, mobility, leisure activities, time-autonomy, respect, religion. Earlier Nussbaum (1995;83-5;2000:78-86) proposed a list of capabilities which has ten dimensions viz. life, bodily health, bodily integrity, sense, imagination and thought, emotions, practical reason, affiliation, other species, play and control over one's environment. Therefore, inequalities in resources can be considered as an important reason of inequalities in capabilities. Agarwal (1994) has argued that "the gender gap in the ownership and control of property is the single most critical contributor to the gender gap in economic well-being, social status, and empowerment". In case of India Naila Kabeer (2015: p.203) clearly affirms that that gender inequality is structured into the organisation of social relations in society, as fundamentally as class is in capitalist societies, as race was in apartheid South Africa, and as caste is in India.

The issue of gender equality has been an important concern in the modernizing and developing societies, including India in the modern period. This is very clearly reflected in the vision and provisions of the Indian Constitution. Moving towards establishing a gender-just society has been a developmental concern for which different policies and programmes have been in operation after Independence of the country. This involves reducing gender-based inequalities in the society in different domains of life – economic, social, cultural, political and thus achieving gender equity.

No doubt the degree of gender discrimination and inequalities has reduced after India's Independence in 1947 as a result of the country's growth and special affirmative policies and measures adopted by the Indian state. Moreover, there has been women's movement in India which has put pressure on the state to ameliorate the condition of Indian women. India's neo-liberal globalisation in recent decades made the country the second fastest growing economy in the world. But it has not been able to stop gender discrimination and inequalities. Besides the conventional domains, new globally-linked spaces have emerged which witness gender discrimination and inequalities. The fact remains even today that women lag far behind men and face inequalities due to continuing gender discrimination which is prevalent in both public and private (family) spheres.

Whatever might be the contradictions and complications in assessing the status of women in India, the fact remains that the overwhelming majority of Indian women are discriminated against and denied their fundamental right to survival, access to resources and control over their production. The practice of prenatal sex selection, higher rates of mortality rates among very young girls, and lower rates of school enrolment for girls as compared with for boys, suggest that 'son preference' is curtailing the access of girl children to food, education and health care. This is often compounded by the increasing use of technologies to determine foetal sex, resulting in abortion of female foetuses. Among those women who do receive the benefits of health and education, many of them unable to contribute fully and productively to the economy because of barriers to their entry into the workforce or barriers to assessing positions of leadership. The available data also reveals that Indian women still remain under-represented in political leadership and decision-making. So, there are several challenges in the way of eliminating discrimination against Indian women, their backwardness and violence against them, and ensuring complete gender justice in all spheres of life – social, economic, cultural, political – covering both the public and private spheres. This would require concerted efforts on the part of the state in particular and the society in general.

The role of women's groups and organisations would be crucial here. Women's organisations and activists would contribute more effectively if they share their best practice exchange and forge partnerships and networks at different levels –local, regional, national and global.

Present volume attempts to understand: (i) what would be the most appropriate theoretical perspective to understand gender discrimination and inequalities in India? (ii) What are the nature, magnitude and causes of gender discrimination and inequalities in contemporary India in different spheres of life? (iii) What approaches and measures have been adopted by the Indian State and women's organisations for promoting gender justice; (iv) What are the challenges and required approach, strategy, policy and programmes to drastically reduce and end gender discrimination and inequalities and achieve complete gender justice in contemporary globalizing India?

SUMMARY OF BOOK CHAPTERS

Chapter 1: Introduction

It, first, briefly discusses the conceptual framework of gender discrimination and inequality drawing from the feminist literature on the subject and thereafter gives details about the chapters included in the volume.

SECTION I: CONCEPTUAL ASPECTS

Section I includes three chapters (i.e. 2-4) which cover the conceptual discourse on gender in social science from a critical angle, including the issue of sexual minorities, and also delves into the philosophical question of gender divisiveness of consciousness.

Chapter 2 contributed by Shiv Kumar Yadav is titled "Gender Discrimination and Inequalities: Status, Causes and Solutions". It views the gender issue a holistic way with a critical eye on its dominant conceptualisation. It goes beyond including only men and women under this concept and includes the third gender i.e. transgender as well who have been traditionally ignored and marginalised in the conceptualisation. It rightly avers that the gender discrimination must be redefined in the new consciousness and ever growing boundaries of humanism. It discusses critically the status of women's discrimination and its causes drawing heavily from literature and suggests holistic solutions to the problem. An appreciable attempt is made to underline the underlying challenges regarding gender discrimination and inequalities in India that are deeply rooted in collective consciousness as well as unconsciousness which is very much contradictory to the ancient concept of 'Ardhnareeshwar' and 'androgyny' of the modern times. The opportunities available today in India are highlighted that lie in the spirit and process of modernisation and globalisation to eradicate the gender discrimination and inequalities which is a crime against half the humanity.

Chapter 3 by Bharti and Misra is titled "Discourse on Gender Discrimination and Inequality in India with Special Reference to Sexual Minorities". It very perceptively examines the concepts of sex and gender, the mention of former being almost a taboo, particularly in public, and highly ignored in academic research, and gender being a social construct. It is noted that the studies on gender are mainly based on viewing male and female as constituting a binary system. It is points out that there are several issues which remain uncovered in the binary conceptualisation of gender and discusses in detail the case of sexual minorities, popularly known as lesbian, gay, bisexual and transgender (LGBT). It views gender discrimination and inequalities as incidences and consequences of differentiating between males and females in society because of certain presumptions, thoughts, behaviours and identity, and most importantly the social norms. It affirms that the binary construction of gender is inadequate to understand all human beings as it isolates and discriminates especially against the LGBTs. Hence, it is aptly noted that the current debates on gender discourse and discrimination/inequality focusing on LGBTs are very rightly breaking the binary view on gender which has been dominant till the recent years.

Nikhil Kumar proceeds beyond the sociological in **Chapter 4** in his chapter on "Gender Discrimination and Inequality: A Case of the Divisiveness of Consciousness". He enters into the philosophical realm wherein he explains the reality of present terrestrial existence of human beings bedeviled with gender discrimination and inequality, its causes and the solution. He examines the issue mainly from the perspective of a celebrated modern Indian philosopher Sri Aurobindo who basically takes an idealist/spiritualist position holding that the terrestrial existence of the man has two parts, at the centre is the Soul, the Divine Self, the Atman which manifests in its instruments that include the body, the life and the mind. At the present evolutionary phase the instrumental selves are in command of the being of man wherein the mental consciousness is under the gravitational pull of Matter i.e. the material world and that causes divisiveness and the assertion of divisive consciousness in the being of man, whose manifestation is found in gender discrimination and inequality. So, the task of putting an end to gender discrimination and inequality shall, Kumar holds, require of man to undergo triple transformation to get rid of the gravitational pull of Matter and thus lose the divisiveness of the mental consciousness and acquire higher state of spiritual 'supramental consciousness' marking an end to the divisive principle of consciousness resolving the conflict between the two genders causing gender discrimination and inequality with the realisation of the One Divine providing perfect harmony between the two genders as visualised in the ancient Indian concept of *ardhanarishwar*, an integral picture of the two genders.

SECTION II: SOCIAL DIMENSION

Section II focuses on discussing the social and cultural dimensions of gender discrimination and inequality. It includes four chapters (i.e. 5-8) dealing with different aspects of the issue ranging from gender discrimination in primary socialisation of children to the modern world of legal profession.

Here, in **Chapter 5**, Ritu Agrawal very succinctly analyses the issue of "Gender Socialisation and Faces of Gender Inequality". She defines gender socialisation as the learning of behavior and attitudes regarded in society as appropriate for a given sex. The socialisation process involves both conscious and unconscious teaching and learning of various social norms and values. Males and females are socialised in the human society. Boys are socialised i.e. taught and learn to be boys and girls to be girls. The socialisation of females stresses on their future primary adult roles as mothers and child-rearers whereas male socialisation on family provider. As a result males and females develop different personality traits, not their biology. She explains two phases of socialisation, viz. primary socialisation process which happens in the childhood and secondary socialisation process which occurs at the later stage in life. She analyses the role of different agencies of socialisation, such as family, education system, religion, mass media, workplace, etc. in reproducing and reinforcing the gender role stereotypes. Moving further, seven faces of gender inequalities in India are explained and some statistical data are provided showing gender inequalities. Major factors responsible for gender inequalities are also indicated. Certain policies and programmes have been implemented by the government for reducing gender inequalities but the problem continues to persist. So, it is affirmed that a new agenda of action is needed to combat and put an end to gender inequalities in the country and move ahead towards all-inclusive growth and development.

Chapter 6 by Anuja is captioned "Social Exclusion of Women: Discriminatory Practices in Contemporary Times" in which she presents an analysis of social discrimination and exclusion of women in contemporary India. She begins with briefly clarifying the concept of social exclusion referring to the nuanced academic debate on the issue. Then she moves on to discussing in detail social exclusion of women in India in several important domains, such as their social identity, education, health, employment, labour force participation and political participation. She clearly shows the gender inequalities still persisting in these spheres of life in the country. It is observed that social discrimination and their exclusion of women begin from the mother's womb and if she is fortunate enough to survive then occurs at home, later at school, at workplace, in politics, and so on. It is held that even though the extent of discrimination and exclusion has declined over the years, women continue to face discrimination and exclusion in different spheres of life. Hence, some steps are suggested to deal with this problem. It is affirmed that the overall policy of inclusion should be such that social justice is achieved for the society as a whole ensuring at the same time inclusion of women in all spheres of social life.

In **Chapter 7**, "Locating the Status of Muslim Women through the Discourse on Marriage and Divorce Laws", Vandana Singh critically examines the socio-economic injustice suffered by Muslim women by especially locating them within the laws governing marriage (issues of *mehr* and polygamy) and divorce. She analyses the widespread tendency to posit women's rights against community rights of Muslims and its adverse impact on Muslim women as individuals in the larger socio-political milieu. It is observed that the state whose support is crucial for promoting the interests of this extremely disadvantaged and vulnerable group too has arguably at least been found wanting in its efforts, if not abdicated its responsibility towards Muslim women . Hence, it emerges that the appropriation of women's issues by a vocal and politically influential male Muslim constituency poses a considerable challenge to Muslim women's rights effectively excluding from consideration the economic, political, and social concerns that define the everyday experiences of Muslim women in India today which needs to be dealt with at the earliest.

In **Chapter 8**, "Gender Inequality and Mobile Phones: Problems and Conclusion for Developing Countries", Faisal Akhtar and Asif Akhtar Khan deal with the broader issue of gender inequality and new technology, mobile phones in this case. Modern technology is said to promote development. But does it do so for both men and women. The authors note that in the beginning mobile phone became mostly accessible to men but slowly it started reaching to women as well. They show that gender gap still prevails in access to mobile phones and hugely so in less developed and developing countries, including India. They affirm that women empowerment facilitates economic development and poverty reduction. They elaborate on how access to mobile phones is benefiting women in multiple ways. Mobile phones are contributing to reduction in gender discrimination and empowering women through education besides providing them easy reach to their parental family and friends in need of crisis. The authors also indicate the major barriers hindering women's access to use the technology which contribute to perpetuating gender inequalities. It is argued here that mobile phones are a boon for women and girls to deal with the present challenges of continuing gender discrimination.

SECTION III: ECONOMIC DIMENSION

Section III focuses on gender discrimination and inequality prevailing in the economic domain of life pertaining to very important economic issues affecting the life of people, viz, land ownership, work participation, wage and also impact of development-induced displacement which is inevitable in the process of increasing industrialisation and urbanisation in the country. This section includes four chapters (i.e. 9-12).

In **Chapter 9** Indrani Mazumdar examines, How does one approach gender, labour and women's work in a country of sub-continental proportions, where across more than 6 decades since independence from colonial rule, the proportions of people living in rural areas has wound down from 83% to 68% (census 2011), but where urban areas still account for just a third of the population; in an endogenously multi-lingual, multi-ethnic country of immense regional diversity that is yet uniquely and almost universally defined by graded hierarchies of caste by birth;and where despite its illegality, stigmatisation of some castes and also of some forms of labour remains a widespread practice; where cultural taboos on women performing some specific tasks such as ploughing set the tone for restrictive gender segregation in work, and employment, but where the last census recorded that 43 per cent of the country's agricultural labourers and 30 per cent of the class of cultivators were women - together constituting 37 per cent of the 263 million people working in agriculture; where certain occupations such as paid domestic work have become rapidly feminised - within a broader pattern of a male dominated industrial and service workforce that has left women with a mere 24 per cent share of the 168 million strong workforce in non-agriculture; or in a country where colonial deindustrialisation and siphoning away of surpluses ensured that a vast base of mass poverty was inbuilt as a foundational context to post-colonial development ; and where after close to seven decades of independence, through two principal stages of state led self-reliance oriented capitalist development (1950s to 1980s) followed by two and a half decades of liberalisation/ globalisation and market led capitalist growth (1991 onwards), the agrarian question and mass poverty have yet to be resolved.

Difficult and full of pitfalls though it is, this paper seeks to present an outline of gendered trends and patterns of employment in contemporary India alongside a quick overview of some of the more longstanding debates around women's work that have emerged from women's studies in India.

In **Chapter 10**, Mallaiah and Singh examine "Gender Discrimination in Distribution of Land and Occupation in Uttar Pradesh". Based on secondary sources of data, they present analysis of gender inequality in distribution of operational landholding and operated area of land across caste groups, viz. general castes, scheduled castes (SCs) and scheduled tribes (STs). Gender gap in occupational distribution of workers belonging to the category of cultivators, agricultural workers, household workers and other workers is discussed for the census period 1971-2011. In addition, it is shown that gender gap in population distribution and in literacy across caste groups continues to be adverse towards women for the same census period. Further, some steps are suggested to address the problem of persisting gender discrimination and inequalities. Analysis of gender gap from the vantage point of caste stratification in society is a distinct feature of this chapter.

In **Chapter 11**, Shivani Tiwari and Sanatan Nayak deliberate upon "Gender Discrimination in Wage and Employment: A Case Study in Lucknow and Rae Bareilly Districts" wherein they cover the issues of land ownership, work participation rate and wages. Based on primary data collected from a sample drawn from Lucknow and Raibareilly districts of Uttar Pradesh, they empirically demonstrate how women suffer from economic discrimination and inequality across caste groups, viz. general, other backward classes (OBCs) and scheduled castes (SCs), and note the status of SC women being the worst. In view of this, they suggest several measures including changes in policy, effective enforcement of existing rules and raising awareness of women gender discrimination about their rights.

In **Chapter 12**, Sahoo and Mishra critically deliberate upon "Development-Induced Displacement, Gender and Women's Movement" under the current regime of globalisation, liberalisation and privatisation. They discuss this issue in general and in the context of Kalinga Nagar Integrated Industrial complex in the state of Orissa in particular. Based on data collected through using the research tools of participant observation, informal interview, focused group discussion and also secondary sources, it is shown how in development-induced displacement gender discrimination has been perpetuated in the policy of resettlement and rehabilitation, despite some recent improvements, as well as in its implementation. Gender discrimination is found to be reflected both in terms of more adverse impact of such displacement on women and in benefits of rehabilitation and resettlement accruing from the development projects.

SECTION IV: DEVELOPMENT POLICIES & PROGRAMMES

In Section IV, there are six chapters which deal with some of the development policies and programmes for promoting development of women and thereby tackling the problem of gender-based discrimination and inequality in the country. In **Chapter 13**, Ginni Braj offers "An Insight into the State Policy and Programmes for Women's Empowerment in India". Here the author provides a brief overview of the constitutional provisions and legislations, policies and programmes meant for women's empowerment. In addition, the author gives some details about the crimes against women which are perpetrated despite several legal provisions, policies and programmes being in place, which shows the need for further efforts required for enhancing gender justice.

In **Chapter 14**, Bhavna Suman discusses the issue of "Rights of Women against Sexual Harassment at the Workplace in India", which has become a matter of great concern with increasing number of women entering the workforce. She begins with referring to the international efforts, particularly by the United Nations in this context, and focuses on the situation in India. Certain important cases of sexual harassment are narrated to highlight the problem. The institutional responses to the problem are dealt with in this regard which cover the earlier existing fragmented legal provisions to the latest comprehensive legislation known as the Protection to Women from Sexual Harassment at Workplace Act 2013. What emerges from the discussion is how far this Act is going to be really effective in eliminating the problem, particularly the patriarchal mindset, remains to be observed.

Next two chapters in this section focus on a different approach to women empowerment i.e. through Self-Help Group (SHG) in which women are provided space and enabled to play the key role in their own betterment rather than depending fully on the government dole for the upliftment of their status as has been the case in conventional state-centric welfarist approach. In this connection, Kailash Chandra Sharma analyses "Gender inequality, Gender Planning and SHG-Bank Linkage Programme in India" in **Chapter 15**. He covers the the issue of gender inequality, gender planning and self-Help Group (SHG)-Bank linkage programme in India which has been pioneered by National Bank for Agricultural and Rural Development (NABARD). Here, the main contention is that economic inequality is the core of gender inequality in general and financial empowerment through SHG-Bank linkage programme leads to economic empowerment thus reducing the extent of gender discrimination within the household and also at community level. First, he briefly discusses various dimensions of gender inequality and then the concept of and approaches to gender planning. Then he analyses the SHG-Bank linkage programme and its gender equity enhancing aspects. Finally, it is affirmed that the programme has proved to be an important tool for financial inclusion of women leading to their economic empowerment but requires further strengthening by overcoming its shortcomings.

In **Chapter 16**, Ballabh and Batra deal with the issue of "Mainstreaming Tribal Women in Development Process through Women SHGs: A Case Study from Jharkhand & Odisha". Here they focus on the intervention made through women SHGs by a reputed national NGO called Professional Assistance for Development Action (PRADAN) which works in seven states of central India which has a large concentration of the Scheduled Tribe population to resurrect the economy of tribal people. They first provide a backdrop of the larger discourse on the divergent approaches, Nehruvian approach vs. Elvin's self-reliant approach, to tribal development, and also the actual development experience of the tribal people since Independence which has led to development-induced large-scale displacement of these people and disruptions and sufferings in their economic, social and cultural life. Then they elaborate on the alternative development framework adopted by PRADAN which relies on capability building of tribal people and local resources blended with modern professional expertise and technology to tackle poverty through enhancing livelihood opportunities. It discusses in detail the case study of women SHGs selected from three districts each from Jharkhand and Odisha. The socio-economic impact of the women SHGs and the impact of livelihood programmes, promoted by PRADAN's professional staff, on the life of the tribal people is assessed and found to be hugely substantial. Finally, it is concluded that building capabilities and putting the instruments of development in the hands of the tribal people would be the most appropriate approach to address their problems, which requires social engineering of the tribal society and bringing institutional innovations which has the capacity to support them as producer, consumer and resource manager.

An initiative by the Indian state in the direction of guaranteeing right to work is the Mahatma Gandhi National Rural Employment Guarantee Act (MGNREGA) wherein poorer women are an important concern. In this context, G.S. Mehta examines "Effectiveness of MGNREGA in Empowering Women" in **Chapter 17**. He discusses the effectiveness of Mahatma Gandhi National Rural Employment Guarantee Act (MGNREGA) in empowering women focusing on a sample of women drawn from four districts of the state of Uttar Pradesh. His empirical analysis examines the extent to which the women belonging to different socio-economic categories, viz. general, backward classes, SC and ST achieved economic empowerment in terms of getting employment and income opportunities, reduction of unemployment and freedom to have control over wages earned through participating in the programme.

Rajeev Kamal Kumar deals with "Utilisation of Public Health Services by Women: A Study of Bihar" in **Chapter 18**. He examines the availability of public health services and its benefits accruing to women in the state of Bihar in general and Vaishali district in particular. First, a brief socio-economic and demographic profile of the state and the district is provided. Then the paper analyses, on the basis of secondary data, the availability and shortfall of health infrastructure and personnel in the state and the district. An attempt is made to assess the utilisation of maternal health services including the ante-natal services and delivery, the family planning services and also the factors affecting the utilisation of public health services especially with a focus on primary data collected from women from two Primary Health Centres (PHCs) in Vaishali district. It is observed in the paper that the state government has been trying hard to provide affordable and quality health services through its network of public health facilities. Still there is shortfall in terms of physical infrastructure at all levels and shortage health services staff in all categories. As a result, the state has not been able to provide the expected level of health services to the women beneficiaries. Moreover, it was found that large majority of women were aware about the different types of public health facilities, but could not actually avail the services much and the extent of availing different types of health services also varied.

SECTION V: VOICES OF PROTESTS

Section V consists of two chapters (i.e. 19-20) which provides glimpses of actual mobilisations and movements by women and also of certain voices of protests in literature pertaining to gender discrimination and inequality in India. Here, in **Chapter 19** Taique Anwer provides a brief overview of "Women's Organisations and Movements in India: Struggle for Gender Equality". It is commonly known that concerns for improving the plight of Indian women were first initiated by social reformers in the modern times. But women entered the public domain in large numbers during the freedom struggle in the country. Also several women's organisations were formed by women themselves to fight against discrimination against them and achieve gender equality. With this backdrop, the chapter first deliberates upon these women's organisations, including their political affiliations and also their mobilisation in trade unions and forums. Then, it gives a snapshot of the recent trends in women's movement in India and also the constitutional provision made for their participation in local governance. Finally, the issues and challenges which confront the women's movement today in India are discussed.

In **Chapter 20** by Neelu Sharma and Gopal Singh is captioned "Rural Women Folks Unite for Gender Equality (A Case Study of '*Khabar Lahariya*"). Here, they discuss the struggle of rural women for gender equality through the means of bringing out on their own a weekly newspaper called *Khabar Lahariya* in five local languages which cover two states, viz. the states of Uttar Pradesh and Bihar. The newspaper is engaged in questioning patriarchal values and norms and trying to transform the consciousness of rural women in particular and the society in general. Based on empirical data collected from founder members, reporters, and readers of Khabar Lahariya the authors present an analysis of the findings of their case study which relate mainly to the problems faced by reporters in collecting data in a male-dominated scenario for running their newspaper and the impact of the newspaper in elimination of social evils, empowering rural women and helping in changing the patriarchal set-up of the society.

References

Alkire, Sabina. 2002. *Valuing Freedoms. Sen's Capability Appraoch and Poverty Reduction*.UK: Oxford, University Press.

Alkire, Sabina and Rufus Black. 1997. "A Practical Reasoning Theory of Development Ethic: Furthering the Capabilities Approach". Journal of International Development 9 (2), pp. 263-279.

Blackden, C. Mark and Chitra Bhanu. 1999. "Gender, Growth and Poverty Reduction: Special Program of assistance for Africa". World Bank Technical Paper No. 428. World Bank.

Derez, Jean & Amartya Sen (2013). *An Uncertain Glory: India and its Contradictions*. London: Allen Lane/Penguin.

Erikson, Robert. 1992. "Descriptions of Inequality: The Swedish Approach to Welfare Research," in Martha Nussbaum and Amartya Sen (eds.). *The Quality of Life*. Oxford, UK: Clarendon Press.

International Labour Organisation. 1995. Gender, Poverty and Employment: Turning Capabilities into Entitlement. Geneva: International Labour Office.

Kabeer Naila (2015). Gender, Poverty, and Inequality: A brief History of Feminist Contributions in the Field of International Development. *Gender & Development*, 23;2, 189-205, Routledge, Taylor & Francis Group.

Mazumdar, Vina (n.d.). Gender Issues and Educational Development: An Overview from Asia.

Nussbaum, Martha. 1995. "Human Capabilities, Female Human Beings" in Martha Nussbaum and Jonathan Glover (eds.) *Women, Culture and Development: A Study of Human Capabilities*, pp. 61-104. Oxford, UK: Clarendon Press.

Nussbaum, Martha. 2000. *Women and Human Development: The Capabilities Approach*. Cambridge, UK: Cambridge University Press.

Sen, Amartya. 1992. *Inequality Reexamined*. Oxford, UK: Oxford University Press.

Robeyns, Ingrid. 2003. "Sen's Capability Approach and Gender Inequality: Selecting Relevant Capabilities". *Feminist Economics* 9 (2-3), pp. 61-92. Routledege (Taylor & Francis Group).

Part - I

CONCEPTUAL DIMENSION

2

Gender Discrimination and Inequalities: Status, Causes and Solutions

— Shiv Kumar Yadav

Introduction

At the surface level, division of gender as male and female seems to be a biological one related to the sexes, but actually it is a kind of hierarchical social division found everywhere in the world. Earlier it was universally accepted as God-ordained division, thus taken as final but as a matter of fact, this division is not based on biology but on social expectations and stereotypes. Thus, this kind of division was extended to work, dress, behaviour, attitude and what not. Since the division is hierarchal in nature, it leads to discriminations and inequalities in all walks of life between male and female. Conceptually the phrase 'gender discrimination' means any kind of discrimination practised on the ground of gender irrespective of being male and female but it has acquired an acceptability as the 'discrimination faced by the female gender' only in the society at the hands of male gender. This discrimination emerges from the notion that both are not equal. This kind of acceptability shows the gravity of injustices that is being practised against the fair sex since the time immemorial.

But the society has been overlooking anxieties and agonies of another gender, who is neither male nor female, known as transgender, despite being an important character of the Mahabharat, Shikhandi, one of the children of Drupad. The world society has not even given them any kind of gender identity till recently. Nepal, being the first country in the world, has given them an identity of third gender in 2007. Then after,Pakistan (2009), Australia (2011), New Zealand (2012), Bangladesh (2013), Germany (2013) and India (2014) have also occorded them status different from male and female. Still, transgenders, who are biologicially hermaphrodite, are generally referred to as eunuch, which is wrong. Actually eunuch is 'a man who has been castrated', as the dictionary defines. So, no one can be born a eunuch. They have been stigmatised just because of God's mistake, if it is a mistake, otherwise it is a new being unlike male and female. Yes, they can't create a family at their own level but they can organize a family by adoption, but even a normal life is a remote dream for them. Again their families where they are born, are the first culprit which start discrimination and then the society which compel them to live separately in a group and live on begging, dancing and singing in public spaces. Now the time has arrived where their pains and sufferings must be recognised and also be redressed so that they feel proud as the citizen of the country. Recently, Bihar has given them the status Other Backward Class(OBC) to bring into mainstream of the society, but it would be only symbolic as they are unable to have normal life among us because we look down upon them.

Womens' Status

Though the world has become a cyber society, but still the female gender feels the intense heat of discriminations and inequalities in almost all aspects of socio-cultural, economic, political life. And this is a global phenomenon with varying degrees of intensity. In India, the level of gender discrimination is not only bad but acutely disproportionate to its political, economic and scientifitic development. This is a clear case of Ogburn's 'cultural lag'. It's true, like any other parts of the globe, India is living in a number of centuries simultaneously, hence the degrees of discrimination in different socio-cultural collectivities are different. This kind of situation demands discerning debate among all the concerned through different angles as the real challenges lie in the religion, patriarchy, the process of acculturation, the notions of family's honour and individual's chastity, the hypocrisy of the victimizers and the victims, which have reduced the female gender to the state of 'Object' and 'Property' that can be possessed. This objectification of female gender is quite contrary to the concepts and values of democracy, liberty, equality, human rights, individualism and human dignity, which are the core concerns of our constitution and of many other developed nations.

Before going to discuss the challenges that are in the way of ensuring gender equality, it would be pertinent to see how the society with the help of patriarchy, has systematically pertpetuated the age-old discriminations and now adamant to ensure the elimination of female from the society with the help of technical experts as well as female herself. This is the effect of patriarchy under which female gender goes against her own species without any objections. Defining the characteristics of patriarchy, M.H. Abrams explains;

> "...... it is male-centered and controlled, and is organised and conducted in such a way as to subordinate women to men in all cultural domains: familial, religion, political, economic, social, legal, and artistic. From the

Hebrew Bible and Greek philosophic writings to the present, the female tends to be defined by negative reference to the male as the human norm, hence as an Other, or kind of non-man, by her lack of the identifying male organ, of male powers, and of the male character traits that are presumed, in the patriarchal view, to have achieved the most scientific and technical inventions and the major works of civilisation and culture. Women themselves are taught, in the process of being socialised, to internalize the reigning patriarchal ideology (that is, the conscious and unconscious presuppositions about male superiority), and so are conditioned to derogate their own sex and to cooperate in their own subordination."[1]

After observing the nature and characteristics of patriarchy, it would not be a surprising fact, in any way, why female acts against her own interests. From womb to tomb, the female gender is being discriminated in our country at every steps of her life:

(a) At the level of mind, she is unwanted as men and women have deep longing for male child. For that those who have affordability and accessibility, they resort to 'sperm washing' with the help of Gender Clinic to ensure only male foetus.

(b) Many others, after conception of zygote they resort to amniocentesis to know the gender of the foetus and if it is female, get it aborted.

(c) After the birth of girl child, she not only gets left -handed compliment from the entire family but sometimes gets killed. Even the mother does not get due attention as regards her health during the post-parturition period,which ultimately affects the breast-fed female child.

(d) During the infant stage, proper nutrition and medical care are not properly extended that leads to weak health of the girls.

(e) At the school-going stage, not only her education is little-cared but she is made to feel inferior to male, which is reflected in the selection of schools. Restrictions are imposed on her physical movement and on her participation in those games and sports which are only supposed to be played by male child. Even in selection of toys, gender bias is clearly visible.

(f) Even much before puberty, she starts feeling the heat of sexual harassment at the hands of close relatives, neighbours and in some cases strangers. Her objectification starts at the age 5 or 6 only and sometimes even below that.

(g) All these harassments are getting properly institutionalised, when they are forced into marriage when they hardly attain the age of puberty and sometimes with comparatively aged person.

(h) Marriage often proves for her an ordeal as she is tortured for dowry and made to work like a domestic help. Harassment heaped on her to the level, where she is forced to commit suicide. Sometimes she is getting killed, often by kitchen fire. Early maternity also creates health problems. Maternal mortality rate can give us enough evidence as to her status in the family.

(i) If someone survives child marriage or gets some education and makes her own choice to have her life-partner, she is not only subjected to torture and confinement, rather getting killed, which is known as honour killing.

(j) The fortunate one, who after being educated and having job also, she is burdened with both domestic job as well as official job unlike her male members of the family.

(k) In many regions, due to age-old superstitions, many women, most often widows are branded as witch and they are heaped with humiliations ,like tonsuring and whitening the head and blackening the face and also makes her move in public space. Mr. Dabholkar of Maharashta was shot dead a year back for his struggle against these kinds of superstitions.

(l) The life of a widow is somewhat hellish. Still she is not allowed to remarry or we can say she is not acceptable as a wife again. Despite having legal right to inherit property from parental side as well as in-law's one, but she seldom gets her share. we find, a tradition is more powerful than the law in our society. She lives a life of destitute or to be at Vrindavan in Mathura (U.P.)

(m) Sexual harassment within home and outside is the most depraved discrimination that is being committed against women and girls. These crimes- illegal or immoral- are being committed by male members of the family at both the destinations – parents and parents' in-law homes. Though appears rarely in newspapers, wife-swapping is also practised.

When she enters the public space to claim her rights to pursue her happiness and comfort, she is being subjected to sexual assault either by intimidation, threat or allurements to obtain her manufactured consent. When she resists the advancement, gets sexually assaulted by force. Reporting of incidents have been coming from political establishments, judicial courtyards, official corridors, public media space, public transport network – railways & city buses, religious Mathhs, juvenile homes/remand homes, educational areas (Schools, Colleges or Universities), hotels and hospitals and cyber Space (e. g. digital rape, nude photos, abusive remarks etc.).

In case of conflicts and riots, women and girls are subjected to mass and gang rapes and after that either abducted or massacred. It is very much obnoxious and nauseating, but very much true, when natural calamities occur, women suffer at the hands of men. Even during the tragedies and tragic situation a male feels entitled to have their bodies for sexual exploitation.

Gravity of the problem in India as to gender harassment can be easily gauged from the fact that out of the first ten episodes of Satyameva Jayate, the four were focused on gender discriminations – female infanticide, dowry system, honour killing and domestic violence.

Causes

This deplorable conditions of women all over the world are not the result of the discrimination and injustice done to them in the recent past rather they were made the culprit of the 'Original Sin' committed by Adam in the Garden of Eden. As God became angry with Adam for having 'forbidden fruit', Golden Apple, so Adam became angry with Eve, who was responsible for inspiring Adam to do the sin. Since Eve was the product of his ribs, so that may be the 'reason' of entitlement taken by men over the body, mind and soul of women. This Biblical story may give the explanations of exploitation of women for the Christians' world, but what about Hinduism who created a concept of God as 'Ardhnareeswar' (Half male and Half female), a modern equivalent of androgynous state or being. Despite having androgynous concept of our God (Shiva) male's entitlement over women's body is still ruling the roost in our society. So reasons or no reasons, but in every religion, for men it is 'reasonable' to claim his entitlement over women.

Since the beginning of all kinds of Civilisation, this entitlement was systematically arranged in religions and related books as well as non-religious literature. This fact is a now an open secret, but some of the quotes as regards this from different religious texts and proverbial sayings are reproduced here to buttress my argument.

"Wives, submit yourselves to your husbands, as to the Lord." -the Bible

"As the Church is subject to Christ, so let the wives to their husbands." St.Paul

"A women's function in life is to provide the male with sexual gratification and progeny." The Koran

"The birth of a girl, grant it elsewhere, here grant a boy." - Atharvaveda–VI

"Blessed be God............. that the child not make me a women" - A jew (male) in his prayer

"As a horse, whether good or bad, requires spurs, so a woman whether good or bad, requires thrashing". - An Italian saying

"There is only one soul among ten women" - A Russian saying

From the texts of great Tradition and the tongues of Little Tradition, we find the presence of deep-rooted gender biases which created stereotypes all over the world. The works of Shakespeare, which are infested with misogynistic practices, has also contributed in hardening the male chauvinistic attitude throughout the world:

"Frailty, thy name is woman". - Hamlet I,2

"For women are roses, whose fair flower
Being once displayed, doth fall that very hour" - Twelfth Night II, 4

"I thank God, I am not a woman to be touched with so many giddy offences". - As you like It III, 2

"Beauty provoketh thievs sooner than gold". - As You like It

"Ay me, how weak a thing
The heart of women is"Julius Caeser II, 4

"She is a woman, therefore to be won." - Henry II,V,3

The person like Jean Jacques Rousseau, the leading philosopher of the Enlightenment had also restrained the freedom of women. He wrote very clearly;

> "The education of women should always be relative to the of men, to please, to be useful to us, to make us love and esteem them to educate us when young to care of us when grown up to advise and console us, to render our life easy and agreeable. These are the duties of women at all times and what they should be taught in their infancy."[2]

At every level the talent, text and tradition have been teaching us the women deserve only secondary position in our life. In Feb'2012, Archbishop Desmond Tutu, a Nobel laureate, who visited India to promote the gender equality, said in his interview;

> "Look, the world has been very silly. Fifty percent of its population consists of women and how can you deny them their rights? God said to Adam it is no good for him to be alone. In order to be truly human, Adam needed a woman. We must not forget that. I believe that we should let women be women, accept them with their feminine traits. I have seen many women leaders who are made to be macho, why? A woman will have to say. "I am a woman, so I have feminine traits. I don't want to be a pretend man." We need that desperately. Also, we need to concentrate more on educating our women because studies have shown that if you want real community development, you need to invest in your women."[3]

It is to be noted here, that the people who are engaged in promoting the cause of gender equality all over the world, harbour such a viewpoint as regards women, which is completely stereo- typical and patriarchal in content. The underlying meaning of his statement is that God created woman to remove the loneliness of man. Here she is being defined as a subordinate not as a coordinate and taken as a supplement to humanity not as a complement. What are the feminine traits ? who should define these traits? Actually, the patriarchal system has been doing this in its favour. How can this world would bring equality in man-woman relationship, is yet to be understood? Further, who will decide the gender traits of the transgender? Actually, these kinds of attitudes are responsible for inequalities and gender discrimination in the so-called developed nations, as they want to ensure their participation of women in all human affairs but as subordinates only.

Perhaps, the subjugation and subordination of women might have started in the very beginning of the civilisation when the human beings were in the food gathering and hunting stage. The wars among the different tribal groups to ensure control over territories might have created a situation in which the conquerors might have abducted women along with other wars' booties. These kinds of occasions, being recuring in nature, might have changed the status of women from human to sub-human and to non-human or slave or objects. Since men and women are biologically mating pairs, so the latter were forced to accept the status of sexual toys, dolls or objects. This objectification of women proved very fatal for the identity, autonomy, voice, right to sexuality and representation, and now for 'life' and 'living' too.

Another development happened, after establishing male's entitlement to female's body, at the level of idea or notion, certainly more dangerous than the former. And this was the concept of honour and prestige of men in regard to 'women's chastity and obediency'. Since 'men' were on complete control of women's body, so they started to regulate their personal and physical conducts in addition to other socio-political and economic ones. This kind of institutionalisation of 'honour' got reinforcement and strength from the other social institutions like 'marriage' 'famliy' .That may be the one ofthe rationales for William Blackstone, Professor of law at Oxford in 18th century, to describe marriage as a 'civil death' of women. He opines, "By marriage, the husband and wife are one person in law, that is, the very being or legal existence of the women is suspended during the marriage, or at least is incorporated and consolidated into that of husband under whose wing, protection and cover she performs everything".[4]

Thus for all practical purpose, women's mind, body and soul became the colony of men. I am afraid, this gender-colonisation can be called the earliest form of any kind of colonisations followed by the slavery system, though the essence of slavery was already present in early stage of women's subjugation. This conceptualisation of 'honour' 'chastity' and 'women's body as sexual objects' completely rejects the relationships like friendship and platonic love between men and women. Herein lays the evidence of mental hegemony over women's personal or intimate space. Since women lost their control over their mind and body in the very beginning of civilisation, Sita's argument was turned down by Ram, when she was to be banished despite having 'Agnipariksha'. She pleaded to Ram that '' being in captivity (of Ravana) she was no longer the master of her person. She would command only her mind and that was always faithful to her husband (Ram)".[5] But her reasoned argument couldn't save her. Still the rape-victims bear the stigma of the crime for which she is not responsible.

Context of Relationship	*Men*	*Women*
Biological	Masculine	Feminine
Social	/ Father, Husband, Brother, Son	Mother/Wife/Sister/daughter
Political	Oppressor/ Ruler	Oppressed/Ruled
Economic	Buyer /Consumer	Producer/ Seller

All these developments as to relationships between men and women, can be presented in figure as below:

As we agree to the fact that this gender- based discrimination and inequalities have been structural in nature since the beginnings, this can be safely postulated that despite all kinds of institutional arrangements to govern the man-women relationships, it has been reduced to biological division where they look like potential mating partners; and all the physio-socio behaviours of the male towards the female throughout the history till the day, are self-explanatory in nature. Perhaps, this may have the reason to help G.B.Shaw in his plays " Mrs warren's Profession", to compare 'marriage' as a 'legalised prostitution'. In support of this postulate, I would like to quote some empirical observations. Arundhati Roy, a writer and activist expresses her experience as to the male's attitude towards female in general:

> "But the talk of a noble working class seemed very, very silly to me. Every time I stepped out of my college campus like other women, I would be brutalised so much by men. It made no difference whether they were proletarian or not, or what their ideology. The problem was the biological nature of these men. The only real conflict seemed to me to be between women and men."[6]

Similar feelings and perception have been put into words by young girl, Estelle Tang, from the US, in her article "An Open Letter to All My Male Friends".

> "It's so (eve teasing, molestation, harassment) predictably a part of my life now that I cringe in anticipation whenever a man looks at me. I internally genuinely bless everyman who turns his face away from me

when I walk part. I've tried dressing down and wearing no make-up when I leave the house, which hasn't helped. It should go without saying that I don't want to be the one who has to alter my behaviour to go unnoticed and I hate that I even felt like I should try—but results say it's a useless exercise, in any ease".[7]

Another remark, from Akhtar Jamil, a famous Urdu writer, born in India, married to a Pakistani, lived and died in Canada in 2011, may be naked truth but a sum total of all other similar viewpoints. She writes while remembering Krishna chandar, her social brother: "Ye bhi achha hi hua ki Allah Mian ne behan-bhai apni marji se bana diye;Varna saari umra bhai dhundhate hi gujar jaati" (It also happened better that God himself has made brother and sister, otherwise whole life would have been spent to find a brother)"[8]

Mira Nair has also some problem when she clearly comments on the depiction of women in Bollywood. She states, "It has always been about the woman as a sexual object who will gyrate herself into your brain and into your loins.I have a problem with that".[9]

If the perceptions of Ms Roy, Ms Tong, Ms Jamal and Ms Nair are even the half truths, as 'no perception comes amiss'[10]. (Virginia Woolf), then the confession of Khushwant Singh, assuming him as a representative of male stereotype can easily convert them into a truth, who confessed; " I have also come to the sad conclusion that I have always been a bit of a lecher"[11]. All above confessions, perceptions and expressions made by them may not be the absolute truth, but even if they are the parts of truths, one can arrive at the conclusion that objectification of women and notions of 'chastity and honour' are actually the root reasons of different kinds of discriminations and inequalities that are being practised against them. In this regard, Simone de Beauvoir in 1953, concluded in her book 'The Second Sex' that,

" She is called the 'sex' by which is meant that she appears essentially to the male as a sexual being. For him she is sex- absolute sex, no less......... She is the incidental; the inessential as opposed to the essential. He is Subject, he is the Absolute- she is the Other."[12]

Thus, ultimately, the male's attitude and rigid consciousness originated from age-old ruling of patriarchy is the confirmed culprit which is responsible for vulnerable status of girl child, young girl and women of India and the world.

Oppurtunities and Solutions

After identifying the challenges in the way of ensuring gender equality and equity in the society, it can be said that the life and living of women in India like any part of the globe, were quite unfortunate and imperfect in the past and is quite problematic but very much encouraging in the present but the future would be certainly much more prospective but not without being tensed, at least in near future.

This problem is like an 'auto-immune disease' which is "caused by substances that usually prevent illness." A family is the first front where discriminations start between boys and girls, which is supposed to be the first field where equality can be ensured but the opposite is true. Outside family, there is complete hostile environment for girls and women. And very surprisingly, these internal and external hostility are not mutually exclusive, hence the vicious circle of discriminations and inequalities comes into being and maintains its perpetuity . That's why to break to vicious circle, multipronged approaches and efforts must be adopted.

In my opinion, at the priority level, education of women and gender-sensitisation of men must be promoted at all levels. Education is the great leveler, which can ensure a level playing field for girls and women to annihilate the sense of male entitlement and accelerate the paces of female empowerment. Educational infrastructures should be developed keeping in view the biological disabilities on the part of women, so that they can feel comfortable at schools and colleges. Apart from many kinds of skills without making them gender biased, there should be 'gender studies' on graded scale on the curriculum from the class fifth itself so that children's mind can be detoxified which they acquire due to their ascribed status which from the family and society. Education can play a big role in gender sensitisation programme like the mass-media of any kind. Here it is a worth-mentioning fact that there should not be a separate schools or colleges for girls and boys.

In order to improve sex-ratio in favour of girl-child and women, the University Grants Commission has launched a scholarship programmer for single girl child of her parents . This should be extended to job-opportunities also in both private and public sectors. Girls' hostel must be a pre-condition to have permission for opening a new school, college and university. Bicycle programme for girls in many states has created a butterfly effect in the stagnated consciousness of urban and rural societies . To ensure maximum visibility of girls and women in the public space many other financial and heath related incentives should be launched and get implemented with religious zeal.

We have enough laws and acts to check all kinds of discriminations and inequalities gainst women but the implementation-side is very-very poor. This reluctancy and biasness of male-dominated law-enforcing agencies, as well as judiciary, have been the real bottlenecks in getting the culprits punished.The police still take crimes like female infanticide, foeticide, child-marriage non-seriously as they treat them as private issues of family and individuals. For this, as short term measures, awareness programmes can only help to some extent. The startling fact about the female foeticide is that it is more a metro-phenomenon, where the 'rich and educated are involved . They commit the crime with impunity as they are resourceful at the level of 'cash' and 'contact'. Hence gender-sensitisation programme among the police officials is a must to inculcate the sense of urgency and socio-civilisation responsibility and this should be the part of their training course. Another culprits regarding female foeticide are medical professionals. Without their active and responsible cooperation it is difficult to curb this menace. The role of Indian Medical Association is quite imperative as self-regulation of their conducts can bring better results.Dowry system is the most glaring example of social hypocrisy that is being practised by the people, parliament and law-enforcing agencies of our country. Actually Indian society has never accepted it as a crime, though the Parliament does. That is the biggest discrepancy exists till the day. Generally 'demanded gifts'(earlier it was only gift) in kinds and cash are dubbed as dowry paid by the parents of the bride to the bridegroom. And its exchange is a matter of prestige and status for both the receiver and the giver. Despite being a crime in eyes of law, both the parties want to make it an open secret, in order to enhance their social prestige .Before marriage, very few cases of dowry are reported to the police just because both the parties are involved in this crime. The policemen appear only after marriage when the bride's side comes in trouble due to more demand made by the groom or for many other reasons. very few marriages in India are being solemnised without dowry. It is because the upper and upper middle class people 'purchase' the talented bachelors from lower middle class for their daughter as grooms with the help of high dowry. The lower middle class people grab this opportunity to change their class and social category. Hence it is a futile exercise to curb it with the help of laws and punishment. But the real victims are women who feel like a square peg in a rould role for many reasons. So some radical change is quite imperative to ensure gender equality and to save the institution of marriage and dignity of women.

My suggestion in this regard is to do away with all kinds of Laws and Acts related to the prevention and prohibition of dowry and at the same time girls' shares in their parental property must be given to them at the time of marriage itself through some legal documents. Marriage certificate should be compulsory which must be enclosed with the legal document which would entitle them to have their share in both the cases whether it is an arranged marriage or love ones.. This is required to help girls to have their share as per law, which seldom gets implemented. A think this step would bring true equality in the society within no time and may prove panacea for money cases of discriminations and sufferings.

Eve- teasing,molestation and sexual assaultl are the most heinous crimes that men commit against women. Reasons are rooted, in the words of Aamir Khan, "we are all born with it:'The feeling that men are superior. We have to deal with the problem in a mature manner."[13]

But the burning question is : why is it not being checked or stopped despite having numerous strong laws at our command? why men don't get afraid of the severe punishment to be awarded for these crimes?It is because of the several primary reasons or assumptions of the culprits: (i) they think that in no case the victim is going to open her month; (ii) if she breaks the silence, she would earn 'bad name' for herself and she would be made responsible for this incident not only by others but by her own family members? (iii) the culprit is very much sure of stigma that would come to her as an additional punishment, that she would not prefer ever; (iv) the family of the culprit would certainly come to rescue him if a victim reports the incident to the people or the police; (v) the patriarchal society always takes the side of the victimizer to perpetuate its dominance; (vi) the post-incident harassment faced by the girl or woman and her family at the hands of police, doctor, lawyer and judge always discourages them to pursue the case to its logical conclusion. This is because the powerful and the rich feel confident of getting out of it with impunity; (vii) which is of utmost importance that stranger rapes form a minisusle percentage of reported cases. The overwhelming number is by acquaintances of the victim despite the fact that if the victimizer is a close relative or acquaintance the cases are generally not reported.

In my opinion, the society cannot eliminate this crime against women unless and until 'silence' is broken with a bang and 'stigma' is to be replaced with self-esteem and 'self congratulation' assuming themselves as the soldiers to fight against the age-old crime being tolerated by the women of the world. It is very vital to change this perspective.For this, I strongly suggest the removal of the provision in the law which prohibits a journalist, police any one to reveal the name, identity and address of victims of sexual assault. This kind of clause is self-evident in nature to prove that society is resporistible for the stigma and not the victim. It is indirectly a social sanction for the silence maintained by victims. This kind of social hypocrisy cannot help eradicate this crime against women. This is not easy in the prevailing rigidity of patriarchy and invisible gender norms, but there is no way out ultimately, as this is the only crime of the world in which the victims are made to feel ashamed and stigmatized. In this regard, the story and steps of Israeli beauty queen Linor Abargil, who visited india in March 2014, to speak against sexual violence, are certainly inspiring and exemplary. She was raped just six weeks before Miss World Beauty Contest' in 1998 at the age of 18, but she never concealed her identify from anyone and got the culprit punished for 16 years imprisonment. She told ' The Associated Press':

"If you go through something very bad or very hard the only pill you can take is to tell, to take it out of your system. Because if you don't, it is like a tumour – it becomes bigger and bigger until it kills you. I feel that I have this privilege to really help other women to open up."[14]

Sooner the better, the identity clause of the victim must be removed so that society can look its face into the mirror of reality.

In this age, when the world civil societies have been relentlessly advancing the argument against the capital punishment for the 'convicted criminals' of different heinous crimes, the Indian patriarchal society is murdering the innocent boys and girls just because they fall in love. who can believe that Lord Krishna was born in India? This is the height of hypoanisy to accept Krishna as God, the Incarnate, who himself helped his sister Subhadra to elope with Arjun for the sake of their love for each other, and at the same time kills the lover and the beloved in this age of globalisation. This crime has another dimension too and that is insidious caste system. At one plane, gender and caste are the same as both the divisions are hierarchical in nature. The concept of family honour has been linked by the patriarchal society to the caste system and to the chastity of women(not men) only. In this way, whole battle of injustice against women has been reduced to the sexual purity and chastity of women itself. Willy or nilly, today or tomorrow one will have to accept it that women are unable to get their all kinds of freedom until and unless they acquire her right to her own body, mind as well as sexuality. Honour Killings get supports from two deadly evils. Patriarchy and caste system, which have slowed down the pace of Indianisiation. And without being Indianised and modernised if we are going to be globalised, casteism, child marriage, female foeticide, domestic violence would go with us, which would defeat the purpose of globalisation of humanity, equality and fraternity. we would not be happy to read the editiorial entitled "The diaspora's dark side" of The Hindu (Kolkata edition. 21 Jan. 2014) which says,

> "From caste discrimination through forced marriages to sex selective abortions, entrenched practices among sections of the British South Asian diaspora pose continuing challenges. .... Technical developments, such as sperm washing to ensure conception of male foetuses complicate the picture. The claim has even been made that a woman has a right to choose the sex of her child."[15]

To stop honour killings, the administration (as we cannot expect any steps from politicians) must come forward in support of 'honoured couples' who break the 'narrow domestic walls' and deal with the cruel murderers heavily in the Court of law.

Domestic volence is prevalent every where cutting across the regions and the class and the communities all over the globe with varying deqrees of intensity. Very recently, an I.P.S. husband of an I.A.S. wife was suspended in Jan 2014 after wife's allegations of domestic violence in Kolkata . This shows that even the empowered woman's status, awarenes and education are of little importance to check this violence. Actually, Vijay Nagaswami's observation, can help in understanding the intricacies of domestic violence;

"The 'masculine woman' has become more acceptable than the 'feminine man' who is still an object of derision. And herein lies the root of the gender conflict – women find it easy to pursue their masculinity; men find it disagreement to even acknowledge, let alone pursue their feminity."[17]

It will take little more time to get man adjusted to new role given by new industrialised and globalised climate.In the meantime, Domestic Violence (prohibition) Act 2007 would have to play the role to check it and for that again women will have to break the silence against the injustice.

As regards political empowerment, it is a worth-mentioning fact that despite having equal political rights and contributions made by women's movements, women as suffers never became a 'nation' at least in political sense. It is a tragedy that even the shared sense of helplessness could unite them as a united force that works in democratic method. In this regard the views expressed by the female law-intern, who broke the silence about her sexual exploitation at the hands of a retired judge of supreme Court can be appreciated. She wrote,

> "If the shared experiences of women cannot be easily understood through a feminist lens, then clearly there is cognitive vacuum that feminism fails to fill."[18]

This it is very important that like Bolivia, Costa Rica, Ecuador, there must be 50% reservation in legislative bodies as done at the panchayats level bodies in many states of India. Women as political heads certainly would affect the governance to some extent. It can be recalled here that in 1970 when Golda Meir, as the chief of Israel's government, suggested during the cabinet's deliberation, which was discussing the way of bringing the rapes down, and among the measure suggested was a curfew on women, preventing them from going out on the streets after dark, an alternative was givn by her- since the rapes were committed by men so the curfew should be placed on men, not women. Ultimately, no curfew was imposed in Israel.

Economic empowerment of women is very much vital for their real freedom and equality.Their's contributions as homemaker have never been recognised as an economic gain and when so-called women's works are changed into paid jobs, men start doing the work like in hotels and restrauants. Their economic independence would also end the division of works on the basis of stereotyped gender's roles. Converting all kinds of work as unisexual in nature would help in empowerment of women as it would expand opportunities for them that would, in turn, ensure socio-cultural freedom and liberate them from the subjugation of inivisible gender norms which are biased in favour of male. After the dismantling of joint family system, women's entitlement to some assets like land, building and shops have been increased .Though this does not give them a sense of ownership but a sense of security does in case of any eventualities. for real economic freedom, their share in parental property is a must and they must be trained with skills as well as endowed with knowledge. The principle of positive discrimination can also be applied in their favour in the realm of economy, administration, judiciary, as well as trade and industries.

Despite all kinds of might, energy and ability shown by women all over the world, there are still many sceptics who are unable to swallow their freedom and choice and argue sometimes vociferously that nature has given women the secondary position on the basis of so-called feminine traits, hence their position must be defined in the light of nature's directives displayed in division of man and woman. Such kind of naturalists are unable to understand that it is science which has helped us to understand that the division of man and woman is a kind of convenience, otherwise there is no difference between the two. Nature never directs that uniformity or order is the only law or system rather often many things in nature are in random position and such kind of discrimination and inequalities cannot be blamed upon the nature as the fate or principle of 'Karma' was being blamed to justify the deprivations of dalits in India.

A time may come in course of scientific development when men will be able to have uterus in his abdomen and women shall be capable to adopt parthenogenesis to have their children without the contribution from male as outlined by Aarathi Prasad in her book "Like a Virgin". In this book she envisages the future of reproduction and rules of sex that are being redesigned which may bring possibility of a solo parent. A woman who might use two of her eggs, converting one into a psuedo-sperm and allowing the foetus to develop in an artificial womb.

Thus, all the foregoing deliberations clearly show that it is in the interest of civilisation and human existence to ensure gender equality in all walks of life, if not, serious consequences may occur for good or bad reasons, such as: burden of unskilled work force would increase; socio –cultural conflicts like divorce, litigation, suicide, torture, tension, and alienation would augment; marriagelessness and livein-relationship would be the realities; childlessness and familylessness would also appear; single mom and unwed mother, single dad and unwed father would be found in number;and many more things yet to be speculated.

The hope of gender equality lies in pushing the boundaries of science and technology, human rights, democracy and globalisation,

References

1. M.H. Abrams, *A Glossary of Lliterary Terms*, Thomson Heinle, 7th Edition, 1999, p. 89.
2. Sudhamani Regunathan, 28.2.2014 "Telling Voices – Engendered Science", *The Hindu*, Kolkata, Friday Review, p. 04.

3. Interview of Desmond Tutu by Sangieta Baroah Pisharoy, Feb 10, 2012, published in *The Hindu*, Kolkata, p. 05.
4. Neena Arora, Nayantara Sahgal and Doris Lessing, 1991, *A Feminist Study in Comparison*, Prestige, New Delhi.
5. A.S. Altekar, 1938 (2nd Edition 1959), Reprint 1995, *The Position of Women in Hindu Civilisation*, 1995, p. 306.
6. Arundhati Roy's Interview to Praveen Swami, *Frontline*, August 8,1997, p. 107.
7. Estelle Tang, 31 may 2014, "An open letter to all my male friends", *The Hindu*, Kolkata, p. 07.
8. Editor, Rajendra Bhatt, Aajkal, Hindi Monthly Magazine, publication Division New Delhi, p. 39.
9. The Hindu, Kolkata, Sunday magazine 7 April 2013, p. 08).
10. Roger Fowler (edt.), 1973/78, *A Dictionary of Modern Critical Terms*, Routledge & Kegal Paul, London, p. 181.
11. The Hindu, Kolkata (Sunday Magazine) 7 April 2013, p. 8.
12. Neena Arora, Nayantara Sahgal and Doris Lessing, 1991, *A Feminist Study in Comparison*, Prestige, New Delhi.
13. *The Hindu* (Sunday magazine), Kolkata, 24 Dec 2013, p. 08.
14. *World View*, Column (by Associated Press) on Linor Abragil, Hindustan Times, Ranchi, 22. March 2014, p. 12.
15. Editorial: 21 Jan 2014, *The Hindu*, Kolkata, p. 06.
16. Vijay Nagaswami, August 31, 2008, 'The WeakerSex' (under the Coulumn "The Shrinking Universe"), *The Hindu*, p. 4.
17. Arun Mohan Sukumar, 16 Nov. 2013, "If it may please the Supreme court", *The Hindu*, Kolkata, p. 09.

3

Discourse on Gender Discrimination and Inequality in India with Special Reference to Sexual Minorities

— *Mukesh Bharati & Preeti Misra*

Introduction

India is known for being multi-cultural, multi-religious, multi-linguistic and other kinds of diversified society. When we talk about gender, gender identities, or any other things related to gender, the knowledge of everything we see, perceive and think can be included in the study of gender because gender is a social construct. Generally, the study of gender rest on the study of male and female binary system but there are lots of issues involved with the study of gender out of that the study of sexual minorities (hereinafter LGBT) is attempted. The understanding of LGBT includes the study of not only gender but also sex.

Gender discrimination and inequality refers the incidences and consequences of differentiating between male and female recipients of society because of certain presumptions, thoughts, behaviours, and identity and most popular the 'social norms'. This is a process by which a person either feels or performs a comparison with other inmates of society. For understanding this, the understanding of sex and gender in a wider sense is needed.

Sex

Generally, we do not talk and discuss about sex mostly in public because of many reasons like immoral; eroticism; absenteeism of sex knowledge from curriculums and prohibited norms of society, that result as an inadequate and improper knowledge of sex among persons and concludes with behavioural problems. 'It is well recognised that sexual health is one of the important component of health in general. It is both the cause and effect of varied behavioural and physical disorders. In spite of this, sexuality research has received only a cursory or negligible interest by Indian researchers. Physicians either show no interest or ignore patients' psychosexual concerns (Avasthi & Nehra, 2000). We lack to great extent the reliable measures and the estimates of sexual disorders (Kulhara & Avasthi, 1995), specialised clinics (Rao. TSS, 2000) special groups,(Rao. TSS,1989), training facilities (Singh et. al, 1987) and concerned practitioners (Avasthi et. al, 1994).'[1]

'There are widely prevalent myths, misconceptions and prejudices concerning sex in our culture (Mishra, 1963) and the so-called 'sex specialists' and 'quacks' have added to the self-perpetuating, iatrogenic disorders.'[2] In her book 'sexuality in India: Teenager and Teacher', 'Kavita Joshi', emphasises various sex and sexuality values and perceptions relating to variables, need for sex education, gender equality, homosexuality, deviant behaviour, etc. for adolescent through inculcating sex and sexuality in different curriculums. 'Dickinson believes that sex is first of all a physical fact.'[3] 'Sex denotes the physical and mental traits that distinguish between males and females; and also the physiology and psychological processes related to procreation and sensual pleasure (Goldenson, 1984).'[4] 'Khujraho temples or Ajanta caves were carved to educate about sex, sex is a matter of one's personal conduct'[5] When says sex, Freud, means 'sex-genitalia and their direct expression'[6] and 'at the same time he comes to the tacit understanding that sex really is nasty, an ignoble slavery to nature.'[7]

When Robyn Ryle asks to her students of sociology about the difference between sex and gender they 'usually agree that sex describes the biological differences between women and men'[8] while using biosocial approach Robyn Ryle discusses that 'sex describes the biological differences between people we call males and people we call females.'[9] Biosocial approach is being applied by the bio-socialists and they particularly focus on the sexual dimorphism which means 'the claim that sex marks a distinction between two physically and genetically discrete categories of people. Sexual dimorphism is the belief that there is something meaningful out there called sex and that we can use certain characteristics to objectively sort people into two categorises called male and female.'[10]

In his book titled "Human Sexuality in a world of diversity" Rathus, pointed out that, 'the word (sex) derives from Latin roots meaning "to cut or divide," signifying the division of organisms into male and female genders. One use of the term sex, then, refers to our gender, or state of being male or female. The word sex (or sexual) is also used to refer to anatomic structures, called sex (or sexual) organs, that play a role in reproduction or sexual pleasure. We may also speak of sex when referring to physical activities involving our sex organs for purposes of reproduction or pleasure: masturbation, hugging, kissing, coitus, and so on. Sex also relates to erotic feelings, experiences, or desires, such as sexual fantasies and thoughts, sexual urges, or feelings of sexual attraction to another person.'[11] 'Sex indicates the difference in Morphology and Anatomy Morphology is which separates from male from female.'[12] Nagpal (2001), 'further opined that sex is gratification and lust is being confused with love.'[13]

Sorenson views 'sex as a biological fact, meaning that it is non cultural, static and scientifically measurable and unproblematic.'[14] According to Michel Faucault, 'the notion of "sex" made it possible to group together, in an artificial unity, anatomical elements, biological functions, conducts, sensations, and pleasures, and it enabled one to make use of this fictitious unity as causal principle, an omnipresent meaning, a secret to be discovered everywhere: sex was thus able to function as a unique signifier and as a universal signified.'[15] Discussing about the understanding of sex, Robyn Ryle point outs that 'sex, then, is a causal factor dictating how gender gets expressed.'[16] 'From a strong constructionist perspective, using sex infers a belief in two kinds of people, male and female. From a biosocial perspective, sex indicates the existence of two different kinds of people, male and female.'[17] Further, 'In English, sex can mean both the biological categories of males and females as well as engaging in some kind of sexual act.'[18] 'LeVay and Baldwin (2009) note that sex is about identity as well as relationships.'[19]

Many authors and writers have contributed in enlargement of knowledge of sex through various perspectives such as biology, anthropology, sociology, psychology, history, medical, science, etc. but we are lacking one perspective which has also contributed in the knowledge of sex. This perspective is known as spiritual perspective and the name of 'Osho' is very famous in this regard. In an article related to Osho 'Sex is a mysterious phenomenon, which has puzzled even great sages.'[20] 'Sex for the Athenians was understood as an action performed always by a social superior on a social inferior. Sex was a deeply asymmetrical act that divided the world into penetrator and penetrated, and these categories were in no way interchangeable.'[21] 'Those deemed socially superior (male citizens) were the penetrators, and those seen as socially inferior (women, children, foreigners, and slaves) were the penetrated.'[22]

The above mention discussion provides us knowledge about sex that reflects sex as biological phenomenon and after having this knowledge it can be said in my own words that sex refers **'the biological identity and its various activities of one or more parts of a person's body in the process of socialisation'.**

Gender

It is that part of study in social science research which has a very long list of work. 'Although much has been written in academic and policy circles on gender, on conflict, and on the impact of conflict on women,'[23] but there has been made an effort to discuss the currently debated issue related to sex, gender and sexuality i.e. homosexuality or same-sex-relationship particularly under Indian criminal justice system. Gender may also be a subject matter of various social scientists, anthropologists, psychologists; human and legal rights activists especially focused on women related issues. Bem & Wharton says, 'that most people in western cultures grow up learning that there are two and only two sexes, male and female, and two and only two genders, feminine and masculine. We are taught that a real woman is feminine, a real man is masculine, and that any deviation or variation is strange or unnatural.'[24]

We have a long list of work on gender within different context as social, economic, political, cultural, and legal & human rights. 'Numerous theories explain how and why gender differentiation and inequality exist in most societies. We cannot describe them all.'[25] Some may be referred here and before going into details of gender studies, we need to 'develop a capacity to see what is hidden by the cultural blinders that we all wear at least some of the time.'[26] Discussing about gender, this term 'defined as the meanings, practices, and relations of femininity and masculinity that people create as they go about their daily lives in different social settings.'[27] Kimmel and Tavris, 'described gender as two "sex" roles- male/masculine and female/feminine by forwarding innate personality characteristics and biological sex characteristic such as hormones and reproductive functions.'[28]

Women are biological inferior to men was debunked by Tavris as women has been regularly participating and producing high level of achievement in comparison of men in different fields of sports. Researchers have tried to find out the 'gender inequality within the economy, family, religion, and other social institutions'[29] of life. Schwalbe, theorises gender is "human-made"[30] and argues that 'gender is a human invention is called social construction.'[31] The situation becomes more complicated when gender is defined within different cultural context as Helliwell, defines 'about the similarity of men and women while Herdt defines gender as flowing and changing across the life span.'[32] In understanding of gender, 'R.W. Connell argued in terms of *hegemonic masculinity and emphasized femininity* that reflects the dominance of men or emphasized femininity is always subordinated to masculinity.'[33]

Now, taking the different categories of individual and institutional level, social scientists Howard & Alamilla, says that at Individual level 'gendered expectations, including stereotypes, are incorporated into how we define ourselves, and shape how we act and react as well as how other perceive us. While, ultimately, gendered identities are the result of larger societal and cultural forces, they are deeply felt, and individuals act upon them.'[34] According to West and Zimmerman, 'gender is "done" in interaction with others in specific situations. They argue that the very process of interaction involves the presentation of a gendered self, the responses of the persons we are interacting with, and our reactions to their anticipated or actual responses. As such gender is an on-going activity that is carried out in interaction with other people, and people vary their gender presentations as they move from situation to situation.'[35] Pleck (1981) defines 'sex role (gender) as, "the set of behaviours and characteristics widely viewed as (1) typical of women or men (sex role stereotypes) and (2) desirable for women or men (sex role norms)".'[36]

Further, some theorists use social constructionism to explain gender at the institutional level. Acker argues, 'that institutions are gendered because "gender is present in the processes, practices, images and ideologies, and distributions of power in the various sectors of social life".'[37] Like Acker, Judith Lorber also combines a social constructionist perspective with the concept of social institutions. She argues that gender be viewed "as a society-wide institution that is built into all major organisations of society:" By viewing gender as an institution, Lorber, sees it as a basis for inequality in society because it is through gender that resources, power, and privilege are distributed. Gender, according to Lorber, is "a process of creating distinguishable social statuses for the assignment of rights and responsibilities."[38] Further, Lorber argued that 'gender is an institution that is embedded in all the social processes of everyday life and social organisations.'[39] Postmodernist theorists ague that 'gender is a product of the discourses within particular social contexts that define and explain gender.'[40] Sorenson views 'gender as a cultural attribute, a means by which people are taught who they are, how to behave, and what their roll will be.'[41] Barbara J. Risman theorises gender 'as a social structure'[42] and examined the construction of gender within individual, intersectional, and institutional dimensions of social life. 'The expression 'gender' denotes 'the social meaning of sex categorisation.'[43]

American sociologist, Betsy Lucal, by giving her own biography and experiences in daily life, consequently provided the two categories i.e. 'issue of identity and issue of interaction'[44] for understanding of gender as social construction. The most common experience "Sir" was emphasised by her. She categorically discussed gender as "perceived gender" and mentioned that gender is pervasive in our society. I cannot choose not to participate in it. Even if I try not to do gender, other people will do it for me. After analysing the incidences she realised that 'gender is a substantial part of her personal identity'. Sharon Preves, a sociologist, has done 'ground-breaking research on what it is like to live in contemporary America with an intersexed body that doesn't confirm to "standard" medical definitions of male and female.'[45] In her study she exclusively targeted the intersex people referred as 'deemed sexually ambiguous'. Through her study, she tried to find out the root causes for gender variation with the help of medical literature. 'Gender is an organizing principle of social life that affects different levels of social reality, not only individual people.'[46]

Another sociologists, anthropologists, researchers and scholars have also added many more knowledge in the area of gender research covering huge range of boundary or limit. The anthropologist, Serena Nanda, discussed in her book multiple sex/gender system around the world about the multiple genders. She emphasised on the variation of gender by taking the example of hijra and other sexual minorities. She categorically argued about gender variation on multiple levels like characteristics, transvestism, occupation, sexuality and power. She concluded her argument with that 'a person who contains both masculine and feminine qualities or one who is transformed from the sex/gender assigned at birth into a different gender in later life manifests some of the many kinds of transformations and ambiguities that are possible, not only for humans, but for animals and objects in the natural environment.'[47]

'Gender refers to the socially constructed roles ascribed to women and men, as opposed to biological and physical characteristics. Gender roles vary according to socioeconomic, political, and cultural contexts, and are affected by other factors, including age, class, and ethnicity. Gender roles are learned and negotiated, or contested. They are therefore changeable.'[48] Judith Butler in her book Gender Trouble (Butler, 1990) seeks to demonstrate that 'Gender is, thus, a construction that regularly conceals its genesis; the tacit collective agreement to perform, produce, and sustain discrete and polar genders as cultural fictions is obscured by the credibility of those productions-and the punishments that attend not agreeing to believe in them; the construction 'compels' our belief in its necessity and naturalness.'[49]

In defining gender, we have different feminists and sociologists who provided their theories. These theories are known as feminist and sociological theories of gender. 'Using the sociological imagination to investigate gender means performing the detailed archaeology of our own biography and learning to identify the larger structural forces at work in our lives surrounding issues of gender.'[50] A network approach of gender provides 'gender is really a product of the networks of relationships we find ourselves embedded in, going all the way back to the very first networks we belonged to as children.'[51] Under feminist theory, 'Gender is considered separately from statuses such as race, ethnicity, age, class, nationality, or sexuality.'[52]

On the basis of these statements, it comes out that gender has a very long list of work and many persons have defined it in their own ways and in defining of gender, they have adopted various approaches and context within the institutions of society. So, it is also very hard to understand and put a specific definition of gender as it keeps changing with the changing of time, context and circumstances. It is rightly said by Lorber and Tavris in understanding of gender that, 'Lorber and Tavris, research shows that the behaviour of real women and men depends on time and place, and context and situation, not on fixed gender differences.'[53]

After this detailed discussion about gender it may presume that an individual is identified with his or her gender identity irrespective of sex at birth and in this social process of gender identity formation everyone not only 'do gender' but also has 'being gender'. Whenever, we think about 'do gender' it relates, how concerned individual feel, think, behave, react and experience for others but in case of 'being gender' it produces the feeling, thinking, behaving, reacting and experiencing of others for individual concerned. In my own view, gender seems an **"Imagination"** in fact **"imagination of person's body and its various activities".**

Sexual Minorities (LGBT)

'We live in a world that is deeply structured by sex and gender. The categorisation of people as 'male' or 'female' permeates our society on every level, including our language, relationships, social institutions, and academic debates. On a social level, biological determinism, or the belief that we act in certain ways because of our physical make-up, is rife. This is the case despite the changes that have occurred over the past century in the way that gender and sexuality are constructed, and high levels of cross-cultural gender and sexual variance.'[54] For a common understanding to society, the status of LGBT is derived from various social, cultural and religious norms followed by law of state i.e. sec. 377 of Indian Penal Code (hereinafter IPC) which is very much centric for my work. The sec. 377 of IPC criminalises the sexual act between same-sex and may be read as:

'Whoever voluntarily has carnal intercourse against the order of nature with any man, woman or animal shall be punished with imprisonment which may extend to ten years, and shall also be liable to fine.

Explanation: Penetration is sufficient to constitute the carnal intercourse necessary to the offence described in this section.'[55]

According to G. R. Dunstan, accepted a sketch of human norm: 'patterns and standards of human relationship, validated widely in ordinary experience, attainable and enjoyed by men and women in varying degrees, and approbated by the conventions, and in some respects by the laws, of societies with a developed awareness of human liberty.'[56] He also discussed that 'there can be no one universal pattern of human sexual behaviour. There must be variety and acceptance of variety.'[57] Moreover, taking a deeper sense of understanding about the 'Variant forms of human sexual behaviour'[58] Rechard Green believed that 'there is probably no limit to the number of 'variant' forms of human sexual lifestyles.'[59]

Forwarding the illustration of Alfred Kinsey, Richard Green pointed out that 'People with an exclusive or major preference for a same-sex sexual partner make up a significant part of the population.'[60] Responding against the developmental mechanism of homosexual behaviour, Richard Green suggested 'prenatal endocrine programming of the central nervous system, various genetic factors, features in the child's family life, such as resolution or non-resolution of the Oedipal conflict ('family romance'), or the impact of early socialisation on 'social learning' as the responsible factors.'[61] Although, he was not sure about the 'genetic loading'[62] behind a homosexual orientation.

'LGBT are dened with reference to two distinct and complex characteristics: sexual orientation and gender identity.'[63] Indian society is diverse and has conservative nature as 'many Indians view transsexualism as a purely Western phenomenon, analogous to homosexuality and lesbianism, created by an overindulgent and over promiscuous society. They gloss over the evils of sexual repression in their own society, and ignore the evidence that homosexuality and lesbianism are as old as man himself, having been written about and discussed in ancient treatises such as the *Kamsutra*.'[64] Talking about the categories such as homosexuality David Halperin, argues that, 'homosexuality are indispensable to the experience of 'being' homosexual and further wants to make clear that such categories do not exist 'outside of history and culture', nor are they some form of 'false consciousness.'[65] A Public Union of Civil Liberties (PUCL)-K fact-finding report about Bangalore says that sexual minorities refer 'people discriminated against due to their sexual identity/ orientation or gender identity. This includes gays, lesbians, bisexuals, hijras, kotis, transgender, etc.'[66]

Marks and Spencer discussed about bullying that 'unwanted behaviour whether physical or verbal which is offensive, humiliating and viewed as unacceptable to the recipient.'[67] 'The Germans and the French call it "the slow poison".'[68] Several recent studies of bullying found that bullying affects the person in many ways out of these 'anxiety, depression, exhaustion, insecurity and self-doubt, shame, embarrassment and guilt, obsessive thinking and nightmares, poor concentration, and sleeplessness'[69] are most prevalent, although the outcomes of bullying are numerous. Now, in my own view, bullying with LGBT persons seems the first interactive activity offered by other persons. LGBT persons are highly vulnerable as far as the bullying is concerned.

Submitted by Georgia Lawrence, on 'The Science of Homosexuality' on Monday, 13-11-2006, 'Homosexuality is an issue that has sparked tumultuous debate in the United States, and has been brought to the forefront in the last fifty to sixty years. While the legal and social implications have captured the attention of the media, the lingering question of biology remains at the core of the debate. Is it possible that one is born with the characteristic of being homosexual, or is it solely a learned behaviour embedded in cultural norms?'[70]

Considering on the study of 'Health and Medicine Week', in 2004, Scientists at Oregon Health and Science University School of Medicine, Simon LeVay and Thomas A. Schoenfeld, Diamant, Louis, Kristof, Nicholas D, Georgia Lawrence concludes with a relationship between biology and sexual behaviour.

Although, the definition of LGBT is not provided in social and legal related studies but there are certain organisations, working groups and authorities who have tried to put definition of terms used under the category of LGBT in express and implied forms. The definitions are discussed out of binary system we know and may be referred here as:

Lesbian

'The word lesbian comes from the Greek Island of Lesbos, where the poet Sappho lived in 600 B.C. Sappho was an intellectual and poet who wrote many love poems to other women'(Reference: Kathy Belge, http://lesbianlife.about.com/bio/Kathy-belge-9380.htm). 'Female, who are erotically attracted to, and desire to form romantic relationship with, other females.'[71] 'A woman who is attracted to women emotionally/sexually/romantically.'[72] Sometimes, lesbians are also called 'homosexual women'. 'A woman who desires other women, the characteristic of people who are female desiring other females.'[73] Deepa V. N. points out her idea about lesbian that 'a lesbian is someone who will have sex with anybody.'[74]

Gay

'Male who are erotically attracted to and desire to form romantic relationship with other male.'[75] 'A man who is attracted to another men emotionally/sexually/physically.'[76] 'Males who desire only other males, the characteristic of same-sex male attraction.'[77]

'A word used to describe a man who is attracted to another men emotionally/sexually/physically.'[78]

Bisexual

'Sigmund Freud admitted the bisexual nature of all human beings, in his system the 'normal' mode of sexual development was heterosexual; explanations were required only when sexual object choices or aims other than reproductive activity with the 'opposite' sex occurred.'[79] Freud has strongly insisted 'on "an original bi-sexuality in every individual" assumes the status of an ethical judgement. His idea of bisexuality presumes an original unity of male and female characteristics and sexual inclination.'[80] 'Bisexual refers, who has erotic attraction to, and interest in developing romantic relationship with, males and females both.'[81] 'Bisexual is sexually responsive to either gender i.e. male or female.'[82] 'A person who is attracted romantically/emotionally/sexually to both men and women.'[83] 'The term 'bisexuality', whilst allowing for polysexual attraction (desire for people of more than one sex).'[84] 'People who are fluid about their desires might identify as bisexual.'[85] 'Alternative types of sexual orientation include those documented by Queen (1997): 'Omni sexual', (attracted to multiple genders), and 'pansexual', a term coined by Firestone (1970) to mean diverse, unbounded desire.'[86] 'Capable of desiring people of more than one gender, or a person who identifies as potentially desiring people of more than one gender. Bisexual has also been given other meanings, such as some who has two gender identities.'[87]

Transgender

'Someone who is anatomically born in a certain sex, but is more comfortable with the gender /sexual identity of a different gender, and chooses to go in for a sex reassignment surgery or hormonal treatment.'[88] 'Transgender is an umbrella term that can be used to refer to anyone for whom the sex she or he was assigned at birth is an incomplete or incorrect description of her or himself. Individuals may use an array of terms to describe their gender identity including transgender woman, transgender man, female-to-male (FTM), male-to-female (MTF), Trans, two-spirit, gender nonconforming (GNC), or persons of transgender experience. Some trans- gender people may identify with the term transsexual and may utilize various interventions to medically transition into the gender they most identify with.'[89] 'An umbrella term which includes cross-dressers, transsexuals, androgynies, drag artists, third and other gender people, and other people with gender identities that are more complex than simply 'male or 'female'.'[90]

Conclusion

Finally, the discussion on gender discourse in general produces the material of male and female study popularly known as binary structure under social construction. Because of having the broader perspective of understanding sex, gender and sexual minorities, we can say that the existing binary social construction for the study of gender is not sufficient and the study of gender itself seems incomplete under such binary construction. Hence, the study of this highly discriminated and isolated community needs to include under the study of sex, gender or person as whole. In legal aspect, the study of LGBT persons is highly debated after some judgements of Indian judiciary. Hence, the study of gender discourse and inequality with reference to LGBT persons is breaking this binary system i.e. male and female study in present circumstance.

References

1. Dr. T. S. Sathyanarayana Rao, "Some Thoughts on Sexualities and Research in India", 46(1) *IJP* 3 (2004).
2. *Ibid.*

3. R. L. Dickinson, *Sexual Adjustment in Marriages-A Pshcho-Medical Approach ix* (Reprint Publication, Dehradun (India) 2004).
4. Kavita Joshi, Sexuality in India: Teenager and Teacher (Kalpaz Publications, Delhi, 2004) at p. 15.
5. *Ibid,* at p. 79.
6. Philip Rieff, Freud: The Mind of the Moralist (University Paperbacks, Methuen: London, 1965) at p. 152.
7. *Ibid,* at p. 154.
8. Robyn Ryle, Questioning Gender: A Sociological Exploration (SAGE Publication, United States of America, 2012) at p. 6.
9. *Ibid.*
10. *Ibid.*
11. Spencer A Rathus, Jeffrey S. Nevid, et. al. (eds.), Human Sexuality in a world of diversity (Allyn and Bacon, United State of America, 4th edn; 2000) at pp. 4-5.
12. Kavita Joshi, Sexuality in India: Teenager and Teacher (Kalpaz Publications, Delhi, 2004) at p. 44.
13. *Ibid,* at p. 59.
14. Joan Z. Spade and Catherine G. Valentine (eds.), The Kaleidoscope of Gender: Prisms, Patterns, and Possibilities (Sage Publications, New Delhi, 2nd edn; 2008) at p. 5.
15. Sara Delamont and Paul Atkinson (eds.), Gender and Research (Sage Publications, New Delhi, Vol. 4; 2008) at p. 107.
16. Robyn Ryle, Questioning Gender: A Sociological Exploration (SAGE Publication, United States of America, 2012) at p. 9.
17. *Ibid,* at pp. 9-10.
18. *Ibid,* at p. 10.
19. Guryinder Kalra, Susham Gupta, et. al; "Sexual variation in India: A view from the west", Indian J Psychiatry, Vol. 52, No. (Suppl 1) (January, 2010) at p. S264–S268.
20. Anil Kumar Mysore Nagaraj, "Osho: Insights on sex", Indian J Psychiatry, Vol. 55, No. Indian Mental Concepts I – Supplement (January 2013) at p. S268.
21. RobynRyle, Questioning Gender: A Sociological Exploration (SAGE Publication, United States of America, 2012) at p. 186.
22. *Ibid.*
23. Tsjeard Bouta, Georg Frerks, et. al. (eds.), Gender, Conflict, and Development (The World Bank, Washington, D.C., 2005) at p. xi.
24. Joan Z. Spade and Catherine G. Valentine (eds.), The Kaleidoscope of Gender: Prisms, Patterns, and Possibilities (Sage Publications, New Delhi, 2nd edn; 2008) at p. 3.
25. *Ibid,* at p. xvii.
26. *Ibid,* at p. xiv.
27. *Ibid,* at p. xiii.
28. *Ibid,* at p. xv.

29. *Ibid,* at p. xvi.
30. *Ibid.*
31. *Ibid.*
32. *Ibid.*
33. Joan Z. Spade and Catherine G. Valentine (eds.), The Kaleidoscope of Gender: Prisms, Patterns, and Possibilities (Sage Publications, New Delhi, 2nd edn; 2008) at p. xvi.
34. *Ibid,* at p. xviii.
35. *Ibid.*
36. Sara Delamont and Paul Atkinson (eds.), Gender and Research (Sage Publications, New Delhi, Vol. 4; 2008) at p. 37.
37. Joan Z. Spade and Catherine G. Valentine (eds.), The Kaleidoscope of Gender: Prisms, Patterns, and Possibilities (Sage Publications, New Delhi, 2nd edn; 2008) at p. xviii.
38. *Ibid,* at p. xix.
39. *Ibid,* at p.10.
40. *Ibid,* at p. xx.
41. *Ibid,* at p. 5.
42. *Ibid,* at p. 9.
43. RajeshTalwar, The Third Sex and Human Rights (Gyan Publishing House, New Delhi, 1999) at p. 24.
44. Joan Z. Spade and Catherine G. Valentine (eds.), The Kaleidoscope of Gender: Prisms, Patterns, and Possibilities (Sage Publications, New Delhi, 2nd edn; 2008) at p. 24.
45. *Ibid,* at p. 33.
46. Tsjeard Bouta, Georg Frerks, et. al. (eds.), Gender, Conflict, and Development (The World Bank, Washington, D.C., 2005) at p. 3.
47. Joan Z. Spade and Catherine G. Valentine (eds.), The Kaleidoscope of Gender: Prisms, Patterns, and Possibilities (Sage Publications, New Delhi, 2nd edn; 2008) at p. 52.
48. Tsjeard Bouta, Georg Frerks, et. al. (eds.), Gender, Conflict, and Development (The World Bank, Washington, D.C., 2005) at p. 3.
49. Sara Delamont and Paul Atkinson (eds.), Gender and Research (Sage Publications, New Delhi, Vol. 4; 2008) at p. 200.
50. Robyn Ryle, Questioning Gender: A Sociological Exploration (SAGE Publication, United States of America, 2012) at p. 32.
51. *Ibid,* at p. 51.
52. *Ibid,* at p. 52.
53. Joan Z. Spade and Catherine G. Valentine (eds.), The Kaleidoscope of Gender: Prisms, Patterns, and Possibilities (Sage Publications, New Delhi, 2nd edn; 2008) at p. 5.
54. Surya Monro, Gender Politics (Pluto Press, London, 2005) at p. 10.

55. Arvind Narrain and Gautam Bhan (eds.), Because I Have a Voice (Yoda Press, New Delhi, 2012) at p. 7.
56. C.R. Austin and R.V. Short, Reproduction in Mammals: Human Sexuality 170 (Cambridge University Press, New York, 1980).
57. *Ibid,* p. 171.
58. *Ibid,* p. 68.
59. C.R. Austin and R.V. Short, Reproduction in Mammals: Human Sexuality 68 (Cambridge University Press, New York, 1980).
60. *Ibid.*
61. *Ibid,* p. 70.
62. *Ibid,* p. 71.
63. Ann P. Haas, PhD, Mickey Eliason, PhD, et. al., "Suicide and Suicide Risk in Lesbian, Gay, Bisexual, and Transgender Populations: Review and Recommendations", Journal of Homosexuality, Vol. 58, (2011) at p. 13.
64. Rajesh Talwar, The Third Sex And Human Rights (Gyan Publishing House, New Delhi, 1999) at p. 12.
65. Robert A. Nye (ed.), Sexuality (Oxford University Press, New York, 2009) at p. 7.
66. A PUCL-K, 2001 fact-finding report about Banglore, Human Rights Violations against Sexuality Minorities in India, at p. 6.
67. *Ibid,* at pp. 2-3.
68. *Ibid,* at p. 2.
69. *Ibid,* at p. 8.
70. http://serendip.brynmawr.edu/exchange/node/33
71. Spencer A Rathus, Jeffrey S. Nevid, et. al. (eds.), Human Sexuality in a world of diversity (Allyn and Bacon, United State of America, 4th edn; 2000) at p. 267.
72. A PUCL-K, 2001 fact-finding report about Bangalore, Human Rights Violations against Sexuality Minorities in India, at p. 6.
73. Surya Monro, Gender Politics (Pluto Press, London, 2005) at p. 194.
74. Arvind Narrain and Gautam Bhan (eds.), Because I Have a Voice (Yoda Press, New Delhi, 2012) at p. 21.
75. Spencer A Rathus, Jeffrey S. Nevid, et. al. (eds.), Human Sexuality in a world of diversity (Allyn and Bacon, United State of America, 4th edn; 2000) at p. 267.
76. A PUCL-K, 2001 fact-finding report about Bangalore, Human Rights Violations against Sexuality Minorities in India, at p. 6.
77. Surya Monro, Gender Politics (Pluto Press, London, 2005) at p. 194.
78. Arvind Narrain, *Queer: Law and Despised Sexualities in India*, Glossary
79. Robert A. Nye (ed.), Sexuality (Oxford University Press, New York, 2009) at p. 10.
80. Philip Rieff, Freud: The Mind of the Moralist (University Paperbacks, Methuen: London, 1965) at p. 185.
81. Spencer A Rathus, Jeffrey S. Nevid, et. al. (eds.), Human Sexuality in a world of diversity (Allyn and Bacon, United State of America, 4th edn; 2000) at p. 267.

82. *Ibid,* at p. 13.
83. A PUCL-K, 2001 fact-finding report about Bangalore, Human Rights Violations against Sexuality Minorities in India, at p. 6.
84. Surya Monro, Gender Politics (Pluto Press, London, 2005) at p. 14.
85. *Ibid,* at p. 16.
86. *Ibid,* at p. 15.
87. Surya Monro, Gender Politics (Pluto Press, London, 2005) at p. 194.
88. *Ibid.*
89. Kevin L. Nadal, Avy Skolnik, et. al., "Interpersonal and Systemic Micro aggression stoward Transgender People: Implications for Counselling", Journal of LGBT Issues in Counselling, Vol. 6, No. 1, (2012) at pp. 55-56.
90. Surya Monro, Gender Politics (Pluto Press, London, 2005) at p. 195.

4

Gender Discrimination and Inequality: A Case of the Divisiveness of Consciousness

— *Nikhil Kumar*

Key Words: *Gender Discrimination, Inequality, Spiritual Consciousness and Supramental Consciousness*

Introduction

There is a Power within that knows beyond
Our knowings; we are greater than our thoughts,
And sometimes earth unveils that vision here.

(Sri Aurobindo 2012: 403)

This is what Sri Aurobindo, a yogi of the unknown eternal heights, discovers. Such a 'Power' is the power of the Soul, the Divine Self, the Self which exists at the centre of our being. It transcends all that is within us. It transcends the body, the life, and the mind which constitute the manifest terrestrial individuality of man. The Soul is a portion of the Divine in us, of which the body, the life and the mind are instruments. The yogis identify us with It, not with these instruments of Soul. For, the Soul, being a portion of the Divine is immortal, the instruments mortal. They have further found the Soul to be the individual poise of the Divine in the being of man. Such individual poise of the Divine, the Soul uses the body, the life and the mind as Its instruments to manifest the Divine in the being of man. Therefore, they come to be the instrumental selves in his being.

On the present evolutionary stage the instrumental selves are in command of the being of man causing mortality therein. Mortality in the being of man is attributed to the truth which Sri Aurobindo makes very clear that the Soul exerts its 'concealed and partial and indirect influence' (1990:225) on them.

But the very 'concealed, partial and indirect influence' of the Soul on them, on the other hand, impels man to rise to the higher evolutionary ladders since it is the individual poise of the Divine, says the Yogi. It comes to be the cause of the success of man in his terrestrial existence. We have, therefore, to let the Soul emerge and take the full and direct control of the instrumental selves for our higher evolutionary journey to have a higher vision of the Divine Truth, and to attain Immortality in course of evolution.

Such a soul-power is required to be evolved for the end of the gender discrimination and inequality prevailing in the human society. On an examination it is found that the gender discrimination and inequality across the globe is the manifestation of the divided consciousness of man, nay, the divisive principle of Consciousness. The divisive consciousness to which the body consciousness, the life consciousness and the mind consciousness of man are receptive on the present evolutionary stage has taken command of his being, nay, the terrestrial existence causing chaos and catastrophe not only in his lives, but on the other spheres, too, of the terrestrial existence. Such truth leads us to shift our attention from gender discrimination and inequality to the consciousness, the divisive principle of which is solely responsible for such gender discrimination and inequality from which the womenfolk are suffering. They are denied their natural rights to survive and evolve in their lives on account of the operation of the divisive principle of the essential consciousness. We, are, therefore, required to rise to the higher planes of consciousness by evolving the soul 'Power within that knows beyond/Our knowings' (2012: 403) to bring about an end of the rule of the divisive consciousness of mind in our being, and consequently of the gender discrimination and inequality. The soul-consciousness with its 'Power' inherent in the being of man is the integral consciousness since it is the portion of the Divine, the individual poise of the Divine. It comes to replace the divisive principle of consciousness in the body, the life, and the mind when It emerges in the being of man from its latent state. Then, man comes to be able to ascend the planes of the spiritual consciousness without any resistance from the hostile forces, the divisiveness of consciousness which exist within the instrumental selves in his being prior to the emergence of the Soul-Consciousness and Its Power. In fact, the evolution of consciousness to its spiritual and, what Sri Aurobindo calls, the 'supramental' planes is the 'central significant motive of the terrestrial existence' (1990:824), the Supramental which exists beyond the plane of creation itself. Of the evolutionary journey of man to the plane of Supramental, the Supramental which is essentially the integral consciousness, he says:

> A spiritual evolution, an evolution of consciousness in Matter in a constant developing self-formation till the form can reveal the indwelling Spirit, is then the key-note, the central significant motive of the terrestrial existence. (1990: 824)

In his yogic consciousness he visualises the manifestation of the Spirit, the Divine Consciousness in the material existence, or to say, Matter. In his epic *Savitri* he expresses the truth poetically:

> The Spirit shall look out through Matter's gaze
> And Matter shall reveal the Spirit's face.
>
> (2012: 715)

He reveals the truth further:

> All earth shall be the Spirit's manifest home,
> Hidden no more by the body and the life,
> Hidden no more by the mind's ignorance;
> An unerring Hand shall shape event and act.
> The Spirit's eyes shall look through Nature's eyes,
> The Spirit's force shall occupy Nature's force.
> This world shall be God's visible garden-house,
> This earth shall be a field and camp of God,
> Man shall forget consent to mortality
> And his embodied frail impermanence.
>
> (2012: 713-14)

Such manifestation of the Divine Consciousness, the Supramental Consciousness which is the destined culmination of evolutionary phenomenon begins to take place when the Soul comes in front in the being of man and takes the reins of the body, the life and the mind in its command for laying down the foundation in him of the irreversible ascent of consciousness to its spiritual and supramental planes.

The Constitution of the Being of Man

We have noted earlier at the outset of the paper that Sri Aurobindo is the Soul who has descended from an unknown eternal heights on the earth, the manifestation of which we find in all his works, especially, in his *The Life Divine*, an epic prose and in his epic *Savitri* besides *The Synthesis of Yoga, Letters on Yoga* etc. since they very poetically record the Divine Truth which evades the vision of the Vedic Rishis and the Gita. Such monumental works of him reveal the descent of the Supramental Consciousness from Its Sovereign Supramental plane of Existence into the terrestrial existence, and the consequent supramental transformation of man, and subsequently of the earth as the culmination of the evolutionary phenomenon. The physical transformation, too, of man and earth will take place as a result of the descent of the Supramental Consciousness from Its Sovereign Supramental plane, the truth which does not come into the vision of the Vedas, the Upanishads and the Gita which are admittedly the highest literary documents of the world-literature.

Sri Aurobindo discovers that we are made up of the body, the life and the mind, at the centre of which exists the Divine Self, the Soul or, what the Vedic Rishis call, Jivatman, or Atman. The Jivatman is the Central Divine Being in man, and is the witness to the evolutionary phenomena in the being of man. It has produced its projection in man, 'psychic being' Sri Aurobindo calls, in course of evolution. It is instrumental in man's physical, vital, mental, spiritual and supramental evolution participating in the evolutionary phenomena. He makes it clear in some of his letters on yoga that what we call 'soul' is the psychic being which is a projection or representative of the Jivatman, the Central Divine Being. He writes in these letters:

> The phrase "central being" in our yoga is usually applied to the portion of the Divine in us which supports all the rest and survives through death and birth. This central being has two forms—above, it is Jivatman, our true being, of which we become aware when the higher self-knowledge comes, —below, it is the psychic being which stands behind mind, body and life. The Jivatman is above the manifestation in life and presides over it; the psychic being stands behind the manifestation in life and supports it. (1979: 265)

He further says:

> *Jivatma* is not the psychic being—we have fixed on *caitya purusa* as the equivalent in Sanskrit of the psychic being. Jivatma is the individual Self—the central being.
>
> The central being is that which is not born, does not evolve, but presides over all the individual manifestation. The psychic is its projection here—for the psychic being is in the evolution and from within supports our whole evolution; it receives the essence of all experience and by that develops the personality Godward. (1979: 267)

He makes the picture of the constitution of the being of man all the more clear when he says:

> The soul, representative of the central being, is a spark of the Divine supporting all individual existence in Nature; the psychic being is a conscious form of that soul growing in the evolution—in the persistent process that develops first life in Matter, mind in life, until finally mind can develop into overmind[1] and overmind into the supramental truth. The soul supports the nature in its evolution through these grades, but is itself not any of these things. (1979: 267-68)

He further says:

> The Jivatman, spark-soul and psychic being are three different forms of the same reality, and they must not be mixed up together, as that confuses the clearness of the inner experience.

> The Jivatman or spirit, as usually it is called in English, is self-existent above the manifested or instrumental being—it is superior to birth and death, always the same, the individual Self or Atman. It is the eternal true being of the individual.
>
> The soul is a spark of the Divine which is not seated above the manifested being, but comes down into the manifestation to support its evolution in the material world. It is at first an undifferentiated power of the Divine Consciousness containing all possibilities which have not yet taken form, but to which it is the function of evolution to give form. This spark is there in all living beings from the lowest to the highest.
>
> The psychic being is formed by the soul in its evolution. It supports the mind, vital, body, grows by their experiences, carries the nature from life to life. It is the psychic or *caitya purusa.* At first it is veiled by mind, vital and body, but as it grows, it becomes capable of coming forward and dominating the mind, life and body; in the ordinary man it depends on them for expression and is not able to take them up and freely use them. The life of the being is animal or human and not divine. When the psychic being can by sadhana become dominant and freely use its instruments, then the impulse towards the Divine becomes complete and the transformation of mind, vital and body, not merely their liberation, becomes possible. (1979: 282-83)

Of the existence of the Jivatman and the Psychic Being *Mundaka Upanishad* speaks symbolically in its verse one of the section I of the chapter III that 'two birds, beautiful of wing, close companions, cling to one common tree; of the two one eats the sweet fruit of the tree, the other eats not but watches his fellow' (1988:205). The bird which eats the 'fruit' is the psychic being. The other bird which 'eats not but watches his fellow' is the Jivatman, the Central Divine Being. The 'one common tree' is man's individual form or outer being. 'Fruit' is the experience of the body, the life and the mind in the being of man in his life. Eating the fruit of the tree is an act of gathering the experiences in the beings of the body, the life and the mind by the psychic being. Of the role of the psychic being in man's evolution of consciousness Sri Aurobindo says:

> Missioned to lead man in the Ignorance towards the light of the Divine Consciousness, it takes the essence of all experience in the Ignorance to form nucleus of soul-growth in the nature; the rest it turns into material for the future growth of the instruments which it has to use until they are ready to be a luminous instrumentation of the Divine. (1990:226)

In the ordinary man the body, the life and the mind are receptive to the divisive consciousness which is the 'Ignorance' (1990:226) Consciousness. The Divisive Consciousness is the Ignorance Consciousness for the reason that it is not able to be conscious of the Divine Truth. The Divine Truth dwelling on the Sovereign Supramental plane is eclipsed to it on account of its divisiveness. A letter of Sri Aurobindo reveals very clearly the role of the Psychic Being:

> It is necessary to understand clearly the difference between the evolving soul (psychic being) and the pure Atman, self or spirit. The pure self is unborn, does not pass through death or birth, is independent of birth or body, mind or life or this manifested Nature. It is not bound by these things, not limited, not affected, even though it assumes and supports them. The soul, on the contrary, is something that comes down into birth and passes through death—although it does not itself die, for it is immortal—from one state to another, from the earth plane to other planes and back again to the earth-existence. It goes on with this progression from life to life through an evolution which leads it up to the human state and evolves through it all a being of itself which we call the psychic being that supports the evolution and develops a physical, a vital, a mental human consciousness as its instruments of world-experience and of a disguised, imperfect, but growing self-expression. All this it does from behind a veil showing something of its divine self only in so far as the imperfection of the instrumental being will allow it. But a time comes when it is able to prepare to come out from behind the veil, to take command and turn all the instrumental nature towards a divine fulfilment. This is the beginning of the true spiritual life. The soul is able to make itself ready for a higher evolution of manifested consciousness than the mental human—it can pass from the mental to the spiritual and through degrees of the spiritual to the supramental state. Till then there is no reason why it should cease from birth, it cannot in fact do so. If having reached the spiritual state, it wills to pass out of the terrestrial manifestation, it may indeed do so—but there is also possible a higher manifestation, in the Knowledge and not in the Ignorance. (1979: 438-39)

The Soul uses the 'instruments' to work out the Divine Will in the terrestrial existence. It is the Will for the Supramental Transformation of the earthly existence. On the present evolutionary stage we are yet to come under the direct governance of the Soul. The Soul exercises 'only a concealed and partial and indirect action' (1990:225) on its instrumental selves as stated earlier at the outset of the paper. Since it exercises 'a concealed and partial and indirect action' on these instrumental selves, we are under the direct control of Mind, or Life which Sri Aurobindo terms the 'Vital Being', or Body, or under the simultaneous control of all these instrumental selves with the result that mortality crops up in our being. They are at the warring state as the divisive consciousness is in command of them on account of which so many mortal manifestations we find in ourselves. The mortal manifestations of the divisive consciousness come to be detrimental to the evolution of our consciousness to the spiritual planes of mind, the spiritual planes where we have the knowledge and realisation of the One Divine, the One Cosmic Self. We are required, as noted earlier, to evolve the 'Power' (2012:403), the Power of the Soul-Consciousness which is latently at the centre of our being in order to bring about an end of the warring state in which the instrumental selves exist on the present evolutionary stage. It is to be noted again that the warring state manifests our divisive consciousness, the divisive consciousness which is at the root of the gender discrimination and inequality. More to say, the divisive consciousness manifests not only in gender discrimination and inequality, but in racial discrimination, communal discrimination, caste discrimination and all other discriminations, too, which have plagued the human lives. Such discriminations hinder our spiritual growth as a result of which we are not able to feel even the touch of the latent 'Power' (2012: 403), and fail to discern, consequently, the Divine Oneness in all the beings of the terrestrial existence. When we are able to see the Divine Oneness at the base of all the forms existing in the terrestrial existence, the forms in the earthly, or to say, material existence come to 'reveal the indwelling Spirit' (1990: 824), the Divine Self in themselves.

Triple Transformation of the Being of Man

Sri Aurobindo speaks of the triple transformation of man 'to effectuate a true manifestation of the embodied Spirit' (1990: 889). It has to result in the emergence of a new race on the earth, the supramental race having a transcendent consciousness. The supramental being has to emerge because, as he says,

> ...there is something not yet accomplished, there becomes clear to view the much that has still to be done, *bhuri aspata kartvam*; there is a height still to be reached, a wideness still to be covered by the eye of vision, the wing of the will, the self-affirmation of the Spirit in the material universe. What the evolutionary Power has done is to make a few individuals aware of their souls, conscious of their selves, aware of the eternal being that they are, to put them into communion with the Divinity or the Reality which is concealed by her appearances: a certain change of nature prepares, accompanies or follows upon this illumination, but it is not the complete and radical change which establishes a secure and settled new principle, a new creation, a permanent new order of being in the field of terrestrial Nature. The spiritual man has evolved, but not the supramental being who shall thenceforward be the leader of that Nature. (1990: 890)

The triple transformation is the transformation firstly of the instrumental selves of man, —the body, the life and the mind. He terms it 'Psychicisation'. It is the psychicisation, or to say, the psychic transformation of these instrumental selves of the Soul in the being of man. Further, he speaks of the spiritualisation, or to say, the spiritual transformation of man, and finally the supramentalisation, or to say, the supramental transformation of man. In order to bring about the triple transformation in our being it is imperative for us to undertake yoga, the yoga which Sri Aurobindo undertook for the successful triple transformation of his being. Such a yoga is, what he calls, the Integral Yoga. The triple transformation of the being of man enables him to see the working of the Divine Mother in the womenfolk. One, then, realises how such a working of the Divine Mother is necessitated for the integral manifestation of the Divine Consciousness in the terrestrial existence with the establishment of the Divine Life therein. In such integral manifestation there is the revelation of the 'indwelling Spirit' in Matter. There will be no riotous state whether it be in the form of gender discrimination or any other discriminations in the earth-nature when the Divine Life is established in the earth-nature. In other words, discrimination comes to its end, and there emerges the picture of a dual harmonious power. A higher consciousness evolves in man. He comes to visualise certain distinctive divine features situated in two genders, female and male. We come to view the dual power of the Divine without which the terrestrial existence cannot emerge out of Its Divine Origin, —the dual Power which is manifest in the two genders of the creatures of the earth. It is as necessary as the two poles of the electric energy, the positive and the negative as we term them, are necessary for the manifestation of the electric Energy. The positive and the negative poles, too, are the dual Power of the electric Energy.

> The incarnate dual Power shall open God's door,
> Eternal supermind touch earthly Time. (2012: 711)

The 'incarnate dual Power' manifests in Satyavan and Savitri in the epic *Savitri.* They have incarnated on the earth to bring down the Supramental Consciousness into the earth-existence from the Sovereign Supramental plane of Existence. In such a higher transcendent consciousness in which the two genders come to be the 'incarnate dual Power' of the Divine, the female figure of Christ comes to be visible to man in Desdemona and Cordelia, — Desdemona and Cordelia who reign supreme in the tragic world of William Shakespeare, the man who has created next to God. They are found to have descended on the earth for the sole purpose of averting the evolutionary crisis and giving impetus to the evolutionary force on the earth shown in the persons of Othello and Lear as it is done by the Avatar, the Incarnation of the Divine on the cosmic plane for the evolutionary ascent of the terrestrial existence. The evolutionary change of consciousness in Othello and Lear takes place as a result of the working out of the force of the Divine Mother in the beings of Desdemona and Cordelia. Such a change is evident when Othello says:

> I kist thee ere I kill'd thee: no way but this,
> (*Falling upon* DESDEMONA.
> Killing myself, to die upon a kiss.
>
> (Shakespeare Othello: V.II.359-60)

Lear's transformation of consciousness is also visible when he realises that Cordelia is 'a soul in bliss' (Lear IV.VII.47). He further says:

You are a spirit, I know...

(King Lear: IV. VIII. 51)

In Sri Aurobindo's *Savitri* Savitri is the incarnation of the Divine Mother. The Divine Mother descends from Her Sovereign World of the Divine in the form of the daughter of King Ashwapati to make the Earth to recover her concealed Divinehood. Satyavan is the symbol of Matter, the Earth. His death is the death of Matter. Savitri, as a result of her successful yogic battle on the supraphysical plane of Existence with the Death-God, Yama, brings back Satyavan to life in his gross physical body. Having seen in the yogic perspective Satyavan's coming back to his life is found to be the emergence of the latent Supramental Consciousness in Matter having got rid of the mortality, the divisive principle of Consciousness. Such an emergence is the supramentalisation of the earth-being. It comes to be possible only by the Mother-force at work in the being of Savitri.

Savitri could be able to do so as she, earlier, by virtue of her yoga of supramentalisation in making her Psychic Being come to be One with her Jivatman brought down the Supramental Consciousness into her being as a result which the Mother-force in her being could come to work for such a high task. Sri Aurobindo has discovered the plane of the Subtle-Matter existing above the plane of the gross Matter in which we live. The plane of the Subtle-Matter which is, in fact, the supraphysical plane of existence has given birth to the plane of the gross Matter. After supramentalising her being she needs to supramentalise the former, the world of the subtle Matter as it is also under the grip of the divisive consciousness. The supramentalisation of the world of the Subtle Matter has to result in the supramentalisation of the world of the gross Matter since it is the origin of the world of the gross Matter. In the event of Satyavan's death she enters into this world to follow him as the soul residing in the subtle body of the man goes first in this world after the death of his gross body (1979: 435). Her supramental consciousness dethrones the divisive consciousness in the world of the Subtle Matter, consequent upon which the Integral Consciousness, the Supramental Consciousness is established into the world of the Subtle Matter. Satyavan's subtle body is supramentalised in this world of the Subtle-Matter consequently. After getting his subtle body supramentalised, that is to say, getting rid of the divisive consciousness in his subtle body his soul comes back into his gross body. Further, under the influence and pressure of his supramentalised subtle body his gross physical body, too, undergoes supramental transformation. Subsequently, the supramental consciousness percolates into the universal world of the gross Matter through his supramentalised gross physical body which results finally into the supramentalisation of the earth-existence.

Sri Aurobindo lays emphasis on psychicisation first. He lays emphasis on psychicisation first for the reason that it makes essential preparation for the irreversible spiritual and supramental transformations of man. It is, in fact, foundation of the integral transformation, the Divine Transformation of man. In its absence the gravitational pull of Matter continues to take place in the body, the life and the mind, and there is, consequently, every possibility of the fall of man from the planes of the spiritual consciousness if he ascends the plane of spiritual consciousness without undergoing the psychicisation. In one of his letters on yoga he writes:

> This psychic development and the psychic change of mind, vital and physical consciousness is of the utmost importance because it makes safe and easy the descent of the higher consciousness and the spiritual transformation without which the supramental must always remain far distant. (1979: 1095)

Such psychic transformation of the mental, the vital and the body consciousnesses opens our 'inner doors' (1990: 933). He says:

> ...if the inner doors are flung sufficiently open, the light from the sanctuary can suffuse the nearest and the farthest chambers of the outer being. (1990: 933)

The psychicisation, or to say, the psychic transformation of the body, the life and the mind which we have earlier noted to be the instrumental selves of the Soul in the being of man, takes place when the Soul takes over the command of these instrumental selves to govern them to turn 'all to the Divine' (1092). They undergo transformation since the Divine Consciousness percolates into them as a result of the taking over of them by the Soul. The percolation of the Divine Consciousness into them makes them receptive to what comes down to them from the planes of the Divine Existence. They come out of the gravitational pull of Matter. They, then, reject most naturally 'that' which goes against the Divine Law. He says:

> ...so a psychicisation will not carry one beyond the present evolution but will make the being ready to respond to all that comes from the Divine or Higher Nature and unwilling to respond to the Asura, Rakshasa, Pishacha or Animal in the being or to any resistance of the lower nature which stands in the way of the divine change. (1979: 1094)

The soul which remains behind these instrumental selves prior to their psychic transformation comes in front in the being of man as a result of their psychic transformation.

It is to be noted here that Sri Aurobindo uses the term 'psychic' as adjective of 'soul'. Therefore, such transformation is also called the 'soul-transformation' of the instrumental selves. It is only after their soul-transformation that they are fit to work out the Divine Will in Nature under the direct governance of the Soul.

Sri Aurobindo, further, speaks of the next inevitable necessity of the spiritual transformation. When man ascends the planes of the spiritual consciousness, the instrumental selves,—the body, the life and the mind—, are, then, capable of receiving the consciousness and power of the planes of the spiritual consciousness.

> ...on that[2] or along with that there must be the spiritual change, the descent of a higher Light, Knowledge, Power, Force, Bliss, Purity into the whole being, even into the lowest recesses of the life and body, even into the darkness of our subconscience. (1990: 891)

In order to make the spiritual transformation intelligible we have to look at the hierarchy of consciousness which Sri Aurobindo discovers in the universe. In such discovery the universe comes to be the graded consciousness. He discovers first, on the plane of Mind Consciousness, the existence of 'physical mind consciousness' as he terms it. He finds Matter and Life, too, to be the planes of consciousness existing below the plane of Mind. In fact, he discovers Matter and Life to be the forms of consciousness, the consciousness which he discovers to be the basic thing in existence. In his another letter on yoga he writes:

> Consciousness is a fundamental thing, the fundamental thing in existence—it is the energy, the motion, the movement of consciousness that creates the universe and all that is in it—not only the macrocosm but the microcosm is nothing but consciousness arranging itself. For instance, when consciousness in its movement or rather a certain stress of movement forgets itself in the action it becomes an apparently "unconscious" energy; when it forgets itself in the form it becomes the electron, the atom, the material object. In reality it is still consciousness that works in the energy and determines the form and the evolution of form. When it wants to liberate itself, slowly, evolutionarily, out of Matter, but still in the form, it emerges as life, as animal, as man and it can go on evolving itself still farther out of its involution and becomes something more than mere man. (1979: 236-37)

In the realm of Physics, too, the Quantum Theory gets unmistakable indication of the existence of consciousness, or what the noted Physicist A.S. Eddington terms, 'mind-stuff' (1929 :276) at the base of the material existence having gone into the deeper depths of Matter, to be more specific, in the sub-atomic world of Matter to discover the ultimate truth behind the duality of wave and particle therein. Eddington says:

> I do not believe that the activity of matter at a certain point of brain stimulates the activity of mind; my view is that in the activity of

> Matter there is a metrical description of certain aspects of the activity of mind. (Eddington 1929: 268)

The other scientists, too, working on the Quantum Theory are occupied with the vision of consciousness at the base of Matter.

> Why should we not expect a reciprocal power of the mental to act upon the material ? (Polkinghorne 2006:51)

They say:

> ...quantum theory is 'observer created'. (2006: 90)

In spite of the fact that the scientific world is not unanimous on the existence of mind-stuff or consciousness at the base of Matter, no scientist is able to refute the scientific arguments made by the scientists like Eddington.

The 'consciousness' factor has taken hold of the scientists' mind so strongly that they have started talking of the concept of *Maya* of the ancient Rishis of India and the Indian Philosophers (2006: 91) to solve the dualism of wave and particle in the sub-atomic plane of Matter. In fact, the scientific mind is required to evolve to see what Sri Aurobindo visualises to enable itself to come out of the trap of the dualism of wave and particle. It is his vision of 'consciousness' at the base of Matter which comes to be the saviour of the scientific mind.

Going above the plane of the physical mind consciousness Sri Aurobindo discovers a plane of mind consciousness which he terms 'the vital mind consciousness' in which the 'life' (1979: 236-37) reigns, the life which, on the present evolutionary stage, is enslaved to the intense separativity which is in operation in the Mind-Consciousness, being capable of experiencing merely the superficiality of the material phenomenon of the Existence. He further discovers another higher plane of consciousness which he terms 'the mental mind consciousness', the mind which makes its own construction of the Truth. The mental mind consciousness, which fails in its construction to present the Truth truly, we recognise as the intellectual mind consciousness. When we go beyond these three planes of the mind-consciousness we enter the plane of the spiritual mind consciousness where, as noted earlier, we have the knowledge and realisation of the One Divine, the One Cosmic Self. When we transcend the spiritual planes, the four successive higher planes, the Higher Mind, the Illumined Mind, the Intuitive Mind and the Overmind, in the Mind Consciousness, we go beyond the plane of Mind. We find ourselves in the world of the Divine Consciousness which he calls 'Supramental Consciousness', the supramental which is the plane of the Integral Consciousness as noted earlier. Sri Aurobindo very categorically says that the mental consciousness, or to say, Mind is the divisive principle of consciousness, and the supramental, or to say, the supermind, the integral principle.

Sri Aurobindo finds that the planes of consciousness below the plane of the spiritual consciousness on the plane of Mind are under the gravitational pull of Matter as discussed earlier. It is to be noted again that the gravitational pull of Matter causes divisiveness and the assertion of the divisiveness of consciousness in the being of man, the manifestation of which we find in the gender discrimination and inequality. Consequent upon their psychicisation or soul-transformation the instrumental selves of man get rid of the gravitational pull of Matter with the result that the divisiveness of the mental consciousness begins to lose its existence, and man enters the domain of the spiritual mind consciousness. With the beginning of the end of the divisiveness of consciousness a movement towards the integral plane of consciousness takes place simultaneously. Such a movement is discovered in the world of the spiritual consciousness on account of which the knowledge and realisation of the One Divine, the One Cosmic Self begins to take place on the aforesaid successive four higher planes of the spiritual consciousness.

The spiritual transformation in the being of man takes place when he enters into the domain of the spiritual planes of the Mind-Consciousness. As he comes up on the spiritual plane, the consciousness and power of the spiritual plane descend into his being. They descend into his instrumental selves,— the body, the life and the mind. Since the gravitational pull of Matter ceases to exist in these instrumental selves as a result of their psychicisation, or to say, psychic transformation, the instrumental selves receive the consciousness and power of the plane of the spiritual consciousness into their beings. No hostility exists in their beings. The latent spiritual consciousness, too, in the being of man gets the opportunity to emerge as a result of the descent of the consciousness and power of the plane of the spiritual consciousness. With the descent of the spiritual consciousness and power from the plane of the spiritual consciousness and the consequent emergence of the latent spiritual consciousness in his being a transformation takes place in the being of man which Sri Aurobindo calls the 'spiritual transformation'. The spiritual transformation of man comes to be, then, irreversible. The spiritual transformation is reversed if the gravitational pull of Matter continues to exist in these instrumental selves in case they do not undergo soul-transformation. He says:

> If the spiritual ascent and descent are not made, the spiritual transformation of the nature cannot happen; if the full psychic opening and connection is not made, the transformation cannot be complete. (1979: 1094)

We have noted that Sri Aurobindo has discovered four planes of the spiritual consciousness on the plane of Mind. They are, what he calls, the Higher Mind, the Illumined Mind, the Intuitive Mind and the Overmind. When man evolves to rise to the summit of the spiritual consciousness, the Overmind Consciousness, he further evolves to transcend the plane of Mind Consciousness, the plane of divisive, or to say, separative consciousness in the furtherance of his evolutionary journey. He transcends the planes of Time and Space which are the creations of the divisive principle of consciousness.

He enters the domain of the Integral Consciousness, the Supramental Consciousness he calls it. It is the plane of Spacelessness and Timelessness, the existence of which has been discovered by Science, too, in Albert Einstein's discovery of the four dimensional plane of existence in his Theory of Special Relativity. His ascent to the plane of the Supramental Consciousness facilitates his supramental transformation. Such supramental transformation takes place when the soul, or to say, the Psychic Being which is a projection of the 'Jivatman', the central being in man as noted earlier, comes to be one with It as a result of the yoga which Savitri undertakes as Sri Aurobindo shows in his epic *Savitri*. Her yoga which is different from the yoga of Ashwapati, her human father is the yoga of supramentalisation of the being of man. The yoga of supramentalisation is transcendent to the yogas of psychicisation and spiritualisation which Ashwapati undertakes since psychicisation and spiritualisation result in the growing nearness between the Psychic Being and Its Divine Origin, the Jivatman.

End of Gender Discrimination and Transcendence of the Consciousness of Gender Division

It is only when the triple transformation of man is effectuated as a result of undertaking the integral yoga of Sri Aurobindo that transcendent consciousness, to use Sri Aurobindo's terminology, the 'Supramental' emerges in the being of man. There comes an end of the operation of the divisive principle of consciousness. The transcendent integral consciousness, that is, the Supramental Consciousness comes into operation. The conflict between the two genders causing the gender discrimination and inequality is, consequently, resolved. The problems with which a man is confronted due to the gender discrimination and inequality begin to be solved as soon as he ascends the spiritual planes of mind-consciousness since a movement towards the integrality of consciousness begins to take place therein. It is on account of the movement towards the integrality of consciousness on the planes of the spiritual mind-consciousness that when man ascends the higher planes of the spiritual mind-consciousness his vision of the Divine Truth becomes lesser and lesser eclipsed, and consequently a more and more harmonious situation between the two genders evolves. The perfect harmony between them comes to be achieved in the Radha-Krishna Consciousness, the Overmind Consciousness as Sri Aurobindo terms it. In the Radha-Krishna Consciousness there is no trace of gender discrimination and inequality. The divine dual power of the Supreme is manifest in this consciousness for the furtherance of the Divine Cause in the terrestrial existence. Such divine dual power is manifest in Lear and Cordelia, too, though *King Lear* is not a work of the Overmind Consciousness[3]:

> ...Come let's away to prison.
> We two alone will sing like birds i'the cage...
>
> (Shakespeare *King Lear*: V.III. 9)

On the plane of the Overmind consciousness which is essentially the cosmic consciousness the 'pre-dominance of the centralising ego-sense is entirely subordinated, lost in the largeness of being and finally abolished' (1990: 950). The ego-consciousness which is the manifestation of the divisive consciousness, being solely responsible, as we have found earlier, for the gender discrimination and inequality is replaced by 'a wide perception and feeling of a boundless universal self and movement' (1990:950). This is what we go to find in the Radha-Krishna Consciousness into which the ego-consciousness is annulled, and such a consciousness, we find, is flooded with Divine Beauty and Ananda. The ego-consciousness is found to have been annulled in Lear, too, as a result of which the dual Power of the Divine works rhythmically.

We two alone will sing like birds i'the cage...

(V.III.9)

Such a rhythm of harmony which gives birth to music and song exists, not only in the conjugal relationship, but in the filial, nay, all human relationship, too, as we find in the case of Lear and his youngest daughter Cordelia.

Consequent upon our higher evolutionary journey when we transcend the spiritual consciousness on the plane of Mind and enter into the world of the Supramental Consciousness, an integral picture of the two genders we discover. The Radha-Krishna Consciousness is transcended in such an integral picture of the two genders. An attempt has been made to sketch such an integral picture of the two genders in, what we call *ardhanarishwar*, an expression for the Lord Shiva. Though it is a mental sketch making a shadow of the integral truth, it is of great help to man to achieve a true picture of the integrality of the two genders. We shall have the true picture when we evolve to the plane of the Transcendent Supramental Consciousness which is essentially the consciousness of the integral nature. Since Sri Aurobindo has found that the 'mental nature and mental thought are based on a consciousness of the finite' (1990: 965) and the 'supramental nature is in its very grain a consciousness and power of the Infinite' (1990: 965), the integral picture of the two genders, the genders which we have earlier noted to be the dual power of the Divine, will emerge in the Supramental Consciousness.

In fact, Lord Shiva is the expression of, what Sri Aurobindo terms, the Supramental Truth. Such supramental consciousness is the need of the hour for the true salvation of the mankind, nay the terrestrial existence.

References

1. Sri Aurobindo: *Savitri*, Helios Books Co. Pvt. Ltd., Chennai, India, 2012;
2. Sri Aurobindo: *The Life Divine*, Sri Aurobindo Ashram, Pondicherry, now, Puducherry, 1990;
3. Sri Aurobindo: *Letters on Yoga*, Parts III & IV, Sri Aurobindo Ashram, Pondicherry, now, Puducherry, 1979;

4. Sri Aurobindo: *Letters on Yoga*, Part I, Sri Aurobindo Ashram, Pondicherry, now, Puducherry, 1979;
5. William Shakespeare: *Othello;*
6. William Shakespeare: *King Lear;*
7. A. S. Eddington: *The Nature of the Physical World*, New York, The Macmillan Company Cambridge, England, 1929;
8. John Polkinghorne: *QUANTUM THEORY: A Very Short Introduction,* Oxford University Press Inc., New York, First Indian Edition, 2006.

Notes

1. The term given by Sri Aurobindo to the highest plane of the spiritual consciousness on the plane of Mind. He has identified four planes of the spiritual consciousness on the plane of Mind and termed them as Higher Mind, Illumined Mind, Intuitive Mind and Overmind. These planes form a hierarchy and exist as successive higher planes.
2. Psychicisation (added by the author).
3. Sri Aurobindo speaks of Overhead Poetry which has the influence of the planes of the spiritual consciousness.

   If some poetry is written from the planes of consciousness existing below the planes of the spiritual consciousness having the touch or something of these spiritual planes, it is the Overhead poetry. Some of the lines of the works of Shakespeare come into the domain of the Overhead Poetry, according to Sri Aurobindo. *King Lear* is no exception.

Part - II

SOCIAL DIMENSION

5

Gender Socialisation and Faces of Gender Inequality

— *Ritu Agarwal*

Gender socialisation and gender roles

Henslin contends that "an important part of socialisation is the learning of culturally defined gender roles." Gender socialisation refers to the learning of behavior and attitudes considered appropriate for a given sex. Boys learn to be boys and girls learn to be girls. This "learning" happens by way of many different agents of socialisation. The family is certainly important in reinforcing gender roles, but so are one's friends, school, work and the mass media. Gender roles are reinforced through "countless subtle and not so subtle ways".

From Conception To Adulthood: Gender Socialisation

It's an obvious - but important - point to note that any human infant is born into a culture that already exists and this culture involves a multitude of social relationships (both inter-personal and institutional). Not only does this mean that a child has to **learn** how to fit into these **existing cultural arrangements**, it also means that the people charged with the task of raising an infant already possess a set of ideas (an "**ideology**") about how to raise that child in line with the various moral and normative expectations of the social groups and society to which they belong.

1. Children learn cultural expectations through a primary socialisation process that involves processes of imitation, gender identification, role learning and conditioning.
2. The socialisation process involves both the conscious teaching and unconscious learning of various values and norms.
3. Males and females are socialised differently in our society. Their socialisation reflects adult perceptions and experiences of the culture in which they live.

4. The socialisation of female stresses their future primary adult roles as mothers and child-rearers. Male socialisation on the other hand stresses a future primary social role as a family provider.
5. Children's toys and books are highly gendered in our society.
6. Males and females develop different personality traits as a result of their differential gender socialisation, not their biology.
7. The processes of primary and secondary socialisation frequently involve different agencies providing contradictory socialising influences.
8. Children are not "passive victims" of a socialisation process. On the contrary, just like adults they play an active part in their own socialisation.
9. Socialisation is not a simple "one-way" process whereby messages are transmitted, received and uncritically accepted.
10. The socialisation process represents a general "structure of rules" relating to acceptable and unacceptable forms of behaviour in our society. People have the ability to obey, reject and change these rules.

Socialisation Into Gender Role Stereotypes.

(1) Childhood Socialisation- Socialisation into gender norms almost always start from the moment the infant is born. Spade and Valentine point out that "[a]lmost every person a child comes into contact with, and virtually all aspects of a child's material world (e.g., toys, books, clothing) reinforce gender". The sex of the newborn is usually the first thing that is checked by the medical team, and the first thing that the parents and family want to know. From then on, the child is brought up in a gendered manner, from the name that he/she is given, to verbal encouragement such as phrases like "what a good boy/girl!", to the toys and activities that he/she is encouraged to play with. As Lindsey notes, "the family is by far the most significant agent of socialisation". Children's toys are usually extremely gendered in nature. Girls' toys are often geared towards nurture and family, such as dolls that require feeding or changing, or cooking sets that reinforce domesticity. Boys' toys, on the other hand, focus more on violence and aggression, such as action figures, weapons and sports equipment. Activities that involve body action or aggressiveness are encouraged in boys, while girls may be chastised for getting their clothes dirty. As a result, boys who play with "feminine" toys such as Barbie dolls may be reprimanded or punished. The clothes that children are made to wear are also extremely gendered. It is often difficult to tell the biological sex of infants and children, as we often assign a sex category to an individual based on his/her secondary sex characteristics and physical appearance. As a result, many parents deliberately dress their children in a gendered fashion, allowing others to correctly identify their child's biological sex. A common understanding for this can be seen in the colour-coding of clothes – parents usually do not dress their infant son in pastel pink, for instance. Girls are put into dresses and skirts, while boys may wear baseball caps and sports jerseys. The infant girl may have bows or ribbons in her hair, while the boys' hair is kept short. Media that is geared towards children is also often heavily gendered. Baker-Sperry and Grauerholz, in their study of children's fairy-tales, found that young women's beauty is heavily emphasised while little mention is made of the handsomeness of men, while Firminger's analysis of teenage girls' magazines reveals that much emphasis is placed on beauty, fashion and the need to know how to attract boys. Girls are treated protectively and boys given more freedom. Girls are valued for their feminity and boys for their masculinity. Children are often treated differently, depending on their sex. For example, girls in rural India may be pushed to work in the household starting much younger than their male counterparts, who are allowed to wake up later or contribute less to the household chores. In America, young boys may be encouraged and pushed into taking up certain sports, while girls may be sent to dance and piano lessons instead. Extreme adoption of masculinity among young girls is also seen as unacceptable. Halberstam notes that among young girls, tomboyism "may even be encouraged to the extent that it remains comfortably linked to a stable sense of a girl identity. Tomboyism is punished, however, when it appears to be the sign of extreme male identification (taking a boy's name or refusing girl clothing of any type) and when it threatens to extend beyond childhood and into adolescence". There is far greater negativity towards young boys who display feminine tendencies. Kane notes that many of the parents in her study expressed discomfort and negativity towards their sons being gender nonconformant, such as the desire to play with nail polish, barbies or wear pink dresses. Kane concludes that such fear was often rooted in the worry that their son would turn out to be gay.

(2) Social Negativity Towards Anything Gender Atypical - Socialisation does not remain only in childhood – stereotypes are reinforced even during adulthood. Conformity to the gender norms thus acts as a form of social control to ensure that the rules are obeyed. For example, sport in the US is seen as a way of reinforcing masculinity for males, especially after the industrial revolution. The advance in technology meant that males were no longer as physically active as they once were, due to the increase in manufacturing and service sectors. As a result, sport became an outlet for men to demonstrate their physical ability. Men who are uninterested in, or unable to play sport, may be viewed as effeminate and gender nonconforming. As adults, the rules are no longer enforced by parents, but by the individual himself/herself and by the people around him. Internalisation of the gender norms has occurred, to the point where the individual can actively or passively enforce the rules on nonconforming others, or even himself/herself. Disapproval from society may encourage a man who wishes to dress in women's clothes to think otherwise about doing so in public, for instance. As a result, individuals survey themselves to ensure that they do not violate gender norms and risk disapproval or discrimination from society.

(3) Mass Media and Advertising - Mass media plays a large, though not necessarily most crucial, role in promoting gender norms and stereotypes. Certainly, the degree to which media is influential depends on the society – media is likely to be more influential in city areas than in rural areas without television or radio access. There are many forms of media, and most involve some sort of advertisement. Mass media can include television, radio, newspaper, magazines, music and books. Femininity is therefore associated with looks and fashion, and a woman needs to be interested in such things in order to qualify as feminine. Advertising, as studied by Goffman, has strong influences upon our thinking and concepts of gender – advertisements include "gender displays", which position men and women in certain gendered ways, which in turn influences our beliefs and ideas. The consumerist society of today reinforces gender stereotypes, where men buy cars to feel ypermasculine, while women are sold "a wondrous array of cosmetic products and procedures that are supposed to turn them into drop-dead beauties". Media therefore encourages both men and women to believe and adhere to certain ideas of masculinity and femininity. It acts as a surveillance tool, where individuals are constantly faced with expectations of a gendered body and so have the power to constantly compare their actual bodies. Media depiction that suggests that women should be passive, weak and sexually available.

Advertising often markets the separate parts of women's bodies eg. Legs, hair, eyes, skin etc.

(4) State laws and policies -In general, the paternal leave granted to men is much shorter than that given to women. This suggests to society that while women do require time to recover from childbirth and men do not, women should continue to stay at home to take care of the child. Maternity leave is not necessarily about the bodily well-being of the mother as it is the connection between the mother and child – breast-feeding, for example, requires the mother's participation, and she therefore needs to spend more time with the child. The shortened paternity leave, however, emphasises the fact that men do not need to spend time with the child except for social and personal needs, and again promotes the notion that men should work to support the family while the mother is needed to remain at home for the child.

(5) Religion – Major world religions such as Judaism, Christianity and Islam tend towards patriarchy and monotheism. As a result, gender roles are often emphasised – for instance, clergy cannot be female under Catholicism, and divorce is not allowed or strongly discouraged. Islam, in certain cultures, encourages women to cover their bodies and faces to protect their modesty.

Even in polytheistic religions, strong gender role stereotypes may exist – the practice of sati in Hinduism, for instance, while legally outlawed in India, still continues to be practiced by some communities. The highly structured, hierarchical nature of some of these religions means that rules about many aspects of life are highly regulated. Gender, being an intrinsic part of society, therefore often falls under the jurisdiction of religion. However, while religion can be a strong factor in pushing society to adhere to the gender stereotypes, it is not necessarily always a factor. Several Christian denominations have embraced homosexuality and homosexual or transgender pastors, while many of these Christian denominations allow for women pastors.

(6) Communication-

Verbal –

The use of language often works to divide society along gender as well. Language is gendered to the point where there are such things as women's and men's speech and language, and one sex should not use the other's. For example, it is more acceptable for men to curse and swear, whereas women's speech is socially more refined and reined in. In many languages, men and women even have different language patterns, such as Thai and Japanese. Lindsey suggests that "while women use language to negotiate relationships and establish connections, men converse to maintain independence and status in a society which is hierarchal". Language also helps to reinforce certain gender stereotypes, such as the negative use of words like "sissy", or often-repeated phrases such as "boys don't cry" or "be a real man". This can also be seen among youth in America, where the term "gay" is often used in a derogatory manner to describe something negative.

Non-Verbal –

Women are encouraged to use their bodies in different ways from men. Iris Young's study, for example, on the ways girls use their bodies to throw balls, deconstructs feminine movements as socially constructed, and emphasises the fact that the girls are taught to rein in their bodies and throw in a way that does not fully utilise all body movements. Girls throw the way they do, she concludes, because of cultural norms and what they are taught, rather than for biological reasons – they are socialised into throwing "like girls".

(7) The Formal Education System- The educational system itself is authoritarian in nature.

Teachers impose different standards of discipline on boys and girls. There are exclusive schools for boys and girls.. Schools and teachers also channel boys and girls towards gender appropriate behaviour and activities.

(8) Economy-The male is breadwinner and provider of family. The female's responsibility is over the reproductive sphere, household and childbearing. There is non valuation of housework..Some jobs are sex specified-

Male- doctor, engineers, politicians and lawyers.Female- nurses, teachers, waitresses, and stewardess.

Gender Inequality in India

It refers to health, education, economic and political inequalities between men and women in India. Various international gender inequality indices rank India differently on each of these factors, as well as on a composite basis. Gender inequalities, and its social causes, impact India's sex ratio, women's health over their lifetimes, their educational attainment, and economic conditions. Gender inequality in India is a multifaceted issue that concerns men and women alike. Some argue that some gender equality measures, place men at a disadvantage. However, when India's population is examined as a whole, women are at a disadvantage in several important ways.

Many Faces of Gender Inequality

Nobel Laureate Amartya Sen's work on gender inequality is of seminal importance. His work on the theory of the household represents the household not as an undifferentiated unit, but as a unit of cooperation as well as of inequality and internal discrimination. He has worked on problems of discrimination against women in the development process, on survivorship differentials between men and women under conditions of social discrimination against women, and on women's agency in the process of social development.

Seven Types of Inequality

It was more than a century ago, in 1870, that Queen Victoria wrote to Sir Theodore Martin complaining about "this mad, wicked folly of 'Woman's Rights'." The formidable empress certainly did not herself need any protection that the acknowledgment of women's rights might offer. Even at the age of eighty, in 1899, she could write to A.J. Balfour, "We are not interested in the possibilities of defeat; they do not exist." That, however, is not the way most people's lives go - reduced and defeated as they frequently are by adversities. And within each community, nationality and class, the burden of hardship often falls disproportionately on women.

The afflicted world in which we live is characterised by deeply unequal sharing of the burden of adversities between women and men. Gender inequality exists in most parts of the world, from Japan to Morocco, from Uzbekistan to the United States of America. However, inequality between women and men can take very many different forms. Indeed, gender inequality is not one homogeneous phenomenon, but a collection of disparate and interlinked problems. Let me illustrate with examples of different kinds of disparity.

(1) Mortality Inequality: In some regions in the world, inequality between women and men directly involves matters of life and death, and takes the brutal form of unusually high mortality rates of women and a consequent preponderance of men in the total population, as opposed to the preponderance of women found in societies with little or no gender bias in health care and nutrition. Mortality inequality has been observed extensively in North Africa and in Asia, including China and South Asia.

(2) Natality Inequality: Given a preference for boys over girls that many male-dominated societies have, gender inequality can manifest itself in the form of the parents wanting the newborn to be a boy rather than a girl. There was a time when this could be no more than a wish (a daydream or a nightmare, depending on one's perspective), but with the availability of modern techniques to determine the gender of the foetus, sex-selective abortion has become common in many countries. It is particularly prevalent in East Asia, in China and South Korea in particular, but also in Singapore and Taiwan, and it is beginning to emerge as a statistically significant phenomenon in India and South Asia as well. This is high-tech sexism.

(3) Basic Facility Inequality: Even when demographic characteristics do not show much or any anti-female bias, there are other ways in which women can have less than a square deal. Afghanistan may be the only country in the world the government of which is keen on actively excluding girls from schooling (it combines this with other features of massive gender inequality), but there are many countries in Asia and Africa, and also in Latin America, where girls have far less opportunity of schooling than boys do. There are other deficiencies in basic facilities available to women, varying from encouragement to cultivate one's natural talents to fair participation in rewarding social functions of the community.

(4) Special Opportunity Inequality: Even when there is relatively little difference in basic facilities including schooling, the opportunities of higher education may be far fewer for young women than for young men. Indeed, gender bias in higher education and professional training can be observed even in some of the richest countries in the world, in Europe and North America.

Sometimes this type of division has been based on the superficially innocuous idea that the respective "provinces" of men and women are just different. This thesis has been championed in different forms over the centuries, and has had much implicit as well as explicit following. It was presented with particular directness more than a hundred years before Queen Victoria's complaint about "woman's rights" by the Revd James Fordyce in his Sermons to Young Women (1766), a book which, as Mary Wollstonecraft noted in her A Vindication of the Rights of Women (1792), had been "long made a part of woman's library." Fordyce warned the young women, to whom his sermons were addressed, against "those masculine women that would plead for your sharing any part of their province with us," identifying the province of men as including not only "war," but also "commerce, politics, exercises of strength and dexterity, abstract philosophy and all the abstruser sciences." Even though such clear-cut beliefs about the provinces of men and women are now rather rare, nevertheless the presence of extensive gender asymmetry can be seen in many areas of education, training and professional work even in Europe and North America.

(5) Professional Inequality: In terms of employment as well as promotion in work and occupation, women often face greater handicap than men. A country like Japan may be quite egalitarian in matters of demography or basic facilities, and even, to a great extent, in higher education, and yet progress to elevated levels of employment and occupation seems to be much more problematic for women than for men.

In the English television series called "Yes, Minister," there is an episode where the Minister, full of reforming zeal, is trying to find out from the immovable permanent secretary, Sir Humphrey, how many women are in really senior positions in the British civil service. Sir Humphrey says that it is very difficult to give an exact number; it would require a lot of investigation. The Minister is still insistent, and wants to know approximately how many women are there in these senior positions. To which Sir Humphrey finally replies, "Approximately, none."

(6) Ownership Iinequality: In many societies the ownership of property can also be very unequal. Even basic assets such as homes and land may be very asymmetrically shared. The absence of claims to property can not only reduce the voice of women, but also make it harder for women to enter and flourish in commercial, economic and even some social activities. This type of inequality has existed in most parts of the world, though there are also local variations. For example, even though traditional property rights have favoured men in the bulk of India, in what is now the State of Kerala, there has been, for a long time, matrilineal inheritance for an influential part of the community, namely the Nairs.

(7) Household Inequality: There are, often enough, basic inequalities in gender relations within the family or the household, which can take many different forms. Even in cases in which there are no overt signs of anti-female bias in, say, survival or son-preference or education, or even in promotion to higher executive positions, the family arrangements can be quite unequal in terms of sharing the burden of housework and child care. It is, for example, quite common in many societies to take it for granted that while men will naturally work outside the home, women could do it if and only if they could combine it with various inescapable and unequally shared household duties. This is sometimes called "division of labour," though women could be forgiven for seeing it as "accumulation of labour." The reach of this inequality includes not only unequal relations within the family, but also derivative inequalities in employment and recognition in the outside world. Also, the established fixity of this type of "division" or "accumulation" of labour can also have far-reaching effects on the knowledge and understanding of different types of work in professional circles. When I first started working on gender inequality, in the 1970s, I remember being struck by the fact that the Handbook of Human Nutrition Requirement of the World Health Organisation (WHO), in presenting "calorie requirements" for different categories of people, chose to classify household work as "sedentary activity," requiring very little deployment of energy. I was, however, not able to determine precisely how this remarkable bit of information had been collected by the patrician leaders of society.

Gender Inequality Index

India is ranked 131 of 189 countries listed in the United Nations Development Programme's latest Human Development Report 2016. Categorised as having achieved 'medium human development', India's HDI value has increased 46 per cent between 1990 and 2015. India is ranked better than most of its SAARC counterparts, including Bhutan (132), Bangladesh (139), Nepal (144), Pakistan (147), Afghanistan (169). On the other hand, Sri Lanka and Maldives fare better and are ranked 73 and 105 respectively, under the 'high human development' category. China is ranked at 90.Norway, Australia, Switzerland, Germany and Denmark are top ranked, while Burundi, Burkina Faso, Chad, Niger and the Central African Republic are ranked lowest.

According to the report, life expectancy at birth in India has increased from 68 years to an average of 68.3 years — 69.9 years for women and 66.9 years for men. Expected years of schooling remains at 11.7 years, while mean years of schooling increased from 5.4 to 6.3 years. The Gross National Income (GNI) based on per capita purchasing power parity (PPP) has risen as well, from $5,497 to $5,663.

The report calculates each country's development value after adjusting its figures for inequalities, known as Inequality-adjusted Human Development Index (IHDI). According to the UNDP "the difference between the HDI and IHDI, expressed as a percentage of the HDI, indicates the loss in human development due to inequality." While India's HDI is pegged at 0.624, it's value falls 27.2 per cent after being adjusted for inequalities, resulting in a HDI value of 0.455. Similarly, life expectancy adjusted with inequalities between 2010 and 2015 fell 24 per cent, resulting in a value of 0.565. In 2015, the percentage of inequality in education was 39.4 per cent or 0.324 and inequality in income 16.1 per cent or 0.512.

India is ranked 125 of 159 countries in the Gender Inequality Index (GII). The ratio of maternal mortality is 174 against every 100,000 live births. Only 12.2 per cent of Parliament seats are held by women. 26.8 per cent of women above the age of 15 years are part of India's labour force — compared to 79.1 per cent men.

Reasons for gender inequalities

Lorber states that gender inequality has been a historic worldwide phenomena, a human invention and based on gender assumptions. It is linked to kinship rules rooted in cultures and gender norms that organizes human social life, human relations, as well as promotes subordination of women in a form of social strata. Amartya Sen highlighted the need to consider the socio-cultural influences that promote gender inequalities In India, cultural influences favour the preference for sons for reasons related to kinship, lineage, inheritance, identity, status, and economic security. This preference cuts across class and caste lines, and it discriminates against girls. In extreme cases, the discrimination takes the form of honour killings where families kill daughters or daughter in laws who fail to conform to gender expectations about marriage and sexuality. When a woman does not conform to expected gender norms she is shamed and humiliated because it impacts both her and her family's honor, and perhaps her ability to marry. The causes of gender inequalities are complex, but a number of cultural factors in India can explain how son preference, a key driver of daughter neglect, is so prevalent.

Patriarchal society

Patriarchy is a social system of privilege in which men are the primary authority figures, occupying roles of political leadership, moral authority, control of property, and authority over women and children. Most of India, with some exceptions, has strong patriarchal and patrilineal customs, where men hold authority over female family members and inherit family property and title. Examples of patriarchy in India include prevailing customs where inheritance passes from father to son, women move in with the husband and his family upon marriage, and marriages include a bride price or dowry. This 'inter-generational contract' provides strong social and economic incentives for raising sons and disincentives for raising daughters.The parents of the woman essentially lose all they have invested in their daughter to her husband's family, which is a disincentive for investing in their girls during youth. Furthermore, sons are expected to support their parents in old age and women have very limited ability to assist their own parents.

Son preference

A key factor driving gender inequality is the preference for sons, as they are deemed more useful than girls. Boys are given the exclusive rights to inherit the family name and properties and they are viewed as additional status for their family. In a survey-based study of 1990s data, scholars found that son are believed to have a higher economic utility as they can provide additional labour in agriculture. Another factor is that of religious practices, which can only be performed by males for their parents' afterlife. All these factors make sons more desirable. Moreover, the prospect of parents 'losing' daughters to the husband's family and expensive dowry of daughters further discourages parents from having daughters. Additionally, sons are often the only person entitled to performing funeral rights for their parents. Thus, a combination of factors has shaped the imbalanced view of sexes in India. A 2005 study in Madurai, India, found that old age security, economic motivation, and to a lesser extent, religious obligations, continuation of the family name, and help in business or farm, were key reasons for son preference. In turn, emotional support and old age security were main reasons for daughter preference. The study underscored a strong belief that a daughter is a liability.

Dowry death rates per 100,000 people map for Indian States and Union Territories in 2012.

Discrimination against girls

While women express a strong preference for having at least one son, the evidence of discrimination against girls after they are born is mixed. A study of 1990s survey data by scholars found less evidence of systematic discrimination in feeding practices between young boys and girls, or gender based nutritional discrimination in India. In impoverished families, these scholars found that daughters face discrimination in the medical treatment of illnesses and in the administration of vaccinations against serious childhood diseases. These practices were a cause of health and survival inequality for girls. While gender discrimination is a universal phonomena in poor nations, a 2005 UN study found that social norms-based gender discrimination leads to gender inequality in India.

Dowry

In India, dowry is the payment in cash or some kind of gifts given to bridegroom's family along with the bride. The practice is widespread across geographic region, class and religions. The dowry system in India contributes to gender inequalities by influencing the perception that girls are a burden on families. Such beliefs limit the resources invested by parents in their girls and limits her bargaining power within the family. The payment of a dowry has been prohibited under The 1961 Dowry Prohibition Act in Indian civil law and subsequently by Sections 304B and 498a of the Indian Penal Code (IPC). Several studies show that while attitudes of people are changing about dowry, the institution has changed very little, and even continues to prevail.

Marriage laws

Men and women have equal rights within marriage under Indian law, with the exception of Muslim men who are allowed to unilaterally divorce their wife. The legal minimum age for marriage is 18 for women and 21 for men, except for those Indians whose religion is Islam for whom child marriage remains legal under India's Mohammedan personal laws. Child marriage is one of the detriments to empowerment of women.

Efforts Made to Reduce Gender Ineqalities

Political and legal reforms

Since its independence, India has made significant strides in addressing gender inequalities, especially in the areas of political participation, education, and legal rights. Policies and legal reforms to address gender inequalities have been pursued by the government of India. For instance, the Constitution of India contains a clause guaranteeing the right of equality and freedom from sexual discrimination. India is also signatory to the Convention for the Elimination of All Forms of Discrimination Against Women, or CEDAW. However, the government maintains some reservations about interfering in the personal affairs of any community without the community's initiative and consent. A listing of specific reforms is presented below.

- Convention on the Elimination of All Forms of Discrimination against Women (CEDAW)
- Prenatal Diagnostic Testing Ban
- The Sexual Harassment of Women at Workplace (Prevention, Prohibition and Redressal) Act, 2013
- Hindu Succession Act, 1956 (Amended in 2005; Gives equal inheritance rights to daughters and sons - applies to Hindus, Buddhists, Jains and Sikhs)
- Muslim Personal Law (Shariat) Application Act of 1937, (The inheritance rights are governed by Sharia and the share of females are less than males as mandated by Quran)

Central and State initiatives to reduce gender inequality

Different states and union territories of India, in cooperation with the central government, have initiated a number of region-specific programs targeted at women to help reduce gender inequality over the 1989-2013 period. Some of these programs include Swarnajayanti Gram Swarozgar Yojana, Sampoorna Gramin Rozgar Yojana, Awareness Generation Projects for Rural and Poor women, Condensed Course of Education for Adult Women, Kishori Shakti Yojana, Swayamsidha Mahila Mandal Programme, Rashtriya Mahila Kosh, Support to Training and Employment Programme for Women, Swawalamban Programme, Swashakti Project, Swayamsidha Scheme, Mahila Samakhya Programme, Integrated Child Development Services, Balika Samriddhi Yojana, National Programme of Nutritional Support to Primary Education (to encourage rural girls to attend primary school daily), National Programme for Education of Girls at Elementary Level, Sarva Shiksha

Abyhiyan, Ladli Laxmi Yojana, Delhi Ladli Scheme. Other women empowerment schemes are Beti Bachao Beti Padhao Scheme, One Stop Centre Scheme, Women Helpline Scheme, UJJAWALA : A Comprehensive Scheme for Prevention of trafficking and Rescue, Rehabilitation and Re-integration of Victims of Trafficking and Commercial Sexual Exploitation, Working Women Hostel, Ministry approves new projects under Ujjawala Scheme and continues existing projects, SWADHAR Greh (A Scheme for Women in Difficult Circumstances), Support to Training and Employment Programme for Women (STEP), NARI SHAKTI PURASKAR, Awardees of Stree Shakti Puruskar, 2014 & Awardees of Nari Shakti Puruskar, Awardees of Rajya Mahila Samman & Zila Mahila Samman, Mahila police Volunteers, Mahila E-Haat, Mahila Shakti Kendras (MSK)

Organisations

- All India Democratic Women's Association
- National Commission on Women
- Ministry of Women Children and Development
- International Center for Research on Women
- UN Women

References

Gender Socialisation and Gender Role1 - socialised to be more ...,https://www.coursehero.com › Broward College › SCIE › SCIE SYG2000

Gender Socialisation, www.sociology.org.uk/notes/fgender2.pdf

Socialisation: The Meaning, Features, Types, Stages and Importance, www.yourarticlelibrary.com/sociology/socialisation-the-meaning-features.../8529

Gender role - Wikipedia, *https://en.wikipedia.org/wiki/Gender_role*

UNICEF - *Early Childhood - Early* Gender Socialisation,*https://*www.unicef.org/*earlychildhood/index_40749.html*

Gender *Home* - World Bank, www.worldbank.org*/en/topic/*gende

India ranks 131 in HDI index: Where do we stand on gender inequality, maternal mortality, schooling?,indianexpress.com India.

MANY FACES OF GENDER INEQUALITY - Frontline, www.frontline.in/static/html/fl1822/18220040.htm

William St. Clair, The Godwins and the Shelleys (New York: Norton, 1989), pp. 504-8.

Bina Agarwal, among others, has investigated the far-reaching effects of landlessness of women in many agricultural economies; see particularly her A Field of One's Own (Cambridge: Cambridge University Press, 1994).

World Health Organisation, Handbook of Human Nutrition Requirement (Geneva: WHO, 1974); this was based on the report of a high-level Expert Committee jointly appointed by the WHO and FAO - the Food and Agriculture Organisation.

Gender inequality in India - Wikipedia,https://en.wikipedia.org/wiki/Gender_inequality_in_Indi.

Lorber, J. (1994). Paradoxes of Gender. Yale University Press, page 2-6, 126-143, 285-290.

Sen, Amartya (2001). "Many Faces of Gender Inequality". Frontline, India's National Magazine. 18 (22): 1–17.

Sekher, TV; Neelambar Hattie (2010). Unwanted Daughters: Gender discrimination in Modern India. Rawat Publications.

"India - Restoring the Sex-ratio Balance". UNDP. Retrieved 12 April 2014.

Appiah, Kwame Anthony. 2010. "Wars Against Women," in The Honor Code: How Moral Revolutions Happen. New York: W.W. Norton and Co., Chapter 4, pp. 137–72.

Gupta, Monica Das. "Selective discrimination against female children in rural Punjab, India". Population and development review. 1987: 77–100. doi:10.2307/1972121.

Kabeer, Naila (1996). "Agency, Wellbeing & Inequality: Reflections on the Gender Dimensions of Poverty". IDS bulletin. 27 (1): 11–21. doi:10.1111/j.1759-5436.1996.mp27001002.x.

Larsen, Mattias, ed. Vulnerable Daughters in India: Culture, Development and Changing Contexts. Routledge, 2011 (pp. 11-12).

Larsen, Mattias, Neelambar Hatti, and Pernille Gooch. "Intergenerational Interests, Uncertainty and Discrimination." (2006).

Rangamuthia Mutharayappa, M. K. (1997). Son Preference and Its Effect on Fertility in India. Mumbai: International Institute for Population Sciences.

Muthulakshmi, R. (1997). Female infanticide, its causes and solutions. New Delhi: Discovery Publishing House.

Sekher and Hatti, 2007 Unwanted Daughters: Gender discrimination in modern india pp. 3-4.

Begum and Singh; CH 7 Sekher and Hatti, 2007 Unwanted Daughters: Gender discrimination in modern India 7.

"Periodic Review: India report 2005" (PDF). United Nations. Retrieved 28 April 2014.

Babu & Babu (2011), Dowry deaths: a neglected public health issue in India, Int. Health, 3 (1): 35-43.

"The Dowry Prohibition Act, 1961". Archived from the original on 9 September 2015. Retrieved 24 December 2006.

Srinivasan, Padma, and Gary R. Lee. "The dowry system in Northern India: Women's attitudes and social change." Journal of Marriage and Family 66.5 (2004): 1108-1117.

Chandrashekhar, Dr Mamta (2016). "Human Rights, Women and Violation". Sex Ratio.

"Supreme Court: False cruelty cases under Section 498A ruining marriages". Indiatimes. 9 December 2014. Retrieved 9 December 2014.

"Nagging wife? Help is at hand!". The Indian Express. Press Trust of India. 11 November 2005. Retrieved 6 April 2014.

"Now, men seek cover under domestic violence law". DNA India. 10 June 2008. Retrieved 22 April 2014.

"Report on the State of Women: India" (PDF). Center for Asia-Pacific Women in Politics. Retrieved 31 March 2014.

Report on the State of Women.

"Convention for the Elimination of All forms of Discrimination Against Women". United Nations. Retrieved 29 April 2014.

Inheritance and Succession, Rights of Women and Daughters under Personal Laws Javed Razack, Lex Orates, Indian Law.

Promotion and strengthening of Mahila Mandals of Haryana.

Mahila Samakhya, UNICEF India.

Delhi Ladli Scheme 2008 Government of Delhi.

Women Empowerment Schemes | Ministry of Women ..., wcd.nic.in/schemes-listing/2405.

6

Social Exclusion of Women: Discriminatory Practices in Contemporary Times

—*Anuja*

I. Introduction

Discrimination is a term used in favour or against a person who belongs to certain category of race, religion, gender identity, disability and many other characteristics. A discriminatory practice exists in every part of the world and it is an age old phenomena which is being practiced against the women on this earth. In the contemporary times the rates of knots of exclusion of women have minimized to some extent but the effect of it since long have sabotaged the whole system of the Indian society. It is very difficult to give a statement or you can say make a conclusion that with the rapid industrialisation or urbanisation and also economic development the processes of class inequalities and exclusion aroused in India. But whatever the reality would be all these processes have affected adversely the various aspects of women's status in the contemporary Indian society. Their participation in politics, their level of education, state of health, their count in the formal and informal sector of labour participation and the wages they get out of it are some areas where women have been continuously excluded to have full participation or equal rights. There are many certain socio- economic or cultural factors where roles of women have remained mostly unrecognised. Women have been subjected to marginality in all realms of life.

The objective to write this paper is to acquaint people with the meaning of social exclusion and how it relates to gender injustice within society, so that they can be in a position to bring out positive changes in their respective communities. Another aim is also to underline the importance of women and their rights in contemporary times. Therefore, an attempt here is to draw attention of the academicians', researchers and policy makers to develop gender just society in which inclusion plays crucial role in securing their life as a human being first and then to fight for equality in all spheres of life. The study is based on the secondary sources of the subject.

II. Social Exclusion: A new approach in academic debate

The debate on exclusion is new in academics in India. It is used frequently as value based concept which means denial of rights and opportunities of a person to achieve power and status in society. As per Economists, exclusion indicates denial of access to opportunities, well being, entitlement failure because of shortage of income and purchasing power (Sen, 1981), prudentially absence of valuable key items (Shaffer, 1998); lack of accessibilities and possession of material and otherwise needed resources, sub-human conditions and facilities required for survival, which are customary or at least widely encouraged and approved in the society to which they belong (Townsend, 1987). This preposition gives an expression that exclusion has only economic criteria and excludes its actual meaning in other criteria like political, social and cultural etc. In short we can say that the excluded are not only deprived of income and purchasing power but also from the mainstream society from participation fully or partially in the social, economic, and political life where they live and the chance of their rights and opportunities of which they are entitled.

The term gained popularity in France during the 1980s (Silver, 1994), the period of economic crisis and restructuring, the crisis of the welfare state, and various social and political crises. Silver traces the diverse lineage of the concept back to the founders of Western social theory, particularly Weber, Durkheim and Marx. She then describes three approaches to social exclusion based on three paradigms of citizenship and social exclusion, which are 'solidarity', 'specialisation', and 'monopoly'. Her explanation of 'solidarity' model draws on the Durkheimian concept of social solidarity, and is contextualised in the political tradition of French Republicanism where citizenship connotes a bunch of civic and political rights and duties, essentials for participation in social and political life. Society is a moral community and social exclusion in such a society is 'the rupture of a social bond between the individual and society'. Such a rupture results in social deviance, anomaly and finally social disintegration, a serious threat to the very existence of society.... (Silver, 1995). "...While 'solidarity' and 'specialisation' models are useful to understand social exclusion in western society, 'monopoly' model is of particular relevance for analyzing social exclusion in Indian society, where exclusion is neither a situation of deviance from dominant social norms, nor is it a result of free interplay of differential endowments of individuals negotiating social, economic and political life in a free society. It is primarily a denial of freedom, equality and free interplay of individual endowments, a consequence of hierarchical society where social boundary is drawn on ascriptive characteristics like caste, tribe, gender, etc. (Pankaj & Pandey, 2014)".

According to Oommen, like all societies, Indian society's stratification is based on age, gender, rural-urban and class, culturally heterogeneity, religious plurality, and caste hierarchy."

"In India, social exclusion has been discussed and debated at two levels (a) social science discourse, and (b) administrative and development policy arena. In social science discourse, the term has been used for understanding the dynamics of hierarchical and stratified Indian society, where social relations are structured on a set of hierarchical principles, and discriminatory social and cultural norms, values and practices. Exclusion is ascriptive, involuntary and transmitted across generations. The forces of modernisation and economic development have created space for their inclusion that has also triggered significant social change. The literature on modernisation and social development in India has explained social integration of the excluded as a yardstick of modernisation and social development (Pankaj & Pandey, 2014)." In Social Science literature, there is a general agreement on the core features of social exclusion, its principal indicators and the manner in which it relates to poverty and inequality (Buvinic, 2005). "Social Exclusion implies... denial of equal opportunities by certain groups on others which prevents an individual's participation in basic political, economic and social functioning of a society. The two characteristics of exclusion are particularly relevant to define the concept. First, deprivation is caused through exclusion (or denial of equal opportunity) in multiple spheres which in turn reveal its multidimensionality. Second it is embedded in societal relations and societal institutions, that is the processes through which individuals or groups are wholly or partially excluded from full participation in the society in which they live (Haan, 1997)." The consequences of social exclusion, thus, depend crucially on the functioning of social institutions and the degree to which they are exclusionary and discriminatory. Social exclusion has a sizeable impact on an individual's access to equal opportunity, if social interactions occur between groups in a power subordinate relationship (Buvinic, 2005).

The grim realities concretize the concept social exclusion as ubiquitous and global. There are no country, rich or poor, "traditional" or "modern", who can credibly claim to be unaffected by social exclusion. They seem to be woven into the fabric of societies, embedded in the system, with deep roots which lead to their continuous reproduction. (www.un.org)

Amartya Sen draws our attention to various meanings and dimensions of the concept of social exclusion. He draws a distinction between the situations wherein some people are being kept out (at least left out) and wherein some people are being included (perhaps even being forcibly included) in greatly unfavourable terms. He described these two situations as 'unfavourable exclusion' and 'unfavourable inclusion', respectively. 'Unfavourable inclusion' with unequal treatment may carry the same adverse effects as unfavourable exclusion' (Sen, 2000).

These developments in social science literature enable us to comprehend the meanings and manifestations of the concept of social exclusion its applicability to gender based exclusion also in Indian perspectives. The concept of social exclusion essentially refers to the processes through which groups are wholly or partially excluded from full participation in the society in which they live. It emphasizes two crucial dimensions which involve the notion of exclusion, namely 'societal institutions' (of exclusion) and their 'outcomes' (in terms of deprivation). In order to understand the dimensions of exclusion, it is necessary to understand the societal interrelations and institutions which lead to exclusion of certain groups and deprivation in multiple spheres- civil, cultural, political and economic. Thus, to acquire a broader understanding of exclusion, it is important to gain insights into the societal processes and institutions of exclusion apart from understanding the outcome in terms of deprivation of certain groups. Exclusion could also manifest itself in diverse ways in terms of 'causes and outcomes' (Thorat, Haan and Sabharwal, 2014). From the above explanation it is clear that social exclusion extends the analytical focus beyond just individuals to social groups.

Another approach to the study of social exclusion is to identify the groups that are known to have been or are in danger of being socially excluded on the basis of their specific attributes and examine the mechanisms of their exclusion and possible ways of increasing their inclusion in the mainstream (Papola, 2012). The words discrimination and exclusion have always been used interchangeably in sociological connotation when used for gender specific issues; therefore, it would be very important to describe the concepts of discrimination and exclusion individually.

The concepts of exclusion and discrimination have emerged from mainstream economics in the context of race and gender. A word about the distinction and relationship between social exclusion and discrimination would be in order here. Discrimination refers to preferential treatment of some over others. But once it is systematically practiced against some groups, it would result in social exclusion. Social exclusion is more intense than discrimination; it may literally imply discrimination in absolute terms, namely boycott. In this sense, the difference between the two is only relative: discrimination is a milder form of social exclusion. The outcomes of either are, however, similar: some groups are placed at a disadvantage in terms of access to assets and jobs, resulting in the poverty and deprivation. And in an analytically meaningful sense, therefore, social exclusion is defined as "discrimination against culturally defined groups" (Haan, 1997, 2007).

As defined by the CEDAW, discrimination is symptomatic of a situation where patterns of structural inequality are maintained by rules, norms and procedures that dictate a subordinate role for women in all spheres of society. This call for an end to all forms of discrimination against women emphasizes the need for a radical re-definition of the process and content of economic, social and political development. It stresses the need for a holistic orientation which acknowledges the vital role of women in development and engineers their integration into development processes as equal partners with men. For this purpose, it is argued that legal and substantive protection at the domestic, regional and international levels must be coordinated for more meaningful enhancement of both the status and situation of women. Within the international human rights literature, the problem of discrimination has been conceptualised as involving the denial of self-determination to women (Okome, 2002).

III. Social Exclusion of Women

Social exclusion is described as a group, or groups of people who are excluded partially or fully from the day to day activities of the society. Women are one such example in developing countries that are socially excluded from mainstream society or can be said that they are being restricted in participating activities in day to day life like economic, politics, social activities and so on. Therefore, in contemporary times

Social Exclusion of Women has become the powerful form of discriminatory practices. Social exclusion of women hinders women to achieve equal rights and status in society. When the elementary fields of nutrition, health, survival and education are not distributed equally among the two sexes of the society, the rights of women are curtailed. Women face inequality in almost every steps of their life, including educational attainment, economic and political participation and female-specific health issues. Asia-Pacific region as whole, and especially South Asia, ranks near the worst in the world in such indicators as nutrition, health, education, employ-ment and political participation (GGI, 2011). As per the record of HDI, India's Gender inequality index, is at the poor 122nd position, among 138 countries. Bangladesh and Pakistan are ranked at 116th and 112nd positions, respectively, indicating that these nations are better in gender equality than India. This also suggests that countries with high gender inequality also have an unequal distribution of human development and vice- versa. Women face discrimination and exclusion and have been victims of exploitation and inequality in education, employment and access to health services.

There are many Feminist discourses on promotion of gender equality and women empowerment. The key concept in feminist thought is gender, which refers to the socially constructed roles played by women and men that are ascribed to them on basis of their sex. Gender analysis is done in order to examine similarities and differences in roles and responsibilities between women and men without direct reference to biology, but rather to the behavior patterns expected from women and men and their cultural reinforcement (United Nations General Assembly, 1996). Feminist theorists understand the term gender not simply as physical and biological differences between males and females, but as a "set of culturally shaped and defined characteristics associated with masculinity and femininity'. The feminist discourse talked about women's oppression as a category and thereby pursuing realisation of women's rights in different spheres such as politics, economy and society (Beauvoir, 1997) With all they were also concerned about their democratic rights too such as right to her body, right to choose a partner in life and right to conceive or not conceive a child, and right to choose safe contraceptives were as important as right to education, employment and political participation

The persistence of inequality between women and men is a problem that is sharper in Asia than in any other continent in the world. It applies even to sex- related mortality rates, with Asia providing the bulk of the estimated "missing women" in the world. It has been empirically noted that the interest of women relates closely to their being excluded from employment opportunities, basic education, and land ownership (Sen, 2007). Structural exclusion experienced by women in Indian society perceives them as subordinate to men in every activity as allocated to them. We generalise social exclusion of women in their marital, health or employment status which is due to unequal power possession and the lack of control over the resources leads them to a greater risk of poverty.

"Women are overrepresented among people living in poverty and suffer from exclusion from basic education, landownership and employment. It has been argued, however, that although anti-poverty policies focusing on women are often seen as attaining development objectives, they may not be very effective in tackling gender-related issues because the subjugation of women is not caused by poverty alone. That is why equality issues should be considered in development programming (Jackson, 1996 in www.un.org, chap IV)." It is not that poverty is the only cause of women's exclusion or keep them away from their rights and power but there are numerous other socio- economic, political as well as cultural factors which time to time perpetuated against them whenever they had tried to gain some rights. The mindset behind this subordination continues unabated.

Social exclusion of women is linked to the cultural perceptions of their role and potential contribution to society. The social exclusion perspective compels us to look beyond gender gaps in education and health. Voice and participation are vital and the cultural perceptions of women that keep them in subordinate status need to be challenged. Creating the conditions that allow women to demand change and influence priorities of State institutions is vital if gender equality and the empowerment of women are to be advanced. Gender identities leading to specific outcomes need to be examined as well. For instance, in many South Asian countries, there is a high mortality among girls, who are subject to aggressive neglect, not to mention foeticide and infanticide. To understand the causes of this phenomenon, a comprehensive analysis of gender identities and relations over the life course is required, exploring forms of marriage exchange and the gendered hierarchies within belief systems (Jackson, 2002 in www.un.org, chap IV). "Excluded groups are disadvantaged in many ways. They are victims of prejudice, are ignored, and are often treated as less than human beings. Inclusiveness is about a growth process which is seen to be 'fair' by different socio- economic groups that constitute our society (Saxena, 2013)."

Women experience and cope with risk completely different from men. Their life itself gives us examples of exclusion such as unequal property rights, being excluded from working due to child bearing, unequal sharing of unpaid care responsibilities, ill health due to lack of nutritional food given in childhood, disability aggrandize their exclusion, unemployment and many more examples.

However, gender differences in different spheres like socio- cultural and economic and education have been taken into consideration. The paper, therefore, highlights on these pertinent issues with regard to gendered nature of women's education, health, labour force participation and above all, their identity.

The social exclusion approach is especially valuable since it enables an acknowledgment and analysis of the dimensions of identity. The demand for sons has not given dignified position to girls in the beginning and women later in the society as a whole and in a family in particular. Sons are given more value because they are preferred to be the future bread earners and also thought as a security for parents whereas, daughters are considered as a liability because she is not going to contribute in future anything to her parents because she will be married off to another family. Therefore, it can be said that our Indian society is patriarchal in nature where men enjoy socially, economically, politically and culturally dominant position but women have no roles to play which could define their position in the society. Whereas, from an early age, boys are helped to acquire masculinity that allows them to assume and maintain their position. On the other hand girls are nurtured in femininity way and their roles are socially constructed. This has become a reality which is not only disappointing but also alarming and need to be checked the response to social discrimination from the time of birth of a child.

Although constitution of India has granted women equal rights but gender disparities remains. This gender disparity slowly- slowly leads to exclusion, negligence of their presence. A strong son preference extends to the denial of girls' right to life. India remains highly patriarchal society where women are marginalised and denied development benefits. The falling sex ratio is a reflection of the existing gender bias. Sex ratio 940 females on average on per 1000 males according to 2011 census (2001– 933/1000). Whereas, overall Sex Ratio has shown improvement since 1991. India's child sex ratio (0- 6 yrs) is 914 females per 1000 males in 2011 and in 2001 it was 927/1000. The fall in the sex ratio for the 0-6 age group is particularly worrisome because it is lowest since Independence. (Fig. 6.1)

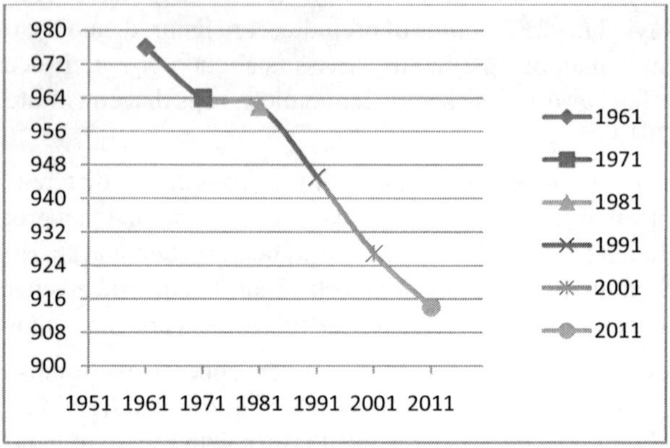

Source: Census, 2011 (Graph created by an author)

Fig. 6.1: Sex Ratio 0-6 yrs

The case is really shocking for Bihar. In 1961, sex ratio was high (1,005) but in due course it has shown regular decline and between 1991 and 2011, the sex ratio has shown maximum decline from 942 in 2001 to 933 in 2011.

The problem of "missing women" in India as conceptualised by Amartya Sen first, has existed for more than a century and a half and is an endemic and persistent feature of Indian society, there are strong reasons to believe that the causes of "missing women" can be strong preferences of son rather than daughter and due to lack of their own identity in the family female were excluded in the decision making process of their own child survival. It means that the process of exclusion starts from the womb of her mother itself. There is a need for Feminists to insist more on the reservation of seats for women in the womb first then to their demand for reservation of seats in parliament because early years of life is most crucial for laying the foundation for inclusion.

Lack of education can be one the pertinent reason for above problem. As we all know that education is the mirror of the society and base of the socio-economic development. It transforms human beings from ignorance to enlightenment, from underdevelopment to faster economic and social development. Education is a vital factor that fuels both social change and economic growth. India is actively pushing forward with its agenda for revamping and restructuring education in the country. Right to Education (RTE) is now a fundamental Right for all children in the age group of 6 to 14 years. But then also the situation of education and especially primary or elementary education is grim in India as a whole and as Bihar particular. Excluding children on the basis of caste, creed, religion and race from accessing school has become a new form of discriminatory attitude of contemporary times. Educational deprivation suppresses their freedom to actively participate in and benefit from elementary education. Henceforth, social exclusion creates barriers to education for both boys and girls, but many of these barriers are higher for girls, therefore, girls in socially excluded groups often suffer from a double disadvantage. Gender disparity in school might have several reasons behind it but poverty put girls at a distinct disadvantage in terms of education.

As Bell Hooks long back talked about this in context of US that poverty hampers the ability of all working class people, especially racial and ethnic groups, to participate in higher education. Therefore, most contemporary published feminist theory in United States has been written by white educated women (Hooks, 1981).

The pace of progress in literacy rate as revealed by decennial census is very slow in India. In the span of fifty years from 1951 to 2001, there has been only marginal increase from 18.33 per cent to 64.83 per cent literacy rate in India. From 1951 to 2001, female literacy shows a mere increase from 8.86 per cent to 53.67 per cent. According to census 2011, the literacy rate of India has gone up to 74.04 per cent. The corresponding figures for male and females are 82.14 and 65.46 per cent respectively. Thus three- fourth of the total population aged 7 years and above is literate in the country. Four out of every five males and two out of every three females in the country are literate. (Fig 6.2)

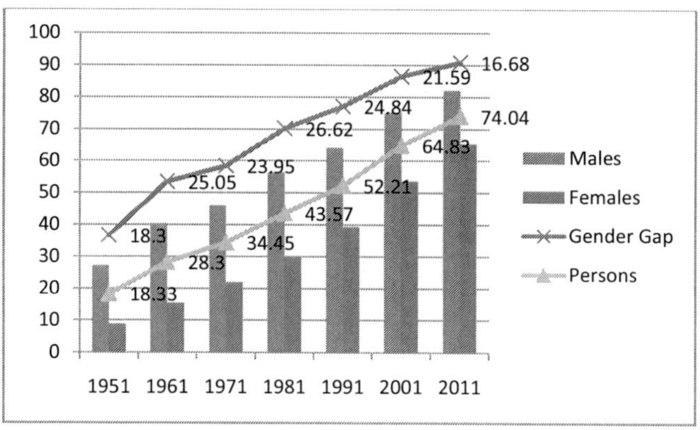

Source: Census, 2011 (Graph created by an author)

Fig. 6.2: Male –Female literacy gap in India (in %)

As shown in the figure here that the gender gap regarding literacy is decreasing but it very slow and due to this the target set by Planning Commission to reduce the gender gap by 10 per cent in 2011-12 has not been achieved. The reduction by 4.99 per cent has been achieved which is a positive stride towards decreasing illiteracy. According to sources, the country has continued its march towards improving literacy rate by recording a jump of 9.21 per cent during 2001-2011. But still 35 per cent of female are illiterate and the gap in literacy rate is 16.68.

When we particularly take case of Bihar, we see that though the data of 2011 of female literacy is showing a positive trend of 53.33 from 33.12 of 2001, but still Bihar stands as second lowest in female literacy. 18.9 million Female are illiterate in Bihar according to 2011 census. Literacy gap is continuously reducing in Bihar but still almost 50% of female population is illiterate in Bihar. (Fig. 6.3)

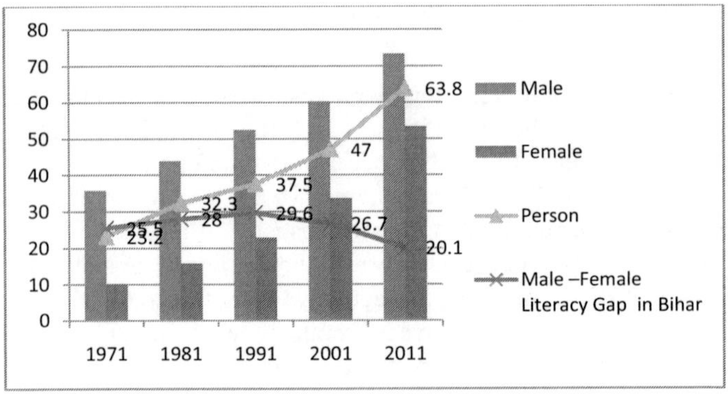

Source: Census, 2011 (Graph created by an author)

Fig. 6.3: Trend of Literacy Rates in Bihar

Education is crucial for the empowerment and emancipation of girls and women, and the realisation of all other human rights. Educating a girl has a transformational effect that changes communities and societies, but society itself to some extent is responsible for this exclusion. Girls often be outside from school to help their parents in domestic work, to look after their siblings, etc. whereas the boys keep their schooling on. Gender differentiated ideologies cut across all social groups, which explains why in all social groups girls lag behind boys in access to and participation in education. Responsibilities for securing domestic water and fuel place tremendous time burdens on women, often shared with younger girls in the family who could otherwise be in school or at rest or play. Family considers girl's education as a financial liability. Early marriage of girls to maintain purity can also be one important reasons of their exclusion from education. Condition of school infrastructure in which bathroom facility comes first for girls where in most of the schools both in rural or urban sector bathroom facility is not available for them which has driven about 50 per cent girl children away from educational facility and the gender gap is still a major issue for the state. Despite all, social customs do not permit them to come out of their homes and attend the classes. Through some reports it has been found that a village woman takes pride in her illiteracy and looks down upon educated women. The age –old superstition that literacy means to invite widowhood is still persisting in many parts of the state. The women's first concern is taken to be her home and it is considered that for running the home and rearing of children literacy is of no use. The men also feel that once women are educated, they lose their hold upon them. A husband of an educated woman in village communities as well as in some urban communities is pitied rather than envied with new awakening in the country. These gender- specific ideologies are responsible for the continued wide gaps in female schooling enrolment and leads to social exclusion of girls from education.

Due to the above reasons, India lag behind in educational attainment with other countries. The average time a kid spends in school in India is 4.4 years, much less than neighbouring Pakistan where the average is 4.9 years (Internet source UNDP). Countries will require increased attention to policies targeted at girls from these groups if they are to meet their Millennium Development Goals for Education and to achieve the social and economic benefits of girls' education (Internet source UNESCO).

It is generally believed that education has an intrinsic relationship with employment but the trend is not the same in India. The labour force indicates the proportion of the population that is economically active, including the employed as well as those unemployed and actively seeking jobs. With regard to female labour force participation (LFPR), India has been witnessing declining trends (Samantroy, 2017).

Gender based discrimination and exclusion is found to be a common phenomenon across the globe. It has been extensity studied and commented upon in its various dimensions including historical sexual division of work, discrimination in hiring, placements and promotions and differences in wages and earnings between women and men. Studies have also focused on differential rates of labour force and workforce participation by women and men and consequent underrepresentation of women in workforce; as well as the sex-based discrimination in family and society in the spheres of education and skill formation and attitudes towards women's work- forms of discrimination that precede discrimination in the labour market and influence the gender based differences in employment and earnings (Papola, 2012). The vast majority of adult male workers (86 per cent) are engaged in a primary economic activity and 65 per cent perform more than one type of work. In the case of women, only a small minority (20 per cent) declare their participation in a primary economic activity because a majority of them consider domestic work as their primary occupation and are, therefore, not included in the labour force. However, 56 per cent of the women have been found to be engaged in a secondary economic activity (IHD Report 2009-10).

The NSS Unit Level data of Round 61st 2004-2005,66th 2009-10 & 68th 2011, showed that in the period 2004-05 to 2009-10 women's labour force participation declined from 33.3 per cent to 26.5 per cent in rural areas and from 17.8 per cent to 14.6 per cent in urban areas (NSSO 2011). According to the International Labour Organisation's Global Employment Trends 2013 report, India is placed at 120th of 131 countries in women's labour force participation. Which violates Article 19 (1) (g): rights to practice any profession, trade and business. The number of actual women workers is high in rural India, in comparison to urban India. The reason behind the contradictory findings is low evolvement of rural women in attending schooling, high demand of female labour in agriculture sector.

Apart from employment lack of access and control over productive assets: like land, livestock, fisheries, technologies, credit, finance, markets etc. women face exclusion due to socio- cultural practices, and also experience gender exclusion in agricultural wages and decisions concerning crop management and marketing. Even though the legal framework on succession has been amended in favour of women but the net result is that daughters still are excluded from the right to inherit agricultural land in actual practice (Saxena, 2013).

The slogan: *Healthy Women, Healthy World,* means women play a critical role in maintaining health and well being of their communities. Unequal access to health care one of the forms of discrimination, have excluded women to have right nutritional diet in their meals which causes infant mortality, female feticide, maternal mortality, malnutrition, not able to work for long (unemployment) etc.

According to NFHS II and NFHS III the proportion of underweight children in 1998-99 was 45.3% for males and 48.9% for females which declined to 41.6% for males and 43.1% for females in 2005-06. Bihar in 1998-99 for male was 35.2% and 37.1% for females which slightly increased in females 38.4%, whereas in boys it declined 34.4% during 2005-06. Causes can be low dietary intake, lack of awareness and also intra household inequality in food distribution, where women suffer most.

Dual discrimination being meted out to women when they are disabled too. Fit and fine women are excluded from the main sphere of the society than women with disability and old age will have no place in the society it seems. Because they cannot fight for themselves in patriarchal structure of society.

The patriarchal structure of Indian society and to some extent to control the power with themselves, women have become the proxy members in politics especially in Panchayati Raj Institutions. In Bihar though women have got 50% reservation in PRIs but their socio- economic and political empowerment continues to be major concerns. Only their name and signature is being used, main works are done by the Mukhiyapati.

The position of women in politics has always been miserable. Political participation means involvement of those affected by decisions in the decision making process. The involvement may include a right to elect representatives, to vote, to campaign and to decide matters, etc. In recent years women's participation in politics actors has improved but their grip over power structure has not been impressive.

The Constitution under Articles 325 and 326, assures political equality to all men and women. Yet the representation of women in Parliament and State assemblies is extremely low in India. Only 11% able to enter Parliament. India stands 108 of 188 in women representation in House (TOI, 2013).

This shows exclusion of women from political participation due to lack of awareness and knowledge of their rights more, than the traditional structure of society. Continuous efforts have been made for 33% seat reservation in all levels of legislature for women. But till date it has not been tabled it in the parliament.

Inclusion in this area could make way for women in other arena too. Full fledge decision making power might change the socio- cultural and economic status of women in future.

Consequently, gender differences and inequalities are a fundamental feature of social exclusion. This is revealed by women's lower employment rate, greater exposure to low pay and more broadly by their lower average earnings. These average gender gaps in employment are more pronounced for particular subgroups, such as employment rates for older workers. Women accumulate lower pension and other benefits where eligibility is earnings-related or based on individual records of employment history because of their lower average earnings, greater likelihood of interrupting their employment or working reduced hours to attend to family care responsibilities, and the higher unemployment rates they experience in many countries. Social welfare systems in most countries still rest on an implicit and outdated policy assumption that women have or should have access to the income of a male 'breadwinner' partner or derived benefits as his dependent spouse. Gender inequalities in employment combined with design inadequacies in social welfare systems produce a situation whereby poverty is disproportionately borne by women or is 'feminised'. However, this gender perspective is often absent from policy debates (Expert Group Manuscript, 2006).

IV. Conclusion: From Exclusion to Inclusion

India is undeniably one of the most unequal societies in the world. There is no other country in the world with such a divergent social plurality and its consequent institutionalised exclusion. There is frequent convergence between social and material inequalities (Hasan, 2009). However, India is also one of the few countries in the post- colonial world that took up the challenge to building an inclusive democracy within its highly divergent socio- economic- political- cultural structure. The democracy and universal adult suffrage in a hierarchical society was the most bold experiment in any country and India remains a major success in that direction (Kohli, 2001).

The rigidity of the social exclusion is structured in the *homo hierarchicus* society, its social and cultural practices and beliefs and values. However, with the progress of time and working of various forces of modernisation, the rigidity of the structural conditions is slowly weakening and so is the rigidity of social exclusion. The rigid and hierarchical social structure has, however, produced a powerful movement for social inclusion that has manifested in Dalit and backward classes movements and more recently women's movement. Women's movement also depended on the identity of gender and the narratives of common sufferings, exploitation and discrimination. Women's movement has still not crystallised in a powerful social force, although women's activists are able to draw cause, issue and incidence based attention to the problem and aspiration of women. Women's issues are now flagged in the public domain, and women's activists and leaders play an important role in this regard.

That is why even though exclusion has been rigid, there is incontrovertible evidence to show that inclusion is also happening. The level of education among women has increased. This has created new opportunities for them to become part of mainstream society (Pankaj & Pandey, 2014).

Inclusiveness is about a growth process which is seen to be fair by different socio- economic groups that constitute our society (Saxena, 2013).

Social Inclusion is a question of rights. Inclusion means integration and integration leads to equality. Fighting with different grass root institutions to get rid of exclusion from the society is quiet difficult. But its is also said that nothing is difficult when your decision is firm enough to fight against social evil. So, when society as a whole takes firm decision to integrate women in society then the disparities mentioned above can only be reduced and later would not even exist in society. It is upto the people of the society, who have full right to take decisions in favour of women and then only gender just society is possible.Gender mainstreaming is an innovative policy for social inclusion of women. Gender sub- plan and inclusive planning is needed. Equality of outcomes should be the main objective of Gender Sub- Plan and not simply equality of opportunities. However, to create a gender-just society, one needs to move from equality of opportunities to equality of outcomes for women and men. There are number of policies implemented by the government like Beti Bachao - Beti Padhao,ujjwala yojana, kishori shakti yojana, dhanalakshmi and many more. All these policies are especially made to empower girl child and women as well. But before empowering them emphasis should be given to the consciousness for whole society on the importance of a girl and women on earth and these policies would have fruitful result then only. Other important thing to be noted that the implementation of the policies related to women or girl done by the government needs time to time monitoring so that it could check the outreach and the target level. The overall policy of inclusion should be to balance the concept of social justice as a whole and which achieve the objective of inclusiveness of women in all dimensions of society.

Beyond this there is need to address the roots of the institutions and structure of women's exclusion as well as discrimination in Indian society in terms of intersectionalities of caste, class and gender identities, which could affect the women's stand in society as a whole.

References

Beauvoir, Simone de, (1997), The second Sex, trans. And ed. By H M Parshley, London, Vintage.

Buvnic, Mayra (2005) Social Exclusion in Latin Aamerica ,in Mayara Buvinic and Jacqueline Mazzaand Ruthanne Deutsch (2005) "Social Inclusion and Economic Development in Latin Aamerica,Inter-Aamerican Development Bank,Newyork.

Constitution of India.

Expert Group on Gender, Social Inclusion and Employment European Commission Directorate-General for Employment, Social Affairs and Equal Opportunities, Manuscript completed in July 2006.

Gender Gap Index, 2011.

Haan A. de., (1997), Poverty and Social Exclusion: A Comparison of debates on Deprivation, *Working Paper*, No. 2 Poverty Research Unit at Sussex; Brighton, University of Sussex.

————(2007), Labelling Works: The Language and Politics of Caste and Tribe in India', in Rosalind Eyben and Joy Moncrieffe (eds.) The Power of Labelling: How People are Categorised and How it Matters, London, Earthscan.

Hasan, Zoya (2009), Politics of Inclusion: Castes, Minorities, and Affirmative Action, New Delhi, Oxford University Press.

Hooks, B., (1981), Ain't I a Women? Black Women and Feminism, Boston: South England Press.

IHD Report 2009-2010.

Kohli, Atul, (ed.) (2001), The Success of Indian Democracy, Cambridge, Cambridge University Press. Views are sited on p. 15.

National Sample Survey Report, 2011.

Okome, M. O., (2002), "Domestic, Regional, and International Protection of Nigerian Women against Discrimination: Constraints and Possibilities" *African Studies Quarterly* | Volume 6, Issue 3.

Oommen, T.K., (2007), Knowledge and Society: Situating Sociology of Social Anthropology, New Delhi: Oxford University Press.

Pandey, A.K., Ashok K. Pankaj (2014), Subalternity, Exclusion and Social Change in India, Cambridge University Press.

Papola, T. S., (2012), Social Exclusion and Discrimination in the Labour Market, ISID *Working Paper* No. 2012/04.

Samantroy, E. (2017), "Understanding Women's Work: Gendered Analysis of Women's Participation in Domestic Duties in North East India", *NLI Research Studies Series*, No: 123/2017.

Saxena, N C, (2013), *Challenges of the Marginalised,* Yojana, August, 2013.

Sen, A. (2000), Social exclusion: Concept, application and scrutiny, *Social Development Papers No. 1: Office of Environment and Social Development, Asian Developmen Bank.*

Sen Amartya, (2007), Social Exclusion: Concept, Application Scrutiny, Critical Quest: New Delhi.

Sen, A, (1981), Poverty and Famines: An Essay on Entitlement and Exclusion, Delhi, Oxford University Press.

Shaffer, P., (1998), *Gender, Poverty and Deprivation: Evidence From Republic of Guinea,* World Development. Vol. 26, No. 12.

Silver, H., (1994), Social Exclusion and Social Solidarity: Three Paradigms, IILS Discussion Ppaers No 69, ILO.

Silver, Hilary (1995), Reconceptualising Social Exclusion: Three Paradigms of Social Exclusion, in *Social Exclusion, Rhetoric, Reality, Responses,* edited by Gerry Rodgers, Chales Gore and Jose B. Figueiredo, Geneva: International Labour Organisation.

Thorat, S. K.,; Arjan de Haan & N. S. Sabharwal (2014), *Exclusion, Deprivation and Human Development: Conceptual Framework to study Excluded Groups (eds)* in Bridging the Social Gap: Perspectives on Dalit Empowerment, Sage Publication: New Delhi.

Times of India, 2013.

Townsend, Peter, (1987), *'Deprivation'*, Journal of Social Policy, Vol. 16, No. 2.

United Nations, General Assembly, (1996), "Implementation of the Outcome of the Fourth World Conference on Women: Report of Secretary General", A/51/322, (www.un.org).

UNDP AND UNESCO Report from internet on Education.

www.un.org, chapter IV.

7

Locating the Status of Muslim Women through the Discourse on Marriage and Divorce Laws

— *Vandana Singh*

Introduction

Islamic Laws in the context of women so far as they propose to situate them in the Muslim society have invariably elicited animated responses, the most fervent debates centered around the interpretations that focus on the Triple Talaq and the practice of Polygamy in Islam. The bona fide voices of alarm favoring the reform on an urgent basis have their concerns beefed up by ones not so converted to the women's' cause making a compelling case to notice the inequity and irrationality embedded in the provisions and which is precisely why the narrative is invested with such stridency and gravity at the same time.The truth is that the general portrayal of Muslim women in India characterizes their status as a product of personal laws, an exercise which more often than not results in according primacy to religious and cultural traditions while furnishing justification of political action by communities and the state in terms of presumed and non-representational notions of communal consensus. Unfortunately, the focus herein is not the women *per se* but the *Shariat* and legal codes that are biased against women at the same time accommodating the religious leaders rather than the women.

The State in the Scheme!

The ShahBano case was a seminal one in the Muslim women's quest for justice and marked the commencement of the political battle over personal law.The decision to revoke the Shah Bano judgment (the argument being that the judgment violated Muslim Personal Law and by implication undermined the identity of the Muslim community predicated on narrow doctrinal principles that distinguished Muslims from others[1]) had far–reaching consequences for Muslim womens'rights. It brought in its wake, strident demands by majoritarian nationalists who invoked secularisation in support of the homogenisation of the family law which was vehemently opposed by Muslim fundamentalists who resisted any legal intervention on the ground that their personal law as not open to legal regulation and in this belligerentstate, women inadvertently became a site of controversy. By assuming that the Muslim leadership (which is predominantly male) was the sole arbiter of Muslim interests, the government circumscribed the political expression of multiple identities, notably gender. More importantly, by accepting personal law as a hallmark of community identity, State policy made it politically incumbent on Muslim women to act as symbolic markers of that identity.[2] Muslim Personal Law has consequently become an important symbol of minority identity whose defense has resulted in the steady corrosion of the rights of Muslim women, systematically subordinated to the perceived interests of the Muslim community. In this process, both the persuasive and contradictory nature of relationship between the State and Muslim women was brought to the fore. While engagement and support are a compelling necessity for advancing the interests of the marginalised and deprived group which Muslim women are, the State appears to have relinquished its duty toward this group, letting the more vociferous, bellicose and dominant male voices to do all the parleying and deliberating on behalf of the women, a prospect which poses a major challenge to Muslim women's' rights which dismayingly have been at best illusory in the absence of empowerment.[3] The Government supported the enactment of the *Muslim Women's (Protection of Rights on Divorce) Act* in May 1986, which provides that section 125 of the Criminal Procedure Code does not apply to divorced Muslim women. The MWA removed Muslim women from the ambit of the general law of maintenance and placed them under a special legislation. However, it also gave Muslim women the right to appeal to the courts if they were not paid the stipulated maintenance. The State conveyed thus, it's ineptitude to protect womens' rights and succumbed to the regressivenotion ofwomen's' identities as being embedded in and subsumed by the community to which they belonged and not as having an autonomous existence. The natural corollary was that their rights would be governed by the Personal Law that more often than not voiced the mindset of the conservative section of the populace. The position of the Government reflects that of the All India Muslim Personal Law Board(AIMPLB) which has appropriated for itself, the right to talk on behalf of the Muslim community, the rhetoric of which body becomesamplified in all scenarios of imagined threats to the Muslim Law.

The primaryjustification and validationfor legal reform in the law is premised in the general norm of the state being the guarantor of equal protection under the law to all citizens. However, advocates of a Uniform Civil Code zero in on personal law, in particular on the issue of gender bias in the existing

Muslim Personal Law (MPL). Their appraisal is centered around those provisions of the MPL that permit a Muslim man to have up to four wives at one time, to divorce his wife extra-judicially, and to be free of responsibility for her maintenance once an approximately three-month post-divorce period *(iddat)* has ended and how these provisions are damaging to womens' interests. The three key concerns of Muslim Personal Law as they relate to women have thus focused on polygamy, unilateral divorce and maintenance and inheritance. It is indisputable that these provisions of the MPL, both as codified and as developed through case law- the accumulated judicial decisions of the various High Courts and the Supreme Court of India over a period of more than two centuries- favor the interests of the male partner. However, it has to be understood that much of the literature on this subject is a strident verbal attack and the evidence presented is often merely sketchy and this renders difficult making valid generalisations about the relative deprivation of Muslim versus Hindu or Christian women in terms of actual legal practice.

Marriage and the Economic Endowment-real or elusive?

Mercifully, the Mulim law of marriage in its inception showed a skewness in favour of women ensuring their economic rights, though it is regrettable thatas they exist today, a clear patriarchal, male-favoring bias in the penal laws and the laws of succession as enjoined upon in the *Shariat*is discernable.Thus, in their conception, Islamic principles could be invoked andemployed to protect the women from spousal scheming and maneuvering towards the objective of encroaching upon these rights, which was very often the case.

Marriage in Islam is a very practically modelled consensual contractual union liberated from the very outset from the sacramental encumbrance of indissolubility or nullification.[4] Marriage was expressed, as was the case with many other transactions, in the language of sale, with no pejorative connotations. *Offer* and *acceptance* formed the basis of the contract, with certain mandatory stipulations built to provide women with additional safeguards. The custom of bride price in tribal Arabia-an amount paid to the father of the bride to recompense him for the loss that accrued to him interms of labor power with his daughter gone off as a result of marriage–was converted into *Mehr* which was meant to be a mark of respect to the woman, and this formed an essential ingredient of a marriage contract. "Dower under the Muhammadan Law is a sum of money or other property promised by the husband to be paid or delivered to the wife in consideration of the marriage, and even where no dower is expressly fixed or mentioned at the marriage ceremony, the law confers the right of dower upon the wife."[5] It is not a 'consideration' in themodern sense of the term but an obligation imposed by the law upon the husband as a mark of respect for the wife.[6] This is made abundantly clear by the author of the *Hedaya* when he says: "The payment of dower is enjoined by the law merely as a token of respect for its object (the woman), wherefore the mention of it is not absolutely essential to the validity of a marriage; and, for the same reason, a marriage is also valid although the man were to engage in the contract on the special condition that there should be no dower."[7]

The Holy Quran invests the women with *Mehr*in the nature of a right. A categorical endorsement of this right is made in all ensuing legal literature. Chapter IV Verse 3 of the Holy Quran stipulates:

> "And give women their dower freely and if they are good enough to remit any of it of their own free will, then enjoy it with a good conscience".

There is also a mention that the Prophet settled 500 dhirams on each of his wives with the exception of OmmBabeebah (from Abyssinia) on whom he settled 4000 dhirams.[8]

The Maliki School of Islamic law even invalidates a marriage without the stipulation of *Mehr*.TheHanafi School lays down that the marriage is valid but if no *Mehr* is stipulated or if the amount stipulated is very low, the woman is entitled to a 'proper' *Mehr, Mehr-el-misl*. The appropriate *Mehr* would have to be arrived upon and quantified depending upon the economic positioning of the husband and the family status of the wife. While a minimum of 10 dhirams is mandatory, the legal texts routinely mention amounts of 1,000 and 2,000 dhirams by way of examples indicating that the Mehr settlements were actually to be far in excess of the lowest stipulated. Augmentations to the amount stipulated at the time of marriage can be effected any time during the course of the marriage. *Mehr* is a mark of respect to the wife and is meant to set off the disability suffered by women under the law of inheritance. Hence, the amount stipulated has to be substantial. A token amount is injustice and wrong as per Islamic principles.

Mehr when prompt is payable on demand but it can also be deferred. In the latter scenario, it can be payed later anytime during the marriage but by all means at the time that the marriage dissolves which could either be by death or by divorce.[9] If at the time of dissolution of marriage the *Mehr* dues are unpaid, the woman is entitled to retain possession of her deceased husband's property. Usually this right is discussed in legal texts as a 'widow's right' but the same principle would apply if the marriage is dissolved by divorce. If the dower is not paid, the wife, and after her death, her heirs may sue for it.

A woman has the right to impose conditions regarding her *Mehr*. For instance she can stipulate that if the husband resides in the same city as her parents then the *Mehr* amount would be 1,000 dhirams, but if he shifts to another city then the amount should be doubled. In such a case if the husband does shift to another city then the wife is entitled to claim 2,000 dhirams.

Mehr need not be stipulated only in cash. Gold ornaments, valuables and other movable and immovable property can also be settled as *Mehr*. *Mehr* is the sole right of the wife and the husband cannot have any claim over it once the marriage is consummated.[10]

The husband can settle his share of family property or a particular house as *Mehr.* The woman would then be entitled to this property or its monetary value. If the woman claims that the matrimonial residence has been given to her in lieu of her *Mehr* debt, it is for the husband to rebut the presumption. If the husband refuses to pay the prompt *Mehr* upon marriage, the woman can refuse to fulfill her marital obligations including cohabitation. She is not bound to obey any of his commands. The wife is entitled to live separately and claim maintenance from her husband during this period. Even if the husband has paid nine dhirams and one dhiram is due, the wife has a right to refuse cohabitation and the husband is not entitled to reclaim the nine dhirams already paid.

If a man agrees to pay a certain amount of *Mehr* conditioned upon her virginity but subsequently discovers that she is not, there is no room for him to renege from his commitment, the entitlementof the woman contracted upon being safely preserved. Once settled, the husband cannot be absolved of his duty to pay the dues, even when there is a subsequent separation which is caused by the wife's action. Even when a Muslim marries a non-Muslim, he is bound to pay her the *Mehr*.

If the husband died without paying his *Mehr* dues, the woman was deemed a creditor, and if she was in possession of her husband's property, she could retain it till her *Mehr* dues were paid. There is substantial case law which holds that the widow's right to retain her deceased husband's property is heritable and alienable[11]. Hence the widow could sell or gift the property or, after her, her heirs could retain it until the *Mehr was* paid.

When the British jurists guided themselves by the Islamic principles while deciding matrimonial disputes, the agreements stood as valid, in the process buttressing a woman's position, recognizing her right to shelter or access to the matriarchal home. But the converse recourse of relying on the British notions of morality and public policy had a poor prognosis and ended up invalidating the agreements.It needs to be appreciated that notions such as morality and public policy were English principles which were stealthily and clandestinely introduced into the Indian family law narrative with adverse consequences so far as the rights of women are concerned as reliance on this premise circumscribed invariably and in a sustained manner, women's right to divorce, to adopt children or to inherit property as mandated by both the texts as well a custom.[12]

In the present times, the personal laws of the post-colonial period are not employed in their original form, their bases on English translations of the original texts, the legal precedents of the British jurists and the local customs and practices leading to the weakening and defacement of these rights beyond measure. *Mehr* is reduced to a mere token, replaced by dowry, an obnoxious custom typical to the Hindusociety which is steadily acquiring currency.[13] The amounts stipulated are as low as Rs 101 to Rs 501, merely a nominal adherence to the Islamic stipulation and only among a very small section does the amount exceed Rs 10,000. The amount of dower paid to the groom is always higher than the *Mehr* whose beneficiary is the woman whereas the practice of pre-marriage agreement has almost ceased to exist. Also, in total disregard to the entire notion of the contractual nature of a Muslim marriage, high amounts of *Mehr* are increasingly looked down upon because of the parallel of a contract of sale that it is reminiscent of. This perhaps is a rub off from the very sacramental nature of the Hindu idea of marriage.This convinient dispensing of the very important economic safeguard which *Mehr* was originally conceived as, has deleterious consequences so far as a Muslim woman's location in her marriage is concerned, very definitely skewing the balance in the favour of the husband in an already patriarchal society, manifesting more profusely and with greater incidence in arbitrary oral divorces, heaping further misery and destitution on the women.

The perfunctory fashion of the contracting of *Mehr* is alarming for it can no more be reckoned as a sufficient protection for women againstimpecunity. An enablement whichmarried women under Islamic Law could take pride of vis-a-vis their counterparts under other legal systems is now a thing of a past and appears nearly surreal in the prevailing social milieu.

Polygamy-Fair and Square?

Polygamy was a practice that predates Islam and the advent of Islam did not abrogate it.Limited polygyny is approved by Islam for exceptional circumstances and with several stringent conditions. It is to the credit of Islam that it modified and reformed the system in existence at the time. Islam put a limit to the numbers of wives that a person can have at one time-maximum of four wives at one time. Secondly, Islam put strict conditions on a person who wanted to marry a second wife. He must be able to provide and maintain the family, and also deal with both on basis of justice and fairness. The tradition says; "If a man has two wives, and does not observe justice between them, he will appear on the Last Day shorn of half of himself." It is incumbent upon him to make an equal partition of his cohabitation among them, irrespective of his marriage with a *sayyibah* (non-virgin) or a virgin.[14]

In Chapter 4 (Surah an-Nisaa), verse 3, after allowing the Muslim men to marry two, three or four wives, the Qur'ãn says:

> *"but if you fear that you will not do justice (between them), then (marry) only one..."* (Surah an-Nisaa, 4:3).

Looking at the psychology of humans, only exceptional people have that quality of justice and fairness. The Qur'ãn itself, in the same Chapter 4, verse 129, says:

> *"And you do not have the ability to do justice between the wives, even though you may wish (to do so)..."* (Surah an-Nisaa, 4:129).

Thus control on polygamy is justified in the light of the impossibility of attainment of perfect impartiality in treatment.

Since Muslim Personal Law permits a Muslim man to take more than one wife, it does not of course recognize as valid, a complaint by the first wife that her husband has married again. Nor does the personal law of the Muslims admit as a ground for complaint,the husband's refusal to divorce the first wife when he marries another. However, a ground for redress exists for an unfairly treated and neglected wife and persistence of such behavior by the husband furnishes a ground for divorce under DMMA.[15]

Whereas a Muslim woman can marry only one husband, a Muslim may marry any number of wives not exceeding four,.[16] And if a Muslim marries a fifth wife, such a marriage is not void but irregular[17] whereas if a Muslim woman marries a second husband, she is liable for bigamy under Section 494 of the India Penal Code, and the offspring of such marriage are illegitimate and cannot be legitimized by any subsequent acknowledgement. [18]

Triple Talaq-The Anathema!

The provision of the Muslim personal law that has ruffled the most feathers and excited the most animated debates, single-handedly triggering the most protracted controversies is the one that allows a man to dissolve his marriage extra-judicially, unilaterally, and automatically by simply pronouncing the word *talaq,* either directly to or with clear reference to his wife. The provision dispenses with the need to even state or establish grounds for this announcement. Such is the arbitrariness embedded in this facility provided to men that even the presence of the woman on whom the pronouncement is to be made is reckoned as non-necessary. In fact, the communication of the information is also superfluous. If he does wish to inform her, he may do so through a third party or in writing! Such a proceeding, although abominable, is nevertheless lawful. *Talaq-e-bidat*which gives Muslim men absolute and unilateral power of divorce is upheld only by the Hanafi School of Islamic Jurisprudence. It involves three declarations (the so-called triple divorce) at one time and one irrevocable declaration (generally in writing).[19] The essential feature of *Talaq-e—bidat* is its irrevocability.The other three schools — Maliki, Shafai and Hanbali — do not approve of it. Besides, *Talaq-e-bidat* where the very word *'bidat'* means 'undesirable or forbidden innovation' or 'any sort of innovation from the path of the Prophet' is not sanctioned by the Koran. It was used as an emergency measure on a few occasions by Caliph Umar who later lamented allowing it. It was widely acknowledged, even by the Hanafi ulema themselves that this method of divorce was not looked upon favorably by the Prophet Muhammad himself. Regrettably, the clerics do not think it desirable for the Indian State or any other body to intercede and put an end to the practice so patently unjust to the women. Missing also are suggestions on measures to lessen its prevalence, other than by trying to motivate men to be better Muslims!

The harshest in matters of divorce and giving the wife nearly no grounds for initiating the dissolution of her marriage is the Hanafi School of Islamic jurisprudence.[20] This is also the schoolfollowed by a majority of Muslims in the subcontinent. If a woman initiated divorce (*Khula*), she would end up forfeiting her right to *Mehr*, very often her only means of support after divorce. This was a major disincentive to women seeking annulment of marriage even in grim circumstances. In the case of *Khula*, the terms of the bargain are a matter of arrangement between the husband and the wife and the wife may, as the consideration, release her *Mehr* and other rights or make any other agreement for the benefit of the husband.[21] Sometimes the husband is emboldened to drive a harder bargain and ask for some additional financial compensation before agreeing to the divorce. He may even coerce her to set asideher right to retain custody of their young children, or to receive child support while they are under her care. Once the terms of *Khula* are agreed upon, the way for the husband to pronounces *talaq-i-bain* (irrevocable divorce) is paved and the marriage is dissolved.[22] To even consider obtaining freedom from an alliance, however manifestly unworkable, when governed by such stipulations would be a daunting and overwhelming proposition indeed!

The Muslim Law empowers the husband to delegate his own right of pronouncing divorce to some third person or to the wife herself. Also held valid is the stipulation that under certain specified circumstances, the wife can pronounce divorce upon herself, on condition that that the option is not absolute and unreserved and the conditions are reasonable and not repugnant to public policy.[23] *Talaq-i-Tafwid* or “this form of delegated divorce is possibly the most effective weapon at the disposal of a Muslim wife for obtaining her freedom without requiring the involvement of any court and is now becoming fairly common in India.”[24] In the reported cases, the stipulations entitling the wife to divorce herself have been conditioned mostly on the husband taking a second wife. Such a conditional option is obviously different from an agreement prohibiting the husband to marry another wife, which according to the Sharaiul Islam [IthnaAshari text] would be void as herein, such a prohibition is expressly stated to be ‘contrary to the (Shiite) law.’

Whatever it’s utility during the past, the law of divorce at least in the Hanafi school was so interpreted as that it became an instrument of tyranny in the hands of the husband.

"The Muslim Dissolution of Marriage Act of 1939 was the legal reform that inarguably had the most noteworthy impact on Muslim women's rights providing for a woman to obtain a divorce from an unwilling or absent husband on ten different grounds including desertion, his suffering from insanity, obstructing her right to practice her religion, disposing of her property without her consent, charging her falsely with adultery, or subjecting her to mental or physical cruelty."[25] Unfortunately, due to the huge social stigma attached to involving oneself in court proceedings, especially those that involve exposing private family affairs to the scrutiny of strangers, the DMMA is rarely taken recourse to by Muslim women. The Family Courts Act enabling arbitration and speedy settlements over protracted adversarial legal action which was typical of the British system requiring one side to prove the matrimonial offence against the other (which causes great hardships and humiliation to women in courts) is also not taken recourse to by Muslim women.

However, it has to be appreciated that if notconcurrentlyallied to the protection of their economic rights, dissolution of marriage and provisions enabling it become counterproductive for women and end up damaging her interests more than augmenting her wellbeing and felicity.

Across the world, in all cultures and socio-political milieus, the Muslims are striving to bring the law in sync with modern ideas of social justice. The All India Muslim Personal Law Board (AIMPLB) was established in 1973 to adopt appropriateapproaches for the protection and continued applicability of Muslim Personal Law in India, especially, the Muslim Personal Law (Shariah) Application Act of 1937. The Board has however faced considerable censure from several quartersin the last few years – fromprominent jurists, scholars and activists especially due to its controversial stand on marriage and divorce – many even accusing a section in the board of "misinterpreting the Islamic laws to the disadvantage of women" and demanding codification of the Muslim Personal Law and an immediate ban on the malpractice of divorce by triple utterance of the word *'Talaaq'*. The All-India Muslim Women's Personal Law Board has, since 2010, advocated the incorporation of Muslim women's rights into the Indian Constitution. These would, at least in law, include protection of Muslim women's inheritance of their fathers' property; the right to education and choice of a career; a ban on underage marriage and forced marriage to men two or three times their age; the right to separation from abusive husbands; definition of rape as punishable by execution; and prohibition of divorce by "triple talaq. ", making void, marriage agreements or divorces transmitted by e-mail or cellphone messagesamong other provisions, Taking upon itself, the onus of reform and responding belatedly to the urgency of it, the Muslim Women (Protection of Rights on Marriage) Bill, 2017 was passed in the Lok Sabha making instant triple talaq or talaq-e-biddat a punishable offence, following the Supreme Court judgment on August 22, 2017 in the case of ShayaraBano vs. Union of India.

Conclusion-it's time we walked the talk!

For any set of lawsto be pertinent and thrive with relevance,whatever their provenance or mandate, theyshould mandatorily be just, gender-fair and humane. Muslim law is decidedly not outside the domain of the judicial process and the issue of *triple talaq* has been subjected to legal recourse, though belatedly. The Muslim Women (Protection of Rights on Marriage) Bill, 2017 voids instant triple talaq in any form, be it spoken, written or by electronic means, thus setting aside a "manifestly arbitrary" practice through the offices of the State. The Dissolution of Muslim Marriage Act, 1939 and the Muslim Women (Protection of Rights on Divorce) Act, 1986 (MWA) are the two other relevant pieces of legislation. However, the Muslim leadership's propensity to make the defense of personal laws as synonymous with the protection of minorities has resulted in Muslim women's' rights remaining a function of collective communal existence rather than a condition of democratic citizenship with the state acquiescing in the scenario in the process circumscribing and constricting the articulation of the gender interests within a narrow specific identity discourse. The very elementarycontradiction between questions of womens' rights and their position within their communities persists as women continue to be located not within the constitution but within their community laws. The waning is not indicative of the Islamic laws of marriage but a woeful measure of the politicisation of women's rights within a communally afflicted male-controlled society. National integration is not going to be endangered if people continue to have multiple personal laws. What is necessary is that the personal laws must be appraised from the standpoint of substantive equality between men and woman and also between women irrespective of their religion. Champions of the faith have repeatedly claimed that Islam prescribes a progressive order for women. The challenge for the AIMPLB is to ensure that the talk is walked by plugging the loopholes in the law. Muslim women in the country have borne the cross of antiquated Shariat law for too long.

References

1. ZoyaHasan, 1994, 'Minority Identity, State Policy and the Political Process', in ZoyaHasan(Ed.), Forging Identities; Gender, Communities and the State in India, Delhi: Kali for Women, pp. 59-73.
2. Syeda S Hamid, 2000, Voice of the Voiceless: Status of Muslim Women in India, Report.
3. MaitreyiMukhopadhyaya, 1998, Legally Dispossessed; Gender, Identity and the Process of Law, Calcutta: Stree.
4. Paras Diwan, 1993, Muslim Law in Modern India, Sixth Edition, Allahabad Law Agency, p. 62.
5. Mahmood J. in Abdul KadirV.Salima(1886) cited in Asaf A. A. Fyzee, Outlines of Muhammadam Law(Fifth Edition), New Delhi: Oxford University Press, 2008, p. 105.

6. Abdur Rahim, 1911,The Principles of Muhammadan Jurisprudence:According to the Hanafi, Maliki, Shafi and Hanbali Schools, Lahore:Kausar Brothers, p. 334.
7. Charles Hamilton's Hedaya,(Second Edition).byS.C Grady, London: W.H Allen, 1870, p. 44.
8. Flavia Agnes, Economic Rights of Women in Islamic Law, Economic and Political Weekly, Vol.31, Issue no.41-42, October 12-19, 1996, p. 2833
9. M. Hidayatullah and Arshad Hidayatullah, 1990, Mulla's Principles of Mahomedan Law, (Nineteenth Edition), Lexis Nexis. Buttersworths, p. 247.
10. Flavia Agnes, Economic Rights of Women in Islamic Law, Economic and Political Weekly, op.cit., p. 2833.
11. MainaBibi vs. Vakil Ahmed, ILR, 1924, 52I. A. 145.
12. Flavia Agnes, Economic Rights of Women in Islamic Law, Economic and Political Weekly, op.cit p. 2834.
13. Newsletter of Women's Research and Action Group, Bombay Vol 1/2 September, 1994, Vol 11/1 February, 1995, Vol 11/2 and 3 August 1995 and Vol 11/4 October, 1995.
14. Arif Ali Khan(Ed.), 2007, Social Philosophy of Islam, New Delhi: Pentagon Press, p. 9.
15. AsafA.Fyzee, 1949, Outlines of Muhammadan Law,Indian Branch, Oxford University Press, p. 175.
16. Roland K. Wilson,1930, Anglo-Muhammadan Law,(Sixth Edition) Lahore: Law Publishing Company, pp. 31-33.
17. Mulla, Mahomedan Law, op.cit., p. 255.
18. Wilson, op.cit., p. 33.
19. Faiz Badrudd in Tyabji, 1968, Muslim Law: The Personal Law of Muslims in India and Pakistan, Bombay: M.N. Tripathi, p. 141.
20. Gail Minault, 2009, Gender, Language and Learning. Essays in Indo-Muslim Cultural History, Delhi: Permanent Black, p. 79.
21. Raheem v. Luteefut-oon-Nissa (1861), 8 MIA 379.
22. In a Minority.Essays on Muslim Women in India. (Eds.) Zoya Hasan & Ritu Menon, New Delhi: Oxford University Press, 2005, p. 37.
23. A.A.A. Fyzee, The Muslim Wife's Right of Dissolving her Marriage, 1936, Vol. 38 Bombay Law Reporter, pp. 113, 120-121.
24. Mulla's Principles of Mahomedan Law, op.cit., p. 267.

8

Gender Inequality and Mobile Phones: Problems and Conclusion for Developing Countries

— ***Faisal Akhtar & Asif Akhtar Khan***

Introduction

Increased gender inequalities, even in the short-run, are having long-term consequences for economic growth and human development (Costa & Silva 2008, 2009). It is only with the help of holistic gender analysis that mobile technologies can fulfill their unlimited potential for improving the lives of women and girls in low income countries. Just one decade ago, women could be facing food problem, or be mis-treated in their husband house by relatives for years before the news reached their parents. Now, phones are helping women in rural India to keep in touch with relatives, and since natal families continue to be the major source of help for married women. (Tenhunen 2008). In many fast emerging economies like India, the privileged live is a highly connected information society, while those at the bottom of the income pyramid (BOP), and especially BOP women, remain disconnected. This means that they are unlucky citizens deprived to access to modern communication devices becouse of rigid and systematic inequities, they are also deprived of the added social and economic benefits of mobile phone access. As the segment of the population experiencing the most impediments, women at the BOP are thus the biggest losers when it comes to mobile phone access and related benefits. This paper is a presentation of challenges of gender discrimination and mobile phone as a boon for women and girls to fight the present challenges of gender discrimination in developing countries with special reference to India.

During the 1990s, researchers were quick to observe that women tend to be latecomers to the digital age (e.g. Dholakia, 1994; NTIA, 1999). As a consequence, the new technology was popularly portrayed as a male domain (Badagliacco, 1990). ICT are seen as yet another toy for the boys (Faulkner, 2001). It was concluded that men are more interested in technology than women, and they are also more tech savvy. (Fallows, 2005). As more statistics became available and Internet and mobile telephony penetration rates began to rise, women started to catch up in many developed countries (Rice and Katz, 2003). In the United States, most new users were women around the year 2000 (Cummings and Krout, 2002). Gender differences remained, but were smaller (Leggon, 2006). But it remains as a sorry story for developing countries, specially for India. The reason behind this sorry state is women inequality. The Mobile phones are a good tool for economic growth, and investing in women really improves the overall wellbeing of the families. Empowering more women with mobile phones can accelerate social and economic development. The mobile phone gender gap is observed as a symptom of broader gender inequalities, apparent in education as well as in the general use and ownership of ICTs (UNESCO 2013).

In higher education males show higher positive attitudes toward using technology for learning than females (You & Cheng 2012, Kahveci 2010; Li & Kirkup 2007). The introduction of technologies has often implicitly been designed to meet the needs of men, not of women (Basu, 2000; Hafkin, 2000). Sharma (2003) points out that – women have less online access than men, for all the usual gender-related reasons – time, money, control, learning opportunities, other commitments, prioritising others' needs.

The Gender Gap around the Globe

Gender equality refers to the extent to which men's and women's opportunities and outcomes are constrained—or enhanced—solely on the basis of their gender. The picture is clearly depicting the current status of gender gap around the globe. While searching the bad percentage, we can get south asia, where gender gap is 37%. We Indian are in red zone in case of gender gap or disccrimination. Becouse the maximum gender gap is found in our territory. It is the result of our rigid thinking.

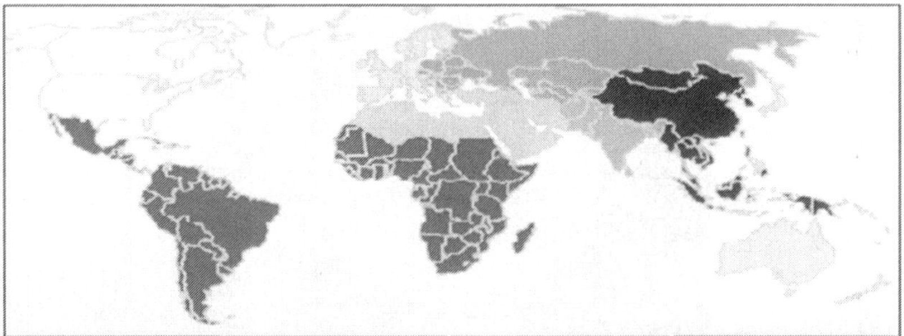

TOTALS	Western Europe (for comparison purposes)	E. Europe & Central Asia	East Asia & Pacific
Gender Gap: 21%, 300 million women	Gender Gap: 0% (estimate)	Gender Gap: 16%, 27 million women	Gender Gap: 17%, 83 million women
Mkt. Opportunity: US$13 billion	2009 subscribers:	Mkt. Opportunity: US$1.6 billion	Mkt. Opportunity: US$4 billion
2009 subscribers:	156 million males 162 million females	2009 subscribers:	2009 subscribers:
1.4 billion males 1.1 billion females	2009 population	150 million males 138 million females	498 million males 393 million females
2009 population	200 million males 208 million females	2009 population	2009 population
2.9 billion males 2.9 billion females		213 million males 233 million females	1 billion males 956 million females
Middle East & N Africa	**Latin America & Caribbean**	**Sub-Saharan Africa**	**South Asia**
Gender Gap: 24%, 25 million women	Gender Gap: 1%, 9 million women	Gender Gap: 23%, 33 million women	Gender Gap: 37%, 124 million women
Mkt. Opportunity: US$1.5 billion	Mkt. Opportunity: US$740 million	Mkt. Opportunity: US$1.9 billion	Mkt. Opportunity: US$3.6 billion
2009 subscribers:	2009 subscribers:	2009 subscribers:	2009 subscribers:
102 million males 76 million females	165 million males 168 million females	145 million males 112 million females	352 million males 208 million females
2009 population	2009 population	2009 population	2009 population
168 million males 165 million females	284 million males 291 million females	419 million males 422 million females	833 million males 786 million females

Source: Rob Conway and Cherie Blair, Women & Mobile: A Global Opportunity, A study on the mobile phone gender gap in low and middle-income countries, can be uploaded from (http://www.gsma.com).

The Mobile Phone Gender Gap Around the Globe

To analise the gender gap, one should understand the breakdown of male and the female subscribers. Today, 1.4 billion, or 48% of the 2.9 billion males in low and middle-income countries, benefit from mobile phone ownership. In contrast, just 1.1 billion, or 38%, of the 2.9 billion females in these countries have mobile phones. This equals a mobile phone gender gap of 300 million women. These 300 million women are adults (14 - 74 years old) who live in areas with mobile network coverage. The difference in figures between the men and women in terms of mobile phone penetration means that women in low and middle-income countries are 21% less likely to own a mobile phone than a man. It is calculated using the given formula. 1.4-1.1=.3 now 0.3is divided by 1.4 = 0.2142 which means 21%.

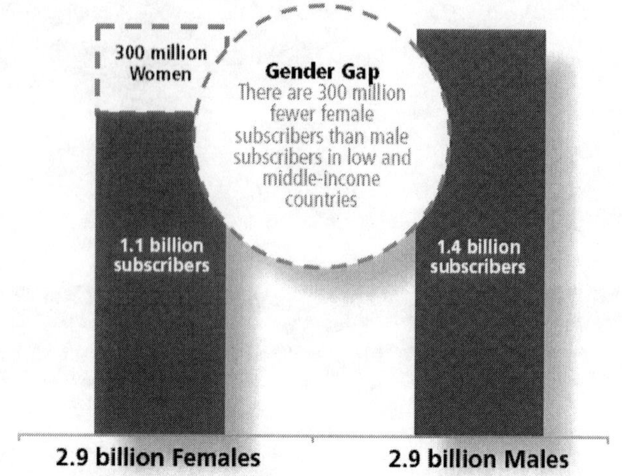

Total number of females and males in low and middle-income countries

$$\frac{\text{Male MobilePhone Owner} - \text{Female MobilePhone Owner}}{\text{Male mobile Phone Owner}} = \text{Gender Gap}$$

Status of Gender Gap in India

India has a very large rural population having 70% of its citizens residing in the rural areas. India also has the largest share of women who are the homemakers (around 70%). Rural women and homemakers have been found to have very low rat of mobile phone ownership than urban women and those

India

2009 GDP per capita	US$1,033
Population	1.2 billion
Adjusted mobile penetration	34%
Female mobile penetration	28%
Male mobile penetration	40%
Mobile gender gap	31%

Low service costs drive female mobile phone usage, but low ownership rates prevail

who work or are in school. Indian demographics, combined with its low overall mobile penetration, help explain why less than 30% of all Indian women currently own a mobile phone. The Indian mobile market is fiercely competitive with some of the lowest service rates in the world. These low rates seem to be helping to drive interest and usage of the mobile phone amongst women.

In addition, most women that do not own a mobile phone borrow phones from family and other friends. Despite large rural and the homemaker populations, Indian women are becoming exposed to and benefiting from mobile phones. Most of the homemakers do get a mobile phone as a gift from their spouse. The figure shows that 94% of homemakers do get a mobile phone from their spouse.

(100% equals all homemakers that received the phone as a gift from their spouses)

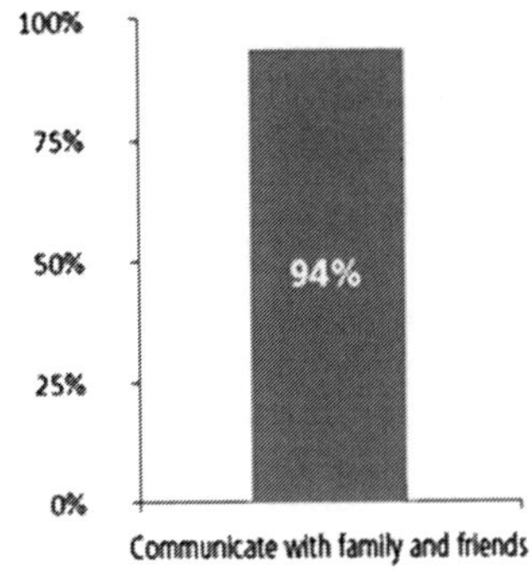

Source: Rob Conway and Cherie Blair, Women & Mobile: A Global Opportunity,A study on the mobile phone gender gap in low and middle-income countries, can be uploaded from http://www.gsma.com.

The Missing Numbers in Gender Gap- Global

	At birth		*Under 5*		*5-14*		*15-49*		*50-59*		*Total (under 60)*	
	1990	*2008*	*1990*	*2008*	*1990*	*2008*	*1990*	*2008*	*1990*	*2008*	*1990*	*2008*
China	890	1,092	259	71	21	5	208	56	92	30	1,470	1,254
India	265	257	428	251	94	45	388	228	81	75	1,255	856
Sub Saharan Africa	42	53	183	203	61	77	302	751	50	99	639	1,182
South Asia (excluding India)	0	1	99	72	32	20	176	161	37	51	346	305
East Asia and Pocific (excluding China)	3	4	14	7	14	9	137	113	48	46	216	179
Middle East and North Africa	5	6	13	7	4	1	43	24	15	15	80	52
East and Central Asia	7	14	3	1	0	0	12	4	4	3	27	23
Latin America and Caribbean	0	0	11	5	3	1	20	10	17	17	51	33
Total	**1.212**	**1,427**	**1,010**	**617**	**230**	**158**	**1,286**	**1,347**	**343**	**334**	**4,082**	**3,882**

Source: World Bank 2011e.

Note: Estimates are based on data from World health Organisation (WHO) 2010, and United Nations Department of Economics and Social Affairs, Population Division UN DESA 2010.

Mobile gender gap in India is 31%. It is calculated using the available numbers but what about the missing numbers. Means the missing females are not calculated to get the exact data on gender discrimination. These missing females had to pay the cost of being female. It is really a horrible affaire. We must rethink on not revising this horror story.

Women Empowerment is Economic Empowerment: A growing body of empirical literature from around the world demonstrates that promoting gender equality is also good development policy—or as stated in the *World Development Report 2012*, "Gender equality is smart economics" (World Bank 2011e). Nobel prize–winning economist Amartya Sen transformed the discourse on development when he argued that development is not only about raising people's incomes or reducing poverty, but, rather, it involves a process of expanding freedoms equally for *all* people.

In most developing countries, women lag behind men in using the Internet, mobile phones, and radios. (Appropriate IT, 2007). The boys are more prone to explore the new functionalities and features while girls tend to focus on communicational functions (Cardoso, 2007; Geser, 2006a; Katz, 2006; Skog, 2002). On the supply side of mobile phone companies also seem to design phones to match the traditional female and male cultures (Skog, 2002). Plant (2001) describes that 60 per cent of the lone women had a mobile phone-a far higher percentage than that of lone men (47 per cent)

A recent study commissioned for the *World Development Report 2012* found that in the East Asia and Pacific region, output per worker could be 7 to 18 percent higher across a range of countries if female entrepreneurs and workers were to work in the same sectors, types of jobs, and activities as men, and have the same access to productive resources (Cuberes and Teignier-Baqué 2011).

Astudies on the relationship between gender and trade suggest that gender inequalities have become financially detrimental for countries in a world of open trade (Do, Levchenko, and Raddatz 2011). To participate effectively in an increasingly competitive world, countries will need to harness their resources efficiently by improving opportunities for all and allocation based on skill instead of gender.

Gender inequality—whether in endowments, economic opportunities, or agency—reduces a country's ability to compete in this increasingly globalised economic environment (World Bank 2011). The expansion of call centers and other economic opportunities for women have been found to increase female educational investment in India (Oster and Millet, 2010, Shastry, 2010, and Munshi and Rosenzweig, 2004).

Mobile Phones are Reducing Poverty

Mobile phones are the tool for the economic growth, and investing in women improves the overall wellbeing of families. Empowering more women with mobile phones can accelerate social and economic development. ICT provide women entrepreneurs with access to worldwide e-business channels, which and can be operated 24 hours a day from home in real-time (Heeks, 2004; Schaefer Davis, 2007; Brodman and Berazneva, 2007).

The One problem shared with the poor in all developing countries is lack of affordable access to relevant information and knowledge services. Mobile phones are the more affordable than computers, require very less infrastructure, do not require the user to have much technological knowledge or even to be able to read and write, and are easy to carry from place to place. They lend themselves to flexible usage (text, voice and two-way communication), do not require special training, and the costs of the connectivity are relatively low. Due to the low cost of labor, mobile phones in developing countries are much cheaper and easier to repair than computers. The use of mobile phones in India and Africa has exploded, and it is now estimated that there are now more mobile phones in use in the developing world than in developed countries.

The proliferation of conferences, websites, and projects on mobile development reflect the rapid growth of interest in this area. For maximizing the potential benefits of mobile technology solutions, very closer attention must be paid to poverty's dynamics, causes, and consequences. Poverty does not result merely from lack of connectedness to the information society. It is also a result of market restrictions, repressive governments, social injustice, and human exploitation. Cultural and social barriers must also be looked at.

Mobile Phones are Reducing Gender Discrimination

The Increased gender inequalities, even in the very short-run, are having long-term consequences for the economic growth and human development (Costa & Silva 2008, 2009). Thus it is not surprising that one of the key target objectives is the promotion of gender equality and women's empowerment. Mobile-based services and systems can be a partial solution to poverty alleviation – but whose poverty? Men and women are often poor for different reasons, and what helps men may further jeopardize the well-being of women and girls (Whitehead 2003).

Will the women remain economically active in the new mobile-powered world, or will men take more control? Will mobiles ultimately narrow or widen the gender opportunity gap? Will the women and girls have access to it, and will it benefit their lives? It is now up to the research community to ensure that the goals of gender equality and the empowerment of women. A major barrier for women's mobile phone use is cultural attitudes which emphasize that it is primarily men who should maintain contact with persons outside the household or community.

This is recognised that the most disadvantaged population group in developing countries are girls. They bear a heavy burden of work at home, receive less education than boys, are channelled into low paying jobs, vulnerable to exploitation and violence, and are pressured to marry young, sometimes even before the age of 15. As the girls enter and move through adolescence, they become very much socially isolated, and this isolation only increases after they marry (Mathur, Greene & Malhotra 2003). Health education and even literacy programs could be set up through text messaging to mobile phones to reach the girls who are socially isolated. The well-being of the girls is important not only from a human rights' standpoint, but also because girls grow up to be mothers, and therefore play a key role in the intergenerational transmission of poverty.

Although material poverty has received the most attention in development research since the 1970s, gender inequality is not just a matter of income and nutritional intake. A more promising approach acknowledges the multi-dimensional nature of gender disadvantage: lack of access to education, marriage customs and age at marriage, violence against women, norms regarding work and responsibility, inheritance and property rights, equal access to housing, control over resources such as land and water, distribution and consumption of resources within the household.

This is only through the holistic gender analysis that mobile technologies can fulfil their enormous potential for improving the lives of women and girls in low income countries. A decade ago, women could be facing food problems, or be mistreated in their husband house for years before the news reached their parents. Now, phones are helping women in rural India to keep in touch with relatives, and since natal families continue to be the major source of help for married women, girls pay attention to whether there is a mobile phone in the house or neighborhood of a potential suitor (Tenhunen 2008, 531).

Mobile phones also carry great promise for alleviating health-related problems, since poverty is both a cause and consequence of illness. Poverty means less access to health services, and women in particular have less access than men. Health services utilizing mobile technologies could help women receive the assistance they need.

In short, mobile phones can be ¯powerful tools for women to overcome discrimination, achieve full equality, well-being and participation in the decisions that determine their lives and the future of their communities.

Mobile Phones are Empowering Women through Education

When it comes to mobile devices and education, most parents believe that mobile devices open up learning opportunities, benefit students' learning and can engage students in the classroom. Many parents also believe that mobiles and apps teach academic skills and content (Grunwald Associates 2013).

Traditional formal learning no longer comprises the majority of our learning. Learning at present is a continuous process and technology rewires our brains (Siemens 2004). Cell phones, eReaders and Tablets are not used in the same way as we use desktop or laptop computers. The type of learning that is appropriate on a mobile phone or smartphone is very different. Mobile phones are common 21st century tools. Most models are equipped with mobile processors that rival even full-sized desktop computers. They are a storage medium, media player, navigation system, encyclopedia, digital camera, game console, appointment book, news portal and a communication platform (JIM 2013). According to Barkham (2012) "it is not wise for schools that cannot afford modern ICT facilities to ignore powerful ICT gadgets in every pupil's pocket" (Barkham 2012).

Using mobile devices for educational purposes is becoming a common expectation of learners (Lan & Huang 2012). "Smartphones are already used extensively in an informal learning context by enthusiasts" (Clough et al 2008). Bachmair (2011) refers to the importance of the assimilation oflearning in informal contexts of everyday life in which students act as naïve native experts. "Mobile devices lend themselves to situated learning, which is often militated against by the fossilised practices of schools. Mobile devices support the notion of learning as meaning-making and they bring into play the life worlds of students and create contexts that lend themselves to replacing the passive transfer of knowledge, which is still in the foreground in the approaches to teaching and learning in many schools" (Bachmair et al. 2011).

More than half of parents believe that schools should make more use of mobile devices in education and look to teachers and schools for guidance on helping children use mobiles and apps for educational purposes (Grunwald Associates 2013).

A team from Alabama University surveyed about 1,000 students aged from 11 - 13 (Cotton et al. 2009). Boys scored higher than girls for using their mobile phones for sending emails, playing games, listening to music, and sharing pictures and videos. Boys are often taught to explore and be more creative with technology; they tend to use mobile devices as a gadget. Girls traditionally have perceived themselves as less skilled in terms of technology. It is argued that it has a lot to do with gender socialisation. "If this perception continues, it can limit young girls. It can impact the types of jobs and courses that girls take', hence it could lead to a different type of digital divide'. They point out that much has to be done to teach girls about the technical and more advanced multimedia features of their mobile devices" (Cotton et al. 2009).

Just this last year, mobile subscriptions increased by 16 percent, compared to just 1.6 percent in the developed world (Source: ITU, 2010). This growth is made possible largely because of the falling costs of simple mobile phones and the sharing of devices among friends and family. Even as mobile penetration has grown exponentially in countries such as India, Kenya and Egypt, the digital divide between citizens in these countries remains an issue.Despite rising access to mobile phones and the steady growth of these countries' economies, gender inequities and income disparities continue to present barriers.

Simulations from Latin America suggest that eliminating occupational and wage discrimination against women could lead to a 9 percent increase in gross domestic product (GDP).(Tzannatos,1999) And a recent World Bank study of India's rapid growth found that states with higher female labor market participation rates enjoyed greater poverty reduction.(Besley, Burgess, and Esteve-Volart, 2005).

In many fast emerging economies like India, the privileged live is a highly connected information society, while those at the bottom of the income pyramid (BOP), and especially BOP women, remain disconnected. This means that not only are some unlucky citizens deprived to access to modern communication devices becouse of rigid and systematic inequities, they are also deprived of the added social and economic benefits of mobile phone access. As the segment of the population experiencing the most impediments, women at the BOP are thus the biggest losers when it comes to mobile phone access and related benefits.

Barriers hindering Women's Access to and Use of Technologies

Exclusion From Technology Education And Design: Not only do men overwhelmingly constitute the users of diverse types of technologies worldwide, but they also dominate the innovation process as developers, creators, and designers. (Clancy, Skutsch, and Batchelor, 2002). Women are often seen only as "users" or "receivers" of technology, not as innovators, (Samson, 2006; Cecleski 2000). and are underrepresented in higher education programs in science, technology, and engineering. (Barber, 1995; O'Rand, 2004; Jorge, 2002; Rathgeber, 2000; Hafkin and Taggart, 2001; Bebbington, 2003). This is partly because women don't have the basic educational foundation for a successful scientific career. Although global gender inequalities in primary and secondary education attendance as a whole have shrunk in recent years, women still make up the majority of the illiterate worldwide. (World Bank, 2009). And many women in developing countries lack the education and skills to access and effectively use technologies, much less build a career around them. (Hafkin and Taggart, 2001); Huyer and Mitter, 2003).

Little Free Time: Across developing countries, women bear a disproportionate burden of household and family responsibilities, such as cooking, cleaning, and fetching fuel or water, as well as child and elder care. These tasks are time- and labor-intensive, leading rural women in some areas to spend from 1 to 5 hours a day gathering biomass for fuel (Cecleski, 2000). and about 1.6 hours a day just collecting water in the dry season. (Scott, 1995, cited in Cecleski, 2000). This heavy burden of unpaid household responsibilities often leads to "time poverty," the absence of discretionary time women can dedicate to personal interests, paid labor, education, or other endeavors. Among those endeavors is learning skills that would allow them to adopt new technologies to improve their productivity or start a small business. (Shelton and John, 1996; Karlsson and McDade, 2001; Hakfin and Taggart, 2001).

Social Norms Favoring Men: Throughout the world, technologies are often considered to be within the purview ofmen.(Cechini and Scott, 2003; Ashby et al. (n.d.). Gender norms aboutmen's control of technology, information, and knowledge limit women's opportunities to learn, use, and benefit fromtechnologies. (Karlsson, 2007; Molony, 2005) At home, husbands might regulate the family radio, mobile phone, or television, controlling when and how other family members use them. At work, men may determine that operating a plow or a computer is not something women should be allowed to learn. Even technology programs that target women can be co-opted bymen once their utility and profitability are established—so women who do gain access to a technology do not see the economic benefits associated with it.(Cecchini and Scott, 2003); Ashby et al. (n.d.); Cecleski, 2000).

Financial And Institutional Constraints: Women tend to lack the financial resources to use, rent, or purchase established and new technologies. (Brew-Hammond and Crole-Rees, 2004; Perera, 2002); Jorge, 2002; Ashby et al. (n.d.); Gurumurthy, 2004; Bamberger, 2006); Zainudeen, Iqbal, Samarajiva, and Ratnadiwakara, 2008). For example, telecenters often provide the only Internet or computer access available in a community but charge a fee that few lower income women can afford. (Jorge, 2002). One of the main reasons women lack access to capital is that laws, policies, and social customs often favor men's ownership of assets. Inheritance laws and social customs in many developing countries prohibit women from owning property, limiting their ability to take out loans that require collateral for large technology purchases.(Clancy, 1999); Lumampao, Mataga, and Parado, 2006). So, would-be women entrepreneurs cannot set up their small businesses. Nor can they buy computers or mechanical equipment that would aid in their work or allow them to train others. This inability to borrow leads to a vicious circle: women cannot develop their skills, which prevents them from earning higher incomes, so they cannot afford the technologies that might boost them to the next rung on the economic ladder.

Conclusion

Mobile phones are life enhancing and income generating tools, but we need ample of promotional programmes so as to make this device reached to every women. Bridging the mobile phone gender gap will bring substantial benefits to women, their families and society at large. By only Targeting campaigns to women to increase female uptake can be a fundamental step toward improving women's lives with mobile phones. In many of the low and middle-income countries, men have significant influence on their wives and daughters' purchases of mobile phones. Addressing men and their concerns – as well as women and their aspirations – through marketing programmes will contribute to boosting adoption of mobile phones by women. The Organisations which is focusing on women's empowerment can directly promote mobile phone ownership as a part of their programmes. Many other initiatives for the

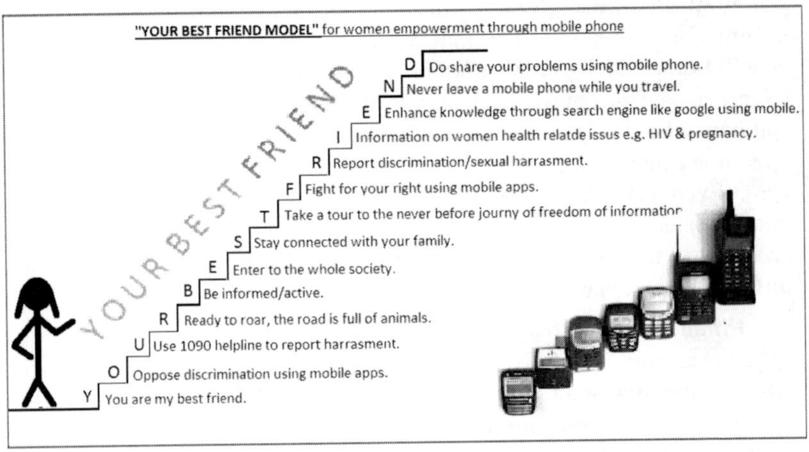

development of mobile services that benefits women is needed. This report never claim to provide an answer to all open questions, but it hopes to stimulate debates, further research and most importantly action so that women, particularty in rural areas, can benefit from the powerful opportunities a mobile phone can provide. What shines out of this study is that Women and Mobile represent great development potential that we need to embrace. I am looking forward to joining with many hands interested on this important initiative.

References

'YOUR BEST FRIEND' is the name of the model for women empowerment through mobile phone. This name is proposed by the writer and limited to this study; hence the use of the name of 'your best friend' model shall not be used in any future writings without prior intimation and authorisation from the writer.

Appropriate IT. (2007, November). Statistics on the gender digital divide. Retrieved October 20, 2009 from http://www.appropriateit.org/2007/11/gender-digital-divide/

Ashby, J., Hartl, M., Lambrou, Y., Larson, G., Lubbock, A., Pehu, E., et al. (n.d.). Investing in women as drivers of agricultural growth (Agriculture and rural development: Gender in agriculture). Washington, DC: World Bank. Available from http://www.ifad.org/gender/pub/sourcebook/flyer.pdf

Badagliacco, J. M. (1990). Gender and Race Differences in Computing Attitudes and Experience. Social Science Computer Review, 8(1), 42-63.

Bamberger, B. (2006). Gender and its place in the energy sector.Women's Policy Journal, 3, 1–19.

Barber, L. A. (1995). U.S. women in science and engineering, 1960–1990: Progress toward equity? Journal of Higher Education, 66(2), 213–234.

Basu, M. (2000). Feminist Perspectives and Gender Link in Development: The Critical Role of Women's Organisations. The Ralph Bunche Institute on the United Nations. Retrieved August 17, 2009.

Bebbington, D. (2003). Women in science, engineering and technology: A review of the issues. Higher Education Quarterly, 56(4), 360–375.

Besley, T., Burgess, R., & Esteve-Volart, B. (2005). Operationalising pro-poor growth: A country case study on India. Joint initiative of AFD, Federal Ministry for Economic Cooperation and Development (BMZ), UK Department for International Development, and theWorld Bank. Retrieved September 4, 2009, fromhttp://siteresources.worldbank.org/ INTPGI/Resources/342674-1115051237044/oppgindia.pdf

Brew-Hammond, A., & Crole-Rees, A. (2004). Reducing rural poverty through increased access to energy services: A review of the multifunctional platform project in Mali. Bamako, Mali: United Nations Development Program.

Brodman, J., & Berazneva, J. (2007). Transformina Opportunities for Women Entrepreneurs. Information Technologies and International Development, Special issue on Women's Empowerment and the Information Society, 4(2), 3-10.

Cardoso, G.; Gomes, M. d. C.; Espanha, R.; Araújo, V. (2007), Mobile Portugal, Lisbon: Obercom.

Cechini, S., & Scott, C. (2003). Can information and communications technology applications contribute to poverty reduction? Lessons from rural India. Information Technology for Development, 10(2), 73–84.

Cecleski, E. (2000). The role of women in sustainable energy development. Golden, CO: National Renewable Energy Laboratory.

Clancy, J. (1999). Policies, projects and the market empowering women? Some initial reactions to development in the energy sector (Working Paper 105). The Netherlands: University of Twente.

Clancy, J., Skutsch, M., & Batchelor, S. (2002). The gender-energy-poverty nexus: Finding the energy to address gender concerns in development. The Netherlands: University of Twente.

COSTA, JOANA & ELYDIA SILVA 2008: The Burden of Gender Inequalities forSociety. –Poverty in Focus 13. Gender Inequality. [Online] International

Poverty Center. < http://www.undp-povertycentre.org/pub/IPCPoverty In Focus 13. pdf > [3.2.2010.]

Cuberes, David, and Marc Teignier-Baqué. 2011. "Gender Inequality and Economic Growth." Background paper for the World Development Report 2012, World Bank, Washington, DC.

Cummings, J. N., & Kraut, R. (2002). Domesticating Computers and the Internet. The Information Society: An International Journal, 18(3), 221.

Dholakia, R. R., Dholakia, N., & Pedersen, B. (1994). Putting a byte in the gender gap. American Demographics, 16(12), 20

Fallows, D. (2005). How Women and Men Use the Internet | Pew Internet & American Life Project. Pew Internet and American Life Project. Retrieved August 16, 2009, from http://www.pewinternet.org/Reports/2005/How-Women-and-Men-Use-the-Internet.aspx.

Faulkner, W. (2001). The technology question in feminism : : A view from feminist technology studies. Women's Studies International Forum, 24(1), 79-95.

Geser, H. (2006a), "Pre-teen Cell Phone Adoption: Consequences for later patterns of phone usage and involvement" [Electronic version], Retrieved February 22, 2004 from http://socio.ch/mobile/t_geser3.htm.

Gurumurthy, A. (2004). Gender and ICTs: Overview report. Brighton, England: Institute of Development Studies.

Hafkin, N. (2000). Convergence of Concepts: Gender and ICTs in Africa. In E. Rathgeber & E. Ofwana Adera (Eds.), Gender and the information revolution in Africa (pp. Chapter 1, document 4). Ottawa: IDRC. Retrieved August 17, 2009, from http://www.idrc.ca/en/ev-32939-201-1-DO_TOPIC.html.

Heeks, R., Arun, S., & Morgan, S. (2004). Researching ICT-based enterprise for women in developing countries: a gender perspective. In Women's ICT-Based Enterprise for Development project. Institute for Development Policy and Management (IDPM), Manchester. Retrieved August 17, 2009, from http://www.womenictenterprise.org/LivelihoodsResearch.doc.

Huyer, S., & Mitter, S. (2003). ICTs, globalisation and poverty reduction: Gender dimensions of the knowledge society. Geneva: Gender Advisory Board, United Nations Commission on Science and Technology for Development.

Jorge, S. (2002). The economics of ICT: Challenges and practical strategies of ICT use for women's economic empowerment. Paper presented at the UNDAW Expert Group meeting, Information and communication technologies and their impact on and use as anbinstrument for the advancement and empowerment of women, Seoul, Republic of Korea.

Karlsson, G. V., & McDade, S. E. (2001). Introduction. In S. Misana and G. V. Karlsson (Eds.), Generating opportunities: Case studies on energy and women (pp. 7–15). New York: United Nations Development Programme.

Katz, J. (2006), Magic is in the Air. Mobile Communication and the Transformation of Social Life, London: Transaction Publishers.

Leggon, C. (2006). Gender, race/ethnicity, and the digital divide. In M. F. Fox, D. G. Johnson, & S. V. Rosser (Eds.), Women, gender, and technology (p. 204). University of Illinois Press.

Lumampao, F. G., Mataga, R.S., & Parado, B.C. (2006). Energizing poor women entrepreneurs. ENERGIA News, 9. Available from http://www.energia.org/resources/newsletter/pdf/ en-122006_lumampao.pdf.

MATHUR, S. MARGARET GREENE & ANJU MALHOTRA 2003: Too Young to Wed: The Lives, Rights and Health of Young Married Girls. Washington, D.C: International Center for Research on Women.

Munshi, Kaivan and Mark Rosenzweig (2004), "Traditional Institutions Meet the Modern World: Caste, Gender, and Schooling Choice in a Globalizing Economy," American Economic Review.

NTIA (National Telecommunications and Information Administration). (1999). Falling through the Net: Defining the Digital Divide. A Report on the Telecommunications and Information Technology Gap in America. Revised. U.S. Government Printing Office, Superintendent of Documents. http://www.ntia.doc.gov/ntiahome/fttn99/contents.html.

O'Rand, A. M. (2004). Women in science: Career processes and outcomes (review). [Review of the book Women in Science: Career Processes and Outcomes, by Y. Xie and K. Shauman.] Social Forces, 82(4), 1669–1671.

Oster, E. and B. Millet. (2010). Do Call Centers Promote School Enrollment? Evidence from India, Mimeo.

Perera, L. (2002). Enabling people to make technologies work for them. In Technology and poverty reduction in Asia and the Pacific (pp. 181–186). Paris: OECD Development Center and Manila: Asian Development Bank.

Plant, S. (2001), On the Mobile: The Effects of Mobile Telephones on Social and Individual Life, Motorola.

Rathgeber, E. M. (2000). Women, men and ICTs in Africa: Why gender is an issue. In E. M. Rathgeber & E. O. Adera (Eds.), Gender and the information revolution in Africa (pp. 17–34). Ottawa, Canada: International Development Research Center.

Rice, R. E., & Katz, J. E. (2003). Comparing internet and mobile phone usage: digital divides of usage, adoption, and dropouts. Telecommunications Policy, 27(8-9), 597-623.

Samson, A. E. (2006). Gender and science, technology, and innovation (Draft paper). Innovation, Policy and Science Program Area, International Development Research Centre, Ottawa, Canada. Retrieved June 10, 2009, from http://www.idrc.ca/uploads/user-S/11707788201Gender_and_STI—FINAL_DRAFT—May_23—AESS1.doc

Schaefer Davis, S. (2007). Empowering Women Weavers? The Internet in Rural Morocco. Information Technologies and International Development, Special issue on Women's Empowerment and the Information Society, 4(2), 17-23.

Sharma, U. (2003). Women Empowerment Through Information Technology. Authors Press.

Shastry, Gauri Kartini, "Human Capital Response to Globalisation: Education and Information Technology in India," mimeo, Wellesley College, 2010.

Shelton, B. A., & John, D. (1996). The division of household labor. Annual Review of Sociology, 22, 299–322.

Skog, B. (2002), "Mobiles and the Norwegian Teen: Identity, gender and class", in J. Katz (ed.), Perpetual Contact: Mobile Communications, Private Talk, Public Performance, Cambridge: Cambridge University Press.

Tenhunen, Sirpa 2008: Mobile technology in the village: ICTs, culture, and social logistics in India. Journal of the Royal Anthropological Institute (N.S.) 14, 515–534.

Tzannatos, Z. (1999). Women and labor market changes in the global economy: Growth helps, inequalities hurt and public policy matters. World Development, 27(3), 551–569.

WHITEHEAD, A. 2003: Failing Women, Sustaining Poverty: Gender in Poverty Reduction. Strategy Papers: Report for the UK Gender and Development Network. London: GADN/Christian Aid.

WDR. (2012) Gender Equality and Development, World Development Report 2012. The World Bank: Washington DC.

World Bank. (2011). Justice for the Poor. The World Bank, Washington DC.

World Bank. (2011e). Defining Gender in the 21st Century: Talking with Women and Men around the World, A Multi-Country Qualitative Study of Gender and Economic Choice. The World Bank: Washington DC.

World Bank, FAO (Food and Agricultural Organisation), & IFAD (International Fund for Agricultural Development). (2009). Gender and agriculture sourcebook. Washington, DC: World Bank.

Zainudeen, A., Iqbal, T., Samarajiva, R., & Ratnadiwakara, D. (2008). Who's got the phone? The gendered use of telephones at the bottom of the pyramid. LIRNEasia. Retrieved April 15, 2009, from http://www.lirneasia.net/wp-content/uploads/2008/05/ica-whos-got-thephone- the-gendered-use-v18.doc.

PART - III

ECONOMIC DIMENSION

9

Gender, Labour and Women's Work: Issues, Experiences and Debates

Indrani Mazumdar

How does one approach gender, labour and women's work in a country of sub-continental proportions, where across more than 6 decades since independence from colonial rule, the proportions of people living in rural areas has wound down from 83% to 68% (census 2011), but where urban areas still account for just a third of the population; in an endogenously multi-lingual, multi-ethnic country of immense regional diversity that is yet uniquely and almost universally defined by graded hierarchies of caste by birth;and where despite its illegality, stigmatisation of some castes and also of some forms of labour remains a widespread practice; where cultural taboos on women performing some specific tasks such as ploughing set the tone for restrictive gender segregation inwork, and employment, but where the last census recorded that 43 per cent of the country's agricultural labourers and 30 per cent of the class of cultivators were women - together constituting 37 per cent of the 263 million people working in agriculture; where certain occupations such as paid domestic work have become rapidly feminised - within a broader pattern of a male dominated industrial and service workforce that has left women with a mere 24 per cent share of the 168 million strong workforce in non-agriculture; or in a country where colonial deindustrialisation and siphoning away of surpluses ensured that a vast base of mass poverty was inbuilt as a foundational context to post-colonial development; and where after close to seven decades of independence, through two principal stages of state led self-reliance oriented capitalist development (1950s to 1980s) followed by two and a half decades of liberalisation/globalisation and market led capitalist growth (1991 onwards), the agrarian question and mass poverty have yet to be resolved.

Difficult and full of pitfalls though it is, this paper seeks to present an outline of gendered trends and patterns of employment in contemporary India alongside a quick overview of some of the more longstanding debates around women's work that have emerged from women's studies in India. Readers will of course note that not all the paradoxes and questions in the introductory paragraph find explicit mention in the rest of this paper. Yet, without some initial contextual frame, it is indeed difficult to grasp some of the issues in debate or to understand the complexities that continue to both concern and challenge scholarship in the field of gender, labour and employment in India.

Repeated Shocks and Continuing Concerns:Falling female employment rates in India

In Indian social sciences, women's work and labour became a separate field for sustained study and debate following publication of the seminal *Towards Equality* report of the Committee on the Status of Women in India (CSWI) in 1974. The findings of the CSWI had been unexpected and shocking, particularly in relation to women's employment. Prior to *Towards Equality*, it had been assumed that 'development' and 'modernisation'of the Indian economy would inevitablylead to (or was leading to) increased employment opportunities for women. Further, among the stated resolves of the preamble to the Indian constitution was that justice, social, economic and political would be secured to all citizens of India, as would equality of status and opportunity. And yet in 1974, 25 years after the adoption of the constitution and forward looking modernisation and development policies, this was found to be clearly not the casefor the majority of women in India. To the members of the CSWI, the statusof women appeared to have actually deteriorated by several measures, and gender inequalities had increased, most strikingly in the sphere of employment.

40 years down the line since then and well into a new century, several issues that first came to light in the seminal CSWI report have continued to remain relevant. Some indeed dog us today with aggravated force. Among other issues raised by the Towards Equality report, the one that is of central relevance to the discussion in this paper is the long termtrend decline - across most of the 20th century - in women's employment rates. The CSWI pointed out that such a decline was observable in terms of women's share in employment as well as the proportions of workers in the female population. In other words – there had been further deterioration intheminority status of women workers relative to male workers as well as in the general population of women themselves. Today,after more than a decade into the 21st century, as we shall see, both the above trends seem to have acquired a renewed and accelerated momentum.Not only have we recently witnessed thelowest ever women's employment rates, but we have alsoseen a shocking fall in the number of women workers by some 20 million across the 5 years that concluded the first decade of the new century (2005-2010). Against the global trend of increasing

levels and rates of female employment, India appears to be moving in an opposite direction, and at a devastating pace. In the 1970s, the declining rate of female employment came as a shock to those who had put their faith in the development paradigm of early post-independence India. So also in the post 1991 period, for those who had put their faith in liberalisation and globalisation as the instruments of progress for Indian women, the sharp fall in women's employment rates has come as an unbelievable shock.

Before opening upa fuller discussion on current trends in women's employment, a few words on sources of data, and some methodological clarifications on how employment statistics are classified and calculated in India may be useful.An enormous size and scale to unregistered and unorganised forms self-employment and wage employment have remained characteristic features of the Indian scenario. Registered institutional reporting based employment figures are therefore far too limited in coverage and reflect only a small fraction of actual employment in India.As such the decennial censuses conducted by the Registrar General of India, and quinquennial employment surveys conducted by the National Sample Survey Office (NSSO) are the principal sources of employment data. It is in such a setting that the census and NSSO ratios of workers to the population (generally presented as number of workers per 1000 in the population)is the key employment statistic in India. Women's employment rates are therefore the ratio of women workers per 1000 females, referred to as female work participation rates. Similar ratios of the self-employed, casual labour and regular workers per 1000 women workers are then givenfor principal status employment and principal + subsidiary status employment by NSSO.In this paper however, all such ratios have been given in percentage terms for ease of understanding for those not used to the way the Indian data is usually presented. In relation to women's employment from NSSO, principal and subsidiary status work is taken togetherthroughout the paper, as it is more inclusive of the forms of work in which women are majorly involved. Although in Census data, the workforce is also divided into main and marginal workers, which might seem to be the same as principal and subsidiary status employment, their definitions are substantially different.All census figures in this paper include both main and marginal workers.

The current employment scenario

Precipitate decline in women's work participation rates and a widening gender gap in employment

As mentioned above, for the contemporary period, the most striking feature in India's employment scenario has been the steep fall in the numbers of women workers from the second half of the first decade of the 21st century. The reduction in numbers of women workers in India by more than 20 million after 2004-05 became evident in following quinquennial survey of NSSO in 2009-10. For some reason, NSSO did another major survey the very next year in 2011-12.Despite the survey of 2011-12 showing a slight increase in the number of women workers over 2009-10, the estimated number of women workers was still showing a fall by more than 19 million between 2004-05 and 2011-12.Further, in 2011-12, female work participation rateshad further dropped to the lowest ever in the history of independent India.

Fig. 9.1 presents a graphic picture of the percentage of workers in rural and urban female populations across six large scale employment surveys conducted by the NSSO. At starting point, the longstanding pattern of higher work participation rates among rural women and far lower rates among urban women is of course striking, although the gap is clearly narrowing down. Such a narrowing is not because of increasing opportunities in urban areas. Rather, it is because, except for an unusual spike in 2004-05, the overall trend has been of steeply falling rates of employment among rural women. Stagnating work participation rates at extremely low levels continues to be the pattern among urban women.

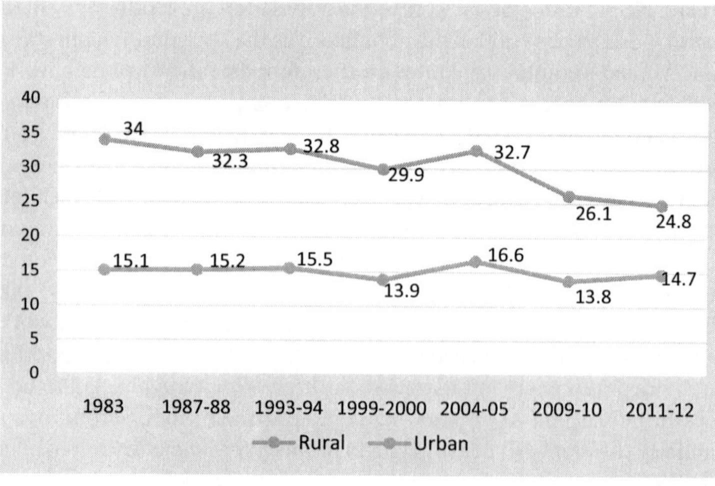

Source: NSSO, various employment survey rounds.

Fig. 9.1: Female Work Participation Rates (1983 to 2011-12) [%]

What is particularly remarkable is that the sharpest fall in women's jobs took place in precisely the period when India's economic growth rates were at their highest. The Liberalisation policy package based on neo-liberal precepts of an open economy,and with its focus on growth enhancement above all, had been put in place since 1991.India's growth story however, actually picked up from 2003-04, when GDP growth rose to an average of 8.8% per annum till 2007-08 compared to an average of 5.4% in the preceding six years. Even following theglobal slowdown after 2007-08, GDP growth in 2009-10 stood at a high 7.44% in India. It later slowed down to around 6.5% in 2011-12, the last year for which we have survey based employment figures at present. The simultaneity of the sharpest ever fall in rates of employment for women and highest ever rates of GDP growth indeed raises questions regarding the assumed positive relationship between GDP growth and employment. At the same time, the broad trend of present day female work participation ratesbeing lower than that of the 1980s, also poses a challenge to the thesis that liberalisation and globalisation leads to feminisation of labour. The feminisation of labour thesis had become a virtual axiom in international discourses on gender and labour from the late 1980s onwards, and for some time had been accepted by many to hold true for India as well. Its continuation at the level of popular discourse amongscholars and activists' who specialize in qualitative micro-studies and are not familiar with the macro-data, has perhaps been one of the reasons that the social effects of the decline in employment rates being experienced by women in India is still a relatively unexplored field.

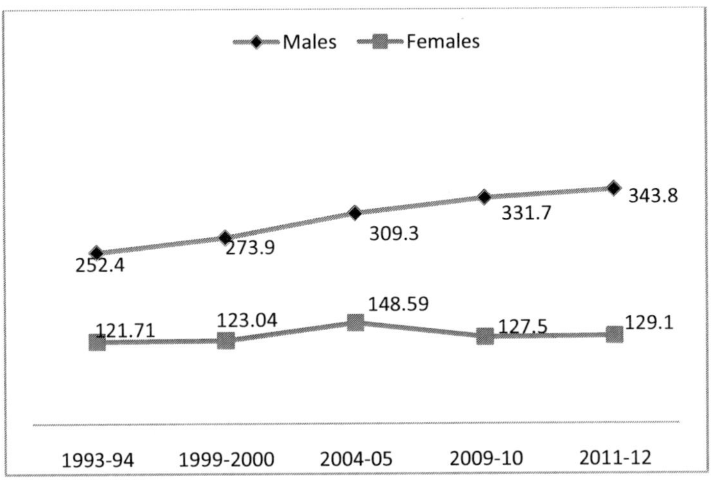

Source: Calculated from various rounds of NSSO.

Fig. 9.2: Male and Female Workers in India 1993-94 to 2011-12 [in millions]

Low employment growth has of course been a general feature of the period of liberalisation in India. However, a particularly striking feature has been that the absolute fall in employment and a declining work participation rate is specific to women. In other words, empirical evidence shows that the gender gap between men and women in employment has been widening. Taking a view of the entire period from when economic policies in India took a neo-liberal turn,workforce figures clearly show that the feminisation of labour thesis does not apply to India at the aggregate level.Instead, women's employment has been lagging and the gender gap in employment has significantlywidened in India. Fig. 9.2 presents a graphic account of India's male and female workforce (in millions) from 1993-94 to 2011-12 which makes this clear. Women's share of overall employment in India has actually fallen from close to 33% in 1993-94 to around 27% in 2011-12.

Among social scientists in India, there are broadlythree explanationsthat have been givenfor the falling female work participation rates. The first two present a positive spin to the phenomenon arguing (1) that the fall in employment, particularly after 2005, is because more women are entering higher education and therefore delaying entry into the workforce, and (2) that rising prosperity is leading to withdrawal of women from poor quality employment. The third explanation is that the decline is primarily due to shrinkingwork opportunities for women who are being otherwise displaced from their traditional avenues of employment, and as some of us have been arguing, this has led to a highly gendered employment crisis.Since policy makers favour the first two explanations, the issue of falling women's employment rates has failed to come into much focus in debates on public policyin India. Within the academic world however,many Indian scholarshave indeed analysed the data and argued for or against one or other of the above positions. There is little point in detailing the way this discussion and debate has played out, since the principal arguments and explanations have beenput together and tested by a team of analysts at the ILO (Steven Kapsos, Andrea Silberman, EvangeliaBourmpoula, 2014).We now have summaryresults for each of the above arguments in relation to the others.The empirical validity and extent to which each of the above arguments can account for the declines in female labour force participation rateswasarrived at using data from five NSSO survey rounds from1993-94 to 2011-12, although consolidated summarised findings have been given till 2010.Across the various survey rounds, data on changes in monthly per capita consumption expenditure of households (a proxy for income), educational levels of the workforce and general populace across age groups, and occupational shifts were correlated with the data on female workforce participation ratesthrough 'a series of scenario exercises, andeconometric analysis'. The summary results provide for a useful account of the relative weight of each factor in explaining the decline in women's employment rates under liberalisation.

Kapsos et al's analysis indicates that each of the threeexplanations have partial validity.However, they show that (A) Increased attendancein educational institutions accounted for only around 9 percent of fall in female work participation rates after 2005, not surprising since the large drop in female participation rates was spread across all age groups. In the relatively longer period from 1994 to 2010, increased participation in education accounted for 14 per cent of the reduced participation in employment. (B) Withdrawal by women from work because of increased household consumption in some sets of households (the prosperity effect), accounted for another 9 per cent of the drop after 2005, and 24 per cent across the full period of 1994-2010. (C) The most significant factor in the decline in female work participation rates across both shorter periods as well as the longer time span from 1994 to 2010 was changes in employment opportunities. Diminished employment opportunities accounted for 66 per cent of the decline in the 1990s, and 52 per cent of the decline in the 2000s.For the whole period between 1994 and 2010, 62 per cent of the decline in female work participation was caused by changes in employment opportunities.

In sum, the above summary analysis indicates thatfor any meaningful appraisal of declining employment rates among women in India, the central issue of diminished opportunities for women in 21st century India's employment structures needs to be addressed.

Sharpest falls in Employment rates among Tribal and Dalit women

N.Neetha's analysis of NSSO data on female work participation rates across social groups from 1999-2000 to 2011-12 has brought some additional insights to the debate. As is well known, hierarchies of economic status in India also have a history of being correlated with caste/community hierarchies inclusive of marginalised social groups such as *adivasis* (autochthonous tribal communities). At the time of adoption of the Indian constitution in 1950, special provisions including quota based reservations in the legislatures, education, and government employment, were made for the members of castes that had for centuries been oppressed with the stigma of untouchability (*dalits)*, recognised in the constitution as 'Scheduled Castes' (SC).Similar provisions were also made for marginalised tribal communities recognised as 'Scheduled Tribes' (ST).A large swathe of middle level castes/communities who have come to be recognised as also having faced a degree of discrimination and marginalisation are included in the category of 'Other Backward Classes' (OBC).Upper castes for whom social discrimination is not considered to be a key issue, are included in what NSSO classifies as 'others'. More recently, issues of marginalisation in the case of Muslims, who constitute the largest religious minority in India, have come to the fore in public debates.

Table 9.1: Female Workforce Participation across Social Groups in India, 1999-2000 to 2011-12.

Rural India	***1999-00***	***2004-05***	***2011-12***	***Difference between 1999-00 and 2011-12***
Scheduled Tribes (ST)	43.8	46.4	36.6	-7.2
Scheduled Castes (SC)	32.5	33.3	26.2	-6.3
Other Backward Classes excluding Muslims (OBC)	31.4	34.7	25.6	-5.8
Muslims	16.1	17.8	15.3	-0.8
Upper castes excluding Muslims	24.6	29.5	21.3	-3.3
Total	**29.7**	**32.7**	**24.8**	**-4.9**
Urban India	***1999-00***	***2004-05***	***2011-12***	***Difference between 1999-00 and 2011-12***
Scheduled Tribes (ST)	20.4	24.5	19.6	-0.8
Scheduled Castes (SC)	18.5	20.0	17.3	-1.3
Other Backward Classes excluding Muslims (OBC)	16.8	19.6	16.5	-0.3
Muslims	9.7	12.1	10.5	0.7
Upper castes excluding Muslims	11.2	14.0	13.4	2.2
Total	**13.9**	**16.6**	**14.7**	**0.8**
Rural+Urban India	***1999-00***	***2004-05***	***2011-12***	***Difference between 1999-00 and 2011-12***
Scheduled Tribes (ST)	41.2	44.4	34.8	-6.4
Scheduled Castes (SC)	29.9	30.8	24.2	-5.7
Other Backward Classes excluding Muslims (OBC)	28.4	31.6	23.3	-5.1
Muslims	14.0	16.0	13.6	-0.4
Upper castes excluding Muslims	19.8	23.4	17.9	-1.9
Total	**25.8**	**28.7**	**21.9**	**-3.8**

Source: Adapted from Table 1 in N. Neetha, 'Crisis in Female Employment: Analysis across Social Groups', *Economic & Political Weekly* Nov. 22, 2014.

In NSSO publications Muslim communities/castes are generally included in the 'others' category along with upper castes, and in the OBC category. In the current list of SC and ST categories, the occasional stray Muslims who may be found are actually negligible. Based on unit level data, Neetha has usefully presented the data separately for Muslims, rather than just including them within the upper caste and OBC social groups. Her analysis of female work participation rates by social groups is presented in Table 9.1.

A preliminary baseline condition, made obvious by Table 9.1, is that female work participation rates have been, and still are, the highest among STs and SCs – communities where restrictions on women going out to work have always been of a lesser order. They are lowest among Muslims followed by upper castes – communities with traditions of cultural taboos on women working outside their homes.The situation among OBCs falls in between these two ends. And yet, it is particularly striking that the fall in female employment rates has been the greatest among STs and SCs - the two social groups, who are among the poorest and most marginalised of all social groups in India. In fact, the table shows that the degree of decline in female work participation rates lessens at each ascending level of the social hierarchy.Neetha has argued that social and cultural inequalities continue to have a strong bearing on employment outcomes, even when the latter are determined by market forces. She suggests that contrary to expectations of the market leading to a weakening ofinequalities based on gender and caste/religion, it actually worsens and reinforces them. Her data shows that any growth in employment opportunities have favoured the more privileged castes, while the less privileged have been losing out much more.

Overall, the work participation data for all women as well as disaggregated by social group suggests that the compelling reasonsfor falling employment rates lie in the agrarian heartland of India. In Fig. 9.1, it was noticeable that while in urban areas, female work participation rates have indeed remained stagnant at abysmally low levels, it is in rural India that the major fall has taken place. Table 9.1 shows that in rural areas, no social group has been able to escape the decline, and women from all groups have been affected, albeit along a scale of graded inequality. In urban areas, on the other hand, upper caste women seem to have kept up their levels of employment and actually slightly improved their work participation rates, while the change for all other social groups has been relatively marginal.

Nevertheless, before approaching the agrarian context, a few words on how and possibly why urban upper caste women seem to be doing better than all other social groups. The distinguishing features of upper caste women's employment that have been highlighted byNeetha's analysis include:

(A) Among upper caste urban women workers, a consistently higher proportion (more than half) have been regular workers with casual workers remaining equally consistently below 8% across all survey rounds (1999-2000 to 2011-12).Among all other social groups in urban areas, the share of regular employment has been increasing, but has yet to reach the halfway mark,while the share of casual labour varies from double the share among upper castes for OBC women workers to 5 times among STs;

(B) A greater proportion of upper caste women workers are employed in the tertiary sector in both rural and urban areas, and relativelygreater proportions are in Educationin comparison to any other social group. Further, among upper caste women working in education, around half are employed in higher education.Among other social groups, the share of higher education was much lessand negligible among SC/ST women;

(C) One third of upper caste womenworkers had written job contracts for more than three years, strikingly more than any of the other social groups. In all, 40% of upper caste women workers had written job contracts of variable durations in contrast to less than 25% in all other social groups. Amazingly, a majority of upper caste women workers were eligible for paid leave (57% in 2011-12), in comparison to around one-third who were similarly entitled among all other social groups.

Taken together, the analysis shows that a greater proportion of upper caste women were in better quality, more stable,and more formal modes of employment in comparison to all other social groups. Importantly such employment includes enabling provisions such as paid leave. The quality of employment that upper caste women are able to access seems to have enabled them to not only retain their position of relative privilege, but also to better withstand the spectre of joblessness or loss of employment.It bears mention that in 2011-12, 46% of India's upper caste population lived in urban areas in comparison to 30% of OBCs, 24% of SCs and barely 11% of STs. Far greater levels of urbanity and therefore of urban embedded social networks, higher educational levels, and relatively greater access tobetter quality employment seem to have given upper caste women a noticeable edge in urban employment. The effects of a slight movement towards reversing the longstanding pattern of relatively smaller proportions of upper caste women entering employment might also be heightened in urban areas where employment rates among women from other social groups are also particularly low.

Structural shifts amidst an agrarian and employment crisis

During the 1990s, as field studies documented increased burdens of work in agriculture by women in a situation where large numbers of men seemed to be migrating out of the sector, scholars and activists had begun talking about feminisation of agriculture in India. Such an understanding was strengthened when the census of 2001 showed that the share of women in the agricultural workforce had increased to 39 per cent from 35 per cent in 1991, and the NSSO showed an even larger increase in women's share of agricultural employmentin 2004-05. Since then, however, the picture appears to have changed. Where the census of 2011 showed a marginal drop in women's share of the agricultural workforce by a little less than 2 per cent over ten years, the NSSO survey that immediately followed showed a steeper fall in the share of women in the agricultural workforce from the all-time high of 42 per cent in 2004-05 to 35 per cent in 2011-12. The differingnumbers between census counts and NSSO estimates of course may appear confusing.Scholars in India generally hold to the NSSO ratios as being more attuned to recording women's work in comparison to the census, but don't necessarily expect the estimated aggregate numbers to be as equally reliable. What is however, relevant for our discussion is that both census and NSSO surveys show a similar pattern of increasing shares of women in the agricultural workforce followed by a reduction.

The reasons for this so-called feminisation followed by defeminisation in agriculture have to be sought in the ongoing agrarian crisis that has been the fallout of neo-liberal policies in India. How policies have spawned this crisis has been fairly well documented. First, as part of the policy of cutbacks in public investment, the state's rural development expenditures were reduced from an average 14.5% of GDP during the period 1985-90 before reforms, to 8% of GDP by the early nineties and further to an average of less than 6% of GDP between 1998 and 2004 (Patnaik, Utsa, 2004). Unsurprisingly, the rate of agricultural growth slowed drastically in the nineties and fell below population growth for the first time in thirty years, while annual employment growth rates in rural India fell to barely half a percent. It was women's employment that was hardest hit.

Secondly, at the very same time that unemployment was growing and real earnings of the rural masses was falling, the government allowed imports of rice, fruit, dairy products, etc. as part of liberalisation of trade, again undermining local producer incomes. Further, the Indian market for seeds and fertilizers was opened to deep penetration by profiteering private companies including multinational corporations. Consequently, the input costs that individual farmers had to pay out became increasingly onerous and debt laden, especially as public sector banks started reducing the number of rural branches and changed the norms of priority sector lending, pushing farmers into the hands of usurious moneylenders (Ramakumar, 2010). Farmers were encouraged to switch to commercial crops linked to global markets, where rising input costs combined with exposure to the volatility in agricultural prices in global markets. In the meantime government administered minimum support prices and state procurement/buying of major food crops were more reluctantly and tardily implemented leaving many farmers lacking processing and storage capacity with little option but to sell at lower prices to traders. When combined with the usurious loans that so many had to take to finance their agricultural inputs and even to fill their periodic consumption deficits, and when farmers were confronted with either a drop in prices of their crop, or failure due to the vagaries of nature, the country witnessed millions of India's peasant farmers falling into irrepayable debt causing hundreds of thousands to take their own lives.

In general, a growing mismatch between higher input costs and relatively low returns ensured increasing non-viability of agriculture based livelihoods and accelerated pauperisation of large sections of the peasantry. This is most strikingly evident in the drop in the absolute numbers of self-cultivators in agriculture – a historical first for India, and a remarkable rise in the number of agricultural labourers across the first decade of the 21st century. Table 9.2 presents the Census counts of female and male cultivators and agricultural labourers for 2001 and 2011.

Table 9.2: Cultivators and Agricultural Workers in Census 2001 and 2011

	Workforce in Agriculture (In millions)		
Indian Census categories	***2001***	***2011***	***Difference***
Female cultivators	41.9	35.9	-5.9
Male cultivators	85.4	82.7	-2.7
Female agricultural labourers	49.5	61.6	+12.1
Male agricultural labourers	57.3	82.7	+25.4
All cultivators and agricultural labourers	234.1	262.9	+28.9

We would argue that pauperisation of the peasantry and the inability of other sectors to absorb those exiting from non-viable farming is what is responsible for what appears as an otherwise inexplicable increase in agricultural labour. Even though, the overall mechanisation level in Indian agriculture is about 40-45%, 90% of the totalfarm power is now contributed by mechanical and electrical power sources. Further, the use of tractors in place of labour, has spread, with tractor sales having tripled between 2001 and 2011-12Mechanisation has thus expanded in Indian agriculture replacing at least some of the demand for labour. Taken together, it becomes obvious that the figures for agricultural workers hide within them high levels of underemployment. Further, the enormous increases in male agricultural labour appear to be crowding women out of the workforce altogether.

Some recognition of the crisis of employment in rural India came in the enactment of the National Rural Employment Guarantee Act (NREGA 2006),that entitled any rural householdwho sought employment to 100 days of manual labour. As NREGA (renamed Mahatma Gandhi NREGA [MNREGA] in 2009) began to be implemented, there was an extraordinary, if unevenly distributed response from women. By 2013, women accounted for more than half of the workdays under MNREGA, indicative of how deeply they had been affected by the agrarian crisis and how much they needed employment. Women still remain the majority off MNREGA workers.

It would be a mistake however, to see the contemporary agrarian crisis in isolation, or to delink it from the dramatic step up in non-agrarian growth, particularly in services, that drove the growth pattern since the 1990s. A creeping or slow agrarian crisis had after all been around in India from the pre-liberalisation period, (even as across the first three decades following independence – India had more or less achieved macro-level self-sufficiency in food grain). Such earlier crisis was typically thought to be caused by land monopoly not having been broken down and the persistence of sub economic modes of exploitation, which in turn meant an inability to substantially reduce the mass poverty concentrated in rural areas. These conditions still continued to operate, if in modified forms, but critical developments and elements related to the neo-liberal globalisation orientation of policy intervened with more immediate force transforming the context and terms of the crisis gripping the countryside, including the marginalisation of agriculture in India's growth story.

Lopsided Economic Growth

For one, the share of agriculture in the country's GDP declined at a more precipitous pace precisely when other sectors of the economy saw accelerated growth. Agriculture's share in India's GDP (at current prices) dropped from 29 per cent in 1990-91 to a mere 14 per cent by 2011-12. [It is worth mentioning here that the decline in agriculture's share continued even during the period of partial recovery in agricultural growth after 2003] Nevertheless, with this 14 per cent share of GDP, agriculture still employs 56% of India's workers (census 2011), even as accelerated rates of mechanisation in agriculture has effectively reduced the number of workdays available for agricultural labourers and particularly women agricultural labourers (Rawal,Vikas, 2010). In other words, 86% of India's GDP currently provides employment for less than half of the country's workers (44% according to the census) that includes just 35% of the female workforce. As per NSSO (which gives the distribution of workers across industries in more detail than the census), around 29% of the male and just 16% of the female workforce were employed in services (including trade, hotels, restaurants, transport, communication, finance, govt., private, personal and all other services) in 2011-12. That same year, services accounted for 58% of India's GDP. Industry's share of GDP (including manufacturing, mining and construction) correlated slightly better with employment. With a 28 per cent share of GDP, industry employed 26% of the male and 20% of the female workforce. It needs to be borne in mind that NSS estimates for employment in agriculture are lower than what the census count shows, but even then the picture is unequivocally clear. Service driven high rates of GDP growth, has not provided commensurate employment growth and the major part of the country's working population still remains concentrated in agriculture.

Further, even the relatively closer match between industry's share in GDP and employment is mostly explained by a major jump in construction employment.A most phenomenal growth in the numbers and proportions of construction workers, emerges from NSSO employment figures, which show the construction workforce as having grown from around 12 million in 1993-94 to over 50 million by 2011-12. Anyone familiar with the nature of construction labour in India would realize that its circulatory migration pattern is such that a large part of this workforce is not making and indeed cannot make anywhere near a permanent move out of agriculture. Construction workers pitch their temporary residences near their sites of work and as they have to keep moving from one worksite to another, so also they have to move their residential quarters. They are workers who epitomize the impermanent daily casual labourer as not even the corporate sector of the industry puts their manual workers on its employee rolls. They are workers mobilised, recruited and supervised by labour contractors, whose prime hunting grounds are inevitably the most socially oppressed/depressed sections of society and whose methods of recruitment and control retain many of the features that were shaped by the discriminatory and racist practices of labour mobilisation under colonial rule. Construction labour is thus perennially unsettled, casual, migratory, and even seasonal in nature since the onset of Indian monsoon rains brings a lull to construction activities, when large numbers of workers return to their villages and to agricultural activities. The same pattern applies to some of its feeder industries – brick kilns, stone quarrying, etc. As for women, despite global figures showing the maximum number of women in construction being in India, they have remained a relatively small minority of the construction workforce (16%), despite a remarkable six-fold increase in their numbers and proportion between 1999-2000 and 2011-12.

Contours of Debates on Women and Work in India

The marginalisation of women in development thesis

In the evolution of the debate on women's employment in Indian social science, the role played by the CSWI's *Towards Equality*report has been touched upon earlier. What remains to be said is that it coincided with and fed a resurgent women's movement, so much so that *Towards Equality*began to be called the 'foundation text' of the women's movement. The debate on women's employment as we know it today cannot be conceived of without taking into account the infusion of the spirit of the women's movement into the scholarly writings and analyses that followed. Widely read by not only scholars, but also activists and political workers– the CSWI report catalysed the bringing together of scholars and activists in what came to be known as the women's studies movement in India. In these early years, work and employment questions lay at the heart of the debates initiated by women's studies.

They began with the long term decline in female work participation being viewed alongside another important finding of the CSWI, namely the declining sex ratio. This led to a critical questioning of development processes and threw up the counterintuitive proposition that women were being marginalised in economic development itself.Theoretically oriented scholars turned to action research as they tried several kinds of experiments in self organizing, particularly by and for women in poverty to counter their marginalisation in the economy.Activists turned to theory and empirical research in joint endeavour.

This then laid the context for a significant body of empirical work – including in the field of action research.In its attempt to understand the processes underpinning the decline in women's work participation, the CSWI had postulated that it was the result of ruination of domestic industry (deindustrialisation) from the colonial period onwards (with relatively greater ruin in the female labour intensive sectors) eroded non-agricultural occupations of women. It had further argued that the externally induced process of limited modernisation had excluded women from the limited opportunities in the modern sector, resulting in a permanent shift of women to the periphery of the economy. Concern regarding marginalisation of women in employment thus became the key issue and action research initiated in the early 1980s was directed atexperiments in women's production collectives attempting to reverse the process of marginalisation.

Underenumerationand Invisibility of women's work

By the late 1980s,as scholars examined the employment data more minutely, the question of actual under-enumeration or undercounting of women's work in national data sets emerged as a significant concern.In a country like India, family based subsistence production is still widespread and women who may not have any independent income, yet perform essential labour in the production process. Statistical systems did recognize that counting only those who receive an income or wage from their labouras workers could not give a real picture of the number of people actually working and laboring, and therefore included many non-monetised subsistence activities in their definition of work. However, the non-monetisedactivities that were female dominated tended to be left out of such definitions. Field evidence indicated that the vast majority of women were certainly not idle and were actively contributed to their household economy. The question wastherefore posed as to why and how the work done by womenwas not getting counted. The invisibility of women's work thus became a major subject of enquiry, and making women's work visible became a cardinal object of research inthe newly developing field of women's studies.Greater attention began to be paid to problems in measurement, and to changes in the definitions of work across censuses and the ensuing problems of comparability. As data was examined more carefully - among specialists, concern with the sharp decline in female work participation rates that had been so central in 'Towards Equality' were overlaid with concerns regarding the *underenumeration* of women's work in the national data systems.Concepts, definitions, arguments, and micro-studies were marshaled for evolvingalternative methods of capturing women's work. The two sectors where such invisibility prevailed to a great extent were agriculture and household industry, and the discussion and debate of this period contributed to generating a greater awareness of the need to make women's work more visible in the macro data, particularly in agriculture (Krishnaraj, 1990, Duvuury, 1989).

Interestingly, in these debates, questions were occasionally raised by some feminists about whether a conceptual separation should at all be made between productive work such as the unpaid economic activities of women, and domestic work within families which was also effectively unpaid work (Jain 1985; Sen 1985). However, on this, the separationbetween economic and non-economic activities has held on quite firmly.Yet, as one might expect, the issue of how domestic family work should be viewed in the economy, tends to crop up again and again in different ways in women's studies, since in the lives of all women, domestic work in their own household remains perennial, whether they are employed elsewhere or not. Recently a renewed focus on unpaid care work by women has been spurred in India by global debates, albeit in theconsiderably changed context brought about by liberalisation.

Women's work and the Informal Sector

Before we turn to more recent trends in women's employment in the changed context of liberalisation, the second pillar of the debate on women's work that began in the earlier period bears mention.This related to the concept of the informal sector.Having evolved out of observation of self employed forms of work and economic activity in the urban setting of some African countries by ILO employment missions and the anthropologist Keith Hart, the informal sector was initially considered a defining feature of underdevelopment. Eluding any clear analytical definition, it became synonymous with the kaleidoscope of unregulated, poorly-skilled and low-paid workers that one may encounter when walking through the streets of towns and cities in developing countries. Its existence and characteristics were thus really defined in contrast and with reference to the formal sector supposedly characterised by regular and written contracts and therefore subject to state regulation.

The concept of the informal sector held great appeal for those interested in bringing the issues of invisible women workers onto the agenda of national policy in India. It seemed to be able to absorb within itself the experience of lack of clear definition or official record of not only several aspects of women's economic activity, but also major contingents of women workers such as homebased workers. In a sense, the concept played a role in highlighting the fact that vast contingents of the working people in developing countries such as India, had remained deprived of the benefits of bare minimum employment security and labour rights, which had been hammered into labour laws over years of industrial struggle in more large scale industries, that increasingly came to be defined as the formal sector. For women, the informal sector/employment acquired even greater significance with the growing realisation that declines in women's employment shares had accompanied the evolution of the formal sector, and that a disproportionately large majority of women workers were concentrated in the more backbreaking forms of labour and work that characterised the informal sector/employment. In India's context, the debates related to the informal sector was thus initiallypioneered by women and women's studies, and the first adoption of the term 'informal sector' in an official report came in the 1988 Report of the National Commission on Self Employed Women and Women in the Informal Sector, titled *Shramshakti.*The link between women's labour and the informal sector gained so much currency that in the early years when the concept had yet to be defined and measured by the statistical systems, an erroneous impression that women dominated informal sector employment became quite prevalent.

With the conceptual advent of the informal sector, the classical developmental dualistic approach comprising agriculture (as the backward subsistence sector) and industry (as the modern sector) came under challenge. As empirical research showed, no longer was it possible for the modern to be equated with the formal sector and the diffused set of occupations and employments that was being termed the informal sector could not always be catalogued and categorised within the dualistic framework. Nor could they be considered residual, given their numerical weight. It was at such a moment that the ground beneath the feet of such critical analysis that located its critical vision within the larger frame of the developmental state and addressed itself towards state led development shifted dramatically, with the rise to dominance of neo-liberalism across the globe, andwith the Indian government's formal accession to the neo-liberal paradigm from 1991 onwards.

In the context of liberalisation and globalisation - labour market oriented approaches to women's employment became preoccupied with the feminisation of labour thesis, with contractualisation, casualisation and outsourcing of formal jobs (informalisation in formal sector work) and feminisation tending to be viewed together.

The feminisation of labour thesis

It was in thelate 1980s that the concept of "feminisation" of labourhad emerged as a somewhat loose attempt to capture the characteristic features of changes taking place in the course of national statutory regulations giving way increasingly to market regulation and globalisation. Particularly in the background of a few developing countries emerging as export manufacturing hubs with increasing proportions of women workers in export oriented garment and electronics industries, feminisation of labour became a central concept around which much of the gender oriented discourses on the impact of globalisation proceeded.

The conception of feminisation of labour included two specific connotations. The first was of course identification of a sharp rise in the share of women in paid employment through either their taking over jobs earlier done by men or, due to relatively faster expansion of sectors (particularly in manufacturing) where female workers predominated. The second connotation included the advance of more generalised precariousness in forms of employment. This was considered to be characteristic of 'flexibilisation' policies in relation to labour, or the trend of employers (large and small) to respond to market uncertainties and increased pressure on costs by reducing their core workforce, and relying increasingly on irregular forms of employment in order to avoid paying wages to workers during economic downturns. The attributes of 'flexible' labour leaned towards a casual nature of the work contract, lower rates of remuneration, lack of security provided, low access to skill etc., all characteristics associated with women's historical pattern of labour force participation (Guy Standing, 1999).

There were of course differing ways in which the feminisation of labour thesis acquired currency in India, with some emphasizing the opening of opportunities for women in the urban labour market [Deshpande & Deshpande, 1992] and others focusing on new methods of exploitation [Vanamala, 2001]. However, by the end of the 1990s, while micro-studies and courses in women's studies often continued to locate their analysis with reference to feminisation of labour, at a macro-level the thesis was faltering before the evidence of a fall in women's work participation in an overall context of low employment growth, and the idea of 'jobless growth' acquired more traction.

Interestingly, the instinctive core of the Indian women's movement reactions to liberalisation did not resonate with the feminisation thesis. However, in more academic circles, the feminisation debate has continued. Within the debates, supporters of liberalisation and globalisation have tended to emphasise (and search for signs of) the first connotation as a positive sign of employment opportunity gains for women. Equivocators generally perceived the changes under way as opening opportunities for some women and the loss of some for others, but concluded that the course of women's own agency and intervention must be directed towards exploration of perceived opportunities within the framework of liberalisation. Opponents emphasised the second connotation, arguing that the forces that propel women into such exploitative conditions of work lie in the increasing burden of poverty or declining incomes of the majority in the era of liberalisation, and called for fundamental change in policy.

What is particularly surprising is that despite overwhelming empirical evidence at the macro-level that in the feminisation of labour thesis is not valid for India, it is routinely trotted out as an axiom for framing analysis of the relationship between women's work/employment and globalisation. It could be argued that the continued prevalence of the feminisation thesis in women's studies courses even today, is based not so much in its validity, but rather on the appeal of the word itself. Thus from feminisation of labour was followed by feminisation of agriculture and feminisation of poverty, etc. Equally, it could be argued that the continued use of a precept that has failed the empirical test is because of a shift in the centre of gravity of conceptualisation and framing of research agendas away from ground realities in India paving the way for a greater reliance on top down theorisation driven by international agencies.

Shifting frames at the international level: WID, WAD, GAD

Parallel to the debates on women's work in India, sometimes feeding into the Indian debates, and sometimes drawing on them, were the shifting frames and approaches in international bodies and institutions to the relationship between women's work and development. From an approach to Women in Development (WID) to Women and Development (WAD) to Gender and Development (GAD), much has been written and debated in international bodies. Although a lot of theorizing surrounds each acronym, in retrospect, it would appear that they all reflected and fed into phases of the development narrative that had maximum currency at the time. Thus, WID largely based its perspective on the assumption that the benefits of modernisation/development was for all, part of the trickle down approach in early development theory. While itcentre staged the issue of equal opportunities for women's employment and opposed the earlier purely social welfare/charity approach to women, in essence it stood in line with early development theories that saw the replacement of the 'traditional sector' by the modern sector as the key process of development. The movement to WAD on the other hand was driven by feminists, with a far greater focus on patriarchy, and theorisation on the relationship between patriarchy and capitalism. WAD therefore conceived of women only development projects/programmes at a time when governments were shifting to programmes/schemes directly geared towards poverty alleviation as the early trickle down development models failed to do so. Ironically, many of the women only programmes that developed out of such a frame, have ultimately fed into an institutionalised use of women as the cheapest and most pliable of labour for various development projects/ programmes. And finally, GAD, with its emphasis on social construction of gender as a power relationship between men and women that subordinated women, on the socially constructed gender division of labour, and emphasis on gender and markets, became the dominant frame during the rise to dominance of neo-liberal policies across the globe.This is not to suggest that the architects of these frames did not challenge the dominant paradigms of development in which they came into existence. However, their close association withprogrammesin developing countries driven/funded by international agencies of various hues were bound to impinge on their conceptualisation. It is perhaps time to reground scholarship on gender, labour and women's work away from frameworks tied to the programmes of international agencies, and are more grounded and derived from women's movements and their experiences.

Concluding Remarks

This paper has attempted to engage with the concerns that have emerged from recent trends in women's employment in India based primarily on what the macro-data tells us. It has raised questions regarding the assumed positive relationship between economic growth and employment. It has shown that a precipitate decline in women's work participation rates and a widening gender gap in employment occurred precisely during the period of highest growth rates in India. Apart from the simultaneity off the sharpest ever fall in employment rates among women and the highest ever GDP growth in India, the paper has shown that the loss of employment opportunities have been maximum for Dalit and tribal women, and supported the argument that the market has worsened and reinforced inequalities based on gender and caste in India. It has argued there has been lopsided growth in India, with the domination of services in India's GDP not being matched by any similar scale of employment in services. It has highlighted the continuing domination of agriculture in employment – particularly in women's employment – at a time when the share of agriculture in GDP has dropped steeply, yet argued that the agrarian crisis and accelerated pauperisation of the peasantry provides the contextual reasons for the steep decline in rural female work participation rates in India. It has outlined how this crisis has been spawned by a slew of policies that are the product of the neo-liberal framework.

In reviewing the debates on women and work in India, kicked off by the seminal *Towards Equality* report of 1974, the paper suggests that the enduring concerns and empirical realities are not adequately reflected or addressed in the current frameworks that dominate international discourses on women, gender, and development.It posits the need to reground scholarship in the field of gender, labour and women's work in the experiences of women's movements in India, rather than follow the programme driven/funded of international agencies.

10

Gender Discrimination in Distribution of Land and Occupation in Uttar Pradesh

— Malti Singh and Lakkineni Mallaiah

Abstract

This paper is to analyse the gender discrimination and inequality mainly in distribution of agricultural land and occupations of workers in Uttar Pradesh and associated gender inequality in population distribution, education and literacy growth. It will also highlight the transformation of labour workforce participation in agricultural sector in the state. This study is confined to only Uttar Pradesh. It is a macro level study. The study is purely based on the secondary data. Gender gap has been used for evaluating the discrimination against women. Population Census reports and NSS reports, Agricultural Census Reports, Annual Plan documents of the Government of U.P, relevant books and research papers in journals are used for the study.

Keywords: *Agriculture, Livelihood, Possession, Education, Cultivator.*

India's Situation

Agriculture is the main occupation of people in India. Around 60 percent of population is depending on agriculture for their livelihood. It provides employment nearly to 58 percent of workforce in the country. It has been contributing 14.6 percent of GDP to the national income. It is the source of livelihood for the population in the country. Economically, around 63 percent of male workers are engaged in agricultural activities as compared to 78 percent of women workers. Almost 50 percent of rural female workers are classified as agricultural laborers and 37 percent as cultivators at the national level (Krishna Rao, 2006). The figures reveals that women play a significant and crucial role in agricultural development and allied field activities including main crop production, live-stock production, horticulture, post harvesting operations, and household industry etc. Having been a significant role in the economic development yet Indian agriculture is still backward and characterised by low productivity, unequal distribution of land among social category wise and in gender wise, illiteracy, high dependency on land, primitive tools and techniques. Hence, there are many factors responsible for the backwardness of agriculture. They are (1) General Factors (2) Institutional factors and (3) Technological factors. The constant population pressure on land leads to sub-division of land. The small and marginal farmers are bound to lose their land and became landless and farming system responsible for the backwardness of agriculture in India. Very few people have possessed high share of land in rural India. The existing small and marginal holdings are one of the evils for the poor agricultural development. After independence, a series of attempts were made to improve the agrarian structure by abolishing large intermediaries, conferring ownership rights to tenants, minimizing the skewed distribution of land through imposition of ceilings on landholdings and redistribution of surplus land to landless and regulating the wages of agricultural labourers. But the progress of the issues was not fulfilling the acquired goal at the national level.

The Situation of Uttar Pradesh

The economy of rural Uttar Pradesh is also based on agriculture, around 65 percent it's population is occupying in the agriculture sector for their livelihood. As per Census 2011, the growth rate of the population is 20.23 percent while it was 25.80 percent in 2001. The state is contributing 16.50 percent population to the country's population in which male population is 52.41 percent and female 47.59 percent. The sex ratio in Uttar Pradesh is 912 female for per 1000 male, which is below national average of 940 as per census 2011 while it was 898 female for per 1000 males in 2001.We can see that gender discrimination is taking place in term of population and in sex ratio also. Women are contributing their assistance in the agriculture field and its allied activities even though they have no proper right to take place in the possession of land holdings in the society.

General Facts: Possession of agricultural land is the symbol of power, prosperity and prestige in the agrarian societies. It is not only a symbol of economic status but also a sign of social phenomena. Indian society is intrinsically based on the hierarchy since a long time. Women are contributing through their participation in agriculture field even though they are discriminated by the social customs since a long time. Inequalities between men and women are apparent themselves in all social-economic areas of development in the Indian society. Hence, securing women's land and property rights is a necessary strategy for ensuring gender equality and advancing women's empowerment worldwide. As a result, the Commission on the Status of Women adopted in 1998, its first resolution on women's housing and land rights, resolution 42/1 on *'Human rights and land rights discrimination,'* recognizing that "secure land rights are the key rights for the economic empowerment of women. During the middle of 2000s, the United Nations Commission on Human Rights now (the Human Rights Council) also adopted a series of resolutions on *'Women's equal ownership of, access to and control over land and the equal rights to own property and to adequate housing.*

The fundamental rights for women to secure rights of land and property are regarded as basic concept to ensure effective and sustainable human development. The Rights of land and property include the right to own, use, access, control, transfer, exclude, inherit and otherwise make decisions about land and related resources. These exercising rights of land should not require consultation or agreement for women beyond that required of men. In this context, there are many views highlighted on ensuring the women's land and property rights in the custom of Indian society.

According to a World Bank report, "Only independent or joint ownership can ensure that women have access and control over land based earnings. Further the World Bank recognizes that the land rights and natural resources may increase the bargaining power of women within the household. It results in increased allocation of household resources to children and women and household welfare. The Swedish International Development Co-operation Agency (SIDA) has also notified that "Women's access to land and property is central to economic empowerment of women. The land serves as a base for food production and income generation in rural economy. Agricultural production and food security also increase when women are granted tenure security. Therefore, women's access to land and property is like a weapon of women's empowerment, food security and poverty alleviation not only at state level but also national level too.

The United Nations Food and Agriculture Organisation (FAO) has also estimated the women strength in the form of ownership of agricultural land. If the women had the same access to productive resources as men, they could increase yields on their farms by 20–30 percent more. This extra grain can provide food to 100–150 million people and make them out of hunger. The United Nations Development Programme (UNDP) has also point out that women's rights to inheritance of property are the crucial factors in reducing women's vulnerability to violence and HIV, as well as empowering to cope with the social and economic evils of the society. The FAO has opinioned that the potential production gains calculated by the gender inequality method are based on the existing distribution of land. This reflects that women control comparatively more agricultural land than men could achieve the greatest potential gains. But overall gender gap in access to agricultural resources is in fact wider where women possessed very less land. The actual gains from closing the gender gap in access to resources would be greater in countries where the gender gap is wider. Increasing women's access to land as well as complementary inputs would generate socio-economic development for the society(Mayra Gomez, and D. Hien Tran, 2012).

Beyond the opinions of institutions on women's Rights to Land, there are some national and regional studies on land distribution and women empowerment and women work participation. Some of the major studies are mentioned here. A.Venkateshwarlu (2003) in his research paper 'Pattern of Land Distribution and Tenancy in Rural Andhra Pradesh' has analysed the changing pattern of distribution of land ownership, tenancy and ownership holdings and operational holdings. He found that average size of both ownership and operational holdings has been declining continuously. Similarly, the share of marginal farmers has been increasing during the period of 1953-54 to 1991-92 while the share of medium and large farmers have decreased in the State. B.B.Mohanty (2008) in his study 'Landholding and Use Pattern among Scheduled Castes and Scheduled Tribes in Maharashtra' has expressed views on changing pattern of land holdings among Scheduled Castes and Schedules Tribes and to assess the impact of land reform measures on landholding structure of the SCs and STSs communities. Finally, the major findings of his study are that the landholders of SCs and STs Communities mostly belong to the small and marginal groups. The number and area of the marginal and small holdings of these communities are in increasing trend while their contribution in medium and large holdings is declining in the state. It is also concluded that the number of large landholders among the Scheduled Castes is negligible. Nageswara Rao (2008) has expressed his opinion on "Dalits and Agricultural Landholdings in Andhra Pradesh" that the distribution of landholdings pattern in Andhra Pradesh is highly skewed. Large and medium land holdings accounts for more than one fifth, the operational area are controlled by only one sixth of the total landholders. There is a positive skewed distribution of agricultural land holdings in the state. Most of the small and marginal operational land holdings refer to Scheduled Castes and Scheduled Tribes in Andhra Pradesh. P. H. Prasad and G.B. Rodgers (1983) have focussed on "Class, Caste and Landholdings in the Analysis of the Rural Economy. This study has the aim to assess the relative merits of each of the three approaches as class, caste and landholdings. Thus, the multivariate analysis of the research paper finds out the result that (i) landholdings, while relevant, were the weakest of the three variables. Distinct effects could be identified associated with tenancy like ownership, (ii) Caste, although weaker than casual empiricism would suggest that caste had significant effects on the most aspects of behaviour, and dominated female labour force participation.(iii) Class was the most consistent, and in a majority of cases the strongest factor. Both landholdings and caste are shown to have independent effects. R. Sharma (1998) in "Distribution of Landholdings in Rural India: A Comparative Study of Scheduled Castes, Tribes and Non- Scheduled Caste and Tribe. The author has an objective to find out the share of total land owned by the households belonging to scheduled caste and tribes and non-scheduled caste and tribes in India. To fill the requirements of the object, the major findings of the study is that during 1980s, the share of land owned by the households belonging to non- scheduled caste and tribes declined by varying degree in all the states except Bihar and Himachal Pradesh. Consequently, scheduled caste and tribes households land holdings increased in all states of India. A. K. Chowdhury and M.H.R. Kashimi (1991) in their study on "Change in Landholdings Pattern and Its Impact among the Bhoksa of Nanital", have evaluated the changes in agricultural land holding pattern and its impact on socio-economic and biological aspects of Bhoksa community of Nanital. The study concludes that a majority of Bhoksa community have possessed 48 percent land from 1 to 5 acre for cultivation while only 1.5 percent number of household families have accounted for more than 20 acre of land holdings. It found that there is a high level of inequality in the distribution of agricultural land in Nanital. VikasRawal (2008) has contributed his views on "Ownership Holdings of Land in Rural India: Putting the Record Straight". In this study, he estimates the landlessness and inequality in terms of ownership of land. The major findings of his study is that over 40% households in rural India do not have own land. The figure shows that about 40% of rural households do not have own land. The distribution of ownership of land holdings in India is extremely unequal. All the studies show that there is an impact of land distribution and occupational distribution on women empowerment and discrimination. Hence, an attempt is made in this paper to analyse 'Gender Discrimination in Distribution of Land and occupation in Uttar Pradesh,' and its impact on socio-economic conditions of female land holders compare to male in terms of land, population, education, literacy and occupational distribution of workers in the State.

Inequality in Land Distributions

Land is the icon of prosperity, power and prestige in the agrarian societies. It is a tantamount of not only an economic status but also a symbol of social status. Indian society has been based on the caste system. The land distribution is also associated with the caste system and with gender discrimination. Since Independence, various measures have been initiated to reduce the inequality in land distribution and make sure land to the tiller. The government has initiated to implement land reforms programmes and women's land and property rights in the state. The main aim of this programmes were to give the ownership of land to the landless or near landless persons. But, land reforms act and land and property right to women could not achieve its goal in Uttar Pradesh also. Still there is a skewed distribution of land and gender discrimination in the State. As, most of the operational holdings and operated area of the land is governed by the General castes people while less area of land has been handled through the SC or ST similarly, male group share is high than female group in all social category since a long time in the State. Table 10.1 shows the percentage of the distribution of operational holdings and operated area in different categories of all size classes during 1970 to 2011. The marginal operational holdings are showing a continuous increasing trend at 66.8 percent to 79.45 percent from 1970-71 to 2010-11. The status of Small holdings is showing a continuous decreasing except the year 1990-91inwhich shows a constant trend. The Semi-medium operational holdings are decreasing from 10.6 percent in 1971 to 5.72 percent in 2011, whereas medium operational holdings are also declining from 4.7 percent to 1.71 percent in the same time. The percentage of large operational holdings is also representing a decline trend at 0.7 to 0.11 from 1970 to 1991but its status was constant during the period of1995-2001after it's percentage fall on at 0.11 from 0.2 in 2011.

The figures are reflecting a very remarkable thing that 66.8 percent marginal operational holdings have only 21.09 percent operated area of land whereas 17.2 percent small operational holdings possessed 20.8 percent of operated area in 1970-71. Similarly, 10.6 percent semi-medium number of operational holdings has possessed 24.99 percent operated area of land and 4.7 percent medium operational holdings possessed 23.22 percent operated. While only 0.7 percent large operational holdings are possessing 9.9 percent of operated land in the year. In 2010-11, 79.45 percent marginal holdings possessed 40.69 percent operated area of land and 13.01 percent small holdings accounted 24.08 percent operated area whereas 5.72 percent semi-medium holdings have 20.59 percent operated area of land. Medium operational holdings 1.71 percent and large operational holdings 0.11 percent accounted 12.48 and 2.16 percent respectively. The percentage of marginal operated area is increasing continuously from 21.09 in 1970-71 to 40.69 percent in 2010-11. Small operated area is showing the increasing trend from 20.8 percent in 1970-71 to 24.4 percent in 1990-91. Accordingly, the percentage of semi-medium operated area, medium and large operated area is decreasing continuously since 1970. The operated area is showing the decreasing status in all size classes. The large size of operated area is now divided into different sizes of holdings in the state. However they are still possessed a high percentage of holdings.

Table 10.2 represent about the percentage distribution of number of operational holdings and operated area of General Castes in U.P among all size classes during the period of 1980-81 to 2010-11. Marginal operational holdings are declining continuously from 81.72 percent in 1981 to 78.68 percent in 2011. Small operational holdings, Semi-medium and Medium operational holding are continuous increasing over the period. But in case of large operational holdings, except 1990-91, it is continuously declining from 96.69 percent to 92.44 percent. In Total holdings, all size classes' of operational holdings are also showing a declining trend from 84.07 percent to 79.38 percent in the State. The table examines the status of possession of land by General

Table 10.1: Percentage Distribution of Number of Operational Holdings and Operated Area in Uttar Pradesh

S. No.	Category of land holdings / Year	*Marginal Holdings*		*Small Holdings*		*Semi - Medium Holdings*		*Medium Holdings*		*Large Holdings*		*Total Holdings*	
		No. of Operational holdings	*Operated Area*	*No. of Opera- tio nal holdings*	*Operated Area*	*No. of Operational holdings*	*Operated Area*	*No. of Operational holdings*	*Operated Area*	*No. of Operational holdings*	*Operated Area*	*No. of Operational holdings*	*Operated Area*
1	1970-71	66.8	21.09	17.2	20.8	10.6	24.99	4.7	23.22	0.7	9.9	100.0	100.0
2	1976-77	69.4	23.9	16.4	21.6	9.6	24.8	4.1	22.3	0.5	7.4	100.0	100.0
3	1980-81	70.6	25.7	16.3	22.6	9	24.6	3.7	21.0	0.4	6.1	100.0	100.0
4	1985-86	72.6	28.3	15.6	23.3	8.3	24.5	3.2	19.1	0.3	4.8	100.0	100.0
5	1990-91	73.8	31.4	15.6	24.4	7.7	23.4	2.7	16.9	0.2	3.9	100.0	100.0
6	1995-96	75.6	34.1	14.5	23.8	7.3	23.1	2.4	15.8	0.2	3.2	100.0	100.0
7	2000-01	76.9	37.0	14.2	24.3	6.6	21.7	2.1	14.3	0.2	2.7	100.0	100.0
8	2005-06	77.96	38.93	13.82	24.24	6.19	21.19	1.91	13.26	0.12	2.38	100.0	100.0

Source: Agricultural Census Reports, Government of Uttar Pradesh, Lucknow.

Note: Marginal Holdings (Below 1.0 Hectare), Small Holdings (1.0-0.2 Hectare), Semi- Medium Holdings (2.0-4.0 Hectare), Medium Holdings (4.0-10.0 Hectare), Large Holdings (Above 10.0 Hectare).

Table 10.2: Category wise Percentages Distribution of Number of Operational Holdings and Operated Area in Uttar Pradesh during 1980 to 2006

S No.	General Castes														
	Size classes	*Year*		*1980-81*		*1985-86*		*1990-91*		*1995-96*		*2000-01*		*2005-06*	
		No.	*Area*	*No.*	*Area*	*No.*	*Area*	*No.*	*Area*	*No.*	*Area*	*No.*	*Area*	*No.*	*Area*
1.	Marginal Holdings	100	100	81.72	83.63	80.43	82.01	80.14	82.45	79.66	82.02	79.24	82.57	79.13	81.58
2.	Small Holdings	100	100	86.78	87.21	86.38	87.06	86.01	87.25	86.29	87.05	87.27	87.91	87.41	86.85
3.	Semi-Medium	100	100	88.75	89.65	88.92	89.06	89.58	90.29	90.10	90.52	92.02	92.10	92.89	93.10
4.	Medium Holdings	100	100	95.18	95.36	94.82	94.97	94.90	95.04	94.99	95.27	95.00	95.78	95.05	94.35
5.	Large Holdings	100	100	96.57	96.69	96.18	96.21	96.98	97.31	96.67	96.77	96.59	96.61	93.06	93.12
6.	Total Holdings	100	100	84.07	89.00	83.01	87.21	82.03	86.30	81.53	85.95	80.31	84.07	79.89	83.62

Source: Agricultural Census Reports, Government of Uttar Pradesh, Lucknow.

category. Operated area of Marginal holdings, Small holdings and Semi-medium holdings are showing a fluctuating trend in the period. After 1991, it is showing a marginal increasing from 95.04 in 1991 to 95.78 percent in 2001 but after it, it is declining by 1.45 percent in 2006. In case of large holdings' operated area of land, the figures shows that except the year 1991, its operated area is continuously decreasing from 96.57 percent in 1981 to 92.58 percent in 2011. Operated area of total holdings is also showing a continuous declining trend from 89 percent in 1981 to 83.09 percent in 2011. Thus, the table shows all size classes are showing a marginal declining trend in number of operational holdings as well as in operated area in the State. However, the general category people have still possessed a higher percentage of land in the state. Table 10.3 examine the percentage of distribution of number of operational holdings and operated area among Scheduled Castes of U.P in all size classes since 1981 to 2011. As number of marginal holdings of Scheduled Castes are increasing continuously since 1980 to 2011 from 17.07 to 19.73 percent but their operated area showing the marginal fluctuate trend over all the period. The marginal holdings operated area of land in SCs community is moving around the figure of 16 percent over the time period. The percentage of small operational holdings of SCs community is increasing slightly at 11.57 to 12.31 from 1981 to 1991but the share of it's percentage is decreasing continuously. The percentage of operated area of small holdings is showing a fluctuating trend over the period among SC community. The percentage of semi-medium operational holdings is fluctuating over the time period whereas its percentage in operated area shows declining from 7.41 in 1986 to 5.36 in 2011. In case of medium holdings, the number of operational holdings is also showing a fluctuating trend. The medium holdings operated area figures reveals the percentage of operated area is decreasing at the rate of 4.37 to 3.39 percent but its percentage increased at 1.48, and 1 percent in 2006 and 2011. The percentage of large operational holdings is also showing fluctuations trend from 1981 to 1996 but after, its percentage increased at 1.98 percent in 2006.The number of SC operational holdings is increasing continuously from 14.34 in 1981 to 18.06 percent in 2011 whereas the operated area of SCs community is also increasing. The percentage of distribution of number of operational holdings and operated area among Scheduled Tribes is analysed in Table 10.4. The percentage of operational holdings of STs in marginal holdings is fluctuating from 1981 to 1996 after it is showing a fluctuating trend over the period. Small operational holdings of STs Community have been showing a fluctuating trend except 2001 year. The operated area is also showing a fluctuating from 1981 to 1996 but after it its share has increased marginally at 0.3 percent in 2006.Semi-medium operational holdings is showing an ups and down trend in the state excluding 2001 year whereas medium operational holdings is increasing continuously from 0.53 percent in 1981 to 0.84 percent in 2001but since 2001, there is found a fluctuate trend in the land holdings.

Table 10.3: Category-wise Percentages Distribution of Number of Operational Holdings and Operated Area in Uttar Pradesh during 1980 to 2006

S No.	Size classes	Scheduled Castes													
		Year		1980-81		1985-86		1990-91		1995-96		2000-01		2005-06	
		No.	Area	No.	Area	No.	Area	No.	Area	No.	Area	No.	Area	No.	Area
1.	Marginal Holdings	100	100	17.07	15.30	18.31	16.75	18.71	16.49	19.07	16.54	19.13	16.08	19.22	16.41
2.	Small Holdings	100	100	11.57	11.13	11.90	11.16	12.31	11.09	11.95	11.17	10.58	10.07	11.08	10.70
3.	Semi-Medium	100	100	8.37	7.36	8.76	7.41	6.22	7.35	6.54	7.27	6.31	7.06	6.01	6.52
4.	Medium Holdings	100	100	4.29	4.11	4.55	4.37	4.36	4.18	4.24	3.92	4.26	3.39	4.20	4.87
5.	Large Holdings	100	100	2.94	2.88	3.20	3.27	2.34	2.13	2.59	2.61	3.35	3.34	5.33	5.54
6.	Total Holdings	100	100	14.34	8.98	15.33	9.72	16.38	10.48	16.79	10.76	17.01	10.78	17.62	12.43

Source: Agricultural Census Reports, Government of Uttar Pradesh, Lucknow.

Table 10.4: Category-wise Percentages Distribution of Number of Operational Holdings and Operated Area in Uttar Pradesh during 1980 to 2006

S	Size classes	Scheduled Tribes											
		Year		*1980-81*		*1985-86*		*1990-91*		*1995-96*		*2000-01*	*2005-06*	
No.		*No.*	*Area*	*No.*	*Area*	*No.*	*Area*	*No.*	*Area*	*No.*	*Area*	*No.*	*Area*	*No.*	*Area*
1.	Marginal Holdings	100	100	1.21	1.07	1.26	1.24	1.15	1.06	1.27	1.44	1.63	1.35	1.65	2.01
2.	Small Holdings	100	100	1.65	1.66	1.72	1.78	1.68	1.66	1.76	1.78	2.15	2.02	1.51	2.45
3.	Semi-Medium	100	100	2.88	2.99	2.32	3.53	4.20	2.36	3.36	2.21	0.83	0.84	1.10	1.21
4.	Medium Holdings	100	100	0.53	0.53	0.63	0.66	0.74	0.78	0.77	0.81	0.84	0.83	0.75	0.78
5.	Large Holdings	100	100	0.49	0.43	0.62	0.52	0.68	0.56	0.74	0.62	0.06	0.05	1.61	1.34
6.	Total Holdings	100	100	1.59	2.02	1.66	3.07	1.59	3.22	1.68	3.29	2.68	5.17	2.49	3.93

Source: Agricultural Census Reports, Government of Uttar Pradesh, Lucknow.

The percentage of semi-medium operated area is decreasing from 3.53 percent in 1986 to 0.84 percent in 2001 but its percentage increased at 0.37 and 0.22 percent in 2006, 2011. In medium holdings, the percentage of operated area is increasing from 0.53 percent in 1981 to 0.83 percent in 2001 however it's percentage slightly decreased at 0.05 percent in 2006 but again increased at 0.07 percent in 2011. The large holdings operated area of STs is also increasing from 0.43 percent in 1981to 0.62 percent in 1996. The percentage of operational holdings is fluctuating during 1981-2006 whereas large holdings operated area is increasing continuously from 2.02 percent to 5.17 percent in 2001. Gender wise percentage of number of operational holdings and operated area among male and female in all social groups of Uttar Pradesh is analysed in Table 10.5. It is observed that the percentage of male group in marginal operational holdings was showing mixed results. The marginal operational holdings of male are declining and female share is increasing. Small and Medium operational holdings are showing fluctuations for both male and female groups. In case of Semi-medium, and Large operational holdings male percentage is decreasing while female percentage is increasing marginally. The operated area for male group in marginal holdings is declining whereas female are better. The marginal operated area of female group increased marginally in 2011. The Small and medium operated area for male and female groups are showing fluctuations. The semi-medium and large operated area of male is declining while female is increasing at the same rate. All size classes represent that operational holdings as well as operated area of male group has decreased and female percentage has increased. Thus, the figures disclose the view that female share is increasing slightly. They are still discriminated because the male percentage in possession of land is still high in the state. Table 10.6 analyse the percentage of number of operational holdings and operated area to male and female groups of Scheduled Castes in Uttar Pradesh. The marginal operational holdings of male are decreasing from 94.38 percent in 1996 to 93.51 percent in 2011. The percentage of operational marginal holdings of female group is increasing from 5.62 percent to 6.49 percent in the same period. In case of small, semi- medium and medium operational holdings, the percentage of male group is declining while female group is increasing. The percentage of large operational holdings for male and female groups is fluctuating. The female percentage is very low in medium as well as large operational holdings whereas the percentage of male is around 97 to 99 percent. The operated area of male of marginal, small, semi-medium and medium is decreasing while female group is enhancing the possession of land. The large operated area of male and female is showing a fluctuating. The percentage of operational holdings and operated area of male group is higher than the female group. The SCs male is also over ruling upon the female group. SCs female group is also discriminated by the SCs male group in the State. Gender wise percentage distribution of number of operational holdings

Table 10.5: Percentage Distribution of Number of Operational Holdings and Operated Area Among Male and Female in U.P.

S. No.	*Size Class*	*Male/ Female*	*No. of Operational holdings*	*Operated Area*	*No. of Operational holdings*	*Operated Area*	*No. of Operational holdings*	*Operated Area*
			1995-96	**1995-96**	**2000-01**	**2000-01**	**2005-06**	**2005-06**
1	Marginal Holdings	Male	94.39	94.68	93.75	94.24	93.14	93.57
		Female	5.61	5.32	6.25	5.76	6.86	6.43
		Total	**100.00**	**100.00**	**100.00**	**100.00**	**100.00**	**100.00**
2	Small Holdings	Male	95.44	95.53	94.89	94.89	95	95.09
		Female	4.56	4.47	5.11	5.11	5.00	4.91
		Total	**100.00**	**100.00**	**100.00**	**100.00**	**100.00**	**100.00**
3	Semi-Medium Holdings	Male	96.26	96.31	96.18	96.24	95.71	95.71
		Female	3.74	3.69	3.92	3.76	4.29	4.29
		Total	**100.00**	**100.00**	**100.00**	**100.00**	**100.00**	**100.00**
4	Medium Holdings	Male	96.92	96.99	96.97	97.05	96.80	96.88
		Female	3.08	3.01	3.03	2.95	3.20	3.12
		Total	**100.00**	**100.00**	**100.00**	**100.00**	**100.00**	**100.00**
5	Large Holdings	Male	97.86	97.89	97.72	97.59	97.69	97.54
		Female	2.14	2.11	2.28	2.41	2.31	2.46
		Total	**100.00**	**100.00**	**100.00**	**100.00**	**100.00**	**100.00**
6	All Classes	Male	94.75	95.73	94.15	95.32	93.63	94.92
		Female	5.25	4.27	5.85	4.68	6.37	5.08
		Total	**100.00**	**100.00**	**100.00**	**100.00**	**100.00**	**100.00**

Source: Agricultural Census Reports, Government of Uttar Pradesh, Lucknow.

Table 10.6: Percentage Distribution of Number of Operational Holdings and Operated Area Among Male and Female in U.P.

S. No.	*Size Class*	*Male/ Female*	*No. of Operational holdings*	*Operated Area*	*No. of Operational holdings*	*Operated Area*	*No. of Operational holdings*	*Operated Area*
			1995-96	**1995-96**	**2000-01**	**2000-01**	**2005-06**	**2005-06**
1.	Marginal Holdings	Male	94.38	94.30	93.80	93.62	93.51	93.49
		Female	5.62	5.70	6.20	6.38	6.49	6.51
		Total	**100.00**	**100.00**	**100.00**	**100.00**	**100.00**	**100.00**
2.	Small Holdings	Male	95.71	95.76	95.48	95.48	95.29	95.27
		Female	4.29	4.24	4.52	4.52	4.71	4.73
		Total	**100.00**	**100.00**	**100.00**	**100.00**	**100.00**	**100.00**
3.	Semi-Medium Holdings	Male	96.49	96.44	96.19	96.17	96.09	96.14
		Female	3.51	3.56	3.81	3.83	3.91	3.86
		Total	**100.00**	**100.00**	**100.00**	**100.00**	**100.00**	**100.00**
4.	Medium Holdings	Male	97.53	97.59	97.47	97.55	97.04	97.08
		Female	2.47	2.41	2.53	2.45	2.96	2.92
		Total	**100.00**	**100.00**	**100.00**	**100.00**	**100.00**	**100.00**
5.	Large Holdings	Male	97.26	97.77	98.61	98.73	98.07	97.87
		Female	2.74	2.23	1.39	1.27	1.93	2.13
		Total	**100.00**	**100.00**	**100.00**	**100.00**	**100.00**	**100.00**
6.	All Classes	Male	94.60	95.23	94.05	94.70	93.74	94.41
		Female	5.40	4.77	5.95	5.30	6.26	5.59
		Total	**100.00**	**100.00**	**100.00**	**100.00**	**100.00**	**100.00**

Source: Agricultural Census Reports, Government of Uttar Pradesh, Lucknow.

Table 10.7: Percentage Distribution of Number of Operational Holdings and Operated Area Among Male and Female in U.P.

(Social Group: Scheduled Tribes)

S. No.	*Size Class*	*Male/ Female*	*No. of Operational holdings*	*Operated Area*	*No. of Operational holdings*	*Operated Area*	*No. of Operational holdings*	*Operated Area*
			1995-96	**1995-96**	**2000-01**	**2000-01**	**2005-06**	**2005-06**
1	Marginal Holdings	Male	95.34	95.57	97.01	97.07	94.68	94.39
		Female	4.66	4.43	2.99	2.93	5.32	5.61
		Total	**100**	**100**	**100**	**100**	**100**	**100**
2	Small Holdings	Male	96.13	96.28	97.19	97.39	95.56	95.61
		Female	3.87	3.72	2.81	2.61	4.44	4.39
		Total	**100**	**100**	**100**	**100**	**100**	**100**
3	Semi-Medium Holdings	Male	97.19	97.26	98.56	98.49	96.09	95.90
		Female	2.81	2.74	1.44	1.51	3.91	4.10
		Total	**100**	**100**	**100**	**100**	**100**	**100**
4	Medium Holdings	Male	98.13	98.22	97.70	97.80	97.20	97.20
		Female	1.87	1.78	2.30	2.20	2.80	2.80
		Total	**100**	**100**	**100**	**100**	**100**	**100**
5	Large Holdings	Male	98.29	98.54	97.80	97.33	98.35	98.43
		Female	1.71	1.46	2.20	2.67	1.65	1.57
		Total	**100**	**100**	**100**	**100**	**100**	**100**
6	All Classes	Male	96.09	97.39	97.27	97.58	95.18	96.03
		Female	3.91	2.61	2.73	2.42	4.82	3.97
		Total	**100**	**100**	**100**	**100**	**100**	**100**

Source: Agricultural Census Reports, Government of Uttar Pradesh, Lucknow.

and operated area among male and female in Scheduled Tribes community of U.P. is represented by Table 10.7. The percentage of male and female group in marginal, small and semi- medium operational holding has been fluctuating. But, the percentage of male medium operational holding is decreasing from 98.13 in 1996 to 97.20 percent in 2011whereas medium operational holdings of ST female group is rising up marginally from 1.87 percent to 2.80 percent. The percentage of operated area of male and female of marginal, small and semi-medium and large holdings has been showing a fluctuating over the time. On the contrary, medium operated area shows that there has come a minor change in the possession of land in STs female from 1.78 percent in 1996 to 2.86 percent in 2011. Now, females are taking interest in the possession of land holdings but their percentage is not sufficient as their presence in the society and their contribution in all holdings moves around1 to 6 percent while male group is possessing land around 95 to 99 percent in the Indian society.

Gender Inequalities

Table 10.8 represents the gender wise population of Uttar Pradesh during 1971-2011. Decadal population of the state has been represented in percentage. The figures reflect that male population is increasing continuously whereas female population is fluctuating. The gender gap reflects that since 1991, female population is increasing whereas the gender gap reflects that there is a declining trend from 7 percent in 1991 to 5 percent found which suggest that now female strength has little improve after globalisation yet male population is still high compare to female in the state. Educational status of Uttar Pradesh is examined by Table 10.9 in percentage. The educational status of male and female has been shown from 1971 to 2011. The figures reveal that male and female educational status is increasing since 1971 up to 2011 but there has a major difference found between them that female educational status has increased from 11 percent in 1971 to 59 percent in 2011while male from 32 percent to 79 percent in the same time. Hence, we can see it that in educational sector females are discriminated by the males. Still female education is below than

Table 10.8: Gender-wise Population of Uttar Pradesh from 1971-2011(in per cent)

S. No.	*Year*	*Total Population*	*Male*	*Per cent*	*Female*	*Per cent*	*Gap*
1.	1971	88341	47016	53.22	41325	46.78	6.44
2.	1981	110862	58819	53.06	52043	46.94	6.11
3.	1991	132062	70396	53.31	61666	46.69	6.61
4.	2001	166174	87560	52.69	78614	47.31	5.38
5.	2011	199582	104597	52.41	94985	47.59	4.82

Source: Annual Plan 2013-14, Vol. 1 (Part-II), State Planning Commission, Govt. of Uttar Pradesh.

male in the Indian society. The percentage of literacy rate and gender gap among all social groups in U.P. has been represented by Table 10.10. Total literacy rate was 21.7 percent in which male literacy rate was 31.5 percent and female 10.6 percent while the gap of literacy rate between them was 21 in 1971. Scheduled Castes literacy was 10.3 percent, in which female literacy rate was only 2.46 percent and male 17.13 percent. In SC community, the gap of literacy between them was 15 percent while the literacy rate in Scheduled Tribes was 14.59 percent in which ST female literacy rate was 6 percent and male was 23 percent having with the gender gap of 17 percent in the same time. In case of SCs total literacy rate increased from 10.3 percent in 1971 to 60 percent in 2011 in which male literacy rate increased from 17 percent to 73 percentwhile female literacy rate also rose up from 3 percent to 46 percent. Thus, SCs female literacy rate increased more during 2001 and 2011 but gender gap shows that SCs female literacy rate gap is declining slightly even though the literacy gap is still high in Scheduled Castes community.

Table 10.9: Gender-wise Educational Status of Uttar Pradesh (in per cent)

Educational Status

S. No.	*Year*	*Male*	*Female*	*Gap*
1.	1971	31.5	10.55	20.95
2.	1981	38.76	14.04	24.72
3.	1991	55.73	25.31	30.42
4.	2001	68.8	42.2	26.6
5.	2011	79.24	59.26	19.98

Source: 11th Five Year Plan, Vol-1 (Part-II), State Planning Commission, Govt. of Uttar Pradesh.

On the other side, in total literacy rate, male literacy was 69 percent in 2001 compared with Scheduled Castes male literacy was 60 percent at the difference of 8 percent. SC's male literacy rate was better than ST's male. Overall the literacy rate in all social groups has increased. Total literacy rate is 69.7 in which male dominates for 79 percent literacy rate while female acquires 59 percent in the State. In case of SCs, total literacy is 60 percent in which male literacy percent is 72 percent whereas female is only 46 percent. Similarly, in STs total literacy rate is 44 in which male administrate for 50 percent literacy rate while female 39 percent. All figures reflect that in all categories of social groups, female literacy rate is less compare to male literacy rate during the whole time period. Of course Central or State government policies for improving the educational level is tremendous even though gender gap of literacy rate between male and female is still high in the state.

Table 10.10: Percentage of Literacy Rate and Gender gap in Uttar Pradesh

Year	Total Literacy				Scheduled Castes Literacy				Scheduled Tribes Literacy			
	Total	Male	Female	Gender gap in lit. rate	Total	Male	Female	Gender gap in lit. rate	Total	Male	Female	Gender gap in lit. rate
1971	21.7	31.5	10.55	21.05	10.3	17.13	2.46	14.67	14.59	22.51	5.58	16.93
1981	27.16	38.76	14.04	24.72	14.96	24.83	3.89	20.94	20.45	31.22	8.69	22.53
1991	41.6	55.73	25.31	30.52	26.85	40.8	10.69	30.11	35.7	49.95	19.86	30.09
2001	56.3	68.8	42.2	26.6	46.3	60.3	30.5	29.8	35.1	48.4	20.7	27.7
2011	69.72	79.24	59.26	19.98	60	72.7	46.4	26.3	44.3	49.9	38.6	11.3

Source: 10th, 11th and 12th Five Year Plan Document, State Planning Commission, Government of Uttar Pradesh.

Table 10.11: Gender-wise Occupational Distribution of Workers in U.P. during 1971-2011 (in Per cent)

S. No.	Year	Cultivator workers				Agricultural workers				Household workers				Other workers			
		P	M	F	Diff. gap	P	M	F	Diff. gap	P	M	F	Diff. gap	P	M	F	Diff. gap
1	1971	59.49	62.42	42.86	19.56	21.56	19.74	45.75	-26.01	8.68	8.24	4.76	3.48	10.27	9.60	6.63	2.97
2	1981	47.42	55.47	39.37	16.10	23.19	13.88	32.50	-18.62	8.18	7.98	8.38	-0.40	21.21	22.67	19.75	2.92
3	1991	53.27	53.94	48.18	5.76	18.94	16.69	35.82	-19.13	2.41	2.27	3.55	-1.28	25.38	27.10	12.45	14.65
4	2001	43.90	42.97	34.32	8.65	19.47	20.13	41.22	-21.09	6.89	4.39	8.30	-3.91	29.74	32.51	16.16	16.35
5	2011	32.48	31.12	22.20	8.92	22.35	27.69	38.43	-10.74	6.34	4.72	9.68	-4.96	39.01	36.47	29.69	6.78

Source: 1971, 1981, 1991, 2001, and 2011, Statistical Abstract U.P., Economics and Statistics Division, State Planning Institute, U.P.

Inequality in Occupational Distribution

The percentage of gender wise occupational distribution of workers in Uttar Pradesh has shown by table 10.11 during the period of 1971 to 2011. The total workers are divided in to four categories such as Cultivators workers, Agricultural workers, Household workers and Other workers. The workers are also divided into male and female category. As male cultivator workers are declining continuously in 1971 from 62 percent to 31 percent and female workers are also declining from 43 percent in 1971 to 22 percent in 2011 while the gap between male and female as a cultivator is marginally increase at 0.27 percent in 2011 whereas the difference was very high in the period of 1971 and 1981. Declining trend of cultivator workers shows that they are losing their agricultural land and shifting to other economic activities in the state.

The male agriculture workers have shown a continuous increasing trend from 14 percent in1981 to 28 percent in 2011 while female workers have been fluctuating over the time period. It is notable thing that in case of gender gap, agricultural women share is high than male agricultural workers in the state. The result reflects in agricultural work, the female agricultural workers are contributing more work compare to male. It is also analysed that male and female cultivators are converted in to agriculture labourers. The percentage of male household workers is increasing from 2 percent in 1991 to 5 percent in 2011. The female workers, percentage is increasing in the same time. But, the negative differential gap shows that in household activities, female share is higher than male.

In other workers, male percentage is rising up continuously from 10 percent in 1971 to 37 percent in 2011 whereas female workers share is fluctuating from 1971 to 2001 but in 2011 female share increased at 14 in 2011 in the state. Similarly, the gender gap in the form of other workers shows that female share is fluctuating in it. As combined, the percentage of both male and female is increasing continuously. There has been seen a change among the occupational distribution of workers in Uttar Pradesh. The cultivators are becoming agricultural workers and agricultural workers are changing into household workers and other workers for the economic activities in the society. As a result, the percentage of household workers and other workers are rising up. Of course female participation has increased in agricultural activities but there has no much change found in the females conditions in the regime of Uttar Pradesh after the globalisation.

Concussion

Female participation is playing a very crucial role in the economic development of the state even though they are discriminated with respect to their fundamental rights in the Indian society. Women are not only doing work in the household activities but also contributing through their assistance in the agriculture activities including main crop production, live-stock production, horticulture, post- harvesting operations, and household industry. Yet females are still discriminated in many ways in the state like landholdings, population share, education, literacy, and in employment as operational workers also. Land distribution is unequal among all social categories along with very high degree of gender discrimination in this respect. In all social categories, female share in land holdings is extreme low while male share is high. It is a very critical condition in the state that at present, majority of the people are controlling the share of land and a small minority of the people are controlling majority share of the land. Now, dependent on land is decreasing in the state which suggests that people are shifting from agriculture sector to no agriculture sector. The percentage of female agricultural workers and female household workers is higher than that of male workers. Further, there is a positive change in the education level over the years but female ratio is less than male.

The economy of rural Uttar Pradesh is also based on agriculture, 65 percent it's population is occupying in the agriculture sector. Possession of agricultural land is the symbol of power, prosperity and prestige in the agrarian societies. It is a not only a symbol of economic status but also a sign of social phenomena. Indian society is intrinsically based on the hierarchy system also since a long time. Women are contributing their participation in agriculture field even though they are discriminated by the social customs since a long time. Inequalities between men and women are apparent themselves in all social-economic areas of development in the Indian society. These Inequalities are most manifest in the area of land, education and occupational workers in the state. Hence, this paper will study the Gender Discrimination in Distribution of Land in Uttar Pradesh. The paper is purely based on secondary data. It is found in the study that in case of land holdings, 94 percent male operational holdings were possessed 95 percent operated area in 1995-96 while 5.25 percent female operational holdings accounted only 4 percent operated area in agriculture field. After a decade, there was seen a marginal change in the possession of land holdings that only one percent increment had been seen in the female operational holdings. The figures represents that female are contributing their assistance in agriculture field even though they are not getting proper right in the possession of land because male are still dominating high share in the agrarian field. Education level of male is also high compare to female in the state. Similarly, it is also concluded in the context of occupational workers that the share of female cultivator workers are declining from 43 percent in 1971 to 22 percent in 2011 while the percentage of agricultural female workers and household female workers are fluctuating over the time period in the state. Similarly, to compare the share of male and female workers in the occupational distribution of workers, cultivator male worker is high than female workers as the ratio 31:22 but in agricultural workers; the share of female workers is high compare to male worker at the ratio of 27:38 in 2011 in the state.

Certain measures need to be taken seriously and systematically to eradicate gender discrimination and inequality. Education is an important component of development. Education is not only improving the skills of people leading to increase in the level of productivity but also acts as an agent of social change. Particularly, technical and vocational education can help the people in securing employment and increase their level of income, consumption and living standard. Given the existing inequalities in literacy rate of different groups it is essential that some educational programme is introduced by the State government to increase the literacy rate among SCs and STs in general and of SC & ST women in particular. Similarly, Land Reforms Act should be restarted with a new zeal by the state government to remove the unequal distribution of land. To make the women empowered in the society, woman's right to land and property must be respected, protected, fulfilled and enforced and this must be done to ensure equality with men. These rights contribute to women's equality, safety and sustainable human development goals, including women's social and economic empowerment, poverty eradication, food security, and sustainable agriculture development in the state of Uttar Pradesh.

References

Krishna Rao., E.(2006), ' Role of Women in Agriculture: A micro Level Study', published in Journal of Global Economy, http://www.rcssindia.org

Government of India (2007), *Uttar Pradesh Development Report*, Vol-1 and Vol-2, Planning Commission, New Delhi.

Government of India, Census Reports 2011,http://censusindia.gov

Mayra Gomez, D. Hien Tran (2012), 'Women's Land and Property Rights and the Post-2015 Development Agenda' published in The Global Initiative for Economic, Social and Cultural Rights and Landesa Center for Women's Land Rights

http://globalinitiative-escr.org

Venkateshwarlu, A. (2003), "*Pattern of Land Distribution and Tenancy in Rural Andhra Pradesh*" Working Paper No. 51, Published in Centre for Economic and Social Studies, Begumpet, Hyderabad.

Mohanty, B.B. (2008), "Landholding and Use Pattern among Scheduled Castes and Scheduled Tribes in Maharashtra", in Deshpande, R.S., Vijay Paul Sharma, R.P.S. Malik, BrijeshJha, S.A. Ansari (eds.), *'Glimpses of Indian Agriculture, (Macro and Micro Aspects)'*, Vol-2, Academic Foundation, New Delhi.

Nageswara Rao, K. (2008), "Dalits and Agricultural Land holdings in Andhra Pradesh", in Karunyakara, L., L.C.Mallaiah, K.B. RatnaKumari (eds.), '*Dalits and Human Development (Contemporary Issues and Emerging Patterns)*', Abhijeet Publications, New Delhi.

Prasad, P.H., Rodgers, G.B. (1983),"*Class, Caste and Landholdings in the Analysis of the Rural Economy*", in Population and Labour Policies Programme, Working Paper No. 140.

Sharma, H. R. (1998) "*Distribution of Landholdings in Rural India: A Comparative Study of Scheduled Castes, Tribes and Non- Scheduled Caste and Tribes",* ArthaVijnana, Vol. XL, No.1, Journal of the Gokhale Institute on Politics & Economics Pune, India.

Agrawal, P.K. (2010), "*Land reforms in states and union Territories in India",* Concept Publishing Company Pvt. Ltd. New Delhi.

Chowdhury, A.K. and Kashimi, M.H.R. (1991), "Change in Landholdings Pattern and Its Impact among the Bhoksa of Nanital", in Upadhyay (eds.), *Scheduled Caste and Scheduled Tribes in India, A Socio-Economic Profile*", Anmol Publications, New Delhi.

Rawal, Vikas. (2008), "*Ownership Holdings of Land in Rural India: Putting the Record Straight"*, Economic & Political Weekly (EPW).

Kumar, Vijendra. (2001), "*Rise of Dalit Power in India*", Published by ABD Publishers, Jaipur (Rajasthan) India.

Planning Commission Report (2002), on *"Labour and Employment",* Published by Academic Foundation.

Agriculture Census 1975-76, Board of Revenue, Uttar Pradesh.

Agriculture Census 1980-81, Board of Revenue, Uttar Pradesh.

Agriculture Census 1985-86, Board of Revenue, Uttar Pradesh.

Agriculture Census 1990-91, Board of Revenue, Uttar Pradesh.

Agriculture Census 1995-96, Board of Revenue, Uttar Pradesh.

Agriculture Census 2000-01, Board of Revenue, Uttar Pradesh.

Agriculture Census 2005-06, Board of Revenue, Uttar Pradesh.

Various Statistical Abstract U.P., Economics and Statistics Division, State Planning Institute, Uttar Pradesh (1971, 1981, 1991, 2001, & 2011).

7thFive Year Plan Document (1985-90), State Planning Commission, Government of U.P.

8thFive Year Plan Document (1992-97), State Planning Commission, Government of U.P.

9thFive Year Plan Document (1997-02), State Planning Commission, Government of U.P.

10thFive Year Plan Document (2002-07), State Planning Commission, Government of U.P.

11thFive Year Plan Document (2007-12), State Planning Commission, Government of U.P.

12thFive Year Plan Document (2012-17), State Planning Commission, Government of U.P.

Annual Plan 2013-14, Vol. 1(Part-I), and(Part-II), State Planning Commission, Government of Uttar Pradesh.

11

Gender Discrimination in Wage and Employment: A Case Study in Lucknow and Rai bareilly Districts

— ***Shivani Tiwari and Sanatan Nayak***

Abstract

Using primary level data in Lucknow and Raibareilly districts in Uttar Pradesh, the study attempts to find out gender discrimination on employment, wages and land ownership. Nearly 200 samples have been collected based on stratified random sampling method in two villages of both the districts. Various statistical techniques such as descriptive statistics and dummy variable models are used to estimate the gender discrimination on wage and employment.

In the study area, 98 percent men are involved in economic activities, while only 21.82 percent women are involved in economic activities. However, nearly 1.65 percent male respondents have reported to be involved in non economic activities, while this is very high for women, i.e. 78.18 percent. Further, 19 percent of rural male workers are self employed in agriculture, while 37.98 percent rural women are found working as housewives. Work Participation rate in India has remained higher for males than for female both in rural and urban areas. Nearly 11.75 percent male work as agricultural labour while 3.96 percent female work as agricultural labour in the study area. Data on the extent of ownership of agricultural land reveals that there is a substantial difference in owning land between men and women in the study area. Village people actively discouraged women, daughters as well as the wife, getting any share in the land or the house. Caste wise ownership of land reveals that the number of general women owning agricultural land is highest, i.e., 19.35 percent followed by 15.49 percent for OBC women in the study area. SC women own minimum area of agricultural land due to their poor land holding capability and illiteracy. Ownership of land was concentrated mostly in the hands of higher castes. Further, it is found that the mean wage of men is Rs 137.29 while the mean wage of women is only Rs 79.80 in the study area. Therefore, social and economic factors on land holding size, wage and employement reveals the existance of substantial gender discrimination in the study area, which needs to be handled with appropriate policy decision.

I. Introduction

Agriculture is a labour intensive activity. Labour accounts for more than 40 percent of the total variable cost of production in most cases. Therefore, availability of labour to work in agriculture is crucial in sustaining agricultural production. The agricultural labour force includes people who are working or looking for work in formal or informal jobs and in paid or unpaid employment in agriculture. That includes self-employed women as well as women working on family farms. It does not include domestic chores such as fetching water and firewood, preparing food and caring for children and other family members (FAO, 2011).

Agricultural Labour constitutes the most neglected class in Indian rural structure. Their income is low and employment is irregular. Since, they possess no skill or training, they have no alternative employment opportunities either (Padhi, 2007, p. 23). Labour is vulnerable to exploitation due to illiteracy and lack of effective bargaining power. This is even worst for the female labour in unorganised sector. Women form an integral part of the Indian workforce. In the rural areas, women are mainly involved as cultivators and agricultural labourers. In the urban areas, almost 80 per cent of the women workers are working in the unorganised sectors such as household industries, petty trades and services, buildings and construction (GoI, 2010, p.101). The entire spectrum of human activity falls into two categories such as economic activities and non-economic activities. Any activity resulting in production of goods and services that add value to national product is considered as an economic activity. Such activities included production of all goods and services for market (i.e. for pay or profit) including those of government services, and the production of primary commodities for own consumption and own account production of fixed assets (NSSO, 2013).

In our study area, 98 percent men are involved in economic activities while only 21.82 percent women are involved in economic activities. As far as non economic activities are concerned, 1.65 percent male respondents are reported to be involved in non economic activities i.e. only 1.65 percent while this is very high for women i.e. 78.18 percent. The reason may be that among rural households, it is widely believed that it is prestigious for a Hindu woman to cook and serve food to her family and guests. A high status is generally associated with the role of housewife in parts of the country that have implicit cultural values associated with Sanskritisation and Brahmanical gender norms (Chakravarti, 1993).

II. Objective & Methodology of the Study

This paper aims to analysis the following aspects of women in agricultural sector in India-

1. To analysis the gender discrimination in employment condition of Indian agricultural women.
2. To explain gender inequality in the wage trend of women in agriculture.

The study is based on primary level data in Lucknow and Raibareilly districts in Uttar Pradesh. The study attempts to find out gender discrimination on employment, wages and land ownership. Nearly 200 samples have been collected based on stratified random sampling method in two villages of both the districts. Various statistical techniques such as descriptive statistics and dummy variable models are used to estimate the gender discrimination on wage and employment.

The paper is divided into seven sections including the introductory section. The second section of the paper deals with the objectives and methodology. Gender inequality in ownership of land is analyzed in the third section. Gender inequality in employment has been presented in the fifth section. In the sixth section empirical analysis of wage differentiation has been discussed. Finally, the concluding section provides a summary of the present study and its main conclusions.

III. Gender Inequality in Ownership of Land

A serious gender gap is found in the distribution of productive resources. Women control less land in comparison to men and that land is also used to be of poorer quality. Indian women contribute a lot in the Gross Development Income. The majority of these women work in the agricultural sector yet agricultural land is usually titled in the name of the male head of the household. This creates a hindrance in their access to development schemes and credit from formal sectors. Lack of ownership of productive resources including agricultural land has been considered as one of the basic causes for perpetuating gender inequalities (Arora & Singhi, 2009).

In many countries, women still lack independent rights to own land, manage property and run business (Christabell, 2009). Data on the extent of ownership of agricultural land reveals that a large proporation of household owns agricultural land i.e. 91.50 percent and the remaining 8.50 percent are landless in the study area. A comparative analysis of the two districts, viz., Lucknow and Rae Bareilly reveals that 90 percent and 93 percent households owned agricultural land in Lucknow and Rae Bareilly respectively (Table 11.1).

Women in India, and worldwide are rarely landowners. This is despite their high level of involvement in agricultural production and dependence on agriculture for their livelihoods (Brown & Chowdhury, 2009). The gender wise ownership of land, reveals that the percentage of female landowners is very low as compared to male landowners. District-wise analysis shows that the number of women owning agricultural land was marginally higher in Lucknow district, i.e 16.67 percent as compared to Rae Bareilly i.e. 15.05 percent (Table 11.1). The reason is that family land pass from fathers to sons traditionally in India. It encourages male members to control over land rights by placing less value on the rights of daughters. Finally, prevailing social custom pressurizes daughters to relinquish their share of inheritance of land to other male family members.

Religion-wise analysis shows that Hindu women are in better position as far as ownership of land is concerned. Nearly 17 percent Hindu women are owning land as compared to 12.20 percent of Muslim women (Table 11.1). Analysis of circumstances under which daughter inherites agricultural land shows that daughter inherites land only when there was no son in the family (Arora & Singhi, 2009).

Table 11.1: Gender wise ownership of Land

District	*Male*	*Female*	*Average*
Rae Bareilly	79 (84.95)	14 (15.05)	93 (100.00)
Lucknow	75 (83.33)	15 (16.67)	90 (100.00)
Religion			
Hindu	118 (83.10)	24 (16.90)	142 (100.00)
Muslim	36 (87.80)	5 (12.20)	41 (100.00)

Source: Estimated from Survey data.

Note: The value in parenthesis show the percentage of total.

Moreover, this situation exists even when the highest government functionaries concerned with land records have taken an interest in ensuring that the names of women are put on record. Village people actively discouraged women, daughters as well as the wife, getting any share in the land or the house. Their reason is simple that a woman getting access to the land or the house would result in dilution of the interest of the male members.

IV. Gender Inequality in Employment

Persons who operate their own farm or non-farm enterprises or are engaged independently in a profession or trade on own-account or with one or a few partners are deemed to be self-employed in household enterprises. The essential feature of the self-employment is that they have autonomy (i.e., how, where and when to produce) and economic independence (i.e., market, scale of operation and money) for carrying out their operation. The fee or remuneration received by them comprise two parts share of their labour and profit of the enterprise.

The landless labourers and marginal farmers pre dominate the rural society. They do not get work most of the days due to seasonal nature of agricultural activities (Government of India, 1999-2000). 19 percent of rural male workers are self employed in agriculture while 37.98 percent rural women are found working as housewives in the study area. As far as unemployed population is concerned, 5.17 percent men and only 0.73 percent women are reported unemployed (Table 11.2). The unemployment rate indicates the proportions of people in the labour force seek work but unable to find any work (Shaw, 2013). The World Development Report 1998 states that women perform two third of the total labour of the world, they earn one tenth of wages and own one hundredth of wealth. Work Participation rate in India has remained higher for males than for female both in rural and urban areas (Gill, 2008). Nearly 11.75 percent male work as agricultural labour while 3.96 percent female work as agricultural labour in the study area (Table 11.2).

Table 11.2: Gender wise Primary Occupation of Respondent (in percent)

Primary Occupation of Respondent	*Male*	*Female*	*Average*
Self-employed in agriculture	136 (19.02)	23 (3.37)	159 (11.38)
Self-employed in non-agriculture	49 (6.85)	2 (0.29)	51 (3.65)
Regular wage/salary earning	58 (8.11)	5 (0.73)	63 (4.51)
Agricultural labour	84 (11.75)	27 (3.96)	111 (7.95)
Non-Agricultural labour	32 (4.48)	22 (3.23)	54 (3.87)
Unemployed	37 (5.17)	5 (0.73)	42 (3.01)
Housewife	00 (00.00)	259 (37.98)	259 (18.54)
Domestic work with some side work	00 (00.00)	24 (3.52)	24 (1.72)

Source: Estimated from Survey data.

Note: The value in parenthesis show the percentage of total.

At present women contribute much for the development of all sectors of the country. Employment gives economic status to women (Ganpati, R.G. et al, 2010, p. 24). Field data shows that women are not aware of their legal power related to land ownership. Land inheritance and entitlement related decisions are taken mainly by male members of the family, villages and the revenue department. In such a given socio-cultural conditions, women find it difficult to assert their land rights. The number of women who have land in their names remains very low; the number of women who have houses in their names is still lower. The number of women having land or houses in the joint names along with their father or husband is almost negligible. This is so despite the fact that almost half of the women are actively involved in agriculture either as cultivators themselves or as labourers.

The main responsibility of women is considered to perform all domestic works such as cooking food, collecting fuel-wood, fetching water and caring of children and the sick. They have to work longer hours than men. This affects women's health negatively. In Asia and Sub- Saharan Africa, women often carry 20-kg headloads, the carrying of such heavy loads usually causes chronic fatigue, spinal and pelvic deformities, and sometimes spontaneous abortion (World Bank, 2010).

V. Gender Discrimination in Wage Pattern

The main reason of low agricultural wages is large disguised unemployment in agricultural sector and low productivity. In rural areas sufficient employment opportunities are not available in other sectors. However, after implementation of Minimum Wages Act and various employment generation policies like MGNREGA, the wages have been increased. The average daily wages for agricultural field labour for ploughing and harvesting at all India level have increased at the rate of 8.7 per cent and 9.2 per cent per annum during 2001-02 to 2010-11 respectively (GoI, 2012-13). However, agricultural wages in general are still much lower than the industrial wages. With skill development this gap will narrow down, putting further pressure on availability and cost of agricultural labour.

Beyond gender, there is little individual variation in the agricultural wage rates by education or social background. The main differences are geographic. Less developed villages have lower agricultural wages than more developed ones. In contrast, non-agricultural wages vary more widely by age, level of education, and social background and somewhat less by location. In our study area the daily wage rates of Lucknow being a developed district is more than Rae Bareilly District. The variation in the daily wages of Lucknow is more than Rae Bareilly.

Table 11.3: District wise Mean Daily Wage

District	*Mean Daily Wage*	*SD Daily Wage*	*Maximum Daily Wage*	*Minimum Daily Wage*
Lucknow	126.37	75.32	694.43	20
Rae Bareilly	123.93	39.93	250	32

Source: Estimated from Survey data.

Even in a state, wage rate varies across selected districts and village clusters. By and large wages in village clusters away from rural town are lower than those in village clusters near town. Through this marginal difference in wages between these two kinds of villages may be due to difference in cost of living (Jha, 2008).

In India wage received was Rs. 149 for males and Rs 103 for females per day in rural areas. Daily wages received by casual laboures of rural areas engaged in public works other than MGNREG public works was Rs. 121.

This was Rs.127 for males and Rs. 111 for females. Daily wages received by casual laboures of rural areas engaged in Mahatma Gandhi National Rural Employment Gurantee (MGNREG) Public works was Rs. 107. This was Rs. 112 for males and Rs.102 for females (NSSO, 69th round). In the study area mean daily wages for men is Rs. 138.10 while it is only Rs.79.25 for wmen labourers (Table 11.4).

Table 11.4: Gender wise Mean Daily Wages

Gender of Respondent	*Mean Daily Wages*	*SD Daily Wages*	*Maximum Daily Wages*	*Minimum Daily Wages*
Male	138.10	61.52	694.43	32.00
Female	79.25	33.84	200	20.00

Source: Estimated from Survey data.

If we see caste wise daily wages, we find that general respondents are getting higher wages i.e. Rs. 135.55 as compared to OBC and SC respondents i.e. Rs.124.05 and Rs. 115.72 respectively. This implies better condition of general households in the study area.

VI. Empirical Analysis of Wage differentiation

Effect of Gender on Daily Wages

In this section it is to see whether gender plays any role in determining daily wages. For this, dummy variable analysis is performed.

Model 1:

Daily wages = f (gender)

$$Y = \beta_1 + \alpha_1 D_1 \text{ gender} + ui$$

$$= 74.52 + 64.06 + ui$$

$$t = (13.44) \qquad (10.20)$$

$$p = (0.00)^{***} \qquad (0.00)^{***}$$

$$R^2 = 0.186 \qquad f = 104.12$$

Here, *** = 1 percent level of significance.

Where,

Y = Daily Wages

D_1 = Male, 0 = Female

The analysis shows that the daily wage of female labour is Rs 74.52 while daily wages of male labour is Rs 138.58. This proves that gender plays a discriminatory role in determining the daily wages of labour.

Effect of Gender on Monthly Income

In this section it is to see whether gender plays any role in determining monthly wages. For this, dummy variable analysis is performed. In this regression female category is the benchmark category.

Model 2:

Monthly Income = f (gender)

$$Y = \beta_1 + \alpha_1 D_1 \text{ gender} + ui$$

$$= 1345.154 + 1812.524 + ui$$

$$t = (7.28) \qquad (8.67)$$

$$p = (0.00)^{***} \qquad (0.00)^{***}$$

$$R^2 = 0.1368 \qquad f = 75.10$$

Here, *** = 1 percent level of significance.

Where,

Y = Monthly Income

D_1 = Male, 0 = Female

The analysis shows that the monthly income of female labour is Rs 1345.15 while monthly income of male labour is Rs 3157.68. This proves that gender also plays a discriminatory role in determining the monthly income of labour.

Factors Determining Low Wage Rates for Female Laboures

The most important reasons for the low rates of wages, particularly for women labour in agriculture are the unorganised nature of farm labour, the ease with which hired labour can be substituted by family labour, the seasonal nature of the demand for labour and the traditional classification of some jobs, as the monopoly of women. Apart from the differentials in wages for the same jobs, discrimination against women is strengthened by having lower rates for the job traditionally done by women, viz., sewing, weeding, transplanting, winnowing, threshing and harvesting, as against ploughing- normally done by men only. The other factor that contributes to the low wages of women is the practice of identifying a workday as equivalent to 7-9 hours. Many women are unable to report for duty on time because of household responsibilities, and do not get the full rates (Singh, 2004, p. 160).

Women Labourers are being paid lower wages for each of the operations in agriculture (Kaul & Singh, 2006, p. 80). If we see the factors that determine low wage rates of females, we found that illiteracy is the main factor which affects the low wage rate of the females. 26 percent respondents said that due to marriage female laboures get few wages (Figure 11.1). Because of marriage most of the women are not in the stable condition to bargain with the land owners.

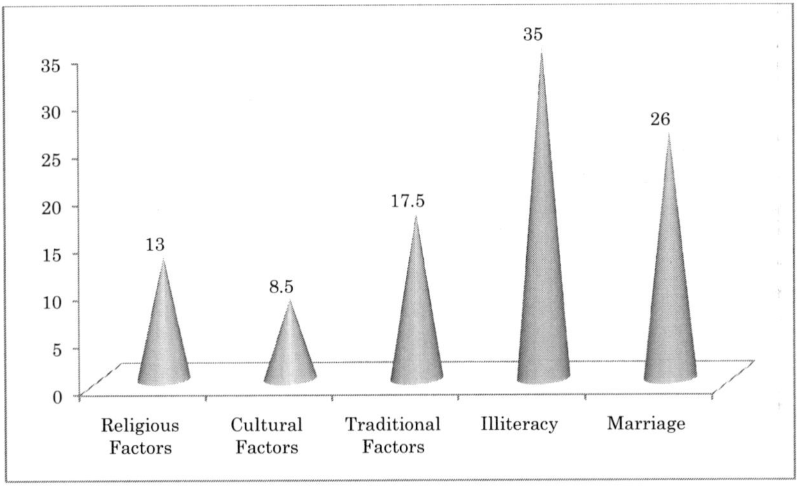

Source: Primary Survey.

Figure 11.1: Factors affecting low Wage Rates of Female Laboures (in percent)

Women agricultural workers are frequently discriminated against in their livelihood security, educa-tion and autonomy (Kelkar, 2011, p.61).

VII. Summary & Conclusion

Women play a very crucial role in agricultural development. In this period of economic liberalisation and globalisation, the quality of women's employment will depend upon several factors. The foremost among these are access to education and opportunities for skill development. The solution lies in creating awareness among women about their legal rights and duties and by providing them adequate opportunities to upgrade their skill levels. The emphasis should be on effective enforcement of the Minimum Wages Act, 1948 and the Equal Remuneration Act, 1976. Proper enforcement of these Acts will create on enabling environment for women workers. Besides these protective measures, policies which encourage education, skill development, and training among women also need to be given priority because Increases in Women's income translate directly in to better health and nutrition for children.

Lack of ownership and control rights to pro-ductive assets is increasingly being linked to negative development outcomes, specifically in relation to gender equality and women's empowerment. Some recent studies point out that there exists a positive correlation between women's ownership of specific assets and reduced vulnerability to experiencing access to productivity increasing technologies. To achieve gender equality and to empower women is very essential for agricultural development and food security.

References

Arora, Saroj & L.C. Singhi, (2009), "Women's Access and Rights to land in Uttar Pradesh" in Prem Chowdhry (eds), *Gender Discrimination in Land Ownership*, SAGE India PVT LTD, New Delhi.

Brown, Jennifer & Sujata Das Chowdhury, (2009), "Analyzing Women's Rights: A Field Study from West Bengal" in Prem Chowdhry (ed), *Gender Discrimination in Land Ownership*, Sage Publications, New Delhi.

Chakravarti, Uma, (1993), "Conceptualizing Brahmanical Patriarchy" in Manoranjan Mohanty (eds), *Class, Caste ,Gender*, Sage Publications Ltd, New Delhi.

Christabell, P.J., (2009), *Women Empowerment through Capacity Building: The Role of Micro Finance*, Concept Publishing Company, New Delhi.

FAO, (2011), *Women in Agriculture: Closing the Gender Gap for Development,* The State of Food and Agriculture, Food and Agriculture Organisation of the United Nations, Rome, Italy.

Ganpati, R.G., J. Murugesan & T. Ramaswamy, (2010), "Regression Model for the Improvement of Economic Status of Self Help Groups", *Journal of Economic and Social Development*, Vol.6, No. 2.

Gill, Kanwaijit Kaur, (2008), "Changing Scenario of Female Work Participation: An Analysis of North-Western States during Pre and Post-Reform Era", *Journal of Economic & Social Development,* Vol. 4, No.1.

Government of India, (1999-2000), *Employment and Unemployment Situation in India*, NSS 55th Round, Ministry of Statistics and Programme Implementation, New Delhi.

Government of India, (2010), *Annual Report 2009-10*, Ministry of Labour and Employment, New Delhi.

Government of India, (2013), State of Indian Agriculture 2012-13, Ministry of Agriculture, Department of Agriculture and Cooperation, Directorate of Economics and Statistics, New Delhi.

Government of India, (2013), *Key Indicators of Employment and Unemployment in India, 2011-12*, NSS KI. (68/10), 68th Round, Ministry of Statistics and Programme Implementation, New Delhi.

Government of India, (2013), *Key Indicators of Drinking Water, Sanitation, Hygiene and Housing Condition in India, July 2012- December 2012,* NSS KI.(69/1.2), 69th Round, Ministry of Statistics and Programme Implementation, New Delhi.

Jha, Brajesh, (2008), "Rural Non-Farm Employment in India", in S M Jharwal (eds), *Glimpses of Indian Agriculture: Macro & Micro Aspects*, Academic Foundation, New Delhi.

Kaul, Sushila & R.K. Singh, (2006), "An Economic Analysis of Wages of Agricultural Labour in Uttar Pradesh", *Manpower Journal*, Vol. XXXXI, No. 1.

Kelkar, Govind, (2011), "Gender and Productive Assets: Implications for Women's Economic Security and Productivity", *Economic and Political Weekly*, Vol.46, No.23.

Padhi, Kulmani, (2007), "Agricultural Labour in India- A Close Look", *Orissa Review*, Feb-March.

Shaw, Abhishek, (2013), "Employment Trends in India: An Overview of NSSO's 68th Round", *Economic and Political Weekly*, Vol.48, No.4.

Singh, Bharat, (2004), 'Working Women in India', Anmol Publications PVT. LTD, New Delhi.

World Bank, (2010), *Social Development & Infrastructure: Making Water Supply and Sanitation Work for Women and Men Tools for Task Teams*, Washington, DC.

12

Development-induced Displacement, Gender and Women's Movement

Dinabandhu Sahoo and Niharranjan Mishra

Abstract

The process of modernity which waved throughout the world due to colonisation of the Non-western societies has led to development and displacement of the native populations. In India the process of development was unleashed via heavy industrialisation, multi-purpose dam construction, mining and infrastructure projects which resulted Development-induced Displacement. Development-induced displacement has caused impoverishment, deprivation and alienation of livelihood resources of majority of native populations throughout the country. Though it has affected all sections of the populations, the enormity of the problem is more severe in case of women than men as they are more connected to nature for their survival. The women's access to land, forests and common property resources have been wiped out without any compensation which undermines women's income and relative social position in society. Moreover, the employment generated in the projects comes under hazardous working conditions, of heavy mechanisation, of low wages and of less employment security, push more and more women to the informal sectors of the economy. Apart from this, displacement also affects women's health and their food security. Drawing from Rawls's theory of justice and based on ethnographic fieldwork in Kalinga Nagar Industrial Complex and secondary data, the paper attempts to understand the kind of impact women face due to development-induced displacement. It tries to know how resettlement and rehabilitation policies have discriminated women, treated unfairly to women and how it is an injustice to women. In addition to this, the paper reflects on how the historical injustice treated to women has given rise to various women's movements against displacement.

Keywords: *Development-induced Displacement, Gender, Discrimination, Justice, Women's Movement.*

With the destruction of forests, water and land, we are losing our life-support systems. This destruction is taking place in the name of 'development' and progress, but there must be something seriously wrong with a concept of progress that threatens survival itself. The violence to nature, which seems intrinsic to the dominant development model, is also associated with violence to women who depend on nature for drawing sustenance for themselves, their families, their societies. This violence against nature and women is built into the very mode of perceiving both, and forms the basis of the current development paradigm.

(Vandana Shiva, Staying Alive: Women, Ecology and Survival in India, 1988, pp. XIV)

I. Introduction

Development via heavy industrialisation, multi-purpose dam construction, mining and infrastructure projects that involves displacement and resettlement of population has long been a subject of major controversies, but in recent years the issue has become particularly contentious. On the one hand, development is considered as a goal worth striving for the greater common good even it inevitably involves displacement and its dire consequences. On the other hand, there are groups that not only oppose the poor resettlement outcomes that cause widespread impoverishment and inequality but denounce the entire current development approach as destructive and discriminatory and demand that no development programmes be undertaken that cause displacement and create people the victims of development. The magnitude of development-induced displacement is very massive and it is being accelerated after neoliberalisation. An authentic estimation suggests that every year about 10 million people bear the costs of displacement throughout the world (Cernea, 1995). The decades following neoliberalisation, the enormity of development-induced displacement in Africa, Latin America, Central Asia, South Asia including India and China is very high (Cotula, Vermeulen, Leonard, and Kelly, 2009; Pearce, 2012). During the last sixty years since Independence, India alone has displaced 60 million people for its development projects. Out of these 60 million displaced people, 75 per cent constitutes adivasis and 25 per cent comprises Dalits (Fernandes, 2008).

In the recent years a paucity of debate among the academic community exists over the issue of gender justice that emerge from the social movement against displacement. Even the rights framework that include human rights justice comprising of economic, social and cultural rights have been neglected by the academicians. Social anthropologists in the mid-twentieth century are among the first to study and document in vivid details the socio-economic and cultural impacts of development projects that involve population displacement and resettlement. It began with the study pioneered by Scudder of the Kariba dam on the Zambezi River and B. K Ray Burman of India of the Rourkela

Steel Plant oustees. The subject has since received great popularity among other social scientists as well. Many studies by development analysts appeared late. NGOs have in recent years carried out their own studies on the plight of the poor who are forcibly evicted. The media too is not lagging behind in reporting stories about projects that causes displacement and its impoverishment outcomes. However the gender dimension of the problem appeared later. It is true that over the years a substantial body of knowledge concerning development-induced displacement has been built up, but many things remain unanswered in this field.

Development and Population displacement if not new has become significant in the neoliberal regime due to the resultant increasing enormity of the problem. Neoliberalism not only brought benefits to the developing countries like India in the form of robust economic growth, but also accelerated the process of development projects and as a result aggravated the problem of forceful eviction of native population mostly rural or tribal population. Development-induced displacement affects people in multiple ways. It dispossesses people from homes, lands, employments, familiar environments, access to education, health and public services, community support networks and a sense of local belonging. Development-induced displacement does not affect men and women equally. The severity of impact is more in case of women than men irrespective of caste, class, religion and region (Mehta, 2009; Sahoo and Mishra, 2016). Further, the negative impact of displacement is felt more among poor, women and girl children, as there exist intra-household inequalities between male and female on the levels of food, nutrition, health and literacy. Amartya Sen (1981) argued that these inequalities are increased at the times of economic stress. Kabeer (1994) states that the gender inequalities that persisted before displacement get manifested and increased in different forms after displacement. In many cases after relocation, women loss access to forests and common property resources that women enjoyed previously. Such a situation paves the way for scarcity of minor forest products and fuel woods which undermines women's income and relative independent social position in society. In recent years industrialisation is followed by heavy mechanisation that adversely affects women's employment (Lahiri-Dutt, 2001; Fernandes 2007; Sahoo and Mishra, 2016). In addition to this, the employment which is provided to displaced women comes under risky working condition and are of low wages and less employment security push more and more women into the informal sectors of the economy (Lahiri-Dutt, 2001; Sahoo and Mishra, 2016). Besides, displacement also adversely affected women's health and their food security. Drawing from Rawls's theory of justice and based on ethnographic fieldwork in Kalinga Nagar Industrial Complex and secondary data, the paper attempts to understand the above issues. The second section of the paper tries to know the kind of impact women face due to development-induced displacement. The third section of the paper describes how resettlement and rehabilitation policies have discriminated women, treated unfairly to women and how it is an injustice to women. The fourth section reflects on the role of women in various displacement movements while the fifth section concludes the above discussions.

II. Development-induced Displacement and Gender

The most wide spread consequences of development-induced displacement is impoverishment risks of a large sections of population (Cernea, 1996, 2000; Mahapatra, 1999b; Mathur and Marsden, 1998). The chief identifiable impoverishment risks that displaced population many a time suffer are: landlessness, joblessness, homelessness, marginalisation, food insecurity, increased morbidity and mortality, loss of access to common property resources and Community disarticulation (Cernea 1995, 2000; Guha 2011; Mathur and Marsden 1998). All these processes get aggravated in the case of relocation of women. Mehta (2009) argues that forced displacement is more severe for women than men, because of difference in caste, class, religion or region. Everywhere women bear the brunt of the forced move a lot more than the male counterparts in their families because of the existence of intra-familial inequalities between male and female on the levels of food, nutrition, health and literacy. The transitional phase of displacement is very problematic for women as all developmental activities got stopped in the project area disrupting the access to previous livelihood resources.

The livelihoods of rural or tribal women depend more or less on common property resources. In case of relocation, the access to common property resources is disrupted thereby causing the loss of fodder and fuel wood availability. This brings an additional burden of workloads and responsibilities for women folk in the family. The loss of access to land and common property resources also affects women's position in their families. Pandey (1998a) asserts that women's access to land and other common property resources declines due to displacement. Further it leads to the disruption of their productive activities which they carry out in home such as livestock rearing, kitchen gardening, fishery, poultry or petty business. Women also lose their earnings from forests, other common property resources and productive activities thereby affecting their position in the family. This decline of access to livelihood resources marginalizes women in labour force, push more and more women to informal sectors or turn them to housewife (Fernandes and Raj, 1992). This process is called *Housewifisation* (Mies, 1998). Housewifisation is another form of women exploitation and is accelerated due to displacement. In Kalinga Nagar Industrial Complex various industries provided only 68 (6.34 per cent) numbers of employments to women out of 1071 employment (see Table No.2). Before industrialisation, the tribal women were equal partner to male in agricultural productive activity. In the post-displacement period due to lack of or limited employment in the industries for women, more and more women have joined informal sectors of employment. Now most of the tribal women are sustaining their livelihood by selling *Handia* (Rice beer) in the industrial complex. Other women who cannot sell *Handia* have become housewives. Displacement accelerates the process of housewifisation.

In the relocated area the loss of food security leads to declining intake of food. Due to intra-household inequality, women and girl children suffer most in food intake which causes malnutrition among the women. Declining intake of food affects women's health. Ganguly Thukral (1996) in her study shows that the per capita food intake has gone down after displacement in Sardar Sarovar Project due lack of employment and low crop productivity. The same situation is also experienced by the Kalinga Nagar tribal displaced people. Malnutrition among tribal women and children is very high in Kalinga Nagar Industrial complex. A local farmer reveals the causes of food insecurity:

> "We are not getting enough water as we got earlier for our land because the water near the plant construction sites is dried up due to the plant construction. Our *Patas* (wetland) and *Nallas* (rivulets) have been dried out due to the industries. We are not able to cultivate Paddy, Mung and Biri and pea nuts due to lack of water. We have left our cultivation. Hence we have to depend on the food supplied by the project authority as resettlement assistance. But most of the time it is temporary and some cases they have stopped the assistance". (Interview 31.10.2014)

Sanitation is another issue which also affects women in relocation sites. The problem of sanitation leads to loss of privacy, frequent quarrel and degrade women's health. Fernandes & Raj (1992) mentions that since NALCO has resettled displaced people without toilet facilities, quarrels between women are frequent because they use a plot which is marked as a pasture by a neighbouring village. Similarly Pandey (1998a) describes that due to less resettlement land and overcrowding, women face the problem of privacy and sanitation and poor health. Women not only face health problems, they also cannot provide their children a secure future by depriving their children the access to education, health and child welfare (Parasuraman, 1993). Fernandes and Raj (1992) mentions that the literacy rate among girl children has drastically gone down in NALCO project after relocation.

Mechanisation has significantly decreased women's employment opportunity in the industry in post-displacement situation. The number of jobs offered to women is less as they lack required education and skills to be employed in an industry. In Kalinga Nagar Industrial Complex it has revealed that a few women, particularly the women headed households or the women kith and kins of the police firing victims have got employment in the projects. Majority of the women have been deprived of getting jobs in the projects. However, due to lack of formal education and skills, the jobs provided to the women are of low wages.

Lack of women's employment and decrease in participation of women in productive activities in relocation affects women's social status. Since women do not have work, they have to leave most of their agro-based rituals or festivals. As women could not contribute to household economy, they could not remain equal partner to men. As a result, women have to lose their independence in case of social and economic affairs in the family as well as political matters (Ray, 1998). It leads to women's dependency on men as well as downward social mobility.

III. Resettlement and Rehabilitation Policies and Gender

Development-induced displacement not only affects women differently, the Resettlement and Rehabilitation policies (hereafter R and R Policy) also treat women unjustly. The R and R policies evolved through the decades in India and in different states is discriminatory and unfair. John Rawls (1971) in his theory of justice viewed 'justice as fairness'. A society is just when it treats men and women equally and fairly. In a social system the formal justice is always just and is adhered to principles. Formal justice is also the rule of law and it supports and secures legitimate expectations.

Before the promulgation of National Resettlement and Rehabilitation Policy 2003 (NRRP), there was a Land Acquisition act 1894 (amended in 1984). The Land Acquisition act did not have any provision of Resettlement or rehabilitation. It only had provision of payment of compensation to the land owners. The act does not provide compensation to those who do not have formal land titles or who depend on common property resources (CPRs). The question of women's right to compensation was absence in the act as women do not have any legal ownership of land or property. Hence, the Land Acquisition act 1894 was unjust and discriminated women. Ganguly Thukral (1996) argued that the Land Acquisition Act, 1894 is gender biased and merely reinforces the existing situation of women's lack of ownership of land and property. The notice of acquisition of land served to a woman in the absence of any male person in the family is considered illegal.

In 2003, India proclaimed its first National Resettlement and Rehabilitation Policy (NRRP 2003). Before the promulgation of NRRP, India had at least five draft policies. Each draft policy was a little improvement over its previous draft policy. Besides, every project has its own R and R policy. A pan India policy was only came in 2003. Although the preamble of the policy has laudable principles, the policy was gender blind. It does not possess the provision of gender issues (NRRP, 2003).

In 2007, India announced its second national rehabilitation policy known as National Rehabilitation and Resettlement Policy (NRP) 2007. The preamble of the policy has excellent provisions. The policy emphasised displacement and deprivation to be minimized. It recognised the limitation of monetary compensation to get rid of the traumatic consequences of displacement and prescribes resettlement and rehabilitation as intrinsic to the development processes (Fernandes, Chetri, Lama, & Joseph, 2012; NRP, 2007). The policy also emphasised the need to rehabilitate "those who do not have legal or recognised rights over the land or upon which they are critically dependent" (NRP, 2007). It includes landless labourers and petty business persons among the displaced persons (DPs). It prescribes social impact assessment (SIA) mandatory. It speaks for a tribal development sub-plan where the tribal DPs predominate. It highlights a time frame for implementation and grievance redressal mechanisms (Fernandes et al. 2012; NRP, 2007).In spite of high and laudable provisions it could not bring desirable results for the marginalised and deprived sections of the society and hence it could not stop resistance to the projects.

Before the coming of the R and R policy 2007, the word gender failed to acquire a significant place in the policy document. Although the R and R policy 2007 recognised gender issues, it is very discriminatory and unfair. The policy does not give fairness to both men and women oustees. The policy while providing compensation and rehabilitation measures include unmarried sisters or daughters in the family, considers an unmarried adult (18 years age or above) son as another family (Fernandes et al. 2012; NRP, 2007). Fernandes (2012) highlights that both the two R and R policies did not deal with the issues concerning women. These policies emphasize land acquisition. They can at best reduce resistance, but cannot rehabilitate people. These two policies are also unjust with regard to Constitutional provisions. These policies violate Article 15 (I) of the Constitution on the grounds of fair treatment against gender. It also contravenes Article 39 (a) of the directive principles of state policy which prescribes securing equal rights both for men and women on the grounds of adequate livelihoods. These policies do not recognise the Constitutional provisions of justice as fairness. There is wide gap between the Constitutional fairness and the reality situation. Moreover, women have been marginalised socially and economically and exposed to violence and abuse after displacement. Hence, Sahaee (2003) argues that R and R policy 2003 is 'gender blind' because it recognizes the male as the head and sole deciding factor for compensation and rehabilitation. While extending rehabilitation benefits it does not mention any separate criteria for women.

In response to the various national level policies different State Governments had brought their respective policies in different period and in different sectors. Table 12.1 shows the promulgation of separate R and R policies for separate Projects in Odisha in different periods.

Table 12.1: Odisha State Resettlement and Rehabilitation Policies.

Year of Promulgation	*Name of the Resettlement and Rehabilitation Policy.*
1973	R and R policy for Rengali Dam project.
1989	Rehabilitation policy for Mahanadi Coal-field Limited (MCL) Areas.
1994	R and R policy for Water Resources Projects.
1997	R and R policy for Kalinga Nagar Industrial Complex.
1998	Rehabilitation policy for Industrial and Mining projects.
2001	Rehabilitation policy for Vedanta Alumina.
2005	New Rehabilitation policy for Kalinga Nagar Industrial Complex.

Source: Government of Odisha.

In addition to these policies, Odisha had 13 project specific policies. In 2006, Odisha proclaimed its Resettlement and Rehabilitation policy as a result of heavy pressure from various anti-displacement movements, civil society and Kalinga Nagar Police firing. Although the policy came as a 'kneejerk reaction' to the Kalinga Nagar police firing and several other high profile movements gaining momentum in Odisha, the policy falls short of the campaigners' demands (Mathur, 2006b). The Kalinga Nagar resistance movement was suppressed with government and company tactics.

The policy which claimed to be among the best in the country is unjust for women. It does not provide justice to women with regard to compensation and rehabilitation. In the context of rehabilitation, one of the most glaring instances of gender discrimination has been the issue of compensation. It does not show fairness on the ground of gender. Odisha R & R policy 2006 considered the unmarried women above 30 years as separate family for R&R benefits, but the same for major sons is 18 years. The discrimination is shown on the legal framework of justice. The Odisha R and R policy 2006 recognizes daughters above 30 years of age, widows and divorced women as separate family for providing rehabilitation. Although the policy recognises a woman divorcee as separate family, it is very problematic for a divorced woman to get a divorce certificate in order to be eligible for getting compensation and rehabilitation benefits. It is the complex legal structure in which a woman divorcee faces a lot of difficulty to issue a divorce certificate. Even nothing has been mentioned about separated women.

Besides, there is another problem evident in the state policy. Though unmarried daughters above the age of 30 years, widow and divorced are considered as separate family at the time of providing resettlement and rehabilitation benefits but they are not considered separately at the time of providing employment opportunities. The policy also violates justice as equality of opportunity. This unjust policy has paved the way for many displaced women to join the informal labour force. In Kalinga Nagar Industrial Complex, most of the tribal displaced women have been pursuing *Handia* (rice beer) selling near the outskirts of various industries and in different local markets held throughout the week in the area. The women selling *Handia* reported that the industrial employment is very limited and it is given to only those who have no sons or whose husbands have killed in the police firing. The industrial jobs in the area are very much mechanised and it is very difficult on the part of an illiterate tribal woman to pursue such a job. Besides the industrial contract jobs offered by many industries located in Kalinga Nagar are very laborious in nature in comparison to *Handia* making and selling which requires small labour. In Kalinga Nagar Industrial Complex out of 659 displaced persons of Nilanchal Ispat Nigam Limited (NINL), 455 employments created for displaced people in which 31 employments have been provided to women. Similarly out of 39 displaced persons Visa Steel has provided employment to 29 displaced persons in which 2 are women. Some other industries like K.J. Ispat, Rohit Ferrotech, Apeejay Logistic, BRPL have not provided any formal employment to the displaced women. Hence, women's employment in the Kalinga Nagar Industrial Complex is very negligible. Industries have not treated women displaced people fairly in providing employment. The distributive justice is unjust for tribal women in post-displacement situation. Women have been marginalised and there is greater injustice in providing employment to women oustees. The Odisha Government also did not accept Asian Development Bank's R and R policy prescription for gender issues suggested in 1998. Table 12.2 below shows the status of employment provided to women in different industries in Kalinga Nagar Industrial Complex.

Table 12.2. Status of Women's employment in Kalinga Nagar Industrial Complex

Name of the industries	*Total No. Of Displaced Persons (DPs)*	*Employment provided*	*No. Of women provided employed*
NINL	659	455	31
Tata Steel	1234	306	19
Visa Steel	39	29	2
MESCO	152	107	5
Jindal Steel	232	153	11
K J Ispat	8	6	0
Rohit Ferrotech	12	11	0
Apeejay Logistic	8	3	0
BRPL	19	1	0

Source: ADM Office, Kalinga Nagar, 2015.

In Odisha, the major industrial projects (Rourkela Steel Plant and National Aluminum Company Limited), thermal power projects (Talcher Super Thermal Power Project under NTPC and Ib Thermal Power Station, a State PSU) and coal mining projects (under Mahanadi Coalfields Limited, a subsidiary of Coal India Limited) have adopted their own R&R policies. However, none of the R&R policies have gender perspective to address gender issues of displacement. In each Project women were not recognised as a separate entity. Even widows, unmarried adult daughters and deserted women were considered as dependents. The State R and R policy is even more gender biased. If a couple holds property separately, they will be considered one unit and will receive one package. In this situation, a woman will have to forego her right to the package as it will be given to the head of the family i.e. to the man. A deserted woman has not even been referred to in any of the state policies. The laws, policies and government procedures also serve discrimination to women. It is the consequence of the unequal social and political set-up that men get preference over women in the matter of land, security, physical space, food intake, jobs, etc. within home, society and in the government (Sahoo and Mishra, 2016).

IV. Development-induced Displacement and Women's movement

Development-induced displacement has severe consequences for women. The policies which have been designed to mitigate the negative consequences of relocation have historically discriminated women. The policies also have not been treated women fairly. All R and R policies have been unjust for women. Although constitutional justice is fair both for men and women, distributive justice is always unfair for women. Since women have been faced historical injustice in both social and political structure, women have been resorted to protest movements against displacement. Many times women have been played key role in anti-displacement movements. A women leader of Kalinga Nagar Resistance movement states that "We are protesting against the injustice treated out by the Government to us. The government never consider men and women equally in both policy and resettlement. We won't bear this injustice anymore". Although women protested against displacement and discrimination, they have been with their men counterparts and think that they are part and parcel of the movement.

Women also played significant roles in protest movement against forceful land acquisition. In Odisha women have played significant roles in different movements both in colonial and post-colonial times. They have played key roles in POSCO and Kalinga Nagar resistance movements in Odisha. In Kalinga Nagar, women also formed a separate women's forum to resist the forceful land acquisition and displacement. In Kalinga Nagar movement large number of women took part in protest movement against Tata project and two women were killed in the police firing on January 2, 2006. Women also have taken quite a significant role in the POSCO movement. Large number of women along with school children protested the POSCO project in sleeping under the scorching sun in Jagatsinghpur district in Odisha. Women also played significant roles in movement against Sardar Sarovar projects, Chipko movement, Baliapal Protest movement and Tehri and Maheswari anti-dam movement. In Odisha the number of women participating in anti-displacement movement is also quite high. Institute for Socio-Economic Development (ISED) found that women have participated in great numbers in protest movements against displacement in Odisha. Women are very quick to respond to any displacement problems. However, the women's movement always remained peaceful. Non-violent Gandhian modes of protest have been always the strategy of women's movement. The women of Kadalimunda village have taken a leading role in a non-violent struggle against the Mahanadi Coalfields Limited (MCL). They also succeeded in bargaining a better rehabilitation package. The women with the support of the men stopped mining operations for three to four days (Pandey, 1998b).

Women invariably had to act under the leadership of women leaders. Almost all the movements had some kind of political affiliation and generally women were hardly given opportunity to react to change of stand by political parties. The upper caste people did not want their women to join the movement apprehending loss of prestige in the society. Although, women participated in large numbers in the protest movements yet they were hardly given due recognition. It is also an urgent need to document the role of women in resistance movement against displacement.

V. Conclusion

In recent years following globalisation and the resistance to neoliberal policies by various grassroots and women's organisations, various states and international agencies have improved their R and R policies. They have given special attention to gender dimensions of the problem. As a result gender aspects in the development processes and in policy frameworks have been added up and are debated. Gender justice is being gradually emphasised. But the increasing mechanisation of the development projects, there is high risks of further marginalisation and discrimination of women particularly where previously women had little skill and education. So the women from indigenous, marginal and backward communities may face high risks of injustice in the development process. In the contemporary time, a growing disparity is being observed as a result of globalisation. This may further perpetuate gender injustice where resettlement is considered a second class citizen. As the employment created by the projects have become hazardous and the work provides low wages, and are without job security, there is greater chance of more and more women to enter into the informal sectors or housewifisation.

Gender injustice is normalised in the structural level as a result of displacement. In the structural level of resettlement policy many countries and funding agencies have adopted specific gender policies in recent years aimed at mainstreaming gender issues in their developmental interventions.

However, gender discrimination still persists in R and R policies. In project planning and implementation gender dimensions of the problems also overlooked. The persistence of patriarchal structure in legal system may increase further gender discrimination in the case of a policy paralysis. Although there is special provision for gender in various policy documents, the patriarchal system of management of resettlement many times can ignore gender equality. In the Orissa resettlement policy 2006 though the needs of women have been emphasised but it is observed that the impacts of projects on gender at most of the phases are ignored. Similar study mentions that Asian Development Bank approved a gender policy in 1998, but the impact on gender at the project preparation and implementation stages were often not considered. In this way gender discrimination is always perpetuated in many forms in case of displacement, resettlement and rehabilitation. However, due to anti-displacement movement by women's agency over a long period of times throughout the state and the country, the gender dimensions of the problem are being emphasised. The concept of gender and gender related aspects gradually have been given emphasis in both policy and implementation levels. But still gender injustice is persisted in displacement situations.

References

Asian Development Bank. (1998). *Handbook on Resettlement: A Guide to Good Practice*. Manila: Asian Development Bank.

Cernea, Michael M. (1995). Understanding and Preventing Impoverishment from Displacement: Reflections on the State of Knowledge. *Journal of Refugee Studies,* 8 (3): 245-264.

_______ (1996). Understanding and Preventing Impoverishment from Displacement: Reflections on the State of Knowledge. In C. McDowell (Ed.), *Understanding Impoverishment:The Consequences of Development-induced Displacement* (pp. 13-32). Oxford: Berghan Books.

_______ (2000). Risks, Safeguards and Reconstruction: A Model for Population Displacement and Resettlement. *Economic and Political Weekly, 35*(41): 3659-3678.

Cotula, L., Vermeulen, S., Leonard, R. & Kelly, James. (2009). *Land grab or Development Opportunity? Agricultural Investment and International Land Deals in Africa*. London: International Institute for Environment and Development.

Fernandes, Walter. (2007, November 19-21). Mines, Mining and Displacement in India. Paper Presented at *First International Mining Conference. Australian National University*: New Delhi.

______ (2008). Sixty Years of Development-induced Displacement in India: Impacts andthe Search for Alternatives. In H. M. Mathur (Ed.), *India Social Development Report 2008: Development and Displacement* (pp.89-102). New Delhi: Council for Social Development and Oxford University Press.

______ (2012, November 17). Displacement and Rehabilitation: The Gender Perspective. Paper presented as Keynote Address at the *National Seminar on Gender Perspective in Displacement, Resettlement and Rehabilitation,* RavenshawUniversity, Cuttack: Odisha.

Fernandes, Walter., Chetri, Shanti., Lama, Satyen. & Joseph, Sherry. (Eds.). (2012). *Progress: At Whose Cost? Development-Induced Displacement in West Bengal 1947-2000*. Guwahati: North Eastern Social Research Centre.

Fernandes, Walter. & Raj, S. Anthony., (1992). *Development, Displacement and Rehabilitation in the Tribal Areas of Orissa*. New Delhi: Indian Social Institute.

Ganguly Thukral, Enakshi. (1996). Development, Displacement and Rehabilitation: Locating Gender. *Economic and Political Weekly, 31* (24): 1500-1503.

Guha, Abhijit. (2011). Special Economic Zones, Land acquisition and civil society in WestBengal. In H. M. Mathur (Ed.), *Resettling Displaced People: Policy and Practice in India* (pp.336-357). New Delhi: Routledge Taylor and Francis Group and Council for Social Development.

Kabeer, Naila. (1994). *Reversed Realities. Gender Hierarchies in Development Thought*. London: Verso.

Lahiri-Dutt, Kuntala. (2001). *Mining and Urbanisation in the Raniganj Coalbelt*, Kolkata: The World Press.

Mahapatra, L. K. (1999b). *Resettlement, Impoverishment and Reconstruction in India: Development for the Deprived,* New Delhi: Vikas Publishing House.

Mathur, Hari Mohan. (2006b, September 11-16). Globalisation, Displacement and Impoverishment Risks: Large Corporations and Tribal Peoples in Orissa, India. Paper Presented at *IAPS/Bibalex Conference on Environment, Health and Sustainable Development of the Session Involuntary Resettlement, Environmental Risks and Social Sustainability*, Library of Alexandria, Alexandria: Egypt.

Mathur, Hari Mohan & Marsden, David. (1998). *Development projects and impoverishment risks: Resettling project-affected people in India*. Oxford University Press.

Mehta, Lyla. (2009). Introduction. In Lyla Mehta (Ed.), *Displaced by Development: Confronting Marginalisation and Gender Injustice* (pp. xxv-xlii). New Delhi: Sage Publications.

Mies, M. (1998). *Patriarchy and accumulation on a world scale: Women in the international division of labour*. Palgrave Macmillan.

National Resettlement and Rehabilitation Policy 2003. (2004). *Ministry of Rural Development (Department of Land Resources).* New Delhi: Ministry of Rural Development.

National Rehabilitation and Resettlement Policy 2007. (2007). *Ministry of Rural Development (Development of Land Resources) (Land Reform Division).* New Delhi: Ministry of Rural Development.

Pandey, B. (1998a). *Depriving the underprivileged for development*. Bhubaneswar, Orissa: Institute for Socio-Economic Development.

______ (1998b). *Displaced development: impact of open cast mining on women*. New Delhi: Friedrich Ebert Stiftung.

Parasuraman, S. (1993). *Impact of Displacement by Development Projects on Women in India*,Working Paper Series No. 159, Institute of Social Studies: The Hague.

Pearce, Fred. (2012). *The Land Grabbers: The New Fight over Who Owns the Earth*. Boston, MD: Beacon Press.

Ray, Rita. (1998). Gender Aspects on Relocation. In P. Mahapatra, A. B. Ota & R. N. Mohanty(Eds.), *Development Induced Displacement and Rehabilitation*. Bhubaneswar: Prachi Prakashan.

Sahaee, Roopee. (2003). National Rehabilitation Policy: Many Loopholes. *Economic and Political Weekly,* 38 (6): 510-512.

Sahoo, Dinabandhu and Mishra, Niharranjan. (2016). Development-Induced Displacement and Gender Injustice: Some Critical Reflectons. *Journal of Politics and Governance,* 5(4): 19-29.

Sen, Amartya. (1981). Family and Food: Sex Bias in Poverty. In P. Bardhan & T. N. Srinivasan (Eds.), *Rural Poverty in South Asia*. (Mimeo) Forthcoming.

Shiva,Vandana. (1988). Staying Alive: Women, Ecology and Survival in India, (pp.xiv), U.K: Zed Books Ltd.

PART - IV

DEVELOPMENT POLICIES AND PROGRAMMES

13

An Insight into the State Policy and Programmes for Women Empowerment in India: State Policy and Programmes for Women's Development in India

— *Ginni Braj*

Introduction

Gender based discriminations prevalent in any of the society are for the disadvantage of both men and women. A society aiming for development and prosperity cannot succeed unless equal status is not ensured to its women.

Sex being the biological difference between men and women and is determined by birth. By gender we understand the socially constructed and culturally determined characteristics related to men and women. Gender indicates the roles and the responsibilities of men and women that are created in our families and our societies. These roles and responsibilities pass from generations to generations and are learned with time. Gender inequality or the subordination of women has been socially constructed and is in no case biologically predetermined. Even though after so many efforts have been taken both at national and international levels the fact remains that even today women are subjected to discrimination both in public and private spheres. There exists a broad agreement that achieving gender parity in the world remains a challenge.

Research Objectives

- To highlight the Indian constitutional provisions provided to end gender based discriminations.
- To highlight the existing legislations in India ensuring protection of women in India.

- To highlight the initiatives taken on the part of successive Indian governments and the benefits ensured to women under various five year plans.

Internationally, efforts have been taken by United Nations to ensure equality with regards to rights for women. The Preamble of UN charter begins by referring faith in fundamental human rights. Article 1(3) of the United Nations Charter declares to achieve international cooperation in promoting respect for human rights and fundamental freedom for all without the distinctions regarding race, sex, language or religion. On 7th November United Nations Convention on the Elimination of Discrimination Against Women was adopted, of which India is a signatory country having ratified it in 1993. In fact out of the eight Millennium Development Goals adopted by United Nations in 2000 one is to promote gender equality and empowerment of women. All the United Nations members and most of the International Organisations are committed to help achieve them by 2015. It becomes obligatory for countries to give due regard to international norms and conventions while framing domestic laws and upholding those ideas and beliefs over which the international community agrees unanimously.

According to United Nations Development Fund for Women (UNIFEM) report *Violence Against Women: Facts and figures, 2013* it is estimated that of all the women killed in 2012, almost half were killed by intimate partners or family members. More often than not, cases of violence against women go unreported. Worldwide, more than 700million women alive today were married as children (below 18 years of age). Women and girls represent 55 percent of the estimated 20.9 million victims of forced labour worldwide, and 98 percent of the estimated 4.5 million forced into sexual exploitation.

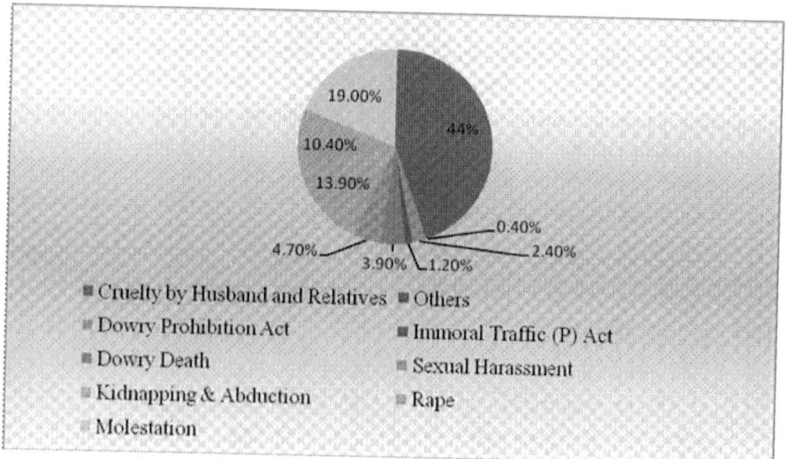

Source: Crimes in India, National Crimes Record Bureau (NCRB), 2011.

Taking India into perspective, the common crimes against women include rape, abduction, gang rape, kidnapping, sexual assault, trafficking, dowry deaths, insult to modesty, child brides, domestic slavery of women, prostitution, sex selection abortion, sex slavery, and acid attack highlight the ugly side of patriarchy in India.

The Indian Constitution strongly upholds the concept of gender equality and has undertaken various initiatives to end gender based discriminations. In the very first session of the Constituent Assembly Pt. Jawaharlal Nehru moved the Objectives Resolution which guaranteed to all the citizens of India justice, social, economic and political; equality of status of opportunity before the law and safeguards to minorities, backward, tribal areas, depressed and Other Backward Classes.

Besides the Objectives Resolution the philosophy of Indian Constitution is further contained in the Preamble. Other than declaring India to be a Sovereign, Socialist, Secular, Democratic Republic the Preamble declares to secure to all its citizens social, economic and political justice. Liberty of thought, expression, belief, faith and worship and equality of status and opportunity.

Part III and Part IV can be regarded as the backbone of the Indian Constitution on which the protective legislations for women has been based. Part III of the constitution contains the Fundamental Rights guaranteeing civil liberties to all the Indians so that they can live their lives in peace and harmony.

Article 13 guarantees that the state shall not make any law which takes away the rights conferred by this part.

Article 14 ensures that the State shall not deny to any person equality before the law and shall provide equal protection within the territory of India.

Article 15 prohibits any discrimination on the grounds of religion, race, caste, sex or place of birth.

Article 16 provides that no citizen shall on any grounds be ineligible for or discriminated against in respect of, any employment or office under the state.

Article 17 abolishes untouchability and makes it an offence punishable in accordance with law.

Article 19 confers six basic freedoms to all the citizens irrespective of gender considerations.

Article 21 except for in accordance to the procedure established by law no person shall be deprived of his life or personal liberty.

Article 21A states that free and compulsory education shall be ensured to all the children of the age of six to fourteen years.

Article 22 protects all the citizens against arrest and unlawful detention

Article 23 strongly prohibits traffic in human beings and forced labour.

Article 24 prescribes that no child below the age of fourteen years shall be employed to work in any factory or mine or engaged in any other hazardous employment.

Other than these **article 25, 26, 27** and **28** ensure religious freedoms to all the citizens while **article 29** and **30** confer cultural and educational rights on the citizens of India. Dr. B.R. Ambedkar considered **article 32** as the heart and soul of the Indian Constitution because it grants the right to every citizen to approach the Supreme Court for the enforcement of his/her Fundamental Rights.

Thus, women are equally entitled for the protection of Fundamental Rights along with men. Other than these rights its is Fundamental Duty to renounce all practices derogatory to the dignity of women, as mentioned in Part IVA of the Indian Constitution. Even the Directive Principles of State Policy aim at securing equal pay for equal work for both men and women and securing suitable employment for men, women and children so that their health is not undermined. **Article 42** establishes provisions for humane conditions of work and maternity relief for women workers. **Article 44** of the Directive Principles calls for the implementation of a Uniform Civil Code the duty of the state. Even though the implementation of a Uniform Civil Code is one of the most controversial topics in the contemporary Indian politics yet it is essential for the achievement of gender justice.

Article 243D and 243T inserted by the Constitution (73rd Amendment) Act, 1992 and the Constitution (74th Amendment) Act, 1992 respectively provide that not less than one-third of the seats shall be reserved for women in every Panchayat and every Municipality. It is further added that, from amongst the seats reserved for the Scheduled Castes (SCs) and the Scheduled Tribes (STs), not less than one-third seats shall be reserved for women belonging to the SCs or STs, as the case may be.

In order to uphold the Indian Constitutional mandate, various legislative measures have been enacted by the states to protect women from social discrimination, atrocities, violence and thereby provide them support. Crimes against women are broadly classified under two categories.

1. **The Crimes which are identified under the Indian Penal Code (IPC)**
   - Rape (Sec.376 IPC)
   - Abduction and Kidnapping for different purposes (Sec. 363-373)
   - Mental and physical torture (Sec. 498-A IPC)
   - Dowry deaths or their attempts (Sec.302-304-B IPC)

- Molestation (Sec. 354 IPC)
- Import of Girls upto 21 years of age
- Sexual Harassment (Sec. 509 IPC)

2. The Crimes which are identified under the Special Laws (SLL)

Various policies and legislations were introduced by successive Indian governments to ascertain protection of women rights. These laws have also been reviewed periodically and amendments made to keep pace with the emerging requirements. To throw light on a few women related and women specific legislations which are currently in existence and are directed towards ensuring advancement, development and empowerment of women are-

The Commission of Sati (Prevention) Act, 1987 seeking to prevent the voluntary or forced burning or burying alive of widows.

The National Commission for Women Act, 1990 mandates the formation of a National Commission for Women to examine, investigate and review the formulation and implementation of various Constitutional provisions, policies and legislations concerning women.

The Indecent Representation of women (Prohibition) Act, 1986 an act prohibiting indecent representation of women through advertisement or in publications, writings, paintings, figures or in any other manner.

The Hindu Marriage Act, 1955 was enacted to amend and codify the law relating to marriage among Hindus. Separation and divorce were also introduced under this act. However, this act does not apply to the state of Goa because there runs a single secular code governing all irrespective of all considerations of religion, ethnicity or linguistic affiliations.

The Dowry Prohibition Act, 1961 prohibits giving and taking of dowry. The act penalizes the parties demanding dowry either directly or indirectly. The person demanding dowry is punishable with imprisonment for not less than six months but can be extended to two years with a fine which may extend up to ten thousand rupees

The Pre-natal Diagnostic Techniques (Regulation and Prevention) of Misuse Act, 1994 attempts to regulate and prevent the misuse of pre-natal diagnostic techniques for the purpose of pre-natal sex determination leading to female foeticide. It puts restrictions on the use of such techniques by genetic counseling centers, genetic laboratories and clinics to determine sex. In 2012 under the Pre-Conception, Pre-Natal and Diagnostics Techniques Act 308 cases were filed in Rajasthan, which was the highest in the country.

The Protection of Women from Domestic Violence Act, 2005 aims to provide effective protection to women who are victims of violence at the hands of relatives, husband or male live-in partner.

The Medical Termination of Pregnancy Act, 1971 was enacted by the Indian Parliament with the intention of reducing the incidences of illegal abortion and consequent maternal mortality and morbidity. The act also states the conditions under which a pregnancy can be ended or aborted, the persons who are qualified to conduct the abortion and the place of implementation. According to estimates unsafe abortions are killing a women every two hours in India. A Lancet paper in 2007 said there were 6.4 million abortions, of which 3.6 million or 56 percent were unsafe.

The Special Marriage Act, 1954 provides a special form of marriage which can be taken advantage of by any person in India and by all Indian Nationals in foreign countries without considering the faith which either party to the marriage may profess. It also discusses about inter-religion marriages and muta marriages.

The Hindu Marriage Act, 1955 discusses about conditions for a Hindu marriage, ceremonies, registration, void and voidable marriages, punishment of bigamy, punishment for contravention of certain other conditions for a Hindu marriage, marriage of a divorced person and others.

The Immoral Traffic (Prevention) Act, is a 1986 amendment of legislation passed in 1956 as a result of India becoming a signatory country of the United Nations' declaration in 1950 on the suppression of trafficking. The laws were intended of initially limiting and eventually abolishing prostitution in India by gradually criminalizing various aspects of sex work.

The Protection of Human Rights Act, 1993 (as amended by the Protection of Human Rights (Amendment) Act, 2006- No. 43 of 2006) provides for the constitution of a National Human Rights Commission, State Human Rights Commission in States and Human Rights Courts for better protection of human rights.

The Minimum Wages Act 1948 is related to Indian labour law that fixes the minimum wages that must be paid to skilled and unskilled labors.

The Indian Parliament has passed The Sexual Harassment of Women at Workplace (Prevention, Prohibition and Redressal) Act, 2013 ensures the right of a women to work in a safe environment free from sexual harassment. The Bill lays down the definition of sexual harassment and aims to provide a mechanism for redressing complaints. The act provides for the constitution of an 'Internal Complaints Committee' at the workplace, and a 'Local Complaints Committee' at the District and Block levels respectively. A district officer shall be responsible for monitoring the activities under the act he can be a District Collector or Deputy Collector.

The Criminal Law (Amendment) Act, 2013was passed in March 2013 provides for the amendment of Indian Penal Code, Indian Evidence Act and Code of Criminal Procedure, 1973 laws related to sexual offences. This act has recognised certain acts as offences such as acid attack, attempt to acid attack, sexual harassment, act with intent to disrobe a woman, Voyeurism and stalking.

Eve Teasing (New Legislation), 1988 proposes protection of women from being harassed usually in public spaces, streets and public transport. This practice has also been referred to as a kind of "little rape" by some of the feminists.

The need was felt to reserve seats for women on the same lines in the House of the People, that is, the Lok Sabha and in the Legislative Assemblies of the States, that is, the Vidhan Sabhas by amending the constitution. Accordingly, on 12th September 1996 the Constitution (81st Amendment) Bill was introduced in the Lok Sabha. The said Bill sought to reserve not less than one-third of the total number of seats filled by direct elections in the Lok Sabha and Legislative Assemblies of the state. But the Bill passed in the Parliament without success. Now The Constitution (108 Amendment) Bill or the Women's Reservation Bill is a pending bill which proposes to amend the Indian Constitution to reserve 33 percent of all seats in the House of the People, the Lok Sabha and in all state Legislative Assemblies, Vidhan Sabha for women.

Thus, these are some of the major legislations adopted by the Indian governments from time to time in order to achieve women empowerment. Apart from these acts some of the other legislations ensuring gender equality in India and thereby ending discriminations are- The Factories Act 1948, The Indian Divorce Act 1969, The Protection of Civil Rights Act 1955, The Maternity Benefit Act 1961, Code of Criminal Procedure 1973, The Equal Remuneration Act 1976, The Muslim Women Protection of Rights on Dowry Act 1986, Juvenile Justice Act 2000, and the amended Married Women's Property Act (1874), The Hindu Succession Act (1956) and others.

Apart from these legislations a small glimpse in the Five Year Plans reveal a number of welfare measures proposed for women welfare. The First Five Year Plan (1951-56) called for the establishment of Central-Social Welfare Board (CSWB), organizing of Mahila Mandals or Women's clubs and the Community Development Programmes were a few major steps in this direction. Social services like health, sanitation, education, rehabilitation and housing were given priority.

The Second Five year plan (1956-61) maternity benefits were extended to women and it was directed towards protecting them from injurious work. The Central Social welfare Board took up welfare extension projects. One in each district in the country each serving a group of 25 villages. The Board had also set up two Advisory Committees to look into the hygiene problems and other women care related services.

The Third Five Year Plan (1961-66) period focused more of its attention on the education of girls. Central and State Welfare Boards assisted about

6000 voluntary organisations in the country to provide health and education related services to Indian women. Community Development programmes were implemented which extended assistance to about 1700 Mahila Mandals Training courses to enable adult women to take up employment. There were provisions of services of maternal and child welfare, education, health, nutrition and family planning.

During The Fourth Five Year Plan (1969-74) period the welfare activities being undertaken by the Central Social Welfare Board continued to exist promoting educational, cultural and recreational activities for women and children. At the Block level welfare centres for women were established and with the help of village panchayats the local mahila mandals were allowed to organize welfare programmes for women.

The Fifth Five Year Plan (1974-79) gave priority to Functional Literacy Programme. During this plan period a new consciousness emerged in India which started considering women as critical inputs for national development rather than to be taken as targets for welfare policies. A committee was appointed by the government in 1971 to examine the status of women in India. The committee report pointed out that the women are still ignorant of their legal rights regarding marriage, divorce, inheritance and maternity benefits, also there exists a wide gap between the enrolment of girls and boys in formal educational institutions, the dropout ratio of girls in schools is very high and the status of women is lowered due to the increasing incidence of dowry. The National Plan of action (1976) identified areas of health, family planning, nutrition, sanitation, education for a planned interference for the improvement of conditions of women in India. In 1976 itself under the Ministry of Social Welfare, Women's Welfare and Development Bureau was established to coordinate programmes and policies and initiate steps for development of women.

In The Sixth Five Year Plan (1980-85)the focus was on the development of women. Attempts were made to improve the working conditions and to raise the economic and social status of Indian women. Scholarships were extended to girls, Vocational Training Centres and Industrial Training Institutes were started. Development of Women and Children in Rural Areas (DWCRA) was started in 1982-83 to train women in wide areas of economic activities. Also under the Integrated Rural Development Programme the beneficiaries covered under TRYSEM were women.

The Seventh Five Year Plan (1985-90) emphasized the need to create new avenues of work for women. During this period the development programmes were implemented with the purpose of providing employment and income generating services. 30 percent reservation of seats is stressed in all elected bodies as a transitionary measure in order to establish that women have equal political status when compared to men.

The Eighth Five Year Plan (1990-95) aimed to extend the reach of services to women in both qualitative and quantitative manner. It aimed to strengthen the women groups at the grass-root levels and offer the packages of services to them, to ensure equal share in parental property, to implement vocational training of women, and to implement programmes for the rehabilitation of destitute women and women in distress.

The Ninth Five Year Plan (1997-2002) focused on growth with social justice and equity. Besides objectives concerning the economic growth the ninth plan aimed at ensuring food and nutritional security for all, particularly vulnerable sections of the society along with empowerment of women an socially disadvantaged groups such as Scheduled Castes, Scheduled Tribes and Other Backward Classes and Minorities s agents of socio-economic change and development.

The Tenth Five Year Plan (2002-07) aims to empower women through the implementation of National Policy for Empowerment of Women (2001) into action, along with it to ensure protection, survival and development of children.

The Eleventh Five Year Plan (2007-12) aimed at raising the sex ratio for the age group 0-6 to 935 by 2011-12 and to 950 by 2016-17. The intention of this plan was also to ensure that women and girl child are 33 percent beneficiaries of all government schemes.

The Twelfth Five Year Plan (2012-17) entitled as 'Faster, Sustainable and more Inclusive Growth' is focusing mainly on the growth rate. The Planning Commission is emphasizing for special dispensation for single women, under various government schemes. Under centrally sponsored schemes special attention has been laid on to reserving a certain percentage of jobs for single women. The focus of the Twelfth Five year plan is basically on four key aspects namely- health, education, urbanisation and governance.

Under particular initiatives taken for women following can be included:

(a) **National Commission for Women** : Setup in January 1992, this statutory body has the authority to supervise and study all issues relating to legal and constitutional safeguards existing for women, thereby reviewing, and suggesting amendments.

(b) **Reservation for Women in Local Self-Government**: passed in 1992 by the Parliament, the 73rd Constitutional Amendment Act ensures one-third of the total seats reserved for women in all elected offices in local bodies in both rural and urban areas.

(c) **The National Plan of Action for the Girl Child (1991-2000):** it is to ensure protection, development and survival of the girl child and the ultimate objective of building a better future for the girl child.

(d) **Beti Bachao Beti Padhao Yojna**: Launched on 22nd January 2015, with the aim to generate awareness of welfare services meant for women and girl child.

Every day, thousands of women and girls become victims of violence, atrocities despite the outward acceptance of women being equal to men - violence against women continues to exist in huge proportions

No City for Women

Crime	*2009*	*2010*	*2011*	*2012*	*2013 (till Oct 15)*
Rape	469	507	572	706	1,330
Molestation	552	601	567	727	2,884
Eve-teasin	238	126	165	236	793
Abduction of women	1,655	1,740	2,085	2,210	2,905
Cruelty by husband, in-laws	1,297	1,410	1,585	2,046	2487
Dowry death	141	143	142	134	123

(*Souce:* affidavit submitted by Delhi Police in Court)

Figures released by the National Crime Records Bureau (NCRB) indicate, a total of rape cases reported in India has gone up to 33,707 in 2013 from 24,923 in 2012. The number of rape cases has doubled in Delhi in 2013 compared to the previous year. According to the National Crime Records Bureau data, Madhya Pradesh at an average records 11 rapes every day, with a total of 4,335 such cases, which is the highest in 2013 among all other states. Madhya Pradesh is followed by Rajasthan with 3,285 cases, Maharashtra with 3,063 and Uttar Pradesh with 3,050 rape cases. As per the Global Voices approximately 90% of the 200,000 humans trafficked in India every year are victims of inter-state trafficking. Rajasthan, Haryana and Punjab are major destinations of trafficked brides. Majority of them belong to scheduled castes, scheduled tribes and lower economic groups. 'Baby Falak case' was an eye-opener where a new way of trafficking came to light.

The ITPA (Immoral Trafficking Prevention Act) is concerned totally with prostitution but all aspects of trafficking is not covered under it. Although IPC sec. 366 offers an effective method to tackle mass abuse, it fails to have a provision for rehabilitating victims of trafficking. In spite of all this the brides who are trafficked are unaware of their own rights because of their little or no exposure to education.

Acid attacks another such act of violence against women has become very prevalent in present times. The Cabinet has passed the Criminal Law (Amendment) Bill, 2012, ensuring provisions for acid victims. Acid attacks have been included under a provision in the Indian Penal Code (IPC) under 326A (hurt by acid attack) and 326B (attempt to throw or administer acid).

The proposed law states that the attacker could get a jail term of 10 years to life for causing hurt using acid as the medium.

Since there is an increment in the cases of rape of minors in India, the present government has approved various measures to amend the Protection of Children from Sexual Offences (POCSO) Act. The ordinance pursues death penalty for rapists of girls below 12 years of age. The minimum punishment in case of rape of women has been increased from 7 to 10 years to life. In case of rape of a girl under 16 years of age, the punishment has been increased from 10 to 20 years, again extendable to life imprisonment. While in cases of gang rape of a girl under 16 years, it will be life imprisonment for the convict with the time limit of six months to dispose of the case.

Conclusion

Women empowerment is a crucial step in achieving gender equality and is therefore essential for equitable development. A short insight into the constitutional provisions, the legislations, the Five Year Plans, programmes and policies introduced by the government reveal that there is no dearth of initiatives being taken on the part of successive governments that lays emphasis on women's safety, and ensure her all round development. We do not need more laws, but proper implementation, efficient enforcement machinery, and willingness on the part of the authorities and society is required to ensure its women to breathe in a safe, protected and discrimination free environment. The loopholes that exist at various levels of government machinery prevent the real beneficiary from receiving the benefits of the policies. Efforts towards economic empowerment, access to quality education, well being and health, end of all types of violence, reproductive rights and their increased participation in politics and political life of the country can bring about a concrete change in their plight.

References

Chawla, Monica. Gender Justice: Women and Law in India. New Delhi: Deep and Deep Publications PVT. LTD, 2006. Print.

Goel, Aruna. Women Empowerment: Myth or Reality. New Delhi: Deep and Deep Publications PVT. LTD. 2009. Print.

Kelkar, Meena. Subordination of women: A New Perspective, New Delhi: Discovery Publishing House, 1995. Print.

Mathu, Anuradha. Gender and Development in India: The Indian Scenario. Delhi: Kalpaz Publications, 2008. Print.

Mehta, Rama. Socio-legal Status of Women in India. Delhi: Mittal Publications, 1987. Print.

Majumdar, Maya. Encyclopedia of Gender Equality Through Women Empowerment. New Delhi: Sarup & Sons, 2005. Print.

Lalneihzovi. Women's Development in India, New Delhi: Mittal Publications, 2007. Print.

Sreeramulu, G. Empowerment of Women Through Self Help Groups, Delhi: Kalpaz Publications, 2006. Print.

http://www.thecho.in/files/Satarupa-Pal.pdf web. d.o.a 08.11.2014

http://www.unescap.org/stat/data/syb2011/I-People/Women-empowerment.asp (statistical year book for Asia and the Pacific 2011) web. d.o.a. 08.11.2014.

http://timesofindia.indiatimes.com/india/92-women-raped-in-India-every-day-4-in-Delhi/articleshow/41704691.cms web. d.o.a. 07.11.2014

https://justiceforwomenindia.wordpress.com/tag/women-trafficking-in-india/ web. d.o.a. 07.11.2014.

http://en.wikipedia.org/wiki/Rape_in_India web. d.o.a. 07.11.2014.

https://justiceforwomenindia.wordpress.com/2012/12/06/acid-attack/ web. d.o.a. 07.11.2014

http://mospi.nic.in/sites/default/files/reports_and_publication/statistical_publication/social_statistics/WM16ConstitutionalLegalRights.pdf

https://timesofindia.indiatimes.com/india/death-penalty-for-rape-of-minors-president-approves-ordinance/articleshow/63873817.cms

https://secure.urkund.com/view/externalSource/redirect/aHR0cHM6Ly9lbi53aWtpcGVkaWEub3JnL3dpa2kvUHJvdGVjdGlvbl9vZl9Xb21lbl9mcm9tX0RvbWVzdGljX1Zpb2xlbmNlX0FjdCxfMjAwNQ2

https://secure.urkund.com/view/externalSource/redirect/aHR0cHM6Ly9pbmRpYW5jaXZpbHMuY29tL21hdGVyaWFsL1NvY2lldHkucGRm0

https://secure.urkund.com/view/externalSource/redirect/aHR0cDovL3d3dy5zdXJhbXlhLmNvbS9pbmRpYS9pbmRpYV9jb25zdGl0dXRpb24ucGhw0

14

Rights of Women against Sexual Harassment at the Workplace in India

— *Bhavna Suman*

Rights of Women against Sexual Harassment at the Workplace in India

Women have been a part of the employment sphere and continue to join in large numbers. The number of women in several kinds of occupations worldwide has been increasing, but they have been burdened with growing inequalities as a result of discriminatory socio-economic practices. This brings into focus the question of women's rights at the workplace. At workplace, women's rights are marked by equal opportunities. Women employees are entitled to equal treatment, equal remuneration and the requisite benefits at the workplace.

However there is discrimination against women at the workplace. It is raised in numerous cases when a woman employee has faced various kinds of discrimination at the workplace. Sexual harassment at the workplace is regarded as one such kind of discrimination and the most common yet dreadful grievance that working women have been facing.

Discrimination and sexual harassment of women at workplace is an unbridled feature which is evident in two significant cases. In Rupan Deol Bajaj vs. K.P.S.Gill and another 1995(6) SCC 0194 case, an IAS officer, Rupan Deol Bajaj claimed that she was sexually harassed by the Director General of Police K.P.S. Gill in 1988. A scrupulous case ensued after an F.I.R. was lodged by Deol and her husband Mr. Bajaj, as a result of which K.P.S. Gill was fined heavily for Rs.2,50,000 in lieu of rigorous imprisonment.

In an important case, Tarun Tejpal, the founder of Tehelka, was charged with rape in an FIR by the Goa police, which sent a team to Delhi to arrest him. A young woman journalist alleged that she was sexually assaulted by him on two days at a Tehelka event in Goa. He was also charged with outraging her modesty and rape, as he had dominance and authority over the woman. Such an offence carries a maximum sentence of life imprisonment and a minimum 10 years in jail.[1] Laws are made in order to look into the atrocities that women face but the vital question which arises is that, they have to be effective in reality and act as a deterrent.

In all these cases, it was recognised that some mechanisms must be at place to look into such violation of women's rights. In both these cases the accused have found a way out of avoiding imprisonment, either owing to a cumbersome or ineffective procedure involved to deal with such cases or their influential position in comparison with the women complainants.

In order to address discrimination of women at the workplace, special rights of women need to be taken into account. This can be substantiated by views of Judith Squires, where she examines a change in focus of contemporary "equality" policies and theories that are marked by a shift in the focus of sameness to difference. The emergence of a commitment to pursuing and theorizing equality has led to the acknowledgment and celebration of differences.[2] Thus, women's rights at the workplace has to be looked at by keeping in mind this respect for difference and should focus at endowing women with special rights and protection mechanisms.

Cases of this kind challenge the literature, discourse and understanding on rights that have been popular since the enlightenment in liberal theory even though it challenges them now. Values such as equality, freedom, rationality, and rights have been central to liberal political theory. It claimed these values on the basis of a conception of individuals as free and equal beings, which in turn led women to reflect on their status *vis-a-vis* men.[3] Later, when feminist theories emerged, they also relied upon some of these assumptions of liberal theory to challenge the patriarchal basis of political power.

At the international level, the United Nations introduced the idea of political and legal rights which was applicable to all individuals. However with time, it was realised that women's rights should be addressed specifically in every field. The Convention on the Elimination of All kinds of Discrimination (CEDAW)[4] demands emphasis on special rights of women, by promoting a substantive model of equality, which includes equality of opportunity for both men and women. The U.N.'s 1995 Conference on Women in Beijing called on nations to "mainstream a gender perspective". According to the *Platform for Action* of the Beijing conference, "the differences between women's and men's achievements and activities are still not recognised in many countries due to their socially constructed gender roles rather than unalterable biological differences".[5]

It was recognised that special rights for women are required because gender roles are socially constructed. However in India where women are increasing in the work place this kind of recognition is lacking. There are special rights for maternity leave and other benefits entitled to women workers like restriction in hours of work at night, safety from physical hazards etc. but for long there was no right for protection against sexual harassment at the workplace. The Sexual Harassment at the Workplace Act came into being in 2013 when it was passed on 26th February 2013 after a long struggle.

Sexual harassment at the workplace

In my paper, I examine the contention that though women have attained formal equal rights but their rights at the workplace seem to be restricted in many ways Firstly, despite the establishment of equality of women in employment in principle, it is far from being implemented. Secondly, disparities put them in a position of vulnerability and dependency. Thirdly, I see how the rights there is also a sense of disadvantage with regard to the kinds of jobs occupied by women as compared to men, and these of women at workplace, how they get violated due to the existing stereotypes in society, and gender discriminatory attitudes. Discrimination against women in modern professions is a complex and multifaceted phenomenon and sexual harassment at workplace is the result of many socio-psychological and cultural factors. It is a degrading experience that women workers have been facing and expresses male power and control over female sexuality that sustain patriarchal relations.[6] Lack of implementation of existing provisions of equal rights was first pointed out by feminist writer Catherine Mckinnon who also examined sexual harassment of women at workplace. Sexual harassment is all about expression of male power over women that sustain patriarchal relations.[7] It reminds women of their vulnerability and subjugated status. In a society where violence against women, both subtle and direct, is borne out of the patriarchal values operating in society, force women's conformity to gendered roles. These patriarchal values and attitudes of both men and women pose the greatest challenge in resolution and prevention of sexual harassment. [8] Several studies find that sexual harassment is still prevalent, concealed, and there in all kinds of organisations.

So far in India, sexual harassment faced by women at workplace was seen as criminal offence however; one of the major challenges in application of this law is the definition of workplace. Laws in the Indian Penal Code (section 294, 354, 509) could be evoked when a woman is sexually harassed but these were framed as offences that either amount to obscenity in public or act that are seen to violate the modesty of women. Over the years these laws and legal categories were severely criticized as a mechanism for normalizing violence against women.

In India, it has been only few years since sexual harassment was for the first time recognised by the Supreme Court as human rights violation that is discrimination based on gender which affects women's Right to Life and Livelihood. The Court defined sexual harassment clearly and provided guidelines for employers to redress and prevent sexual harassment at workplace. The evolution of sexual harassment law in India began with the landmark case of **Vishaka vs. State of Rajasthan**[9] in 1997, which has been credited with establishing sexual harassment as illegal. The Supreme Court judgment in 1997 made a remarkable intervention in recommending reform of the law in this direction and which marked a discursive break with the categories used in the past. This judgment claimed that there was a need for legal intervention to ensure constitutional rights of women. Even when the Supreme Court has given mandatory guidelines, known as Vishaka Guidelines, for resolution and prevention of sexual harassment enjoining employers by holding them responsible for providing safe work environment for women, the issue still remains in the lurch for most women and employers.

"Vishaka guidelines apply to both organised and unorganised work sectors and to all women whether working part time, on contract or in voluntary/ honorary capacity. The guidelines worked as a broad framework, which put emphasis on prevention and within which all appropriate preventive measures can be adopted."[10]

"Sexual Harassment of Women at Work place (Prevention, Prohibition and Redressal) Bill, 2006drawn out by National Commission for Women (NCW), conferred upon women the right to protection against sexual harassment and the right to livelihood."[11] It also provided for the prevention and redressal of sexual harassment of women. International conventions and instruments like Convention on the Elimination of All Forms of Discrimination against Women (CEDAW)[12] too recognise the "right to protection from sexual harassment and the right to work with dignity" as universal human rights and these rights have been ratified by the Government of India. There was a long wait for a law to come into place, with the sexual harassment at the workplace Bill languishing on paper since 2004 when it was first introduced by NCW and the Lawyers' Collective. The bill underwent amendments in 2006, 2008 and finally 2010 before it was tabled in the Indian Parliament i.e. Lok Sabha. It was passed by the Lok Sabha in September 2012 and the Rajya Sabha on 26th February 2013. It got a final approval by the President of India in April 2013.

A new debate on violence against women in the form of rape, criminal offence and sexual assault has emerged in the light of the recent rape and death of a 23 year-old woman in New Delhi and the public outrage and widespread protests by the people. This case of gruesome sexual assault of a woman, named 'Nirbhaya' by the media and civil society has garnered a voice that could not be ignored by the government and the law-makers of this country. Laws relating to sexual assault in all forms have come under scrutiny by activists, lawyers and decision makers so amendments and primacy was given to constitution of new laws. The Criminal Law (Amendment) Act, 2013 looks at a wide range of crimes against women and the Sexual Harassment of Women at the Workplace (Prevention and Redressal) Act, 2013 [13] brings in its ambit even domestic workers and agriculture labour, both organised and unorganised sectors. As per the act, sexual harassment includes any one or more of unwelcome acts or behaviour like physical contact and advances, a demand or request for sexual favours or making sexually coloured remarks or showing pornography. [14]

Legal provisions for Sexual harassment at the Workplace in India

As women have moved from the private sphere to the public domain several new laws are needed for their protection. In this context women's rights at workplace are paramount for giving them equality with men. So, evolving laws for women for prevention of atrocities like sexual harassment at the workplace or for gender justice is necessary for protection of women's rights.

An approach by feminist legal scholars states that women have a subordinate status in society where patriarchal attitudes and norms are deep-rooted and thus, women inherently become weak and vulnerable to acts of violence. In this situation, feminist scholars develop a protectionist attitude towards women whereby they seek legal resolutions to deal with the intrinsically weak and subjugated position of women. Ratna Kapur refers to this conception as patriarchal discourses.[15] She argues that the protectionist approach accepts the traditional and patriarchal discourses that construct women as weak, biologically inferior, modest and incapable of decision-making. Such so-called feminine characteristics are perceived as natural, immutable and thus, as the appropriate starting place for legal regulation.[16] When we refer to discrimination faced by women, feminists, activists and lawyers propose legislations or legal provisions in order to protect women which, in the process are expected to ultimately enable protection and equal rights to them.

Ratna Kapur and Brenda Cossman have examined the relationship between women and law in promoting equality and advancing women's equality. However, they also argue that law which has been instrumental in women's struggles for social change can have its own limitations. Thus, the main concern should be for reform of discriminatory laws.

The question of implementation of laws emerges as another important aspect dealt by feminist scholars like Nandita Haksar who examines the way in which law has reflected patriarchal oppression.[17] Lina Gonsalves focuses on the enforcement of laws that were intended to benefit women, and argues that law enforcers discriminate between men and women and unconsciously tend to reflect traditional and rigid attitudes towards women.[18] Similarly, Flavia

Agnes interrogates the impact of law reforms on women and questions whether laws intended for women's benefit have lived up to their promise.[19] As far as the law enforcement agencies, it is often observed that there are scores of legislations that are directed to facilitate rights of women. But how far are these utilised for delivering justice to women is a valid question.

So, identifying the tensions between laws only providing for a formal equality to women unable to impart a substantive equality; and the existing social stereotypes of inequality, patriarchy and subordination of women, there are two important aspects that need to be looked at. First, whether laws have the capacity of prohibiting sexual harassment at the workplace at community level and raise awareness about this issue in the real sense. Second, it is required to continually interpret and improve the strength of these laws which have evolved through legislation, and court-made laws, and have found a pertinent place within the debate on affirmative action in India.

Law has played an important role in advancement of women's rights, evident in different phases of development of women's movements in India since colonial times, whether it was the protectionist role of the social reformers or enfranchisement of women later. After this, women's organisations had begun to pursue their demands to include legislative reform in inheritance and marriage. According to Jana M. Everett, the main strategy followed in India 'was the passage of legislations guaranteeing sex equality and special provisions for women in the areas of employment, politics, education and personal law'.[20] In late 1970s, law played a prominent role in dealing with issues of rape and dowry. The most discussed issue post-1990s has been violence against women and sexual assault and harassment.[21]

Despite the path followed by the women's organisations through varied interventions for protection of women against discrimination and violence, the contemporary women's movement's commitment for law has been contradictory in character. Even after successful campaigns by feminist activists for reforms of civil and criminal law, the legislative enactments were inadequate according to the demands of the movement. It met with success in creating public awareness on issues of violence and discrimination against women but when it came to the role of these legislations in combating such numerous kinds of discrimination, there was disillusionment with law.

The guidelines for seeking protection of women's rights, developed by women's groups and women's commissions, were premised on two views : women as a class are non - working spouses and their only contribution is unpaid domestic labour; or men and women are equal partners and hence their rights, duties and responsibilities are equal and of a similar nature.[22] The second view of Flavia Agnes seems to be important and relevant to my idea of women's equality which is intrinsically sought after. The pursuit of equality of women could not ignore unequal power relations existing within the public as well as private spheres of our society which always culminates into unequal treatment of women in all endeavors of life.

There was no specific law on sexual harassment but the existing criminal, social, civil and labour laws dealt with this subject. The Indian Penal Code (1860), labour legislations like the Factories Act (1948), The Maternity Benefit Act, 1961, The Employees State's Insurance Act (1948), Mines Act (1952), Plantation Act (1951) and Equal Remuneration Act (1976)[23] protect the rights of women workers and ensured equality in employment that were to provide a dignified life, but these provisions did not deal with sexual harassment directly. Sections 354 and 509 of the Indian Penal Code provides for punishment in form of imprisonment or fine in case of any obscene act in public places in the form of a song, ballad or words or use of criminal force against any woman, intending to outrage her modesty.[24] Eve teasing' can also be punished under this provision.

The role of judiciary assumed greater importance due to this absence of enacted law to provide for effective enforcement of a guarantee against sexual harassment at workplace, the supreme court had laid down guidelines and norms that were to be observed at all workplaces or other institutions, till the time a legislation came about. The Supreme Court in a landmark judgment, the Vishakha case, declared sexual harassment as a criminal offence. It took into account constitutional provisions/legislations of the India and the Beijing Statement of Principles of the Independence of the Judiciary 1995 and the Convention on the Elimination of All Forms of Discrimination against Women (CEDAW)[25] to lay down the guidelines on sexual harassment.[26]

The Supreme Court's judgment directed organisations to include an appropriate code of conduct in their services conditions and contracts and set up a complaint mechanism according to its decision. For example, several organisations were urged to constitute a complaints mechanism like in the Ministry of Stataistics. According to the Ministry office memorandum, "it is necessary and expedient for employers in workplaces to observe certain guidelines to ensure prevention of sexual harassment of women." [27] It has made it obligatory on a company that employs women to set up Committee, with at least one woman as a member to sort out grievances and complaints of this nature. By this, responsibility would be imposed on the employer and other responsible persons in workplaces or other institutions to prevent or dissuade the acts of sexual harassment and also offer procedures for the resolutions, settlement, or prosecution of acts of sexual harassment by taking all steps required. Thus, the preservation and enforcement of the women's right to equality in all workplaces.

Since the judgment in the Vishaka case, several cases regarding sexual harassment at the workplace have come up and have been dealt with, based on Supreme Court guidelines. Cases of sexual harassment at workplace have evolved by way of reference to the Vishaka case and following the definition of sexual harassment stated in this landmark case.

Important Cases against Sexual Harassment in India

In the case, *Chairman Railway board and others v. Chandrima Das and others*, it was held that the right of the victim, under Article 21 was violated and the state was under the constitutional duty to pay her compensation. In *Apparel Export promotion Council v. A.K.Chopra* [28]*(1999) 1 SCC 759* sexual harassment was committed by a superior ranking employee against a lower ranking employee. The allegation was that Ms. Suchitra Vishnoi was taken to a room on the pretext of taking dictation from the Chairman of the Apparel Export Promotion Council by his private secretary, A.K. Chopra. In the High Court, the appeal filed by the Apparel Export Promotion Council was dismissed, and the appeal filed by A. K. Chopra was partly allowed. On appeal to the Supreme Court the chief justice said that any action, a gesture whether directly or by implication, aims at or has the tendency to outrage the modesty of a female employee, must fall under the general concept of the definition of sexual harassment.

Thus, in the APOC decision, the order of the High Court was set aside and the punishment as imposed by the Disciplinary Authority and upheld by the Department Appellate Authority of removal of the chairman from service was upheld and restored.[29] The Supreme Court justified that any reduction in punishment is bound to have a demoralizing effect on women employees and is a retrograde step. This case brought out the definition of sexual harassment by pointing out that physical contact is not essential to comprise sexual harassment at workplace. There are certain indicators given in the Supreme guidelines which prove an action amounting to sexual harassment at workplace.[30]

In the judgment delivered by the Andhra Pradesh High Court in *K.S.Triveni and others v. Union of India and others* 2002 III CLR 690[31], following Madras High Court, the courts have allowed employment of women during night shift and the two High Courts have struck down the clause (b) of sub-section (1) of section 66 of the aforesaid Act as unconstitutional. *K.S.Triveni case* brought changes to section 66 of Factories Act, wherein the restrictions on the working hours of women were relaxed for certain industries, empowering the State Governments to draft time limitations or completely relax the restrictions for certain industries like software technology. But even though the state governments allowed women to work during night shifts, the onus of responsibility lay on the employers to provide adequate security to women employees. The security concerns and rights of women employees against sexual harassment can be understood by referring to the Som Mittal vs. Government of Karnataka Criminal Appeal No.206 of 2008 wherein Pratibha Murthy, a BPO employee working for Hewitt and Packard Global Software

Ltd., Bangalore who was raped and murdered by the cab driver while going for her duty. In this case the company failed to comply with the adequate safety and security measures drafted by the Government in the Gazette for women working during night shifts. The Court relied on the definition of an 'employer' which states that an employer who is a person being in charge of or owning ultimate control over affairs of an establishment.[32]

In *Shenaz Mudbhatkal v.Saudi Arabian Airlines (1998)*, the Bombay High Court in India was for the first time confronted with a sexual harassment case. Shenaz was an employee of Saudi Arabian Airlines and the harasser was Station Manager (Airport) Abdul Allah Bahrani. Shenaz decided to put an end to the continuous sexual harassment by taking up the matter with the higher authorities of the petitioner Company at its Head Office in Jeddah, Saudi Arabia. The high court decided the case in favour of the victim. The petitioner challenged the said order but his special leave petition was dismissed by the Supreme Court.[33]

Rupan Deol Bajaj and another v K.P.S.Gill and another (1989) involved sexual harassment of the subordinate employee by her superior. Rupan Deol Bajaj, an Officer of the Indian Administrative Service (I.A.S) of the Punjab Cadre and then working as the Special Secretary, Finance, filed a complaint with the Inspector General of Police, Chandigarh Union Territory charging offences under Sections 341, 342, 352, 354, and 509 of the Indian Penal Code (IPC) committed by Mr. K.P.S. Gill, the Director General of Police, Punjab on July 18, 1988 at a dinner party. Mr. Gill moved the High Court by filing a petition under Section 482 Cr. P.C. for quashing the F.I.R. and the complaint. The Supreme Court was of the view that "the High Court had committed a gross error of law in quashing the FIR and the complaint and K.P.S. Gill was convicted and was fined Rupees 2, 50,000 in lieu of 3 months rigorous imprisonment."[34]

All these cases can be attributed as landmark cases on sexual harassment at the workplace and have re-identified the meaning of sexual harassment as given in the definition as per the guidelines of Vishaka judgment. They have in fact, provided a significant momentum to reporting and complaints of sexual harassment at the workplace in a big way and expressed the need for legislation to limit sexual harassment at the workplace.

Institutional Responses to Sexual Harassment at the Workplace

Keeping in mind the importance of institutions in dealing with violation of rights of women, I sought to explore how the institutional environment handles discrimination at employment, mainly cases of sexual harassment of women at their workplace. Here I would also like to mention that by 'institutions' I am referring to several kinds of institutions. To begin with, the concerned institutions (both public and private workplaces) are liable to tackle the issue of gender discrimination and sexual harassment through their policies and code of conduct manuals. These institutions have to comply with the legal guidelines that are enlisted in the formal legal system of our country and were also expected to intervene in cases of violations of laws. In order to monitor these processes the role of national level institutions like National Commission for Women (henceforth NCW) and National Human Right Commission (henceforth NHRC) becomes significant. As a result of pressure created by the active women's movement in the 1980s on the state regarding women's interests through legislation and other means, a demand for an institutional set up came upon the state to improve the status of women. Legal reforms were accompanied by the establishment of the NCW in the early 1990s which was expected to engage in gender equality and empowerment of women. The lack of constitutional machinery, judicial ability and social interest formed the impetus and need for the formation of these institutions.

The National Commission for Women (NCW) constituted under the National Commission for Women Act, 1990 has been quite active in highlighting the issue of sexual harassment and creating awareness among the general public. Similarly, the National Human Rights Commission (NHRC) is competent to inquire suo motu or on a petition presented to it by a victim or any person on his or her behalf into a complaint of violation of human rights or abetment thereof.[35] Both the commissions follow the judicial approach as manifested in Vishaka's case (1997).

There have been instances when sexual harassment issues have come to the Commissions for grievance redress and have been resolved by direct counselling by the institution and by setting up inquiry committees and directing it towards the organisation where a harassment case has taken place. NCW has recognised such cases and tried to resolve them with the powers and resources that it possesses. One such instance is of Sangeeta Sharma, a 33-year-old advocate practicing at the Andhra Pradesh High Court, committed suicide by consuming pesticide. The bright young lawyer took the extreme step as she could no longer bear the constant sexual harassment by her male colleagues and senior advocates. The victimised woman advocate had to resign and suffer professionally to put an end to her ordeal and she ended her life. In her suicide note, Sangeeta named advocates Vijay Kumar and G. Narasimha Naidu besides 15 others for sexual harassment and abetment to suicide. As a follow-up, the NCW had written to the Bar Council of India (BCI) and bar councils of all the states to expeditiously set up sexual harassment committees in the High Courts and the Supreme Court. But the response has been disappointing and reflected on "the insensitivity towards women's issues in the judiciary as the Andhra Pradesh Bar Council—which ideally should have taken up the initiative after Sangeeta's tragic suicide—wrote back to the commission to approach the registrar of the Andhra Pradesh High Court to set up such a committee."

The NCW in its 'Search for a Vision Statement on Women Empowerment vis-à-vis Legislation and Judicial Decisions' prepared by Indian Trust for innovation and Social Change (NCW), focussed at the statutory benefits in favour of women and stated that judicial activism through a process of affirmative action and protective discrimination.

While looking at an institutional framework, the role of another set of 'institutions' or civil society institutions/organisations i.e. the Non Governmental Organisations (henceforth NGOs) is indispensable, especially the women's rights based groups, which effectively undertake sexual harassment as their cause or agenda. Delhi based NGOs Sakshi and Saheli have been actively involved with protection of women's rights in all respects and they have strongly advocated the rights of women against sexual harassment at the workplace. Sanhita, a Kolkata based NGO, an initiative of women activists, has been instrumental in pressurising the institutions and redress mechanism to deal with sexual harassment issues. The Centre for Women's Development Studies (CWDS), a research centre working for realisation of women's equality and development and Maitreyi, another such organisation develops a feminist perspective in understanding women's issues and the women's movement, and gender sensitisation.

Efforts for Sexual Harassment Legislations

For women, sexual harassment remains an impediment to equal opportunity, dignity and security at the workplace, the absence of law or its inadequacy relegates gender specific violations of women workers to a private problem that is to be negotiated by individual risks and costs. Legal recognition does not put an end to the problem of sexual harassment but its labeling as a legal injury does establish normative standards for acceptable workplace conduct and employer responsibility. The issue of sexual harassment at workplace requires multi- sectoral interventions that help develop a culture of intolerance towards it rather than denial of the phenomena. Civil law enables scope for developing such a culture as well as providing redress. It can enable cross-sectoral participation in addressing sexual harassment and provide non-punitive and non- adversarial responses.[36]

With increasing visibility and attention drawn to sexual harassment, the issues in fixing the legal liability reflect on different perspectives of influencing the outcome and its ability to deliver gender justice. The perspectives range from using male standards, to protectionist approaches which stereotype women. There is also a move towards taking into account the subjectivity of the victim rather than using stereotypes of any kind. This evolution in standards marks a shift towards a substantive application of equality, one that accommodates the subjective experience of the victim in a particular context rather than imposing a uniform standard.[37] There have been difficulties in proving sexual harassment and also the reluctance of courts to award damages against the wrongdoers in deterrent amount. In many other cases, it has been observed that criminal sanctions against sexual harassment have proved inadequate.

The Supreme Court's decision in Vishaka is a remarkable instance of judicial law-making and activism. However, this judgement had its own limitations: only indirect references regarding compensation and relief are made under public law available to the victim. The courts in India are not concerned with developing jurisprudence of compensation based on tort. A general theory for sexual harassment other than educational and employment areas could not be developed. The Supreme Court also did not address the question of the victim's difficulties of proving a case of sexual harassment. According to D.K. Srivastava there is a problem with the application of the objective test. On one hand, there is a possibility that the conservative element of society might consider women complaining of sexual harassment as having invited it by their conduct. On the other hand, there is a possibility that certain groups of people are likely to hold different and perhaps unconventional views. They may dismiss many complaints as being frivolous. Similarly, delays in reporting may be caused because of the complainant's desire to seek advice from family or friends or because of other considerations. Such delays could prove fatal to her claim.

Despite the institutional measures and recommendations there have been certain drawbacks and laxity by the organisation in dealing with sexual harassment at the workplace. There is lack of reporting of sexual harassment at workplace for which there can be several reasons. Delays and reluctance on part of the employers on one hand and fear and hesitation of the employees on the other hand, which prevents them to come out with their complaints. Second reason could be attributed to the existing patriarchal attitudes of the employers which remain unchanged.

In order to effectiveness of institutions, there is a need to consider factors such as the institutional design[38], patterns of recruitment, quality of personnel, organisational culture, internal conflicts for distribution of power and allocation of resources within the institution, systems of autonomy and accountability. As for their advisory role in the policymaking area, the commission has been treated as a purely recommendatory body whose recommendations are not binding. Sheba Tejani observes that sometimes Complaints Committee is not instituted properly, also there are times when most of these committees have not adhered to the guidelines and when the Complaints Committee fails in its duty then the private sectors employees' only alternative is to file a civil suit in a court of law.[39]

Protection to Women from Sexual Harassment at Work Place Act, 2013[40]

In the cases of sexual harassment at workplace, we see that the same debates and issues come up and the victims are not able to get a proper redress mechanism. There are bodies or institutions which look at this aspect and have followed guidelines and principles dealing with such cases, owing to the existing landmark judgments. However several issues come up in this area as numerous limitations of the Vishaka judgment have been examined. Women's groups have been trying to arrive at a solution to expand and determine the workplace and its nature. They have also clearly sought to create structures of redress for different categories of workers. As a result, a bill in order to prevent, protect and redress sexual harassment of women at the workplace was drawn out by the Lawyers' Collective and a thorough debate on the draft of the bill was undertaken in 2003. After the limitations of the proposed bill were discussed and overcome, the National Commission for Women (NCW) proposed Sexual Harassment Bill (2006). [41]

The revised version of this bill i.e. the Protection of Women against Sexual Harassment at Workplace Bill, 2010 had been introduced in the Lok Sabha by the Ministry Women and Child Development and its objective was to enact a comprehensive legislation to provide safe, secure and enabling environment free from all forms of sexual harassment to every woman, irrespective of her age or employment status. Finally, in September 2012, the Sexual Harassment at the Workplace bill, 2010 was passed by the Parliament.[42] This bill was guided by Women and Child Development Minister Krishna Tirath, and passed without discussion.[43] Finally, the new law on sexual harassment at the workplace was enforced in April 2013 after the assent of the President.

The Protection of Women against Sexual Harassment at the Workplace Act, 2013 by recognising the social discomfort that the complainant experiences, proposes that no information about the complainant or the complaint can be made known to the media or public in any manner even in response to the RTI applications. The Act will apply to all companies and institutions – both public and private – to establish female-led internal committees to follow up on sexual harassment complaints. The act gave a definition of "aggrieved woman" referring to those women who would get protection under the Act. The act was applicable to all women, irrespective of their age or employment status, both in the organised or unorganised sectors, public or private sectors. The Act has clients, customers and domestic workers too in its purview as it included the 'unorganised sector' where the number of such workers is generally less than 10 like in hospitals, nursing homes, educational institutions, sports institutes, stadiums, sports complex. It also rendered any place visited by the employee during the course of employment including the transportation and specified it as a 'workplace'. According to the Act, every employer is required to constitute an Internal Complaints Committee at each office or branch with 10 or more employees. The District Officer is required to constitute a Local Complaints Committee at each district, and at the block level if there was a requirement. The Committee is supposed to complete the inquiry within a time period of 90 days and after the completion of the inquiry, the report to be sent to the employer or the District Officer, depending on the case, and how it is to be handled was determined within 60 days. Complaints Committees have the powers of civil courts for gathering evidence and are required to provide for conciliation before initiating an inquiry, if requested by the complainant. The Act prescribes penalties for employers. Non-compliance with the provisions of the Act shall be punishable with a fine of up to ₹50,000. Repeated violations may lead to higher penalties and cancellation of licence or registration to conduct business. In the case of false or malicious complaint, the Act provides for action against the complainant in accordance with service rules and in any other manner in case no service rules exist.[44]

There are some sections of this legislation which has drawn sharp criticism from women's rights groups. This Act says that women, whose complaint is found to be untrue, will be punished. This will act as a restraint to the filing of complaints and goes against the spirit of the Act. The composition of the committees is also not satisfactory and there is no guarantee that the process will be time-bound. AIDWA pointed out that the "project workers" such as ICDS, ASHA and Midday meal workers have been left out of the ambit of the Act, which are largest and fastest growing groups of working women and their conditions of work make them extremely vulnerable to abuse and violence.[45] Naina Kapur, a Delhi based lawyer pointed out that the Act "is badly drafted and offers us mediocrity". Other critics like former Chief Justice J.S. Verma[46] have been opposed to the provision requiring conciliation before an inquiry, saying that it is "yet another way in which the dignity of women is undermined".

The law leaves it up to the internal committee to decide a monetary fine to be paid by the perpetrator, depending on their "the income and financial status". So, as Albeena Shakil, a women's rights activist from New Delhi says it finally comes to this, that low-level executive will likely pay a lower fine for harassment than a senior executive. The law also does not define the range of financial penalties.[47] The worst lacuna lay in a provision in the law that calls for punishment for making a false complaint. Women with legitimate grievances may keep quiet, fearing that they will not be able to prove their allegations and may instead be hounded for making false claims, says Suneeta Dhar, director at Delhi-based women's group Jagori.[48]

The Sexual Harassment at the workplace Act was a much anticipated development and was a pertinent pathway towards ensuring women a safe and healthy work environment. As far as the implementation of this Act is concerned, there are certain obstacles that have come into discussion ever since the Act came into force one and a half years back. Lack of awareness about what constitutes sexual harassment is the biggest hurdle that comes into forefront. There is a need to educate employees about the provisions enlisted in the Act and made aware of what constitutes the 'act of sexual harassment'.

Several workshop sessions were organised by Centre for Transformimg India that is a non – profit trust.[49] In this programme Human Resources managers asked a number of questions regarding what constitutes sexual harassment at the workplace and how should a company go about its internal investigation regarding sexual harassment at workplace complaints. Another important aspect was regarding how an organisation should handle if victim files a police complaint and also when the accusation was found to be false. It discussed the definition of an 'extended workplace' like company arranged transportation and business trips. The new sexual harassment law covered many things like verbal and non- verbal 'conduct of sexual nature'. Several organisations and non- governmental organisations NGOs were required to form an internal complaints committees that were supposed to receive written complaints, investigate them and make recommendations to the employer.

Indira Jaising recommended a formal procedure to be laid out in the form of an Internal Complaints Committee (ICC) in all organisations as it would enable a conduct of enquiry objectively i.e. without giving in to misunder standings and help in protection of women from sexual harassment at workplace.[50]

Finally, activists note that while the new law starts by advocating prevention of sexual harassment, it dilutes the responsibility of the employer in preventing it. Since the fine for an offence has to be paid by the employee, it does not give companies much incentive to take active steps to create a harassment-free environment at work, say activists. "The penalty for not setting up the internal committee is a maximum of 50,000 rupees ($919). This is much less as compared to the U.S.,where women can sue their companies for turning a blind eye to sexual harassment and get compensation of up to $300,000, depending on the size of the company."[51]

Activists realised that the legislation is not strong enough to empower these women and even if it did, how to enforce it in informal, unregulated workplaces would remain a pertinent question. At this juncture, therefore, seeking a guarantee of speedy and effective implementation of law is the most crucial deliberation and as suggested by lawyers and activists, there is a need for special tribunals for hearing appeals regarding sexual harassment at the workplace.

Thus, it is realised that women's difference is an imperative consideration in rethinking the basic conceptions of legislative policies as the question that comes up here is as to what is that the feminists and the legal approach is seeking as equality. The framing of gender equality as equal treatment in law excludes all forms of discrimination of individuals as members of social groups that are disadvantaged. In the discussion on discrimination of women and equality, it is important to look at the two aspects of equality. Equality can be classified into formal and substantive equality. Formal equality is a principle of equal treatment: individuals who are alike should be treated alike, according to their actual characteristics rather than stereotypical assumptions made about them. It is a principle that can be applied either to a single individual, whose right to be treated on his or her own merits can be viewed as a right of individual autonomy, or to a group, whose members seek the same treatment as members of other, similarly situated groups.[52] While formal sex equality judges the form of a rule, requiring that it treat women and men on the same terms without special barriers or favours on account of their sex, substantive equality looks to a rule's results or effects. Formal rule equality often does not produce equal results because of significant differences in the characteristics and circumstances of women and men.[53] Equal treatment of women in the real sense will come about by laying stress on substantive equality. In this paper, I have dealt with the need for equal rights of women at the workplace with regard to equality and special rights of women against discrimination.

Tyson Smith and Michael Kimmel observe that while workplace discrimination cases emerge from a definition of equality that requires that we treat those who are like as if they were alike, sexual harassment proceeds from a different assumption about equality: it recognises essential differences and therefore relies on the notion that equality also requires that we treat 'unlikes' as if they were unlike.[54] Sexual harassment is examined on the basis of principles of impartiality and non-biasness towards others. Thus we see that the meaning of equal treatment with regard to gender is confounded by the fact that the law is unable to account for actual differences between women and men which would mean that similar treatment might be discriminatory and treating them differently on the other hand would be discriminate.

So, neutral laws and policies treating men and women at par may seem to be non-discriminatory, but could be discriminatory because women may be at a disadvantage as compared to men due to existing inequalities. This approach helps us to identify the weaknesses of formal or laws and policies as they are neutral in application. So we see that the opportunities presented through formal equality, which manifest themselves in gender-neutral policy or law, may actually discriminate against women.

Thus, the new Sexual harassment at the workplace (Prevention and Protection) Act, 2013, is one such formal guiding principle that certainly hopes to offer positive light to the issue of workplace harassment and may change the scenario of grievance redress mechanism in cases of sexual harassment at the workplace in the country, however how far it will help in bringing about a change in the existing patriarchal attitudes is a unfathomable question. The level of success that it can bring in tackling sexual harassment at workplace differently, than it has been done in the past, can be gauged once its existing inadequacies are overcome rightfully.

References

Primary Sources

India gets new law against sexual harassment of women at workplaces', Press Trust of India, April 25, 2013 at www.ibnlive.in.com.

'Sexual Harassment of Women at Workplace (Prevention, Protection, Redressal) Bill 2006' at www.ncw.nic.in.

'Sexual harassment of women at workplace bill passed amidst coal-gate chaos', Press Trust of India Updated: September 03, 2012, at www.ndtv.com.

All India Meeting of Chief Justices of High Courts on Women at www.ncw.nic.in.

Apparel Export Promotion Council vs A.K. Chopra on 20 January, 1999 at www.indiankanoon.org/doc/856194. This case has been quoted in NCW report, also at www.indlaw.com .

International Women's Rights Action Watch Asia Pacific (IWRAW) (2005), *IWRAW Asia Pacific Occasional Papers Series No. 7*, Kuala Lumpur, Malaysia, 1.

Justice J. S. Verma Report. 'Report of the committee on Amendments to Criminal Law' (Justice J.S. Verma, Justice Leila Seth and Gopal Subramanium), January 23, 2013 at *blogs.wsj.com.*

List of various Central Government Acts, Ministry of Labour and Employment, Government of India at www.labour.nic.in/act/welcome.html.

National Commission for Women Act (Act No. 20 of 1990), Govt. of India and See Sec.12, Protection of Human Rights Act, 1993 of National Human Rights Commission (NHRC) published by NCW and NHRC on their websites www.ncw.nic.in and www.nhrc.nic.in(accessed July 16, 2009).

Platform of Action, Report of the Fourth World Conference on Women (4-15 September 1995) Beijing, Paragraph 27 at www.un.org/esa/gopher-data/conf/fwcw/off/a—20.en .

Rupan *deol Bajaj and Anr. v. K.P.S.Gill* and another 1995(6) SCC 0194 at www.indlaw.com .

Sexual harassment at the workplace Act, 2013 at www.ncw.nic.in.

The Convention on the Elimination of All kinds of Discrimination (CEDAW), 1979 at www.un.org/womenwatch/daw/cedaw/ .

Supreme Court Judgements at www.indiankanoon.org.

Secondary Sources

Agnes Flavia, 'Protecting Women Against Violence- Review of a Decade of Legislation', 1980-89, *EPW*, April 25,(1992), 19.

Agnes Flavia, *Law and Gender Equality-The Politics of Women's Rights in India*,New Delhi: O.U.P., 2000.

Arya Sadhna, National Commission of Women- Assessing its Performance, Vol. XLVIII No. 18 *EPW*, May 4, 2013, 112-118.

Biswas Shreya, '17% of working women report to have faced acts of sexual harassment at work place: Oxfam poll', November 27, 2012 at www.articles.economictimes.-indiatimes.com.

Chandhoke Deepalee, 'Laws on Sexual Harassment- Indian Laws dealing with this Crime' at www.doccentre.org/.../sexual-harassment/harassment-law-I.htm .

Deshpande Prasanna, 'Restriction on working hours of Women in IT/ITES', September 1, 2008 at www.vertolex.com.

Elshtain Jean B., *Public Man, Private Woman,* Princeton, New Jersey: Princeton University Press, 1981.

Everett Jana Matson, *Women and Social Change in India*, New Delhi: Heritage, 1979.

Gonsalves Lina, *Women and the Law*, New Delhi: Lancer, 1993.

Haksar Nandita and Singh Anju, *The Demystification of Law for Women*, New Delhi: Lancer, 1986.

Kapur Ratna, 'Challenging the Liberal Subject: Law and Gender Justice in South Asia' in Maitrayee Mukhopadhyay and Navsharan Singh, ed., *Gender Justice, Citizenship and Development*, New Delhi: Zubaan, an imprint of Kali for Women, 2007, 116-170.

Kapur Ratna and Cossman Brenda, *Subversive Sites- Feminist Engagement with Law in India*, ed., New Delhi, London : Sage, 1996.

Kishwar Madhu, 'Sexual Harassment and Slander as Weapons of Subjugation', *Manushi* 68, January - February 1992.

Kurup Deepa, 'New law a weapon to combat sexual harassment at work', *The Hindu*, March 9, 2013, Bangalore.

Mackinnon Catherine, *Sexual Harassment of Working Women*, (New Haven: Yale University Press, 1979), 151-154.

Mathew Mini, 'Sexual Harassment at Workplace', (paper presented at the 'Orientation Program on Women's Rights: Laws that Protect', India Centre for Human Rights and Law, Mumbai, 6–7 August 2001).

Patel Vibhuti, 'A Brief History of the battle against Sexual Harassment at the Workplace', InfoChange News & Features, November 2005 at www.infochange-india.org. (This paper was presented at a Round Table on 'Sexual Harassment-Free Workplace for Women', on October 17-18, 2005, at Sahyadri Guest House, organised by the Maharashtra State Commission for Women, Mumbai).

Phillips Anne, *Feminism and Equality,* ed.,Oxford: Basil Blackwell Ltd., 1987.

Raymond Neeta, 'Sexual Harassment at work', *Combat Law, the human rights magazine* (special edition on violence against women), September-October, 2003 at www.combatlaw.org.

Sharma Pankaj, 'India's first Workplace Sexual Harassment Survey reveals Startling Revelations', Centre for Transforming India, November 13, 2010 at www.release-news.com.

Squires Judith, "Equality and Difference" in *The Oxford Handbook of Political Theory*, ed. John S. Dryzek, Bonnie Hong, Anne Philips, (New York: Oxford University Press, 2006), 470-471.

Tejani Sheba, 'Sexual Harassment at the Workplace- Emerging Problems and Debates', *EPW*, October 9, 2004, 4491.

Vasant Khusita, 'New Workplace Sexual Harassment Law 'Already Out Of Date', April 29, 2013 at *blogs.wsj.com/.../2013/.../new-workplace-sexual-harassment-law.*

Notes

1. 'Tehelka case : FIR charges Tarun Tejpal with rape', November 22, 2013 at www.ndtv.com (accessed November 23, 2013).
2. Judith Squires, "Equality and Difference" in *The Oxford Handbook of Political Theory*, ed. John S. Dryzek, Bonnie Hong, Anne Philips, (New York: Oxford University Press, 2006), 470-471.
3. Anne Phillips, *Feminism and Equality,* ed,. (Oxford: Basil Blackwell Ltd., 1987), 1-23.
4. The Convention on the Elimination of All kinds of Discrimination (CEDAW) adopted in 1979 by the UN General Assembly is often described as an international bill of rights for women. Consisting of a preamble and 30 articles, it defines what constitutes discrimination against women and sets up an agenda for national action to end such discrimination. See www.un.org/womenwatch/ daw/cedaw/ *(accessed November, 30 2008).*
5. Platform of Action, Report of the Fourth World Conference on Women (4-15 September 1995) Beijing, Paragraph 27 at www.un.org/esa/gopher-data/conf/ fwcw/off/a—20.en (accessed March14, 2009).
6. Catherine Mackinnon, *Sexual Harassment of Working Women*, (New Haven: Yale University Press, 1979), 151-154. She argues that sexual harassment should be examined under a theory of inequality that would recognize the systematic subordination of women.
7. Catherine Mackinnon, *Sexual Harassment of Working Women*, (New Haven: Yale University Press, 1979), 151-154. She argues that sexual harassment should be examined under a theory of inequality that would recognize the systematic subordination of women.
8. Madhu Kishwar, 'Sexual Harassment and Slander as Weapons of Subjugation', *Manushi* 68, January - February 1992.
9. Vishaka Guidelines against Sexual Harassment in the Workplace *came* on the 13th august 1997 as a result of this historic case where the gang rape of a *saathin* who was trying to prevent child marriages, in 1992 in the state of Rajasthan. A group of women organisations came forward to file public interest litigation. Vishaka Judgement [1997(7) SCC.323] at www.legalserviceindia.com/.../l217-Vishakha-Judgement'.html *(accessed April 29, 2007).*
10. *Ibid.*
11. The Sexual Harassment of Women at the Workplace (Prevention and Redressal) Bill, 2004 (revised in 2006) at www.ncw.nic.in (accessed November 26, 2008).
12. The *Convention on the Elimination of All Forms of Discrimination against Women (CEDAW)*, adopted in 1979 by the UN General Assembly, is often described as an international bill of rights for women. It defines what constitutes discrimination against women and sets up an agenda for national action to end such discrimination in its preamble and 30 articles at www.un.org/womenwatch/ daw/cedaw/cedaw.htm *(accessed* November *26,* 2008).
13. http://www.iitbbs.ac.in/notice/sexual-harrassment-of-women-act-and-rules-2013.pdf.

14. 'India gets new law against sexual harassment of women at workplaces', *Press Trust of India*, April 25, 2013 at www.ibnlive.in.com (accessed May 6, 2013).
15. Ratna Kapur and Brenda Cossman, *Subversive Sites- Feminist Engagement with Law in India*, ed., (New Delhi, London: Sage, 1996), 23.
16. Ratna Kapur, 'Challenging the Liberal Subject: Law and Gender Justice in South Asia' in Maitrayee Mukhopadhyay and Navsharan Singh, ed., *Gender Justice, Citizenship and Development*, (New Delhi: Zubaan, an imprint of Kali for Women, 2007), 116-170.
17. Nandita Haksar and Anju Singh, *The Demystification of Law for Women*, (New Delhi: Lancer, 1986), 70-80.
18. Lina Gonsalves, *Women and the Law*,(New Delhi : Lancer, 1993), 108.
19. Flavia Agnes, 'Protecting Women Against Violence- Review of a Decade of Legislation', 1980-89, *EPW*, April 25, (1992), 19.
20. Jana Matson Everett, *Women and Social Change in India*, (New Delhi: Heritage, 1979), 99.
21. A national campaign emerged around the rape case of Mathura, a young tribal girl who was raped in police custody and the accused was acquitted by the court's decision that held the victim 'of loose morals'. A public outcry of miscarriage of justice was a national campaign to reform the rape laws ensued.
22. Flavia Agnes, *Law and Gender Equality-The Politics of Women's Rights in India*, (New Delhi: O.U.P., 2000), 188.
23. List of various Central Government Acts, Ministry of Labour and Employment, Government of India at www.labour.nic.in/act/welcome.html (accessed October 16, 2012).
24. Rupan *deol Bajaj and Anr. v. K.P.S.Gill* and another 1995(6) SCC 0194 at www.indlaw.com.
25. The *Convention on the Elimination of All Forms of Discrimination against Women (CEDAW)*, adopted in 1979 by the UN General Assembly, is often described as an international bill of rights for women. It defines what constitutes discrimination against women and sets up an agenda for national action to end such discrimination in its preamble and 30 articles at www.un.org/womenwatch/daw/cedaw/cedaw.htm *(accessed* November *26,* 2008).
26. Vishaka Guidelines against Sexual Harassment in the Workplace *came* on the 13th august 1997 as a result of this historic case where the gang rape of a *saathin* who was trying to prevent child marriages, in 1992 in the state of Rajasthan. A group of women organisations came forward to file public interest litigation. Vishaka Judgement [1997(7) SCC.323] at www.legalserviceindia.com/.../l217-Vishakha-Judgement'.html *(accessed April 29, 2007).*
27. Office memorandum of Ministry of Statistics and Programme Implementation at http://www.mospi.gov.in/sites/default/files/iss-circular/O_Memorandum_24apr17_0.pdf
28. Apparel Export Promotion Council vs A.K. Chopra on 20 January, 1999 at www.indiankanoon.org/doc/856194. This case has been quoted in NCW report, also at www.indlaw.com (accessed July 16, 2009).

29. Laws to prevent sexual harassment of women at the workplace, indianlaw-watch.com/practice/laws-prevent-sexual-harassment-women-work-place/
30. *Ibid.*
31. See *Andhra Pradesh High Court in K.S.Triveni and others v. Union of India and others* (AIR 1979 AP 1) in All India Meeting of Chief Justices of High Courts on Women at www.ncw.nic.in (accessed July 16, 2009).
32. Prasanna Deshpande, 'Restriction on working hours of Women in IT/ITES', September 1, 2008 at www.vertolex.com (accessed December 18, 2008).
33. See http://shodhganga.inflibnet.ac.in/bitstream/10603/12832/15/16_chapter% 207.pdf
34. Rupan Deol Bajaj & another. v. Kanwar Pal Singh Gill & another, Date of Judgment 12/10/1995.
35. See National Commission for Women Act (Act No. 20 of 1990), Govt. of India and See Sec.12, Protection of Human Rights Act, 1993 of National Human Rights Commission (NHRC) published by NCW and NHRC on their websites www.ncw.nic.in and www.nhrc.nic.in(accessed July 16, 2009).
36. International Women's Rights Action Watch Asia Pacific (IWRAW) (2005), *IWRAW Asia Pacific Occasional Papers Series No. 7*, Kuala Lumpur, Malaysia, 1.
37. *Ibid,* 9.
38. Sadhna Arya, National Commission of Women- Assessing its Performance, Vol. XLVIII No. 18 *EPW*, May 4, 2013, 112-118.
39. Sheba Tejani, 'Sexual Harassment at the Workplace- Emerging Problems and Debates', *EPW*, October 9, 2004, 4491.
40. The Sexual Harassment of Women at the Workplace (Prevention and Redressal) Act in The Gazette of india, Ministry of Law and Justice at http://www.nitc.ac.in/app/webroot/img/upload/77331401.pdf
41. See 'Sexual Harassment of Women at Workplace (Prevention, Protection, Redressal) Bill 2006' at www.ncw.nic.in (accessed September 8, 2012). See the NCW website for the Sexual harassment at the workplace Act 2013.
42. 'India"s New Labour Law- Prevention of sexual harassment at the workplace at http://www.mondaq.com/india/x/238076/Discrimination+Disability+Sexual+Harassment/Indias+New+Labour+Law+Prevention+Of+Sexual+Harassment+At+The+Workplace
43. 'Sexual harassment of women at workplace bill passed amidst coal-gate chaos', Press Trust of India Updated: September 03, 2012, at www.ndtv.com (accessed February 5, 2013).
44. Law Resource India- the Protection Of women from sexual harassment at the workplace bill, 2010 at https://indialawyers.wordpress.com/2011/05/27/the-protection-of-women-against-sexual-harassment-at-work-place-bill-2010/
45. Deepa Kurup, 'New law a weapon to combat sexual harassment at work', *The Hindu*, March 9, 2013, Bangalore.
46. See Justice J. S. Verma Report. 'Report of the committee on Amendments to Criminal Law' (Justice J.S. Verma, Justice Leila Seth and Gopal Subramanium), January 23, 2013 at *blogs.wsj.com (*accessed *June 17, 2013).*

47. Khusita Vasant, 'New Workplace Sexual Harassment Law 'Already Out Of Date', April 29, 2013 at *blogs.wsj.com/.../2013/.../new-workplace-sexual-harassment-law (accessed June17, 2013).*
48. *Ibid.*
49. See https://cftingo.wordpress.com/
50. Indira Jaising, Sexual Harassment at workplace, Universal law Publication, New Delhi, 2014, pp. 17-18.
51. Khushita Vasant, 'New Workplace Sexual Harassment Law 'Already Out Of Date', April 29, 2013 at *blogs.wsj.com/.../2013/.../new-workplace-sexual-harassment-law (accessed June17, 2013).*
52. Katharine T. Bartlett and Angela Harris, 'Gender and Law: Theory, Doctrine, Commentary', (1998), 101-102 at www.academic.udayton.edu/Gender/02Unit/index.htm (accessed November 2, 2013).
53. *Ibid.,* 261-262 at www.academic.udayton.edu/Gender/03Unit/index.htm . *See Iris M. Young (1989) and Anne Philips s(1991).*
54. Tyson Smith and Michael Kimmel, 'The Hidden Discourse of Masculinity in Gender Discrimination Law', *Signs: Journal of Women in Culture and Society*, In Press, (2005), 1827-1849.

15

Gender Inequality, Gender Planning and SHG Bank Linkage Programme in India

— ***Kailash Chandra Sharma***

Abstract

The paper acknowledges gender inequality as an important concern in development literature. Gender inequality or gap or discrimination may be viewed in terms of rights (social, economic, political and legal); access and control of resources; economic opportunity; power and political voice. Understanding the concepts relating to gender roles and gender planning is essential for launching suitable development interventions. It is of crucial importance to inculcate the gender sensitivity in the approach of development professionals, policy makers and public at large to mitigate the gender bias prevailing in society so that the gender gap is eliminated for good and a harmonious society evolves with respect and dignity for all men and women.

The self help group (SHG) bank linkage programme pioneered by National Bank for Agriculture and Rural Development (NABARD) has been a powerful way to achieve women's empowerment to an extent leading to reduction in gender inequality at household and community level. It has been a significant tool for financial inclusion of women leading to their empowerment. The underlying message is that economic inequality is the core of gender inequality in general and financial empowerment through SGH bank linkage leads to economic empowerment thus reducing the extent of gender discrimination within the household and also at community level. The programme has been a notable tool for financial inclusion of women leading to their economic empowerment and, therefore, requires further strengthening by overcoming its shortcomings.

Acknowledgement: *The author would like to thank the participants of the National Seminar for their comments and observations. The views expressed are those of the author and do not represent the views of the organisation he belongs to.*

1.0 Introduction

Gender is primarily a social variable which has significant economic consequences, therefore, gender and gender related issues have assumed significance for socio-economic research and policy. This paper considers gender inequality as a serious development concern in the context of India. Further, gender planning and gender sensitive programmes become crucial for reducing gender inequality in society. Aspects relating to gender inequality, gender planning and Self Help Group (SHG) Bank Linkage Programme of India are the subject of this paper.

The paper is organised in five sections. The first introductory Section considers gender as an important variable in development literature and describes various dimensions of gender inequality in society with special reference to India. The concept of gender planning is explained in Section 2. Policy approaches for gender planning are discussed in Section 3. Self help group bank linkage programme (SBLP) and its gender equity enhancing aspects are elaborated in Section 4. Section 5 provides conclusion of the paper.

Gender refers to the roles and responsibilities of women and men that are socially determined. Gender is related to how individuals are perceived and expected to think and act as women and men because of the way society is organised, not because of their biological differences. A distinction is now generally made between sex and gender. Sex is the condition of being male or female on the basis of biological characteristics, and gender is the socially constructed ways of being masculine or feminine. This distinction is made to infer that the biological differences are natural and permanent whereas the attributes of men and women are socially constituted and thus changeable over time and space.

The social nature of gender is evident in the variation between attributes and activities that are considered male and female when comparisons are made across cultures, between classes and ethnic groups in the same culture or over time. Two persistent facts, however, are observed across time and place: First, the importance of gender as a basis of social division of labour, men and women do different types of tasks and have different jobs within the family, in household production and in the marketplace. Second, women have less access than men to resources, rewards and power. For example, it is reported that about half of world's population is female, they contribute two third of total working hours and produce half of world agricultural production. However, in terms of their earnings, they earn one third of world income and own about one per cent of world property.

Sen (2001) describes seven types of gender inequality with special reference to India. These relate to: mortality – death rate is higher for females compared to males; natality – before birth, elimination of female foetus; basic facility – literacy is lower for females compared to males; special opportunity

– higher education access is lower for females compared to males; professional inequality – less women in professional jobs compared to men; ownership inequality – property in the names of fewer women compared to men; household inequality – within household work sharing is not equal, women tend to work longer hours than men. Ground realties, by and large, confirm that women are at more disadvantaged position compared to men in general.

Gender inequality or gap or discrimination can also be viewed in terms of rights (social, economic, political and legal); access and control of resources; economic opportunity; power and political voice. United Nations Women, Agency of United Nations Organisation (2011) reports that the number of countries with more than 30%, the global minimum for political voice, of Members of Parliament (MPs) is only 28 in the world. It further states that 117 countries have equal pay laws but women are paid less in the range of 10-30%. However, women across the world enjoy more freedom and opportunity than ever before. Still women are denied a fair deal due to failure in implementation of laws, lack of resources, lack of will or cultural reasons across the world.

Therefore, gender inequality is not an issue of emotions; it is an issue of justice and priority. Gender planning is a tool to address gender inequality in society. The following section deals with some aspects of gender planning.

2.0 Gender Planning

Gender planning is required to address the issue of gender inequality. Gender planning involves gender analysis that refers to a systematic way of looking at the different potential and actual impacts of development on women and men. It involves answering the following questions. Who does what? Who gets what? Who gains? Who loses? Gender analysis requires separating data by sex, and understanding how labour is divided and valued. Gender analysis is to be done at all stages of the development process; it seeks to answer how a particular activity; decision or plan will affect women differently compared to men.

Gender analysis and planning, in other words, involve understanding gender roles and needs. Women usually play three roles: First, reproductive role i.e. all work and activities involving child-bearing and rearing, and the care of other family members and dependents, all household and domestic tasks including preparation and processing of food, collecting fuel and water, etc. are covered under the reproductive role of women. Second is, productive role that covers work done for payment in cash or kind and includes anything with a potential exchange value, whether for market or for home use. Third, community role that includes activities undertaken at the community level within the framework of local, regional and national levels- local government activities, village-level decision-making, etc. Community role is generally rewarded either directly or indirectly, through status. Compared to women, men usually perform productive and community roles. The burden of reproductive role is largely borne by women in society though there is some role sharing under this category in recent years.

Gender needs are about the specific needs of women vis-à-vis men. Though, everyone has needs - for food, housing, income, education, health, etc., however, women have gender needs because of their nature of work and lower status in society. Women's gender needs arise from the gender division of labour, and from their subordinate position relative to men in society. There are two types of gender needs- practical gender needs and strategic gender needs. Practical gender needs are needs women identify to assist them perform better the tasks they are already doing. Practical gender needs are concerned with inadequacies in living conditions such as water provision, health care and employment, and enlarging their access to resources or free time. They are practical in nature and are a response to immediate perceived necessity. Meeting practical gender needs improves the quality of women's lives and enables them to be more efficient in what they already do, but it does not challenge the gender divisions of labour or women's subordinate position in society.

Strategic gender needs are the needs which women identify because of their subordinate position in terms of their relationship to men in society. Strategic gender needs vary according to particular contexts. They may relate to the gender division of labour, or to power and control of resources. They may also include such issues as legal rights, equal wages, domestic violence, women's control over their own bodies and fertility. Meeting strategic gender needs helps women to achieve greater equity, seeks to change existing gender roles, and therefore challenges women's subordinate position vis-a-vis men in society.

The aim of gender planning is to bring women into mainstream development process on equal terms with men, both as agents and as well as beneficiaries. It recognises that there is a gender division of labour and that women usually in all societies have less access to resources, power and control over their lives relative to their men counterparts. Main policy approaches to gender planning are the subject of the next section.

3.0 Policy Approaches to Gender Planning

Policy Approaches to Gender Planning are mainly two. These are: Women in Development (WID); and Gender and Development (GAD).

Women in Development (WID)

Development worker's and planners' concentration on Women in Development (WID) issues arose from a realisation that women's contributions were being ignored and that this led to many failures in development efforts. WID projects, frequently involving only women as participants and beneficiaries, were an outcome of this realisation. Within this WID approach, there are three strands as follows:

Welfare: This strand focuses on women's role as wives and mothers offering household support. It considers that women are beneficiaries of, but not active participants in development. They benefit from development through resources in support of their needs in the domestic arena, such as nutrition, education, family planning, health facilities, food aid, fuel and water availability, etc. The welfare approach focuses on the reproductive role and meets practical gender needs mentioned earlier.

Anti-Poverty: The anti-poverty strand focuses on women's problems as the 'poorest of the poor' and the solution as poverty alleviation, not equality with men. This approach, therefore, aims to increase women's income-earning capacity by income generating projects, skills training, introduction of appropriate technologies, literacy, etc. The Anti-poverty approach focuses on the productive role and meets practical gender needs of women discussed earlier.

Efficiency: The efficiency strand sees women essentially not as beneficiaries of intervention, but as a major resource in development. It points to women being half the world's population, already contributing to all economies, but not always sufficiently used. If development is to become more efficient, it must include the participation of women. Women have the capacity to compensate for declining social services by the use of their "free" time. It puts women into mainstream development, and assumes that if they participate they will automatically benefit and contribute to national economy. The efficiency approach recognises women's triple role with a focus on the productive role and meets practical gender needs indicated above.

Gender and Development (GAD)

The Gender and Development (GAD) approach shifts the focus from women as a group to the socially determined relations between women and men. A GAD approach focuses on the social, economic, political and cultural forces that determine how men and women might participate in, benefit from and control project resources and activities differently. Within this GAD approach, there are two main strands as follows:

Equity: This approach seeks to promote women's status, power and control. It also recognises women's active role in development, particularly through their productive role. It seeks to challenge the power of men over women, and to end discrimination. It is an interventionist approach, working through changes in legislation, and through mobilisation of activities concerned with women's rights. The equity approach recognises women's triple role i.e. reproductive, productive and societal, and meets strategic gender needs.

Empowerment: The Empowerment approach comes from women's groups who seek to empower themselves through greater self-reliance. Women seek to influence their own change, and the right to determine their own choice of life. They also seek to gain control of and access to resources. This approach differs from the equity approach in origin and strategies. It emerges from women who have been involved in liberation struggles and grass-root women's organisations, and is articulated in the writings of women leaders of developing countries. It concerns property rights, skill upgradation, access to education, health, credit, etc.

In recent years, Gender budgeting or Gender-responsive budgeting (GRB), a concept popularised by United Nations (UN) is being used for gender planning and is about mainstreaming gender concerns in the development process. Gender-responsive budgeting (GRB) is about government planning, programming and budgeting that contributes to the advancement of gender equality and the fulfillment of women's rights. It entails identifying and reflecting needed interventions to address gender gaps in specific sectors, government policies, plans and budgets. GRB also aims to analyze the gender-differentiated impact of revenue-raising policies and the allocation of domestic resources and official development assistance. GRB initiatives seek to create enabling policy frameworks, build capacity and strengthen monitoring mechanisms to support accountability to women's development.

In India, the concept of GRB is introduced in 11th FYP (2007-12). It is called gender responsive budgeting or gender budgeting. It is a step forward from "special plan for women" in Indian Planning. GRB means making budgetary allocation for women development programmes by various ministries as per policy of the Government.

The issue of gender inequality in India is a real one and requires commitment and action at all levels. Though, efforts have been made in the past, much more needs to be done in this regard. Setting gender equity right is important in India and economic empowerment of women is the key to gender equity. Further, key factor in economic empowerment is financial empowerment. Financial exclusion of women is severe in India (394 saving bank accounts for women / 1000 saving bank accounts for men) as per RBI data as on March 2012 (The Hindu, August 30, 2014). The specific constraints regarding financial services to women are - lack of awareness, education among women; accessibility; lack of collateral; suitable financial products; cumbersome procedures; lack of entrepreneurial skills/initiatives, production and marketing management; small size of enterprises- high transaction cost; and not so positive attitude of bank staff.

One interesting programme called Self Help Group (SHG) bank linkage programme pioneered by National Bank for Agriculture and Rural Development (NABARD) has been a huge success in terms of gender empowerment of women in India. The following section deals with the SHG bank linkage programm and its gender dimension in India.

4.0 SHG Bank Linkage Programme (SBLP) In India

The SHG Bank Linkage Programme (SBLP) in India is spearheaded by NABARD, though started as a financial inclusion programme way back in 1992; it has turned out to be a gender sensitive programme wherein women participation and contribution has been significant. The programme addresses practical as well as strategic gender needs of women and adopts empowerment approach for bringing gender equity mentioned earlier.

Concept of SHG and some aspects of gender equity contributions of SBLP are elaborated in this section.

SHG and SHG Bank Linkage Programm (SBLP)

A Self Help Group (SHG) is a homogeneous group, comprising 10-20 members (mostly poor women), where members first pool in their savings and give out small loans to needy members. Once the SHG successfully undertakes savings and credit operations from its own resources, it can borrow from a bank through SHG Bank Linkage Programme (SBLP) to enhance its pool of resources. Banks usually give four to ten times of SHG's pooled savings as loan for a year as a cash credit limit after proper appraisal of the SHG. Government of India has recently announced that these loans will be given by banks at the rate of 7% per annum. The loan to the group is made in the name of SHG and is operated by its two nominated representatives. There is an inter se agreement between the SHG and the bank regarding the repayment of the loan wherein all SHG members are collectively responsible for the repayment of the loan. Loans to individual members are given at the group level. Therefore, the SHG acts as a grass root level financial institution providing saving and credit facilities to its members.

Specific objectives of SHG Bank Linkage Programme are: sustainable access to financial services; stronger livelihood support systems; enhancement of collective bargaining power; self reliance and sense of dignity; improvement of overall standard of living. All these eventually lead to empowerment of group members who are mainly women.

The SBLP has two stages of bank linkage. First is called saving linkage when the SHG opens a saving account with the bank and the second is called credit linkage when the SHG is able to avail credit from the bank. Reserve Bank of India (RBI) and NABARD have issued instructions to banks for opening saving and credit accounts of SHGs with relevant documents relating to the SHG.

As mentioned earlier, NABARD pioneered the SBLP as a strategy for increasing the outreach of banking services among the poor in rural areas. The process involved formation of SHGs of poor, encouraging them to pool their thrift regularly and using the pooled funds for loaning small amounts to members. In the process, poor became aware of the importance of financial discipline. With a modest beginning with 500 SHGs in 1992, the SBLP has become a movement with 74.30 lakh SHGs with saving bank accounts with various banks and 41.97 lakh SHGs having loan accounts with various banks as on 31 March 2014. The experience of banks with women SHGs under SBLP has been extremely encouraging in terms of timely repayment of loans. Seeing the success of SBLP, the concept of SHG has been used by Government of India (GOI) in its poverty alleviating programmes such as Swarn Jayanti Gram Swarojgar Yojana (SGSY) and now National Rural Livelihood Mission (NRLM).

Gender and SHG Bank Linkage Programm (SBLP)

It is interesting to note that SBLP has a strong gender orientation and it may be observed in terms of proportion of women SHGs in total SHGs that are saving linked and credit linked as on March 2014 as shown in Table 15.1 below:

Table 15.1: Percent of Women SHGs Saving and Credit Linked under SBLP (March 2014)

Indicator	*% of All SHGs*
Women SHGs Saving linked	84.14
Women SHGs Credit Linked	81.15
Women SHGs Credit Linked during 2013-14	84.33

Source: Drawn from NABARD (2014)

Although, the programme was started with reaching the un-reached in terms of banking services, the experience has been significant in terms of participation of women in an overwhelming manner. 84.14% of all SHGs are women SHGs as on March 2014 as seen in Table 15.1. Also, the percentage of credit linked women SHGs overall and during 2013-14 is also in the same range indicating the strong gender orientation of SBLP till date (Table 15.1). Thus the trend of credit linkage continues to be in favour of women SHGs as shown in Table 15.1.

The experience in Uttar Pradesh is that women SHGs have been more sustainable than men SHG (Sharma et al. 2005). Parida et al (2010) explore the performance and sustainability of SHG program in India at the group level. The study is based on data from a survey carried out in six states in India. Overall, the performance analysis reveals that all-women SHGs perform best.

The women SHGs are doing particularly well in terms of recovery of loans and per capita saving. The quantitative results indicate that only all-women SHGs are sustainable. The factors that determine the sustainability include recovery of loans, per capita savings, and linkage with an SHG federation.

SHG Bank Linkage Programm (SBLP) and Women Empowerment

A study by NCAER (2008) covering six states (Andhra Pradesh, Karnataka, Maharashtra, Odisha, Uttar Pradesh and Assam) reported that 80% SHGs have only women members. Further, the study showed significant improvement in rural poor's access to financial sources as a result of SBLP. The study also showed that SBLP empowered women members in terms of enhancing self confidence substantially. Table 15.2 shows some indicators of empowerment of women as a result of SBLP.

Table 15.2: Women SHG Members Reporting Empowerment (%)

Indicator of Empowerment	***% of women SHG Members Reporting Improvement***
Household Decision Making	80.0
Self Confidence	79.5
Ability to face problems	73.6
Control over use of Money in the Household	62.2
Participation in Village Affairs	51.4

Source: Adapted from NCAER (2008).

Table 15.2 shows that a significant proportion of women SHG members have reported improvement in their role in household decision making, self confidence, ability to face problems, control over use of money in the household and participation in villages matters. However, change in ownership of production and consumer assets is not reported by women SGH members.

Similar findings are reported by Chitagubbi et al (2011) who studied the socio- economic status of self help group members to evaluate the social impact of membership of SHGs on the empowerment of women group members. The membership of SHGs made the women members aware of the gender inequality and led to economic, social and political independence of members. It also improved the position of women members in the patriarchal family system through gaining knowledge of legal system and enabled the members to involve in family decision making. Moreover, the members also developed the leadership qualities through the sense of devotion to work, duty consciousness and self confidence.

Sa-Dhan (2011), an umbrella organisation of microfinance institutions in India reports that SHGs have made a lasting impact on the lives of the women in rural areas. Their quality of life has improved. There is an increase in their income, savings and consumption expenditure. The women have gained confidence. They can speak in front of large group of people. They got recognition in the family and society. SHGs have also given women greater role in household decision making

It is worthwhile to note the significant contribution of SBLP to gender empowerment in India as mentioned above. However, it is also important to mention that there are challenges in SBLP. These challenges relate to quality of SHGs, increase in number of dormant and defunct SHGs, hassle free financial intermediation by banks, increasing NPAs and uneven spread of SBLP across different regions of the country.

It is an ongoing challenge to ensure well functioning SHGs where group meetings are held regularly, members save regularly, loan repayment is timely, account keeping is up to date and group functioning is democratic. Adequate support from banks is also an ongoing issue as even now many bankers do not fully support SBLP by providing hassle free services for opening of saving and credit accounts. It has also happened that SHGs have been formed and credit linked but have defaulted in their repayment and have created non-performing assets for banks. Finally, SBLP has been largely a south ward movement whereas the need is more in north and north eastern region of the country. In spite of these massive challenges, there is no denying that SBLP has been a significant player in women empowerment in the country.

Therefore, the need of the hour is to strengthen the SBLP in the areas identified above by suitable interventions such as support for reviving dormant and defunct SHGs, second tier institution building, microenterprise development by SHGs through capacity building, capacity building of bankers for attitudinal change and incentivizing bankers for doing good work in rural areas under SBLP. NABARD has initiated some of these interventions and need to be supported further. National Rural Livelihood Mission (NRLM) interventions such as availability of loan to SHGs at 7% rate of interest need to be made available all SHGs in all development blocks of the country.

5.0 Conclusion

Gender is an important variable in development literature. It is important to note that gender is a social variable which means different things to different people. Sex denotes the biological differences between male and female whereas gender is about the social roles and responsibilities handled by men and women in society. Understanding the concepts relating to gender roles and gender planning is essential for launching suitable development interventions. It is of crucial importance to inculcate the gender sensitivity in the approach of development professionals and policy makers to mitigate the gender bias prevailing in society so that the gender gap is eliminated for good and a harmonious society evolves with respect and dignity for all men and women.

The self help group (SHG) bank linkage programme pioneered by National Bank for Agriculture and Rural Development (NABARD) has been a powerful method to achieve women's empowerment to an extent leading to reduction in gender inequality at household and community level. The underlying lesson is that economic inequality is the core of gender inequality in general and financial empowerment through SGH bank linkage leads to economic empowerment thus reducing the extent of gender discrimination within the household and also at village level. The programme has a strong gender orientation and needs further strengthening.

Acknowledgement: The author would like to thank the participants of the National Seminar for their comments and observations. The views expressed are those of the author and do not represent the views of the organisation he belongs to.

References

Chitagubbi, G., Shivalli, R. and Devendrappa,S. (2011), A Study on the Usefulness of Self Help Group Membership to Women for Empowerment, *Journal of Farm Sciences,* Vol. 1, No. 1, pp. 112-119.

NABARD (2014), Status of Microfinance in India 2013-14, MCID, NABARD, Mumbai.

NCAER (2008), Impact and Sustainability of SHG Bank Linkage Programme, NCAER, New Delhi.

Parida, P. C. and Sinha, A. (2010) Performance and Sustainability of Self-Help Groups in India: A Gender Perspective, Asian Development Review, Vol. 27, No. 1, pp. 80-103.

Sa-Dhan (2011) Bharat Microfinance Report 2011 Side by Side, Sa-Dhan, New Delhi.

Sen, Amartya (2001), Many Faces of Gender Inequality An essay, Frontline, Vol 18, No. 22, Oct 29-Nov 09, 2001.

Sharma, K.C. et al. (2005) Micro Credit Action Research Project Experiences and Lessons learnt, BIRD, Working Paper 29, BIRD, Lucknow.

The Hindu, Allahabad Edition, 30 August 2014 (Daily News Paper).

United Nations Women, Agency of United Nations (2011), Progress of the World's Women 2011–2012: In Pursuit of Justice, New York.

16

Mainstreaming Tribal Women in Development Process through Women SHGs: A Case study of Jharkhand and Odisha

— *Vishwa Ballabh and Pooja Batra*

Abstract

The Scheduled Tribe community in India are characterised by economic and social marginalisation, primitive existence, geographical isolation and educational backwardness. They have been displaced by industrialisation, power plants, mining and multipurpose large/medium dams so called 'temples of modern India' but have become 'temple of doom' for the displaced people. Post-independence several plans and schemes were prepared to bring the tribals under the main development strap but most did not touch even the fringe of their problems and more often than not failed. The reasons are not difficult to find since it has not taken into consideration the cultural milieu of the tribals.

Against this back drop, we present in this paper the experience of PRADAN, an NGO, which is working in the central tribal belt of India to reconstruct the economy of the tribal people. PRADAN is working through women Self Help Groups (SHGs) across 41 districts in the seven states (Bihar, Chhattisgarh, Jharkhand, Madhya Pradesh, Odisha, Rajasthan, and West Bengal) of India. PRADAN'S core philosophy in working with the poor tribal women is in path to conquering economic poverty through enhancing livelihood opportunities. In this process PRADAN'S Professionals enable poor women to break free from their past, develop an alternative vision for their future and set achievable goals. It makes effort to develop the poor with technical, organisational, negotiating skills that facilitate attainment of their goals. In doing so PRADAN emphasizes in women's collective wisdom and recognizes their respect in environment and builds on local resources enhancing people's capability, using local people (CSP and CRP) with PRADAN professionals for communication. Some of the factors identified for PRADAN'S success are (i) emphasizing on collectivism and forming women SHGs (ii) capacity building of the SHGs depending on the capacity and learning ability of each member (iii) identification of leadership at initial stage nurturing and sustaining the leadership (iv)the pace at which livelihood programmes are developed is well spaced and (v) PRADAN'S trained professionals are working directly with the local resource persons in different village who speak the local dialect.

I. Introduction

As per the 2011 Census, India's tribal constitute 8.61 per cent of the total population of the country, numbering 104.28 million Government of India, 2013) and 70 per cent of them live in the 'Central belt' extending from Gujarat and Rajasthan in west across the states of Maharashtra, Madhya Pradesh, Chhattisgarh, Bihar, Jharkhand and Odisha to West Bengal in east. The area is rich in forest, bio-diversity and mineral resources. The tribal people form an integral part of the central belt and their development is *sine qua non* for inclusive development of the region.

The issue concerning the tribal development was brought into the center of agenda immediately after independence. There are evidences that prior to and after independence an intense debate for the development of tribals took place. It was because of these concerns that the Prime Minister, Pt. Jawaharlal Nehru had appointed Verrier Elwin as an Anthropological Advisor to the Government of India. Nehru acknowledged that he learnt a lot from Elwin about life, culture and issues concerning the tribal people. Beyond this however, both of them differed, the disagreement was mainly on four counts (Guha 2001:149; cf Rath 2006:70) – (i) Are the tribes different from caste society? (ii) Are their history different? (iii) What are the relationship between caste society and tribes? and (iv) What should be the approaches for their development?.

Nehru strongly disagreed that the caste and tribes are different from each other. The sociologist and anthropologist including Elwin at that time believed that caste is organic and tribe is segmentary that their land holding structure is kinship based and the transfer of land is restricted to kinship only whereas such a restriction does not exist in caste society. Similarly Nehru also differed with many, about the historical difference between caste and tribes and was of the view that most colonial writings sought only to reflect disunity among human beings and is based on conjectures that needs reexamination. Nehru also questioned the authenticity of foreign writers to open up the mysteries of savage cultures on Indian soil without understanding the social coherence between tribes and non-tribes. Nehru argued that the difference between tribes and non-tribes is not structural, whatever difference between them is observed are a result of settlement of these people in two different time periods in the history of civilisation (Rath 2006: 67).

Elwin, however, strongly differed with Nehru on this count. He argued that the relationship between caste and tribe, if any, is exploitative, the caste society has not contributed positively to the development of tribes (Rustomji 2001:237). Nehru believed that the commercialisation of tribal produce was not only an appropriate strategy but also income generating means, which would mitigate tribal people's poverty and misery. Elwin on the other hand was concerned about the exploitation of tribals by the moneylenders, traders and contractors and therefore argued for protectionist approach[2] to be given for tribal development. Though Nehru agreed for special attention to the tribes in specific contexts but strongly opposed that National Planning Commission should be burdened with it. Thus Nehru strongly advocated and followed integrative approach for mainstreaming tribals in the development process and their special case of context specific were largely ignored (Rath 2006:79).

From the above brief review it is evident that the mainstream political system was concerned about the issues relating to the development of the tribal people but it did not recognize their special circumstances and problems. Thus it is important to examine the experience of these development efforts of the tribals.

II. Experience with Development

The development of dams, hydro-electric projects, power plants were in high on agenda immediately after independence. As a result a large mass of population was displaced. There is no precise estimate however approximately 60 - 65 million people have been displaced in India since Independence, the highest number of people uprooted for development projects in the world. This amounts to around one million displaced every year since Independence," says a report released recently by the Working Group on Human Rights in India and the UN (WGHR). "Of these displaced, over 40 per cent are tribals and another 20 per cent consist of dalits (Scheduled Caste)and other rural poor who live on and off on common property resources" and hardly 20 per cent have been rehabilitated as per the WGHR report (cited from Times of India June 4, 2012). Tribals have been uprooted from their homes and huts, displaced from their farms, jungles and rivers and sacrificed at the altar of national interest. These millions bear witness to the destruction of their own lives, livelihoods and lifestyles. Thus, there are two faces of the temples of modern India as argued by Fernandes, 2008. "One, the glorification of development; the other the fact that like monuments of the past, these present–day temples too are built on the blood and sweat of millions of people. Whilst slaves and prisoners built the former, todays farmers and others who leave off the land, forests and other resources are being improvised in the name of 'development' (Fernandes 2008: 8).

A large number of research articles have been published about the plight displaced and project affected people (Ahmad and Dutt, 2006; Areeparampil

2010 1996: 1524-1528; Asthana 2012:96-102; Dhru 2010; Fernandes 2007; Goyal 1996: 1461-1467; Kabra 2003: 3073-3078; Mishra 2002: 197-208; Mohanty 2011: 67-73; Negi and Ganguly 2010; Pandey and Kumar Rout 2004; Ray 2000; Sarkar 2007: 1435-1442; Sen 1995: 963-966; Sharma and Singh 2009:62-68). Almost each of them (barring a few) identify that the displaced people have suffered unprecedent risks not imagined at the time of implementation of the project. Therefore the protests and contestation against any project which involves displacement of people have become common. Therefore, consensus seems to be emerging that development-induced displacement causes considerable social, economic and cultural disruption and losses to both individuals and communities (Dreze et al 1997; Dwivedi 1999 43-78; Parsuram 1993:3; Thukral 1992; Oliver-Smith 1991; World Commission on Dams 2000. Michael Cernea proposes that the onset of impoverishment can be represented through a model of eight interlinked potential risks intrinsic to displacement: landlessness, joblessness, homelessness, marginalisation, food insecurity, increased morbidity and mortality, loss of access to common property and social integration (Michael Cernea 2000: 16). The loss of access to community services and violation of human rights could be added to the model, since people lose their neighbourhood in resettlements process and bear the brunt of violation of human rights (Downing 2002:8-9).

In the case of tribals, the experience of displacement is more monstrous. It all begins with landlessness and slowly turns into joblessness, loss of income, lack of access to healthcare and to other forms of deprivation, it forces the parents even to pull school going children out of it. For example, the predominantly tribal DPs of the Salandi dam in the Keonjhar district of Orissa who were earlier living close to a town that had some schools, so most of the children went to school. They were resettled in a forest area in which they were given some land and a house but no school was built for a few years. By the time schools were built the children had lost the habit of going to school. Besides, poverty had increased among them because land allotted to them was of poor quality and they could not grow enough food and had to purchase much of it. In the absence of other sources of livelihood they had to turn their children into child labourers in order to earn an income (Fernandes 2007:4). In most cases impoverishment itself forces the parents to put their children to work full time to maintain the family. As per studies, 49 per cent of the displaced or deprived families in West Bengal and 56 per cent in Assam (Fernandes and Bharali 2006: 125-126) have pulled their children out of school in order to turn them into child labourers.

The tribals encounter tremendous odds in dealing with the market economy. Their unfamiliarity with modern technology and skills coupled with official indifference to their entry into the mainstream economy, pushes a majority of them into conditions of servility and bondage. As stated above, access to work declines after the project alienates the land if the project gives jobs, except in women headed families they go almost exclusively to men considered heads of families. If they are rehabilitated, land is allotted to men. So the domestic power passes fully to the man and from him to his son (Thekkekara 1993: 29). As result of displacement joblessness is higher among women than among men. Most of the rehabilitation policies provide a job per family or self-employment. Besides one job per family is not an alternative because after land alienation the remaining members do not have resources for self-employment. So women from the families that are excluded are bound to be doubly marginalised. The women shift from being a housewife and depending on the man's single salary who spends maximum part of his salary on alcohol. Therefore for survival of the fittest they are forced into menial and marginalised form of labour as maids and servants, as constructing labourers or into prostitution which are highly unorganised and socially humiliating (Bhanumathi 2007:4). The negative impact continues in other aspects too, health being one of them. All the studies show an enormous rise in water borne, malnutrition and environmental degradation related diseases among the DP/PAPs.

In some of the research studies the proponents of development argued that the monetary income of the displaced person improves after the resettlements. However there are empirical studies which infact contradict such observation, for example, one study reports that out of 700 persons from 13 projects who are interviewed in Andhra Pradesh, monetary income had improved in less than 30 cases. It deteriorated in remaining cases, at times by more than 80 per cent (Ray 2000:37). It has also been argued that even when monetary income rises, the life style of the displaced people does not necessarily improve. Some of them who measure the change through the improvement of monetary income ignore the fact that before displacement a large number of the DPs belonged to the non-monetized and many of these communities sustained themselves on the Common Property Resources (CPRs) or by rendering community services to the village or as agricultural labourers. Their lost livelihood is not compensated or replaced. So even when monetary income rises after displacement, they tend to become insolvent because the CPRs and other sources of their non-monetized livelihood are not replaced. (Fernandes 2008:188). A document comprising of testimonials of tribals from Singrauli region in Central India, draws our attention towards the quandary of forest dwellers, "who were formerly dependent on forest produce for their for their livelihood but after displacement they hardly have any access to the forest produce and have been pushed to the fringe by the expansion of coal mines in the area".

One of the testimonials from Amravati of a mother of six children, who has lived in Moher forest (Singrauli area) with her family for more than a decade remarked- "*prior to the work for mine began I used collect forest produce for livelihood but now boundaries have been established and no villagers are allowed to penetrate into the forest*". Another testimonial highlighting the plight of the villagers who use to collect "mahua and other forest produce like tendu leaves, chironji, harra, bamboo and mushroom" for their daily survival, found themselves in unrest on hearing of, these forest being handed over to companies for coal mining. They quoted *"if the government takes this initiative the means of livelihood for us would be lost and we may not even get any compensation as we have no rights over these forests"*. Similarly Ramadhar Saket from same region in his testimonial remarked every year during the Mahua season we shut down my house in Amelia village and come and stay in the Mahan forests for about a month to collect Mahua, which we sell for Rs. 17-20 / per kg. We also collect other forest produce like tendu leaves, chironji, harra, bamboo, mushroom and others. However, we are now hearing that these forests will be given to the company for mining coal. If the Government gives away these forests we would have no other means to live and we will not even get any compensation because we have no rights over these forests (Jayashree Nandi, TNN Oct 15, 2012). Such cases are abundant.

In a poignant remark on this 'Wild Economics of Displacement' Arundhati Roy says, "many of those who have been resettled are people who have lived all their lives deep in the forest and have . gathered their food, fuel, fodder, rope, gum, tobacco, tooth powder, medicinal herbs and housing material. Instead of a river, now they have a hand pump. In their old village they had no money but they were insured. If the rains failed they had the forests or the river to fish or livestock as their fixed deposit for survival .Without all this, they are a heartbeat away from destitution" (Roy 2005; Revolutionary frontline).

In addition to the plight of displaced people, the developmental efforts designed for the tribal communities also did not succeed (Barik 2006; Basu 2006: 149) due to their sectarian approach of the state. The development policy of the State is based more on the power relations between different social groups (Barik 2006:108) and the tribals of Jharkhand and Odisha did not have such powers. Thus overall developmental experiences of tribal people have been adverse because their concerns were largely neglected. Thus, Nehru's dream of mainstreaming the tribal in the national economy remains unfulfilled.

III. Socio –Economic status of STs in Jharkhand and Odisha

Both Jharkhand and Odisha are located in east coast of India and are famous for its rich mineral resources and forest. With a geographical area of 74,677 sq.km in Jharkhand and 155,707 sq.km in Odisha 29.45 per cent (Jharkhand) and 32.33 per cent (Odisha) area are under forest cover in these respective states. According to the 2011 Census the total population of

Jharkhand is 32 million where the share of tribal population is 26.2 per cent and 41 million with a share of 22.8 per cent in Odisha. Jharkhand and Odisha contribute 8.3 per cent and 9.2 per cent ST population respectively to the total ST population of the country. There are thirty-two tribes in Jharkhand, major among them being Santhal, Munda, Oraon and Ho. Eight out of the thirty-two tribes of Jharkhand fall under Primitive Tribal Group (PTG) . They are Asur, Birhor, Birajia, Korwa, Savar, Pahariya (Baiga), Mal Pahariya and Souriya Pahariya. Of all the states of India, Odisha has the largest number of distinctive tribes, as many as sixty-two. Khond is the most populous tribe followed by Gond, Santal, Kolha, Munda, Saora, Shabar and Bhottada, Bhumij, Bhuiya, Oraon, Paroja and Kisan. Out of the sixty-two notified STs only eight are declared as PTG namely Juang, Bondo Poraja, Lodha, Didayi, Mankidia, Birhor, Kharai and Soura.

As per the 2011 census the sex ratio of the tribal population in Jharkhand is 1003 and of Odisha is 1029 compared to national total average of 943 females per 1000 males. Except the sex ratio, the socio economic status of the tribals in Jharkhand and Odisha lags behind the other social groups (Table 16.1).

Table 16.1: Socio –Economic Status of Tribals vis –a- vis others in Jharkhand and Odisha

S. No	*Particulars*	*Jharkhand*		*Odisha*	
		Total	*ST*	*Total*	*ST*
1.	**Sex Ratio (per 1000 males) (Census 2011)**	948	1003	979	1029
2.	**Percentage of population living below poverty line (2011-2012)[a]**	40.8	51.6	35.7	63.5
3.	**Literacy Rate (Census 2011)[b]**	66.4	57.1	72.9	52.2
4.	**Infant Mortality Rate (IMR)[c] (per 1,000 live births)**	68.7	93.0	64.7	78.7
5.	**Under –Five Mortality Rate (U5MR)[c] (per 1,000 live births)**	93.0	138.5	90.6	136.3
6.	**Life Expectancy at Birth[d] (2001)**	61.94*	62.6	59.17	58.5

Source a: www.indiastats.com; b: Registrar general of India, Census 2011; c: NFHS-3, 2005-06; Ministry of Health & Family Welfare, Government of India; d: Estimates from Census of India, 2001.

Notes- *: Jharkhand was a newly carved state from Bihar and the data given are for the combined state of Bihar.

Both states have high incidence of poverty among the tribal community with 51.6 per cent (Jharkhand) and 63.5 per cent (Odisha) of tribal population living below the poverty line whereas the figure for overall rural population are 40.8 per cent in Jharkhand and 35.7 per cent in Odisha. It should be noted that the total rural population also includes tribals, and if we remove the tribals from the total rural population the gap between tribal and non-tribal would increase. Similar observations are made for literacy, infant mortality, under five child mortality and life expectancy at birth. The average literacy rate of the tribals is 57 per cent in Jharkhand and 52 per cent in Odisha. The health scenario is pathetic as four out of every 10 women are malnourished and most of the new borne babies are underweight.

Due to such low socio-economic development among STs, Government has made affirmative policies, programmes and enacted laws. There are many Constitutional safeguards for the welfare, development and protection of STs in the country. In spite of these affirmative actions, tribals in India face insurmountable problems and their social status continues to remain poor. In order to break free from economic poverty and enhance their livelihood capabilities PRADAN intervenes with a belief that professionals involvement will facilitate in expanding opportunities for poor people through innovation and by adapting and demystifying technology, building and nurturing fair service linkages and beneficial networks, fostering collaboration among tribal people and between them and the rest of the world and helping tribal people enhance their capabilities.

IV. Mainstreaming Tribal Women for Development

This section deals with "social engineering" carried out by a national level NGO – namely Professional Assistance for Development Action (popularly known as PRADAN) working in the eastern tribal belt areas of Madhya Pradesh, Chhattisgarh, Jharkhand, Bihar, Odisha and West Bengal. Founded in 1983, PRADAN is a non- profit organisation, registered under the Societies Registration Act with headquarters in New Delhi. It was pioneered by a group of young professionals, who were inspired by the conviction that individuals with knowledge resources and empathy for the marginalised must work with communities at the grassroot levels in order to help them overcome poverty.

PRADAN'S operation in Jharkhand and Odisha is spread across 59 blocks in 16 districts of Jharkhand and 21 blocks in 6 districts of Odisha. Agro climatically PRADAN'S operational area is sub divided into three Agro Climatic zones each in both the states. In Jharkhand the three agro climatic regions are Central North Eastern Plateau (Bokaro, Dumka and Godda); Western Plateau (Gumla and Lohardaga) and South Eastern Plateau (Khunti and Saraikela Kharsawan) while in Odisha its North–Eastern Ghats (Kandhamal, Rayagada and Koraput); North Central Plateau (Keonjhar and Mayurbhanj) and West Undulating Zone (Kalahandi). These climatic zones and regions vary on various parameters like rainfall, soil type and extent of the forest land etc. but an unifying feature of these regions is that the rainfall is quite substantial (above 1200mm), but erratic in time and space. The soils in both states are lithological and poor in nutrient. The entire area of operation in Jharkhand and Odisha is traditionally mono-cropping and paddy is the main staple crop which is grown mostly under the rain fed conditions. The forest degradation along with the uncertainty of agriculture has led to food insecurity forcing people to migrate outside in search of livelihood support. The development of irrigation, infrastructure is also poor due to poor groundwater and steep slopes. This was a common feature of the area before the intervention of PRADAN as narrated by village after village during our visits for the survey.

For this case study, one district from each agro-climatic zone was randomly selected. Thus from Jharkhand, Dumka (Central North Eastern Plateau); Gumla (Western Plateau) and Khunti (South Eastern Plateau) and from Odisha, Kandhamal (North–Eastern Ghats); Mayurbhanj (North Central Plateau) and Kalahandi (West Undulating Zone) were chosen. Since our objective was to examine the impact on the tribal economy therefore two villages each representing (0 – 5) years of intervention, (5 – 10) years of intervention and more than 10 years of intervention from each district were randomly selected. Thus overall 32 villages of where PRADAN operates were studied from Jharkhand and Odisha. The data collection was done using pretested questionnaire for household, village and SHG levels. Multiple approaches such as Participatory Rural Appraisal (PRA/ RRA (Rapid Rural Appraisal)), Focus Group Discussions (FGDs) and household survey were used to obtain the information.

4.1 Conceptual Framework of PRADAN's Intervention

PRADAN'S core has been to create livelihood options for the poor tribal women and the development of their livelihood to make it sustainable. On the top of this framework is entry through SHGs in the villages and bank linkages which help Women's group to overcome high indebtedness, exorbitant interest rates and set the stage for larger development (Figure 16.1). Once this is achieved, livelihood enhancement activities are initiated through improvement in agricultural practices, wasteland development and introduction of new agricultural and horticultural crops on one hand and micro-enterprises development like goat rearing, poultry, tasar silk cooperatives and linkages with the market on the other. Collaboration and setting up of networks with Civil Society Organisations (CSOs) are also done for better market linkages and availing higher remunerative prices for their products. Capacity building trainings are also organised on technical and non-technical aspects for the members of SHG engaged in livelihood intervention. This process intends to ensure food security by increasing local employment and thus reducing migration. The micro-enterprises like goat rearing, poultry, tasar silk-worm farming further enhances the income leading to better health and schooling for the children which in turn is expected to improve overall human development (Figure 16.1). The essence of PRADAN'S developmental model is in achieving higher human development and enhancing human capacities.

PRADAN'S interventions are accomplished in three phases in a particular village. In the first phase, it forms, promotes and nurtures the SHG as a viable financial intermediary between its members and commercial banks. As a part of its activities it initiates capacity building trainings for the office bearers and members of the SHG. The organisation has developed a robust stage by stage and step-by-step methodology for developing, nurturing and promoting SHGs as an independent functionary (Figure 16.2). In the primary stage, the first step for an SHG is to begin as a mutual aid association of poor women. This is an informal association of 10-20 poor women belonging to the same village and sharing a common socio-economic background. This is done through frequent and regular visits and interactions in groups and with individuals by PRADAN professionals. During the first 2-3 months of the formation of the SHG, a one-day module on awareness generation is conducted with the group members. In the second step, after four months of group formation exposure visits are organised.

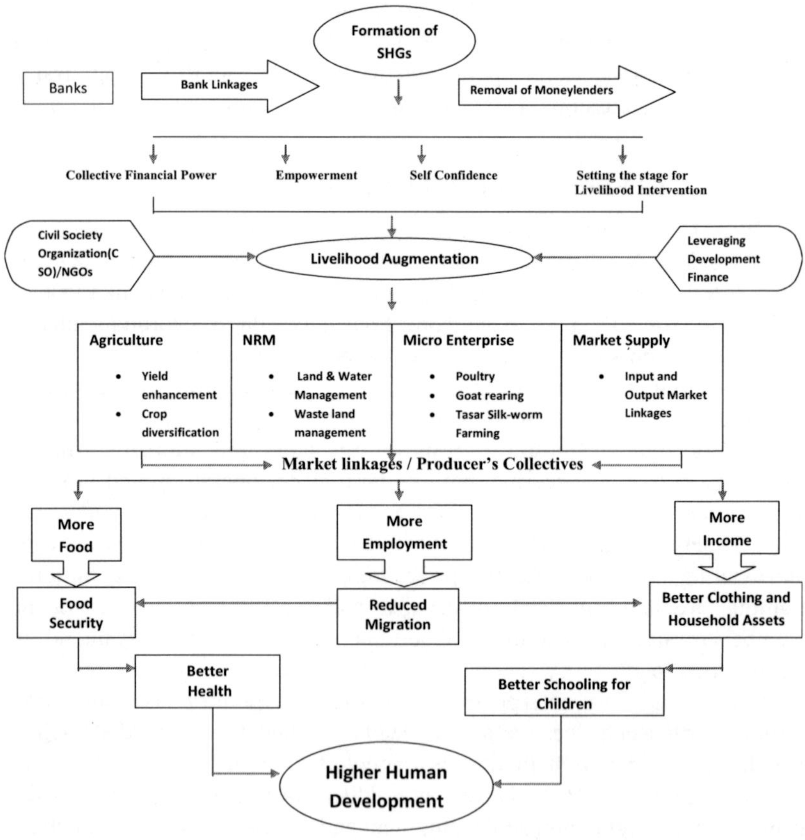

Figure 16.1: PRADAN's Developmental Model.

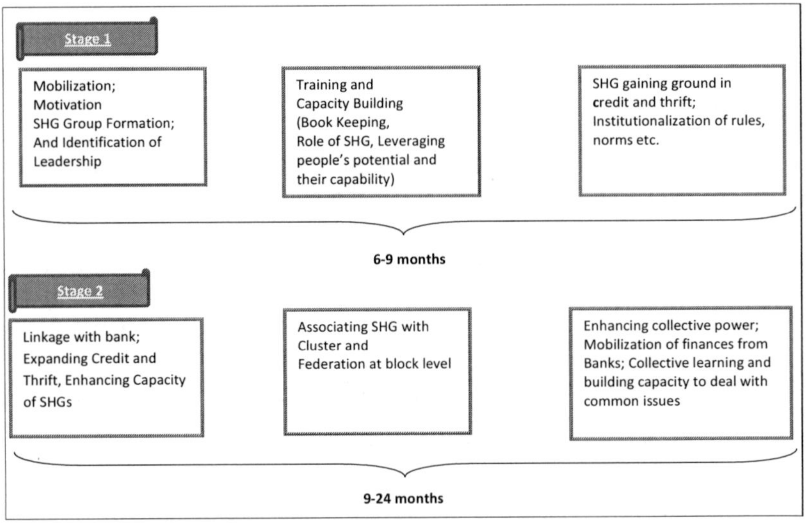

Figure 16.2: Process for grooming an SHG by PRADAN

Women, belonging to a particular SHG, pool in Rs. 10 to Rs. 20 each on a weekly basis, to create a collective fund. After six months of the formation of the group, 4-5 members from each group are given 3-4 days residential training. This training focuses on the importance of SHG in the larger social context and an attempt is made to help the members build a larger perspective of SHG in their lives. The members share their responsibility and design strategies to strengthen their SHGs. The other trainings include– accounts training, motivational training and credit planning.

In the second phase, PRADAN helps to develop the livelihood options for members of SHG through intensive analysis of various opportunities, potential and constraints. PRADAN supports enhancing productivity of natural resources and promoting micro-enterprises. It intervenes in the field of agriculture (improved paddy cultivation, cultivation of new crops and vermicomposting); horticulture (vegetables, mango plantation, floriculture, development of local nursery); livestock (goat rearing and rearing of livestock); forest based livelihoods (lac cultivation, siali leaf plate and tasar cultivation); small scale irrigation (construction of ponds, check dams and pump sets) and watershed development (lift irrigation-wasteland plantation and soil moisture conservation structure). PRADAN also promotes micro-enterprises such as poultry, tasar silk processing and rearing. Of the total households, majority of them have participated in one or more livelihood activities; the choice of options is often guided by the availability of local natural resource base and/or skill base, but at times the potential to exploit the synergy between livelihood options is also considered. Some members are encouraged to practice diversified agricultural activities while others have taken up forest based activity, livestock and other micro entrepreneurial activities to enhance their livelihood support systems.

In the final phase, PRADAN intervenes by leveraging development finance by linking the SHGs to government programmes and banks. It also promotes various kinds of people's organisations and links them with NGOs to scale up their established models and builds new livelihood opportunities. Finances are necessary for the rural poor to create livelihood assets and as working capital, enhancing the productivity and carrying capacity of resources, creating service infrastructure, and building people's skills and capabilities. PRADAN leverages support to livelihood projects by linking the rural poor to government programmes/agencies at the District, State and Central levels and with development banks like NABARD and act as a facilitator in them. In order to scale up the livelihood activity, PRADAN promotes and nurtures Producer's Collectives as an institutional support to poor farmers. It works with the producers so that they can play an effective role in the critical aspects of governance, management and operations of the existing collectives. This provides a large-scale expansion of agriculture based livelihoods and positions producer collectives to effectively channelize production, marketing and financial services to its members. In order to deepen its partnership it networks with other Civil Society Organisations like Vikash Bazar.Net in Jharkhand and South Odisha Development Initiative (SODI) in Odisha.

These three phases have distinct but intertwined objectives. In the first phase, PRADAN seeks entry in the village/hamlet, builds confidence and forms Women Self Help Groups (SHGs). Not only does PRADAN make them realize their collective potential but it also makes them believe that their current situation and predicament is not because of their sins or some curse but due to socio-political situation. They also help them believe that with persistence and collective efforts positive changes can be made. Only when the Women's group feel confident does the livelihood augmentation begins. In the final stage PRADAN has begun to network with NGOs (like Vikash Bazar.Net and SODI) to strengthen their reach in the market segment and to leverage and augment the resource available with other NGOs. This process helps the tribal groups to realize better prices for their products and help them increase their collective bargaining capacity in both import as well as export markets.

In most of the development activities, PRADAN operates with the supporting hand of Community Service Providers (CSPs) and Community Resource Persons (CRPs). Both these agents play different roles. Community Service providers (CSP) are young men and women from the community who are "trained" by PRADAN'S team on certain areas like developing norms of SHG, Package Of Practice (POP) of crops, vaccination and primary healthcare to animals/birds, etc. They provide handholding support particularly on skill, knowledge and information about the product so that the community gains. On the other hand, the CRPs are individuals from the same community who have already gained experience from PRADAN'S intervention. After gaining experience from PRADAN'S intervention they share their experiences with other community members to get them convinced and motivated thereby acting as leaders. Thus having overall knowledge of the village they act as representatives to the village. They also organize the procurement and distribution of inputs like seeds, fertilizers, pesticides and provide technical guidance to the farmers and also take care of marketing of the produce. They directly contact the SHG farmers who have volunteered to take part in this activity. A CSP can take up the services of more than one activity depending upon the timing of the activities and his /her own skills and capabilities. Most of the CSPs are men, but initiatives are being taken up to encourage women to take up this role as well. Today a remarkable number of women are taking up initiatives to engage in the development process and play service provider's role in their localities. For example in some of the villages of Jharkhand (Dumka and Gumla) the CSPs are women. PRADAN intervenes by organizing various types of technical and non -technical trainings to build the capacity of the SHGs, CSP/CRP, households and the community as a whole. At times PRADAN'S team trains a pool of CRPs which in turn train the SHGs and also their functionaries at the cluster level. This process helps improving local human resources and improves their capabilities.

4.2 Motivation, Management and Impact of SHGs

The success of an SHG depends upon the real motivation of the members in coming together. Initially the villagers were not convinced with the idea of forming an SHG they were scared that they would lose their savings. It was PRADAN'S team who convinced and motivated them to form an SHG. Seeing the successful formation, functioning and reaping the benefits of the first SHG other SHGs were formed in the same villages or nearby localities. In both the states in terms of caste, majority of the SHG members belong to the ST community followed by SC, OBC and Others. In Jharkhand out of the 41 Women SHGs studied 85 per cent belong to the Scheduled Tribe (ST) community while the remaining belong to OBC, SC, Others category or Sarna group with a mixed composition of caste. While in Odisha out of the 36 SHGs studied, 75 per cent of the members belong to ST community while the rest belong to OBC and SC community (Table 16.2). The number of members in an SHG varies from minimum 10 to maximum 21. In most of the SHGs in both the states, the numbers of members have increased since their formation. In Jharkhand the savings per member was Rs.3,495 while in Odisha it was Rs.2,887. Similarly the loan outstanding per SHG member in Jharkhand was Rs.1,699 while for Odisha it was Rs.3,971.

Table 16.2: Salient features of SHG in Jharkhand and Odisha

	Jharkhand	*Odisha*
Total SHGs in Sampled Villages	79	51
Number of SHG (*Sampled*)	41	36
Membership	(10-21)	(8-18)
Total No. of SHG Members	595	446
Composition of SHG		
(i) **Tribal**	35	27
(ii) **Non-Tribal or Mixed**	6	9
Total Deposits	20,79,693	12,87,835
(i) **Savings per SHG**	53,325	36,795
(ii) **Savings per Member**	3,495	2,887
Total Outstanding	10,11,052	1183310[1]
(i) **Loan per SHG**	25,924	51,,448
(ii) **Loan per Member**	1,699	3,971
Number of SHG linked to the Bank	34	29
Main occupation	Agriculture, Wage labour	Agriculture, Animal Husbandry, NTFP Collection

For 12 SHGs we could not get the total outstanding amount, hence the data pertains to only 39 SHGs.

4.3 Management of SHGs

The financial affairs of an SHG are managed by the office bearers- President, Secretary and treasurer- who are representatives to the bank, but most decisions are taken in the presence of all members which demonstrates that members believe in collective responsibility. The President, Secretary and Treasurer play an important role as signatories for withdrawal of money or taking loans from the bank. The office bearers are selected by the members on the basis of their educational qualification, technical know-how (maintenance of books of accounts) and communication skills. The SHG collects the savings and deposit it in the nearby located bank[3]. All the SHGs also keep a part of their savings in a box which helps them to meet their immediate needs. One person is responsible for keeping the box and other member keeps the key of the box. This helps them to keep a dual control over financial assets and safeguards their savings (Picture 16.1).

It is observed that for 80 per cent SHGs in Jharkhand and 67 per cent SHGs in Odisha there was no change in the leadership role and the same people continued in their positions since the inception of the SHG. However, in some villages it was found that leaders changed after specific period of time. Overall, thus we found continuity and original leadership except in a few cases where efforts to evolve alternative leadership was observed. Most of the SHGs in both the states have a fixed day and time for their weekly meetings but it varies from SHG to SHG. The meetings are held usually outside homestead under a tree in an open space, in school, on terrace, community hall or in the house of any SHG member. The SHG members are charged a fine of Re.1 - Rs.2 if they come late for the meeting or a fine of Rs.2- Rs.5 if they were unable to attend the meeting. The collection of monthly savings is the only major activity of the SHGs. In an SHG in Jharkhand (Gumla), members along with depositing money also give one glass of rice. If a member is unable to give rice in one of the meeting, then she gave two glasses of rice in the next meeting. The saved rice is sold and the money is used for buying registers, pens, etc. (Picture 16.2).

Picture 16.1: An SHG in Debidih village, Gumla which keeps their savings in a box

Picture 16.2: Rice collection drive during SHG meeting in Gumla

In Jharkhand and Odisha of 83 per cent and 81 per cent of SHGs are linked to banks. The interest rate on loans obtained from banks in both the states varies from 4 - 12 per cent per annum depending on the nature of loan obtained from the banks. Besides mobilizing savings, another important activity of SHGs as instruments of financial intermediation is to extend credit to members for the purpose of consumption, production, festivals or asset purchase. The SHGs charges interest which varies from 1 - 4 per cent per month and in case of defaults or late payments, the interest doubles. Thus interest earned becomes collective earnings of the group. The time period of loan varies from 1 month - 1 year depending on the loan amount, the repaying capacity of the borrower, purpose and timing of the loan. A villager who is not a member of SHG can also avail the loan with an interest rate of 4 per cent on a monthly basis. In Jharkhand 0.3 per cent of SHG members had defaulted while in Odisha 0.9 per cent were unable to repay the loan which is extremely low as compared to the default rate in commercial banks in relatively developed regions (default rate 40 per cent). As stated above, if a member does not repay the loan on time, the interest rate doubles which works as a deterrent.

For the smooth functioning of the SHG in Jharkhand and Odisha, PRADAN helps to form secondary organisations such as Clusters[4] and Federations[5]. A Cluster is a crucial link between the Federation and SHGs. It helps in the better administration as well as in fostering a feeling of unity and solidarity among the group members. Overall, review and monitoring of the SHGs take place at the Cluster level. While the federation is an apex body of SHG and Cluster comprising of a general body and an executive committee. The executive committee is constituted by elected/selected representatives of cluster who are the implementing and administrative body for handling day to day functions. The Federation is also responsible for the overall dissemination of information, implementation of livelihood plan, monitoring and evaluation of the microfinance operations. Through this, tribal women's collective bargaining and outreach gets enhanced.

4.4 Economic and Social Impact of SHGs

All in all the SHGs that we interacted, we found the SHGs have undoubtedly made a positive impact and proved as a blessing on the lives of poor women. Economic independence which was only a dream for the tribal women has come true. In general, following impacts have been observed:

Development of a healthy financial behaviour: The formation and promotion of SHG has led to the development of a healthy financial behavior. The flexibility in the amount of savings and repayment period has assisted the poorer communities to participate and reap the benefits. The initial loans in the SHGs were small and usually taken for meeting the domestic consumption needs but now members take loan for production, asset purchase and in some cases, for setting up their own enterprise. With each repayment the confidence grows and larger loans have been sought and repaid.

Security of women: The access to financial services has increased the security of women by releasing them from high interest debts and the clutches of moneylenders; it has allowed them to take advantage of market opportunities and develop a livelihood strategy that builds on their specific needs. It has also increased their employment security by allowing them and their families to diversify their occupational opportunities like- tasar silk reeling, poultry, etc. This in turn has ensured better clothing and income security.

Improved Role in decision making: An exposure to financial transaction, access to credit and a feeling that they are contributing to the family's financial and income security has given the women a sense of confidence and improved their status within the household. Women have a relatively greater say in the use of the money that they have earned and a greater respect in their families. Their increased ability to articulate their needs at various levels and their improved managerial skills have also earned them respect of their men.

Expansion of Horizons: The SHGs have expanded the women's world view, with more and more members and leaders stepping out for Cluster meetings and exposure visits to nearby towns and villages. At the Cluster and Federation meetings, their representation has given them a sense of pride and has also increased their self-respect. Some of them are even able to deal with senior bureaucrats and Public Developmental Officials. Women SHG members no longer want to remain confined within the four walls of their house.

Women Empowerment: Women have come together as a group and represented issues of interest to them as a class, demonstrating empowerment and collective strength. SHG act as community platform as women become active in village affairs contesting for local elections, taking action to address social or community issues like domestic violence, alcoholism, dowry system, schools and water supply. For instance in one of the village of Jharkhand we found that the SHG was instrumental in making a rapist surrender and due action was taken against him.

Personal Growth: Many women members of SHG who were shy, reticent and under confident, today they have emerged as leaders and are more articulate having a better self-perception and confidence. In most of the SHGs that we interacted with, women spoke of the need for certain specific livelihood related initiatives, improvement of infrastructure in their village varying from quality schools, health centers, electricity, drinking water and pucca roads, etc. These women also see themselves as agents of change and are of the opinion that these changes cannot be brought out without collective wisdom and efforts.

Gender Equation: The relationship with their men has improved and both share the workload of their house. According to them, they discuss household problems and prioritize the activities needed for improving family welfare.

Thus the SHGs promoted by PRADAN are not just microfinance organisation but they play different roles through different stages of evolution-mutual help; financial intermediation; livelihood planning and social empowerment. Today the women in these villages are acting as agents of change and have created a platform to share and demonstrate their affinity towards each other and mutuality. One only needs to visit these villages and SHGs to understand the changes brought out in their social status which is no less than a 'social revolution' in their lives, if their words are to be believed.

4.5 Livelihood Programmes and their impact

Livelihood development programmes open opportunities for the rural poor to engage in meaningful occupations. PRADAN'S livelihood programmes in Jharkhand and Odisha based on the nature of its activities may be classified into Agriculture (Food Crops & Cash Crops), Land and Water development, Forest based livelihoods, Poultry, Livestock and Micro-Enterprises. Over 67 per cent of the total households are involved in more than one livelihood activity and of these 48 per cent are involved in diversified agriculture, 14 per cent forest based activity, 31 per cent livestock, 5 per cent poultry and 12 per cent undertake micro enterprise related activities.

Improvement in Agriculture - Since in most of the villages of Jharkhand and Odisha, paddy is a staple crop and 60 per cent of the cultivated area is occupied with paddy, hence increasing its productivity is *sine qua non* for enhancing their livelihood. And therefore, PRADAN has rightly chosen to improve the productivity of rice cultivation. In order to increase the yield of paddy it is trying to disseminate System of Rice Intensification (SRI)[6] technology and improved variety of seeds in the area of operation. Some of the villagers are also using improved traditional method for paddy cultivation which has resulted in improving the productivity of paddy.

Enhancing productivity and diversification are the core strategies of PRADAN'S agriculture programmes. Specific activities are increasing the productivity of the main cereal crops to improve food security and *diversify into cash crops* such as pulses, oil seeds and vegetables. In some villages in Jharkhand pigeon-pea, cow pea and maize have been identified as suitable and additional crops to finger millet, gundli and kodo which were grown earlier. Some villagers are using fertilizers and poultry litter to increase the production of maize. Pigeon–pea is being promoted and cultivated as it supplements the protein content in the diet of the local people and it also has a strong potential to improve the quality of soil through nitrogen fixation by root nodules and augmentation of organic matter through leaf-fall and control of soil erosion. In Odisha in some villages before PRADAN intervened, kandula, black gram, mustard and finger millet were grown but now days additional crops like turmeric and pumpkin are being cultivated. Villagers are being exposed and trained on turmeric boiling which is of great additional value with less labour, water and fuel wood requirement. In addition to diversification of alternate crops in both the states, it is also encouraging the farmers to take up *vegetable cultivation* on their small-scale homesteads and near dug wells. In both states PRADAN has intervened by growing new vegetables in large quantities for household consumption and for commercial purposes. For example in some villages of Jharkhand earlier paddy, pulses and oilseeds were grown and now, in addition, vegetables such as ridge gourd, bitter gourd, mustard, cucumber, spinach potato, onion, tomato, chilly and lady's finger are being cultivated. However, in villages of Odisha PRADAN has intervened by motivating the SHG members to cultivate potato and engaging them into backyard vegetation. Varieties of vegetables are being planted and fenced using organic manure and pesticides. Thus diversification of crops into pulses and vegetables has resulted in adding nutritional value to their food and bringing cash in the hand of the community. In order to protect the young plants from insect vectors and viral diseases, setting up of *collective nurseries on vegetables*[7] are being promoted by PRADAN'S team in some villages of Jharkhand. In addition to the diversification into alternate crops and vegetables, *mango plantation* along with intercropping is also being encouraged. It is one of the fastest growing livelihoods option in both the states. *Floriculture* activity is also being practiced as a source of income in a village in Jharkhand but on a small scale.

Forest Based Livelihoods-PRADAN mostly works with the rural poor who live near forests and for whom forests and trees have been an important source of livelihood. In Jharkhand and Odisha, forest and tree-based livelihood interventions comprise of trading of siali leaf plates, lac cultivation and tasar cocoon production. *Siali leaf plate-making* is a source of supplementary income for poor people in these villages. PRADAN works in some of the villages with the tribal women, engaging them in making loose leaf and rough stitched leaf plates. The SHG members opting for this activity have been formed into a cooperative which provides support in the form of inputs, technical services and marketing of the produce. Another traditional occupation which has proved to be an important source of income for the tribals is *lac cultivation*. It has been identified as one of the leading NTFP activity. And in Jharkhand it is being cultivated on a large scale. Of the selected villages studied most of the households were involved in *tasar cocoon production*. Tasar rearing is being undertaken in some villages of Jharkhand and the rearers are being trained on improved rearing techniques which has reduced the risks and increased the overall productivity.

Livestock -PRADAN works with rural families in the promotion of goat rearing activities in the selected villages of Jharkhand and Odisha. It intervenes by bringing in better-quality breeds, veterinary care at the same time, developing a reliable cadre of village-based service providers and marketing systems. Village youths have been trained as paravets to provide technical services to the families at their door step. The paravets are responsible for ongoing supervision to improve production efficiency, by ways of ensuring timely vaccination and de-worming, measuring weight gain, regular health checkups of animal stock and treatment of some common diseases. In some villages of Jharkhand and Odisha, goat rearing practice is still in its prototype stage.

Poultry -PRADAN has developed a model of decentralised small holder poultry rearing which has emerged as a powerful tool for the livelihood promotion of rural poor women. The women from tribal and other poor families are organised into cooperatives to serve the growing needs of small town and urban markets. PRADAN is providing the women – through the cooperatives – hands-on training (technical), management support, assistance in securing finances from either banks or government programmes and market linkages. The women's cooperatives organised by PRADAN are providing inputs like feeds, chicks and medicines. At the same time, the cooperatives are making arrangements to market the birds. Some of the producers are also being trained to provide veterinary care and manage linkages on behalf of the cooperative.

Natural Resource Management-With an aim to enhance productivity, income and achieve sustainable livelihoods it promotes the Integrated Natural Resource Management (INRM) of land, water, forest and biological resources to achieve and sustain potential agricultural productivity. It uses participatory planning with the people; develop systems and treatment measures that are most suitable to the resources available. It combines managing the use of natural resources along with their conservation and sustenance. In Jharkhand and Odisha, PRADAN has intervened in creation of irrigation infrastructure and land development. Funds have been mobilised by the Government of India under various schemes for the construction of ponds, wells, for land leveling and lift irrigation. For example in a village in Odisha water is being supplied to households by diverting water from upstream at their door step for domestic use along with irrigation. This has reduced the drudgery of women who had to commute for a long distance to fetch water for domestic purposes.

Micro-Enterprise-PRADAN is promoting home-based microenterprises such as poultry rearing, tasar yarn production in Jharkhand and Odisha. For example in one of the village in Jharkhand a tasar reeling center has been initiated which is providing employment to 20 women. These women are working for 3 hours a day and earning an income on a monthly basis. Similarly in one of the villages in Odisha, broiler poultry farming is being encouraged.

4.6 Overall Assessment of Change

In an attempt at assessing the change of particular strategies, two points need to be kept in mind. One is the difficulty in establishing the casual link between a particular outcome and its cause when more than one factor work. In case of the changes that have taken place in villages of Jharkhand and Odisha, for instance one can identify different causes – government sponsored tribal development programmes, watershed development programmes, irrigation and forestry development programmes. The other point is the tendency to confine impact analysis exclusively to quantifiable variables, to neglect of often more significant qualitative changes. The criteria used in Table 16.3a, 16.3b, 16.3c to assess the changes brought about in villages of Jharkhand and Odisha under different time periods of intervention are therefore to be considered as indicative rather than exhaustive. The changes, grouped into on-farm changes, changes in the levels of living asset structure and occupational pattern, have been subjected to "pre" and "post" intervention analysis.

The indicators of *on-farm changes* point to the improvement in the primary source of livelihood of the villagers, viz. capacity to grow new and more crops. There has been a significant improvement in agriculture as the yield of paddy has doubled almost in all the villages of Jharkhand and Odisha. Although the yield varies year after year depending upon rainfall but this has led to improvement in food availability, change in cropping pattern and diversification of agriculture. Thus, for instance the yield of paddy has increased from 4-6 quintal /acre to 9-14 quintal/acre.

The improvement in the livelihood base is reflected in the changes in the standards of living. The ability to secure two meals a day (*food security*) remains one of the most revealing indexes of a household's living condition and the data points to a substantial improvement in this. In all the time frames of intervention before PRADAN intervened, the households had food available for 4-6 months and during the rest of the months they survived by borrowing from moneylenders, other villagers migrated to nearby towns but post intervention new livelihood opportunities have been created and food is available throughout the year. For example in a village in Jharkhand earlier the villagers ate finger millet, rice and salt now they eat rice with vegetables and dal. A phenomenal improvement in the *household assets* is also noticed. Pre intervention the households were poor without fans, chairs and tables, television and mobile phone; had utensils of mud and one cycle. Now mostly all the households have these necessities- utensils of brass, copper and steel; more than one mobile phone and cycle and few households have television with cable connection too. To be aware of the developments in society the villagers have started reading newspapers. In most of the villages in both states, the additional income generated by intervention has been used to purchase new sets of clothes. Thereby, the pair of clothes for each member has increased.

Table 16.3 (a): Developmental Intervention and Socio-economic change in sampled villages of Jharkhand and Odisha (< 5 years of Intervention)

	JHARKHAND		*ODISHA*	
	Pre Intervention	***Post Intervention***	***Pre Intervention***	***Post Intervention***
	1. On-farm Changes			
i. Paddy Cultivation				
-Method	Traditional	SRI, Improved traditional	Traditional	SRI, Traditional
-Yield	4-6 Q/ Acre	9 -14 Q/ Acre	3 – 5 Q/Acre	8-11 Q/Acre
ii. Diversification of Agriculture	Paddy, millet crops, pulses (urad), vegetables for household consumption	Paddy (SRI, Improved traditional, Variety of seeds), maize, pulses, oil seeds, vegetables for household and for sale	Paddy, millet crops, pulses, turmeric, few vegetables for household consumption	Paddy (traditional, SRI), vegetables, wheat, turmeric at commercial level
iii. Cropping Pattern	Paddy, fallow	Paddy, intercropping of varieties of vegetables	Paddy and turmeric	More diversified with cultivation in summer also
iv. Cropping Intensity	Low cropping intensity	80-112 per cent	Low cropping intensity	91-121 per cent
	2. Changes in Levels of Living			
i. Availability of food grains				
-During Normal year	4-6 months	8-12 months	3-6 months. Worst situation in Kaliani village (Mayurbhan)j whereas in Baripada village (Kandhamal), sufficient food available throughout the year	9-12 months. Also, rice availability under BPL programme ensures food security
-During Scarcity Year	4-8 months	6-10 months	Only for 1-2 months, rampant migration and high indebtedness	For 2-3 months, rampant migration and indebtedness
ii. Two full meals a day (% HHs)	50 per cent	80 per cent	Yes from migration and daily labor, food is secured	Yes , manageable
iii. Source of Drinking water	Wells, stream and ponds	Hand pumps, wells	Tube wells, river ,wells, spring water	Tube wells, wells, spring water
	3. Changes in the Asset Structure and Occupational Pattern			
i. Water Harvesting Structures -Check Dams	No Dam	Dam in Kurdega village (Gumla)	Dam in Kenduguda village (Kalahandi)	Same
- Cooperative Lift irrigation	Nil	Nil	Nil	Nil
ii. New trees/plants in the village	Nil	Mango, Arjun and Asan (for sericulture), Semialata (for lac)	Nil	Plantation done
iii. Occupation	Agriculture, seasonal migration for wage labor	Agriculture, Wage labor	Agriculture Service in Kenduguda village (Kalahandi) and Wage labor in Ramasali village (Mayurbhanj)	Agriculture Service in Kenduguda village (Kalahandi) and wage labor in Ramasali village (Mayurbhanj)
iv. Migration (% HHs)	50 per cent	10-13 per cent	40-60 per cent	Reduced to 25-30 per cent

Table 16.3 (b): Developmental Intervention and Socio-economic change in sampled villages of Jharkhand and Odisha (5-10 years of Intervention)

	JHARKHAND		***ODISHA***	
	Pre Intervention	***Post Intervention***	***Pre Intervention***	***Post Intervention***
1. On-farm Changes				
i. Paddy Cultivation				
- Method	Traditional	SRI, Improved, Variety of seed	Traditional	SRI, Traditional
-Yield	4-6 Q/ Acre	9-14 Q/Acre	4- 10 Q/ Acre	8-11 Q/Acre
ii. Diversification of Agriculture	Paddy, millet crops, pulses, few vegetables for household consumption	Paddy (improved traditional, SRI, hybrid), hybrid maize, pulses, vegetables, collective nursery for commercial purpose	Paddy, millet crops, pulses, turmeric, few vegetables for household consumption	Paddy (SRI), wheat, sunflower, vegetables for household and for sale, turmeric for commercial purpose
iii. Cropping Pattern	Paddy and millet crops only	More diversified with cultivation in summer also	Paddy and turmeric	More diversified with cultivation in summer also
iv. Cropping Intensity	Low cropping intensity	85-138 per cent	Low cropping intensity	110-126 per cent
2. Changes in Levels of Living				
i. Availability of food grains				
- During Normal year	4-8 months	10-12 months	4-8 months	6-12 months
- During Scarcity Year	2-5 months	4-7 months	2-3 months	2-4 months
ii. Two full meals a day (%HHs)	90 per cent	100 per cent	90 per cent	100 per cent
iii. Source of Drinking water	Well, Chhua, Hand pump	Same	River, well, open stream	Hand pump, well, gravity flow from stream
3. Changes in the Asset Structure and Occupational Pattern				
i. Water Harvesting Structures -Check Dams	No dam	Dam in Pathargora village (Dumka)	Nil	1 under construction in Deuli village (Mayurbhanj)
-Cooperative Lift Irrigation	No	1 in Luru village (Gumla)	Nil	Nil
ii. New trees/plants in the village	Nil	Plantation done	Nil	Plantation done
iii. Occupation	Agriculture, seasonal migration for wage labor	Agriculture, Wage labor, Poultry farm in Jhatnitola village (Khunti)	Agriculture, Labor	Agriculture, Poultry, Goat rearing
iv. Migration (% HHs)	50 per cent	Reduced to 5- 10 per cent	40-50 per cent	Reduced to 10 per cent

Table 16.3 (c): Developmental Intervention and Socio-economic change in sampled villages of Jharkhand and Odisha (>10 years of Intervention)

	JHARKHAND		*ODISHA*	
	Pre Intervention	***Post Intervention***	***Pre Intervention***	***Post Intervention***
1. On-farm Changes				
i. Paddy Cultivation				
- Method	Traditional	SRI, Improved traditional	Traditional	SRI, Improved traditional
-Yield	2-6 Q/ Acre	12-18 Q/Acre	4- 6 Q/Acre	7-12 Q/Acre
ii. Diversification of Agriculture	Paddy, millet crops, few vegetables only for household consumption	Paddy (improved, SRI, hybrid), additional vegetables	Paddy, few vegetables only for household consumption	Paddy, additional vegetables, oilseed, pulses
iii. Cropping Pattern	Paddy and millet crops	More diversified with cultivation in summer also	Paddy , millet crops and turmeric	More diversified with cultivation in summer also
iv. Cropping Intensity	Low cropping intensity	73-118 per cent	Low cropping intensity	97-111 per cent
2. Changes in Levels of Living				
i. Availability of food grains				
- During Normal year	4-8 months	9-12 months	2-6 months	5-8 months
-During Scarcity year	3-6 months	3-7 months	1-2 months	3-8 months
ii. Two full meals a day (% HHs)	90 per cent	100 per cent	Yes because of credit from moneylenders or selling of siali leaves	No change
iii. Source of Drinking water	Well, river	Well, Hand pump	Wells, ponds, tube well, canal, stream	Wells, tube wells
3. Changes in the Asset Structure and Occupational Pattern				
i. Water Harvesting Structures - Check Dams	2 dams in Budhudih village and 1 in Gandhrakhpur village (Dumka).	3 in Budhudhih village (Dumka) (1 given by MNREGA). 3 dams in Gandhrakpur village (Dumka) Dam did exists in Debidih village (Gumla) but it has got damaged	Nil	Nil
- Cooperative Lift Irrigation	Nil	1 each in Debidih and Luru villages (Gumla). In Turiyadih village (Gumla) the lift irrigation does not work.	Nil	Diesel pump given to group in Nahudesaru and 1 Lift irrigation in Ballisuga village (Kandhamal)
ii. New trees/plants in the village	Nil	Plantation done	Nil	Plantation done
iii. Occupation	Agriculture, seasonal migration for wage labor	Agriculture, wage labor, government job, poultry farm in Budhudih	Agriculture, labor, forest dependent	Agriculture, forest dependent, labor
iii. Migration(% HHs)	50 per cent	Reduced to 5-10 per cent	40 per cent	Reduced to 10-15 per cent

Earlier the women wore a sari without blouse, roamed barefoot, used nagra mitti[8] to wash their hair and were shy to present themselves in public. But post intervention their life style has changed. The women have a matching blouse for each saree, each member of the family has at least 2-3 pairs of chappals/shoes, wash their hair with shampoo and dress up well to visit the nearby market.

The extent to which the above improvements are sustainable depends on the changes that have taken place in the means of production. The data on the improvements in the three key resources –land, water and trees show that significant investments have been made in consolidation of these resources. In this, land and water development hold a pre-eminent position, since they contribute in reducing the ecological vulnerability and increasing the cropping intensity. The changes in the occupational pattern to which the data point are another proof of the improvement that has been brought about in the resource base of the villages. The fact that the percentage of labour force dependent on migrant labour has reduced from 50 per cent to 10 per cent in sampled households of Jharkhand and from 40- 60 per cent to 25-30 per cent in Odisha. This proves that the productivity of the land and other resources has been restored to a degree that the village is able to feed its people and its people need no longer wander around in the nearby towns and other states to eke out a living.

PRADAN'S intervention has brought about a change in the thought process of the villagers in both the states. They are more concerned about the education of their children and the heath of their families. In mostly all families today joint decisions are taken by men and women concerning the future of their children. The increased income generated from various livelihood options is being invested in quality education and health of the family members. Majority of the women are concerned about the quality of education thereby are transferring their children from missionary to private schools. They have understood the importance of education and are motivating and supporting their children to pursue higher education in nearby towns and states. The health scenario has also undergone a change. Earlier when any family member used to fall ill people, due to their superstitious beliefs, thought it to be symptoms of black magic. Thereby, they did Jhad Phuk[9] . Now whenever any person falls ill they rush them to the nearby healthcare center. Villagers are aware of the health issues and are consuming nutritious food under proper sanitation conditions.

Overall, thus, the impact of PRADAN has been multipronged. Firstly, it has helped the women groups to build their confidence among themselves to realize their latent potential which in turn has led to removal of indebtedness and freed them from the clutches of moneylenders. Secondly, the intervention in agriculture, land and water management and introduction of micro-enterprises has enhanced their food and income security and finally, it has reduced the dependence on migration as a source of income and livelihood.

V. Concluding Remarks

Before we conclude, we would like to draw attention on perspective of tribal development as the onset of India's independence. Since independence (even prior to independence) there has been intense debate on development discourses and development of tribals. At the time of independence, industrialisation was at the center of development discourse and Nehru, the first Prime Minister of India, as an architect of modern India designed five year plans for speedy development of the entire nation. His appointed Anthropological Advisor to the Government of India, Verrier Elwin, a British Indian citizen, wanted that the tribes should be left alone. This meant allowing them to live their own way, not infringing on their economic space and permitting them to grow in their self-created and self-designed paradigm.[10] Elwin did not oppose Nehru for his industrialisation programme so long it did not affect the tribal but Elwin strongly believed that the tribals were exploited by the outsiders – so called a more civilised caste society – whenever they penetrated in tribal areas. Nehru of course did not agree with Elwin that the tribes should be kept in isolation, away from the mainstream, and argued that the plans should be designed to bring the tribes in mainstream of development. Elwin differed with Nehru and supported Gandhi's stand on self-reliant village republic and tribals right on forest land as well as the use of their own indigenous technology in the production process.

Since the early planning era, several Commissions and Committees were constituted to look after the tribal community's problems and needs and suggest appropriate strategies to solve them. However none succeeded and several even affected them adversely. For instance, maximum money was invested in mines and development of industrial plants in the tribal areas due to the rich resources available there. These investments affected tribals adversely since they were uprooted from their habitations (Ballabh and Batra, 2013). Experience with economic planning and development was equally disappointing and the overall condition of the tribals in Jharkhand and Odisha continued to lag behind the other social groups including Scheduled Castes.

Against this back drop where most public interventions for tribal development in central India did not bear any fruit, we presented a case study of PRADAN an NGO which is silently revolutionizing the development process through Women Self Help Groups (SHGs). PRADAN'S core philosophy in working with the poor tribal women is in path to conquering economic poverty through enhancing livelihood opportunities. In this process PRADAN'S Professionals enable poor women to break free from their past, develop an alternative vision for their future and set achievable goals. It makes effort to develop the poor with technical, organisational, negotiating skills that facilitate attainment of their goals.

It is not difficult to find as to why PRADAN succeeded, first and foremost, the focus is on collectivism as opposed to the individual tribe. Historically, the tribal society was known for their egalitarianism, sharing and caring for the sustenance of their society. Though true egalitarianism may not be present in the present world and some inequality has infected the tribal community as well, the fact that most of them continue to be poor by any economic standard but once they saw the opportunity to improve through collective SHGs they accepted it. Added to it, PRADAN chose to make entry in any village through Women's Self Help Group which proved a blessing in disguise. Tribal women were the most vulnerable section of society and have suffered in a worse manner from underdevelopment, indebtedness, alcoholism, illiteracy and under and malnourishment. These women saw collective SHGs as an opportunity to improve their economic and social status. Second, the pace at which PRADAN professionals move, step by step, in the formation, nurturing and introduction of livelihood programmes also contributes to their success. Here emphasis was more to enrich the capacity of women members rather than meeting the targets. This pace varies across villages and within the village with different SHGs. Meeting the target and spending the fund has never been a major concern for PRADAN which is quite common in public supported developmental programmes. Thus, PRADAN professionals concentrate more on capability development of individuals and their organisations like SHGs, clusters and federations. This has led to further contribution towards human and social capital formation within the tribal society. Third the identification of leadership was also critical at various levels of SHGs, clusters and federations. Since most of the first generation SHG members are illiterate, this becomes a very critical factor. Their learning ability in book keeping, management of funds, communication and trust of other members were identified as some of the critical issues for election/selection of the office bearers. Hence mutual discussion and understanding the members was an important factor during the formation of SHGs which were carefully crafted. Thus most SHGs continue with original selected leaders for sustenance of the SHGs. Fourth the organisation recruits young professionals from top institutions and universities who hold specialised degrees in subjects like management, engineering, agriculture, social sciences and deploys them at the grassroots level, inducting, nurturing and developing them to operate in a wide spectrum with diversified roles and responsibilities. These professionals not only are trained to directly interact with the tribal people but also help to develop local Community Resource Persons (CRPs) and Community Service Providers (CSPs). While selecting the CSP and CRP extreme care is taken by PRADAN'S professionals as CRPs and CSPs are local persons from the community who speak same local dialect and hence communicate effectively. Finally, the tribal people and their organisations themselves prepared plan for their development – in agriculture, horticulture, poultry and tasar silkworm reeling and whatever was possible in their local condition and with the resources available through public or private sources. They learned the new technologies and methods – and even introduced new enterprise in some areas – and networked with organisations. Their illiteracy and other disabilities did not prevent their ability to learn and apply the same.

Both Nehru and Elwin died in 1964, had they been alive, would have realised that they were fundamentally wrong or at best only partially correct. Elwin of course would have realised that keeping the tribes in isolation did not prevent their deprivation and protect them from exploitation. He would have also realised that the tribes do not have any inherent incapability to learn new technologies or newer ways of producing goods. At the same time Nehru's industrialisation also did not help the tribal community; it only brought misery, deprivation and even uprooted them. Both of them would have realised that building people's capabilities and putting the instrument of development in the hands of the tribals would have been a better approach to address problems of tribal communities. This requires social engineering of the tribal society and bringing institutional innovations which has the capacity to support them as producer, consumer and resource manager.

References

Ahmed, N. and Lahiri Dutt K (2006), "*Engendering Mining Communities: Examining the Missing Gender Concerns in Coal Mining Displacement and Rehabilitation in India*", New Delhi: Sage Publications.

Areeparampil, M (1996), "Displacement due to Mining in Jharkhand", *Economic and Political Weekly*, Vol 31, No. 24(15) : 1524-1528.

Asthana V (2012), "Forced Displacement- A Gendered Analysis of the Teri Dam Project", *Economic and Political Weekly*, Vol XLVII(47-48): 96-102.

Ballabh, V and Batra P (2013), "Development Induced Displacement: Second Generation Problems". Paper presented at IAJBS conference on Sustainability & Business Practices: Implications for Business Schools; Saint Louis University, John Cook School of Business, USA - July 14 - 16, 2013.

Barik, R. K (2006), "Faulty Planning in a Tribal Region: The Dandakaranya Development Authority" in Govind Chandra Rath (ed), *Tribal Development in India-The Contemporary Debate*, New Delhi: Sage Publications, pp. 92-111.

Bhanumathi, K (2007), "Status of Women Affected by Mining in India", www.samataindia.org.in. accessed on May 20, 2015.

Cernea, M (2000), "Impoverishment Risks, Risks, Safeguards and Reconstruction: A Model for Population Displacement and Resettlement" in M Cernea and Christopher McDowell (ed.), *Risks and Reconstruction: Experiences of Resettlers and Refugees* ,Washington: The World Bank: 1-52.

Dhru Kelly A (2010), "*Acquisition of land for 'development' projects in India: The Road Ahead*", Ahmedabad: Research Foundation for Governance.

Downing E. Theodore (2002), "*Avoiding New Poverty: Mining-Induced displacement and Resettlement*", paper series No.58 London: International Institute for Environment and Development.

Dreze,J, M Samson and S.Singh. ed.(1997), "*The Dams and the Nation*", New Delhi: Oxford University Press.

Dwivedi, R (1999), "Displacement, Risks and Resistance: Local Perceptions and Actions in the Sardar Sarovar", *Development and Change*, 30(1): pp. 43-78.

Fernandes, W and G Bharali (2006), "Development-Induced Displacement in Assam 1947-2000: A Quantitative and Qualitative Study of Its Extent and Nature", Working paper Guwahati: North Eastern Social Research Centre.

Fernandes, W (2007), "Development-Induced Displacement: The Class and Gender Perspective", Paper presented at the International Conference on *The Emerging Woman in the Indian Economy.* Christ College, Bangalore, November 26-27, 2007.

- (2007), "Mines, Mining and Displacement in India", *International Mining Conference.* New Delhi: Indian School of Mining, Dhanbad with Australian National University and the University of New South Wales, November 19-21,2007.

- (2008), "Paying the Price for Someone Else's Displacement", Working Paper Guwahati: North Eastern Social Research Centre.

- (2008),"India's Forced Displacement Policy and Practice Is Compensation up to its Functions?", Michael M. Cernea and Hari Mohan Mathus (eds). *Can Compensation Prevent Impoverishment? Reforming Resettlement through Investments and Benefit-Sharing*, Oxford University Press: 181-207.

Government of India,(2013), *Statistical Profile of Scheduled Tribes in India*, Ministry of Tribal Affairs, Statistical Division, New Delhi :Government of India.

Goyal, S (1996),"Economic Perspectives on Resettlement-and Rehabilitation", *Economic and Political Weekly*, Vol XXXI (24) :1461-1467.

Guha, Ramachandra. 2001 [1999]. *Savaging the Civilised: Verrier Elwin, His Tribals, and India.* New Delhi: Oxford University Press.

Ghurye, G.S (1943), *The Aborigines –So Called and Their Future*. Poona: Gokhale Institute of Politics and Economics, (cited from Rath 2006).

Kabra (2003), "Displacement and Rehabilitation of an Adivasi Settlement", *Economic and Political Weekly*, Vol XXXVIII (29) : 3073-3078.

Maheshwari (2006),"Preparing to repeat a dammed history", www.videovolunteers.org/petition. accessed on May 20, 2015.

Mishra (2002), "Development, Displacement and Rehabilitation of Tribal People: A Case Study of Orissa", *Journal of Social Sciences*, 6(3): 197-208.

Mohanty, R (2011), "Impact of Development Projects on the Displaced Tribals: A Case Study of a Development Project in Eastern India", *Orissa Review*, Government of Odisha LXVIII (2& 3) :67-73.

Nandi, J (2012), "Coalmines displace forest tribal dwellers in Central India", *Time of India*, http://articles.timesofindia.indiatimes.com/2012-10-15/india/34471405_1_forest-dwellers-mahan-forests-forest-rights-act

Negi S. and Ganguly S (2010), "*Development Projects vs. Internally Displaced Population in India*", paper presented at the ESF- UniBi- ZiF research conference on 'Environmental Change and Migration : From Vulnerabilities to Capabilities', Bad Salzuflen, Germany, December 5-9, 2010.

Oliver-Smith, A (1991), *Displacement Resistance and the Critique of Development: From the Grassroots to the Global,* Final Report for ESCOR, Refugee Studies Centre, Oxford :University of Oxford.

Pandey, B and Rout B.K (2004), "*Development Induced Displacement in India: Impact on Women*", New Delhi: National Commission for Women.

Parasuram, S (1993), "*Impact of Displacement by Development Projects on Women in India*", Working Paper Series No 159, The Hague: Institute of Social Studies (ISS).

Ray, P (2000), "Development Induced Displacement", *South African Resource Watch,* Vol 2(1): 33-41.

Rath G.C (2006), "Nehru and Elwin on Tribal Development: Contrasting Perspectives" in Govind Chandra Rath (ed), *Tribal Development in India-The Contemporary Debate*, New Delhi: Sage Publications: 52-91.

Roy, A (2005), "Revolutionary Frontline", http://revolutionaryfrontlines.wordpress.com accessed on May 20, 2015

Rustomji, Nari (ed.).2001[1989].*Verrier Elwin: Philanthropologist*. New Delhi: Oxford University Press,(cited from Rath 2006).

Sarkar, A (2007), "Development and Displacement", *Economic and Political Weekly*, Vol XLII (16):1435-1442.

Sen, J (1995),"Displacement and Rehabilitation – Some points towards Changing Course of Current Thinking", *Economic and Political Weekly*, Vol XXX (17) : 963-966.

Sharma, R N and Singh Shashi R (2009), "Displacement in Singrauli Region: Entitlements and Rehabilitation", *Economic and Political Weekly*, Vol XLIV (51): 62-68.

Srinivas, M.N.1944, 'Review of the Aboriginals', *Journal of the University of Bombay (History, Economics and Sociology)*, New Series ,12:4, January,91-94.(cited from Rath 2006).

Thukral, E (1992), "*Big Dams, Displaced Peoples: Rivers of Sorrow, Rivers of Joy",* New Delhi: Sage Publications.

Thekkekara, M. (1993), "Tribal Women: The Trauma of Transition", *Social Action* 43(1): 23–31.

World Commission on Dams (2000), *"Dams and Development: A New Framework for Decision making",* The Report of the World Commission on Dams, London, VA: Earthscan Publications

Notes

1. Revised paper presented in the National Seminar on "Gender Discrimination and Inequalities in Contemporary India: Status Causes and Solutions" organised by the Department of Sociology, Babasaheb Bhimrao Ambedkar (Central) University, Lucknow, November 11-12, 2014.

2. Indian academia also criticised the park and isolationist approach on the ground that property right in land and land market was created by the British colonial rulers. Such property right was not developed for the central Indian region which led to their continuance of communal ownership (see Ghurey, 1943 and Srinivas 1944 cited from Rath 2006).
3. It should be noted that the literacy rate among first generation SHG members is quite low and whosoever can read and write are given priority in the selection of the office bearer.
4. A cluster is a group of 10-15 contiguous SHGs within a geographical proximity. The members of the SHG are the representatives to the general body of cluster who in turn elect President and Secretary for the Cluster. It is a forum of peer learning, cross learning, problem solving and as an interface with panchayat, bank and relevant stakeholders. They also help SHGs in preparing their finance and livelihood plans. The proposals for linkages with banks are prepared and discussed in the meetings.
5. Federations are generally formed at block level to create a platform for solidarity, identity, dealing with various socio- economic issues the SHG members face and it also ensures self-sustenance of the SHGs.
6. SRI is a package of practice consisting of six elements – seed treatment and seed rate, transplanting within 7-14 days, seedlings taken out with mud, one seedling per hill, maintaining line to line and plant to plant distance and making sure weed-free field by weeding 2-3 times.
7. It is a group of 15 to 70 farmers who are raising vegetable nursery together in the best suited common place protected with nylon nets.
8. Clay found near the river belt and has a texture of fuller's earth.
9. Jhad Phuk is black magic a traditional method to cure sickness and ills.
10. For details see Rath (2006). Nehru and Elwin on Tribal Development; Contrasting Perspectives.

17

Effectiveness of MGNREGA in Empowering Women

—G.S. Mehta

I. Introduction; Since independence, various initiatives have been undertaken for improving the socio-economic status and empowering different disadvantaged groups of population, especially women in India. To begin with, the Constitutional provision was made for socio-economic, cultural and political equality and to provide equal rights for availing different opportunities to all social groups of population. Further increasing emphasis has also been provided in the past development plans to introduce a variety of women specific development programmes and schemes with an attempt to ensure the maximum participation of women in these programmes. Even at the policy level, various legal reforms and resolutions in the form of social acts have also been introduced to bring improvements in the social empowerment of women. A great emphasis has also been laid on the maximisation of participation of women in different levels of education so that they may become aware about their rights, responsibilities and social standing and maximize their participation in different social, political and economic activities.

However, over the years the participation of women in all available opportunities including education and employment is lagging far behind that of their male counterparts. This has been clearly highlighted in the National Human Development Report, 2002. In fact, the women have the disadvantages of around 6 percent in the availment of education with a cumulative inequality of 5 percent against men (Mehta, 1990) and the total disadvantage of women in employment depress their position to an extent of 68 percent from the point of equality with men (Papola, 1982). The National Human Development Report (2001) also points out that the gender disparity index in India has increased from 0.62 points in 1981 to 0.68 points in 1991. Prevailing social evils, traditional social system, biased attitude of society and family against women have been recognised as the main factors limiting the scope of women to participate in different Grover 2001). In this sense, various social evils and cultural backwardness, which are so deep rooted since ages, cannot be removed merely through the socio-economic and political activities and in availing certain opportunities.

Now, it has been well accepted that the effectiveness of laws, social reforms and acts may succeed only in a situation when there is social sanction, social acceptance and mass supports in their implementation (Aggrawal and introduction of laws and acts. To tackle these problems, Nayyar (1987) advocated introducing certain socially acceptable programmes and approaches. It was generally believed that mere legislation would not be enough for women's development. The legislation and acts have to be backed by proper implementation and strong public supports (Bhagwati, 1985)

In background of the undesirable achievements visualised with the introduction of various programmes on achieving empowerment among women during different plans in the past the National Rural Employment Guarantee Act (NREGA) was enacted to reinforce the commitment towards empowering women through making a mandatory provision of providing at least one third of the total employment to be generated under NREAGA for women in rural areas during each year. In addition, the Act emphasized for not making any discrimination against women in wage payment, ensuring maximum participation of women in different decision making process of NREGA related activities etc.

II. The Present Study; In this light the present paper attempts to examine at the extent to which the women of different socio –economic groups had achieved economic empowerment through participating in MGNREGA activities. This has been analyzed in terms of getting employment and income opportunities, reducing unemployment and freedom availed in keeping their wages after participating in MGNREGA activities. The paper is based on a sample of 158 women consisting 68 participant and non-participant women of MGNREGA, randomly selected from four districts of the state of Uttar Pradesh.

1. Impact of MGNREGA on Employment and Unemployment; The impact of the introduction of MGNREGA in creation of additional employment and its contribution in reducing the incidence of un-employment among women has been assessed in terms of its share in the gross working days and un-employment days of the women during last year. This analysis has been attempted at district level and according to different socio – economic parameters of woman participant and non – participant households.

(i) **Across the Districts**; Looking at the contribution of MGNREGA in providing employment it revealed that the participant women were only getting employment for 5 percent of working days in different works created under MGNREGA while a highest proportion of 47 percent working days were lost under the condition of unemployment. Remaining 35 percent and 13 percent working days were utilizing under the self employment and other non – MGNREGA employment. Across the district level the proportion of working days of women under MGNREGA were highest at 7 percent in Chitrakoot followed by 6 percent in Hardoi. Among the participants and non–participants the proportion of working days under non – MGNREGA employment were relatively higher for former groups than the latter group of respondents in totality terms and across most of the districts except in Chandauli. But the proportion of working days employed as self employed were noted higher in favor of non–participants in each of the district.

Overall impact of MGNREGA has been very positive in providing additional employment and reducing unemployment of women who has been participating in MGNREGA employment. It is evident by the fact that as a result of getting employment of participant women for over 9 percent of additional working days over the non–participants the differences in the proportion of unemployment days of participants has been gone down over 56 percent as compared to non–participants. Across the districts, the differences in getting additional days of employment of participant women in MGNREGA over their non–participant women was reaches to the highest points of 15 percent of working days in Hardoi and the differences in the proportion of unemployment days were down at 41 percent to 58 percent for participant women over the non – participant women.

(ii) **Across the Castes of Households;** The sample of women participants was from only SC and BC communities. The contribution of MGNREGA in providing employment had gone more in favor of BC women than the SC women. As the proportion of working days under MGNREGA for former group of women was reported 12 percent as against 6 percent for latter group of women. Even the former groups of women were getting higher days of employment than the latter group of women but less than non-participants. But days of employment as self employment were relatively higher for SC than the BC women but the same were higher for both the groups of non–participants women

The impact of MGNREGA has also been positive in terms of providing additional employment of lowest from 11 percent to highest at 13 percent days among the participant women over the non -participant women. But a negative impact against all the castes of participant women over the non- participant women was revealed

Table 17.1: Impact on Employment and Unemployment Across the Districts

Proportion of Working Days	*Participant Households*					*Non-Participant Households*				
	Hardoi	*Kheri Lakhimpur*	*Chandauli*	*Chitrakoot*	*Total*	*Hardoi*	*Kheri Lakhimpur*	*Chandauli*	*Chitrakoot*	*Total*
Under MGNREGS	6.06	0	0.5	7.22	4.79	0	0	0	0	0
Under Non MGNREGS	30.67	7.72	4.5	11.08	13.11	0	3.08	6.94	7.7	4.5
Under Self employment	16.06	52.08	51.71	31.73	35.16	60.4	64.58	61.11	51.89	58.95
Unemployed days	47.2	40.21	43.3	49.97	46.95	39.6	32.34	31.94	40.41	36.56
Total days available for work	100	100	100	100	100	100	100	100	100	100

Table 17.2: Impact on Employment and Unemployment by Caste of Households

Proportion of Working Day	*Participants*				*Non-Participants*				*Difference*			
	SC	*ST*	*BC*	*Gen*	*SC*	*ST*	*BC*	*Gen*	*SC*	*ST*	*BC*	*Gen*
Under MGNREGS	5.98	0.00	12.05	0.00	0.00	0.00	0.00	0.00	7.20	0.00	15.80	0.00
Under-Non MGNREGS	13.36	0.00	14.39	0.00	24.52	0.00	24.31	13.49	11.09	0.00	11.30	13.49
Under-Self employment	43.73	0.00	38.63	0.00	45.48	0.00	44.44	54.76	-43.37	0.00.	-36.82	-54.76
Unemploy-ment days	36.93	0.00	34.93	0.00	30.00	0.00	31.25	31.75	38.34	0.00	36.08	31.75
Total working days	100.00	0.00	100.00	0.00	100.00	0.00	100.00	100.00	100.00	0.00	100.00	100.00

in the days of employment as self employment in non-MGNREGA activities. Even the proportion of UN – employment days for all the castes of women participants were noted higher than their non–participants counterpart of women.

(iii) Among Men and Women; Further, there revealed a clear-cut discrimination in providing employment opportunities against women in MGNREGA. This was evident by the fact that the proportion of employment days provided for women accounted to 5 percent as against 10 percent days for men. In fact the proportion of working days under both non – MGNREGA and self-employment were indicated higher for both participant and non – participant men as copmpared to women. Its direct impact was seen in terms of higher proportion of un – employment days for women among both participants and non–participants than their men counterparts.

However, because of participation of women in MGNREGA, they have been getting over 9 percent additional days of employment over the non–participant women. Even the concern impact was revealed more significant in favor of men participants than the women participants and also over their non –participant counterparts. As the men participants were getting 35 percent of additional days of employment over the non–participant men.

2. Impact of MGNREGA in Generation of Income; Further the analysis has been carried out to examine the contribution of MGNREGA in the total income generated from different sources in the participant and non–participant households of women at district level and among the different socio-economic groups of households during the year 2007-08. Also, attempts has been made to examine the differences emerging in the contribution of income generated from different sources between the households of participant and non–participant households on one hand the implication of NREGA income generated in the women participant households over the non–participant households.

Looking at the contribution of MGNREGA in the total income generated at the level of participant households this share seems to be quite significant in the sense that the share of MGNREGA employment was 9.12 percent as against 10.76 percent share in MGNREGA income of women participants. The overall impact of income generated from MGNREGA has also been positive in favor of women participants in terms of achieving higher contribution over their non-participant counterpart in the total income of households in almost the districts. In other words, because of 11 percent income additional income generated from MGNREGA employment the overall contribution of women participant has increased to over 37 percent higher

Table 17.3: Impact on Employment and Unemployment by Sex

Proportion of working Days	*Participant Households*			*Non–Participant Households*			*Difference*		
	Male	*Female*	*Total*	*Male*	*Female*	*Total*	*Male*	*Female*	*Total*
(a) Under NREGA	9.74	4.76	8.59	0.00	0.00	0.00	34.74	8.94	25.37
(b) Under Non-NREGS	24.85	12.88	22.09	12.89	4.50	11.52	55.58	20.24	42.74
(c) Self employment days	35.76	35.94	35.80	60.04	58.95	59.86	-26.61	15.76	-11.22
(d) Un-employment days	29.65	46.42	33.52	27.07	36.56	28.62	36.28	55.07	43.11
(e) Total days available for work	100.00	100.00	100.00	100.00	100.00	100.00	100.00	100.00	100.00

Table 17.4: Contribution of Women MGNREGA Income Across the Districts

Percentage Share in HH income by Source	*Participant Households*					*Non–participant Households*				
	Hardoi	*Kheri lakhimpur*	*Chandauli*	*Chitrakoot*	*Total*	*Hardoi*	*Kheri lakhimpur*	*Chandauli*	*Chitrakoot*	*Total*
NREGS Income	2.19	0.00	8.07	23.85	10.76	0	0	0	0	0
Non-NREGS	16.76	0.00	51.30	85.04	44.85	3.33	0.00	3.13	2.08	2.30
Total Household Income	2.28	0.00	9.15	21.79	9.33	3.33	0.00	3.13	2.08	2.30

Table 17.5: Contribution of Women MGNREGA Income By Caste of Households

Percentage Share in HH Income by Source	*Participants Households*				*Non-Participants Households*			
	SC	*ST*	*BC*	*Gen*	*SC*	*ST*	*BC*	*Gen*
Wage Income During All Sources of 2007-08								
Proportion of Female MGNREGS Income in total MGNREGS Income	9.07	0.00	14.21	0.00	0	0	0	0
Proportion of Female Non-MGNREGS Income in total MGNREGS Income	52.41	0.00	37.49	0.00	4.72	0	1.91	1.29
Proportion of Female Wage Income in total Household Wage Income	9.73	0.00	10.33	0.00	4.72	0	1.91	1.29

than the contribution of non –participant women in the total income of their respective households.

(i) **Across the District Level;** Looking at the contribution of MGNREGA in the total income generated at the level of participant households this share seems to be quite significant in the sense that the share of women in MGNREGA employment was 9.12 percent as against 10.76 percent share in MGNREGA income. Across the districts level, the situation was almost same. Even, in Chitrakoot the share in income and employment of women was 24 percent and 15 percent respectively. The contribution of women in income earned from non–MGNREGA employment has been indicated quite significant in totality term and across almost the districts except in Hardoi while its comparison was done with the share of women in non –MGNREGA employment.

Moreover, the overall impact of income generated from NREGA has been positive in favor of women participants in terms of achieving higher contribution over their non -participant counterpart in the total income of households in almost the districts. In other words, because of 11 percent income additional income generated from MGNREGA employment the overall contribution of women participant has increased to over 37 percent higher than the contribution of non –participant women in the total income of their respective households.

(ii) **Across the Caste of Households;** Since the sample women participants were from only SC and BC community of households the both the caste group of women were contributing a significant proportion of income in their households through participating in NREGA employment. However, this share was significantly higher for BC women than the SC women accounting for 14 percent and 9 percent respectively. But the contribution of non–MGNREGA was found many folds higher than the Non–MGNREGA income in the total income of both the castes of household. However, as a result of additional income generated from MGNREGA employment by the participant women over the non –participant women the overall contribution of former group of women has gone up remarkably much higher than the latter group of women in the total income of their respective group of households

3. Access to Freedom for Keeping Wages; In the process of examining at the extent the women were in a position to achieve improvement in their empowerment after participation in the works of MGNREGA. The analysis in this context is centered around to assess the differences emerging between

Table 17.6: Women Keeping and Not Keeping Wages Across the Districts

Description	Participants					Non-Participants				
	Hardoi	*Kheri Lakhmpur*	*Chandauli*	*Chitrakoot*	*Total*	*Hardoi*	*Kheri Lakhimpur*	*Chandauli*	*Chitrakoot*	*Total*
No.of Women Sample H.H	1 (100.00)	-	18(100.00)	49 (100.00)	68 (100. 0)	30 (100.0)	22 (100.0)	19 (100.00)	19 (100.00)	90 (100.00)
Women keeping wages	1 (100.00)	-	8 (44.44)	22 (44.90)	31 (45.59)	14 (46.67)	4 (18.18)	8 (42.11)	7 (36.84)	33 (36.67)
Women not keeping wages	-	-	10 (55.56)	27 (55.10)	37 (54.41)	16 (53.33)	18 (81.22)	11 (57.89)	12 (63.16)	57 (63.33)

Table 17.7: Participant and Non-participant Women keeping and not keeping Wages by Caste

Description	Participants					Non-Participants				
	SC	*ST*	*BC*	*General*	*Total*	*SC*	*ST*	*BC*	*General*	*Total*
No. of Women Sample H.H	40(100.00)	2(100.00)	25(100.00)	1(100.00)	68(100.00)	32(100.00)	0	45(100.00)	13(100.00)	90(100.00)
Women keeping wages	19(47.50)	0	11(44.00)	1(100.00)	31(45.59)	9(28.13)	0	17(37.78)	7(53.85)	33(36.67)
Women not keeping wages	21(52.50)	2(100.00)	14(56.00)	0	37(54.41)	23(71.87)	0	28(62.22)	6(56.15)	57(63.33)

participant and non –participant women in getting freedom from their households to keep wages which were generated from MGNREGA and other sources and its uses under different heads.

(i) Across the District Level; The participant women constituted to those who participated in both the works while the non–participant women had participated in only Non-MGNREGA works. In totality terms, only 42 percent women had the freedom to keep their own wages with them. Even the Proportion of such women was as low as 18 percent in Kheri Lakhimpur though it was highest at 48 percent in Hardoi. However, the impact of participation of women in MGNREGA has been quite positive in terms of getting freedom by them in this context. As the proportion of participant women keeping their wages with them were 46 percent as against 37 percent non–participant women. Even this proportion of participant women reached at 100 percent in Hardoi.

(ii) Across the Caste of Households; The freedom to keep their wages was generally provided to almost the castes of women by their households but these proportion women were varying from highest at 57 percent for general castes followed 40 percent BC to lowest at 39 percent for SC women. However, among the participant and non–participant women the proportion of them keeping wages with them was significantly higher among all the castes of former group of women than the latter group of women. This indicates the fact that initiating maximum participation of women in MGNREGA could be an important measure to bring improvement in the empowerment of women especially disadvantaged groups of women in the near future.

Conclusions; There has been at least some extent of impact of MGNREGA in creation of additional employment for women participants during the last two years of its implementation in the state. Unemployment days of participants have gone down over 56 percent as compared to non –participants. Among the different castes, the contribution of MGNREGA in providing employment had largely gone in favor of BC women followed by SC women. Again the former group of women were getting higher days of employment than the latter group of women but less than non participants in Non-MGNREGA activities. The participant women were empowered to get additional employment of 11 percent to 13 percent days over the non -participants.

Further, there revealed a larger difference in providing employment opportunities among men and **women i**n MGNREGA. The proportion of employment days provided to women accounted to 5 percent as against 10 percent days to men. Also, the proportion of unemployment days for women among both participants and non – participants were noted higher than their men counterpart. However as a result of participation of women in MGNREG its contribution has been noted in providing over 9 percent of the additional days of employment to the participant women over the non – participant women. Though, the concern impact was revealed more significant in favor of men participants than the women participants.

In terms of the extent of empowerment achieved by women in driving earning the participant women were contributing 11 percent additional income over the non –participant women for their household by way of getting MGNREGA employment. But still, the contribution of non- MGNREGA income has been significantly higher than the MGNREGA income in the households of both participant and non–participant women in almost the districts. But the overall contribution of women participants has increased to over 37 percent higher than the contribution of non –participant women in the total income of their respective households after getting MGNREGA employment. However, this contribution was noted significantly higher in case of BC women than the SC women accounting for 14 percent and 9 percent respectively.

The impact of participation of women in MGNREGA has been in providing freedom 46 participant women to keep their wages with them. But, a very high proportion of 78 percent women were utilizing it in the purchase of food items while a lowest proportion of 19 percent of them were using it for personal purposes. Relatively higher proportion of all castes of participant than their non –participant counterpart of women had availed the freedom to keep their wages with them. This indicates the fact that maximizing participation of women in MGNREGA could be a important measure to bring improvement in their empowerment in the near future. Moreover, the women participants representing different socio- economic background of households in general and landless, low income groups and ST/SC households had gained over their non –participants in getting higher days of employment and thereby reducing in proportion of unemployment days and contributing higher income for their households after the introduction of MGNREGA in every sample districts of the state.(Mehta, 2009)

References

Aggarwal D. Grover I and Grover D (2002), Political Empowerment of Women Panchayat Members: Study from Haryana, in Grover I and Grover D. (ed.), *Empowerment of Women,* Agro Tech Pub. Co., Udaipur.

Banerjee Nirmala (1989), 'Trends in Women Employment, Some Micro Level Observations', *Economic and Political Weekly*, April 29.

Bhagwati Jagdish (1985), 'Family Court Needs More Powers', *Hindustan Times*, August-11, 1985.

Mehta G.S. (1990), 'Disadvantages against Women', *Man and Development*, Vol. XI, No. 2.

Mehta G.S. (2009); Management of MGNREGA, Issues and Challenges; Giri Institute of Development Studies, Lucknow.

Nayyar Rohini (1987), 'Female Participation Rate in Rural India', *Economic and Political Weekly*, December 9.

Papola T.S. (1982), *Women Workers in Urban Labour Market: A Study of Segregation and Discrimination in Employment*, GIDS, Lucknow.

18

Utilisation of Public Health Services by Women: A Study of Bihar

— ***Rajeev K. Kumar***

Abstract

Health is a state of complete physical, mental and social well-being and not merely the absence of disease or infirmity' (WHO, 1946). The concept of health and diseases are not absolute. These vary from one culture to another and from one geographical region to another. The need for health services vary for men and women and the availability and accessibility to health care services also vary for them. Women require health services more frequent than men as their requirement is more due to their physiological needs. The present study tries to understand the utilisation of maternal health services including the ante-natal services and delivery and also the family planning services in the Vaishali district of Bihar state. The specific objectives of the study are- to analyze the availability and shortfalls of infrastructure and health personnel in the state and district; accessibility and utilisation of maternal health services; and also to study the factors affecting the utilisation of public health services. This study is based on both primary data and secondary data. The primary data collection was made from two block Primary Health Centers (PHCs) namely Rajapakar PHC and Patepur PHC of Vaishali district of Bihar. The secondary data was collected from various sources.

The Government has been trying hard to provide affordable and quality health services through its network of public health facilities. But it has been found in the study that the State of Bihar has been lagging far behind in providing the proper health facilities. The shortfall in terms of the physical infrastructure at all the levels (district hospital, sub-divisional hospital, CHC, PHC, APHC and HSC) and health personnel in all the categories of the staffs (medical, Para-medical and nursing staffs) is evident.

Other issue which comes out distinctly is the utilisation of different health services in the district. It was found that the district was not able to cover the expected level of beneficiaries for most of the services. The shortfall of the infrastructure and health personnel is the main reasons. It has also emerged from the study of women respondents of the two PHCs that most of them know about the public health facilities but unable to avail the services.

Declaration and Acknowledgement:

The contribution submitted herewith is original, not copied from any other source, and not submitted elsewhere for publication. It has also undergone plagiarism test, all the references have been cited correctly and I accept the responsibility for releasing this material. I would also want to acknowledge the efforts of T. Khandade in collecting the data and with whom a paper titled "Ability to Take Health Care Decisions: A Case of Rural Women of Vaishali district of Bihar", in Relocating Women equal Role in Indian Society, *(Eds. P Kumar & S Gupta), 2015, Rawat Publications, Jaipur, (ISBN 978-81-316-0742-8) has been published.*

The present paper deals with the availability and utilisation of public health facilities by women in Bihar. The paper is mainly consisted of three parts. First part deals with the status of public health institutions, its availability and shortfall in the state. It also includes a brief introduction of the subject, studied area and methodology. The second part consists of utilisation of different maternal and child health services by the women. The last part of the paper focuses on the findings of the utilisation of health services at two block PHCs of Vaishali district of Bihar. At the end of the paper, a few suggestions are also put forth for the improvement of utilisation of health services by women in the state.

1. Status of Public Health Facilities in Bihar

1.1 Introduction

Health is the level of functional or metabolic efficiency of a living organism. In general parlance health means proper functioning of the body i.e. a person is able to carry out the routine work without any stress. Health is defined by World Health Organisation (WHO, 1946) as 'a state of complete physical, mental and social well-being and not merely the absence of disease or infirmity'. The concept of health and diseases are not absolute. These vary from one culture to another and from one geographical region to another. Health is also dependent upon a number of other factors such as socio-economic and cultural factors, environmental, biological and other factors.

Women have a different relationship to the heath care system than men. Women are more likely to use the health care services than men because of their health status, higher incidence of chronic health problems, and lifetime need for reproductive and related services. There are also considerable differences in how different groups of women use the health care system that are driven by economic factors, age and health status, and health needs. Many women experience a range of barriers to care that are logistical and economic in nature (Salganicoff, Ranji and Wyn, 2005).

The need for health services vary for men and women and the availability and accessibility to health care services also vary for them. Women require health services more frequent than men as their requirement is more due to their physiological needs. It has also found from different studies that despite the more needs of health care the women have limited access to health care services due to various socio-economic reasons. If the women are denied to health care services particularly the women of reproductive age group we also deny the health services to the infant and children dependent on them. Good health and well being of the women plays a great role in the development and emancipation of women. It also contributes to the development of family and society. Good health is a fundamental goal of development and it has been realised that targeting health as part of development is an effective way of improving the welfare of people including the women (Kumar & Kapoor, 2009).

Children and women, especially the young children, are the most vulnerable group of population in matters of survival and health. The productive capacity of individual is directly related to their physical and mental development which is shaped by the attention and care individual receives during his or her formative years – the childhood period. The most critical role in the survival, growth and development of the child is played by the mother. The physical and mental status of the mother contributes very significantly towards the survival, growth and development of the child. Enhancing the physical and mental capacity of mother is therefore critical for ensuring survival of the child and its normal growth and development (Chaurasia, 2006).

Beside this, Women have unique health issues. And some of the health issues that affect both men and women can affect women differently for example, women are more likely to die following a heart attack than men, women are more likely to show signs of depression and anxiety than men, the effects of sexually transmitted diseases can be more serious in women, osteoarthritis affects more women than men, women are more likely to have urinary tract problems. Unique issues include pregnancy, menopause, and conditions of the female organs. Women can have a healthy pregnancy by getting early and regular prenatal care. They should also get recommended breast cancer, cervical cancer, and bone density screenings (http://www.nlm.nih.gov/medlineplus/womenshealth.html). Addressing women's reproductive health in totality is important for understanding gender issues as they reveal how gender norms affect reproductive health services, differential exposure to risk, access to services and their benefits, to information, and to resources (Basu and Mitra, 1992).

The role of public health in improving the health status of women and children is immense. This can be further improved by increasing the access and availability of public health care services to the women, especially in rural areas of the state. Public health has been mainly concerned with preventing disease, prolonging life and promoting health care through the organised efforts of the community as well as state.

It has been observed that most of the rural people are dependent on the public health institutions of the area, but its utilisation by the women depends on several factors such as awareness about the health facilities, proximity of the health facility, educational level, working status etc. Educated women are likely to have proper knowledge and information on modern medical treatment and have greater capacity to recognize specific illness (Caldwell, Reddy & Caldwell, 1983). Similarly, working women are expected to have greater control over resources in the household. They are likely to have greater knowledge about pregnancy and childbirth due to greater freedom of movement. However, it is also argued that women's work in developing countries is poverty induced and therefore likely to have negative impact on the use of their health care services (Berman et al., 1997).

It is believed that the people living in urban areas have better facility of health services but accessibility and affordability are still a major concern particularly for the poor. Women living in urban slums have more difficulty as they do not have basic sanitation and toilet facilities. Rao and Somayajulu (2004) observed that though the urban areas, compared to the rural, are better equipped for providing the health services but in spite of this, the urban poor especially women and adolescent girls do not have the access. They attributed the poor health status of the women to several factors such as unhygienic practices, childbearing practices, unavailability of toilets, drainage system, less awareness and women enjoying moderate level of autonomy in view of their role in decision making. They also found that in spite of universal awareness about the contraceptive methods, only half of the studied women reported to be using any method.

1.2 Methodology

The present paper tries to understand the utilisation of maternal health services including the ante-natal services and delivery and the family planning services in the Vaishali district of Bihar state. The specific objective of the study is- to analyze the availability and shortfalls of infrastructure and health personnel in the state and district; accessibility and utilisation of maternal health services (ANC and delivery) and family planning services in Vaishali district; and also to put forth some programmatic suggestions to improve the utilisation of public health services by women.

This study is based on both primary as well as secondary data. The primary data collection was made from two block Primary Health Centers (PHCs) namely Rajapakar PHC and Patepur PHC of Vaishali district of Bihar. The secondary data was collected from various sources such as Census-2011, SRS-2011, District Health Information System (version- 2), Bihar Development Report-2012, State Project Implementation Plan (SPIP) of State Health Society of Bihar, Govt. of Bihar and other documents and reports of health department.

The field work for the primary data collection was carried out in the month of Oct, 2012 by the study team members. A total of 140 respondents were interviewed consisting of 70 respondents each from both the above PHCs (Rajapakar and Patepur). After editing and cleaning the data, 10 incomplete schedules were discarded from the study sample and thus the responses of 130 women were analyzed. All the respondents were female patients who had come to the Govt. health facilities to avail the health services. The data was collected through a structured interview schedule. Most of the questions in the interview schedule were close ended and focused on the respondents' socio-economic profile, educational status, awareness about the Govt. health facilities and the accessibility of these facilities by the respondents. After the data collection, the data were fully validated in terms of internal consistency before it was analyzed. The data were analyzed using SPSS software, version-17.

1.3 Background Characteristics of Studied State and District

Bihar is an entirely land-locked state and located in the eastern part of the country (between 83°-30' to 88°-00' longitudes). It has a total area of 94,163 sq. km. after the division of the state. As per census- 2011, the total population of the state is 103,804,637 and it ranks third in country in term of population. The population growth of the state of Bihar is very high as the average annual population growth rate is 2.26 percent and the decadal growth rate is 25.07 percent during 2001 and 2011. This is much higher as compared to the national average of decadal growth rate (17.64 percent). Majority of the population of the state resides in rural area (88.70 percent). Rate of urbanisation in the state is only 11.30 percent.

The annual per capita income of the state is only Rs. 13,362 which is one of the lowest in the country. Bihar has the adverse geographical situation and it faces either drought or flood or both in the same year leading to a halted progress of the state. The rate of the urbanisation of the state is also very low (only 11.30 percent). The urbanisation is directly correlated to industrialisation and the scope of industry is less. Most of the industries are based on the agriculture and hence the rate of urbanisation is much slower. The biggest advantage for the state is its large young population and the availability of natural resources but there are several constrains as well in the path of development such as acute climatic conditions, land locked area, and low industrialisation etc.

The density of the population is 1102 persons per sq. km, which is much higher than the national average of 382 persons per sq. km. The decline in sex ratio has also been observed for the state. It is only 916 females per 1000 males (rural- 926 and urban- 868). The child sex ratio (0-6 years) is 933 in the state. The total literacy rate of the state is again a major concern. It is only 63.8 percent for the state while the literacy rate of the country is 11 percent more than the state (74.04 percent). Male literacy rate is 73.3 percent while the female literacy rate is only 53.3 percent in Bihar. Gender gap in literacy rate for Bihar as well as Vaishali district is also very wide. It is almost 20 percent for the state and 19 percent for the Vaishali district. Infant Mortality Rate (IMR) i.e. number of deaths per 1000 birth was 52 in the year 2011-12 which is slightly higher than India (50). Crude birth rate and death rate for Bihar are 28.5 percent and 7.0 percent respectively while for India the figures are 22.5 percent and 7.3 percent respectively (table 18.1).

Table 18.1: Background Characteristics of the state and studied district

Indicators	*Bihar*	*Vaishali*
Area (sq. km.)	94163	2036
No. of Community Development Blocks	534	21
Annual per capita income 2011-12 (Rs.)	13362	—
Average Annual growth rate (%)	2.26	2.9
Decadal growth rate (%)	25.07	28.58
Total Population	103804637	3495249
Rural	92075028	3262715
Urban	11729609	232534
Sex Ratio (no. of females/ 1000 males)	916	892
Rural	926	893
Urban	868	878
Child Sex Ratio (0-6 years)	933	894
Population density per sq. km.	1100	1717
Rural	23.9	28.87
Urban	35.11	24.58
Birth Rate (SRS-2011)	28.5	—
Death Rate (SRS-2011)	7.0	—
Natural Growth Rate (SRS-2011)	21.5	—
IMR –no of deaths per 1000 birth (2011-12)	52	45
Percentage of urbanisation	11.30	6.67
Total Literacy Rate (Census, 2011)	63.82	66.60
Male Literacy Rate (Census, 2011)	73.29	75.41
Female Literacy Rate (Census, 2011)	53.33	56.73

Source: Census, 2011; Bihar Development Report-2012; SRS-2011; State Health Society Bihar.

The studied district Vaishali is one of the 38 districts of Bihar with an area of 2,036 sq. km. It became a district when it was split from Muzaffarpur district of Bihar in 1972. Vaishali district is a part of Tirhut division and Hajipur town is the district headquarters. In 2006 the Ministry of Panchayati Raj named Vaishali as one of the country's 250 most backward districts (out of a total of 640 total districts in the country). It has three Sub-Divisions namely-Hajipur, Mahnar, and Mahua and 21 blocks namely- Mahnar, Sahadai Buzurg, Vaishali, Bidupur, Goraul, Raghopur, Lalganj, Hazipur, Mahua, Jandaha, Patepur, Sahdeibuzurg, Rajapakar, Bhagwanpur, Chehrakala, Premraj, Patedhi-Belshar, Desri, Taiyyopur, Sarai, Manibhakurahar. Vaishali is also important districts due to its close location with the state capital.

According to the 2011 census, Vaishali district has a population of 3,495,249 ranking 86th in India (out of a total of 640 districts). The district population comprised of 3.36 percent of the total population of the state. Both the population density and growth rate of the population of the district are much higher than the state. The district has a population density of 1,717 persons per sq. km while the population growth rate over the decade 2001-2011 was 28.58%. Also the decadal growth rate of the district in rural areas is (28.58 percent) is higher than the urban areas (24.58 percent). This is also in contrast to the state where the decadal growth for the urban areas is higher. The district also falls much behind the state in terms of percentage urbanisation. It is only 6.67 percent in the district as compared to the 11.30 percent for the state. The sex ratio of the district is only 892 females for every 1000 males which is again very low as compared to the state and country. The child sex ratio (0-6 years) is not very encouraging as well for the district (only 894). The literacy rate of the district is slightly higher than the state. It is 66.60 percent (male- 75.41 percent and female- 56.73 percent). Here also the gender gap in literacy is too wide.

Bihar is one of the most backward states of the country. This is also seen in the above data which shows that the state is fairing very poorly on most of the major demographic and socio-economic indicators such as annual and decadal population growth rates, sex ratio, population density, birth rate, death rate, rate of urbanisation, natural growth rate, literacy rate etc. If we compare these data with the last census, we see the deterioration. The situation of the studied district is even worst.

1.4 Public Health Facilities in the State and District

The constraints in providing the qualitative and affordable public health services have been felt for a longer period of time in the state as the shortfall of the health facilities, basic infrastructure facilities in the public health institutions and skilled and trained manpower are evident in the data. The shortfalls of the facilities and the manpower are felt in all the categories of the health facilities. These facilities are not increased with the increasing population and demand and not even upgraded in the state. These facilities are not even equipped with skilled manpower and infrastructure as per the Indian Public Health Standard (IPHS).

Poor health infrastructure is also reported in the 5th CRM report. At present the state has 9696 HSCs, which is about 60% of the total required. The lack of infrastructure for service delivery is a limiting problem in the state. In addition to a mismatch between required, sanctioned, and those in place; the quality and completeness of facilities is also a major challenge. There are major physical infrastructure constraints at the field level. The pace of civil works is very slow. Most of the HSCs are situated in either at rented building or having no buildings. The load on the Block PHC is high in comparison to availability of resources and adequate infrastructure, hence there is an urgent requirement of up-gradation of BPHCs into CHC to reduce the load and enhance the quality of care. Running water, electricity and toilet facilities are missing at most APHCs and HSCs. Non availability of residential accommodation is a major lacuna since no new additions of staff quarters between 2005 and now. Construction of health facilities is not as per IPHS standard. Currently there is no infrastructure and finance wing both at the state and district level (CRM - 2011).

The following figure and table present the availability of different types of public health facilities in the state. It also gives the required facilities as per the population and IPHS norms and percentage shortfall of these facilities. If we observe the table, the shortfall of public health facilities is distinctly visible in all the categories except Primary Health Centers. The overall shortfall is 47.64 percent. The maximum shortfall is observed in the category of Community Health Care Centers and Referral Hospitals (88.41 percent) and minimum for the District Hospitals (5.26 percent). More than 50 percent shortfall is also observed for Medical College and Hospitals (65.0 percent) and Additional Primary Health Centers (55.40 percent). Health Sub Center,

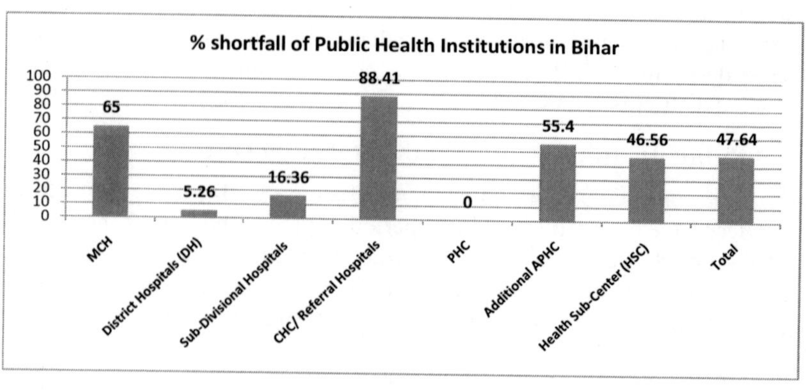

located at the village level, is the first contact point with the community. A huge gap is also observed in the HSC (46.56 percent).

Table 18.2: Availability and Shortfall of the Public Health Institutions in Bihar

Type of Facilities	*Required*	*Existing*	*Shortfall*	*% shortfall*
Medical College and Hospital (MCH)	20	7	13	65.00
District Hospitals (DH)	38	36	2	5.26
Sub-Divisional Hospitals (SDH)	55	46	9	16.36
CHC/ Referral Hospitals (RH)	604	70	534	88.41
Primary Health Center (PHC)	534	534	0	0.00
Additional Primary Health Center (APHC)	2787	1243	1544	55.40
Health Sub-Center (HSC)	16576	8858	7718	46.56
Total	***20614***	***10794***	***9820***	***47.64***

Source: SPIP-2012-13, State Health Society Bihar, Govt. of Bihar.

The following table 18.3 gives the status of availability and shortfall of the medical and Para-medical staffs in the state. It is evident from the following table that the health personnel in all the categories i.e. medical, nursing and Para- medical staffs are very less in numbers. The overall shortfall of these health staffs is 34.73 percent. Maximum shortfall is observed in Lady Health Visitors (regular LHV) which is 57.56 percent and minimum shortfall is observed in Auxiliary Nursing Midwives (regular ANMs; only 18 percent). More than 50 percent shortfall is observed in the categories of – regular LHV (57.56 percent), regular Nurse Grade- A (56.18 percent), contractual Nurse Grade- A (56.52 percent), Multi- Purpose Workers (52.47 percent), and Laboratory Technicians (51.32 percent).

Thus, the shortage of the health personnel in all the categories is very high. Most of the regular positions are vacant for a long time. The recruitment of regular staffs has not been made for a long time. One of the major grave concerns of Public Health Delivery System in Bihar is the huge shortfall of medical and nursing staffs. Due to this the existing health staffs have high patient load. The shortfall in the categories of LHVs also affects the quality of work done by ANMs who are posted at HSCs. These LHVs are supposed to play the role of supervisors and supervise the ANMs work but due to work load and paucity of LHVs, they are unable to supervise the ANMs.

To make the system run somehow the Government appoints these staffs on contract basis. This is an ad-hoc arrangement. Now the state has two cadres of staffs, regular and contractual, in all the categories. The percentage of all the contractual health personnel (doctors, Nurse Grade-A, and ANM) is almost 40 percent of the total existing staffs which is quite high. It is also found that the contractual staffs are made to work more on less (consolidated) payment. These categories also gave birth to several practical problems related to the

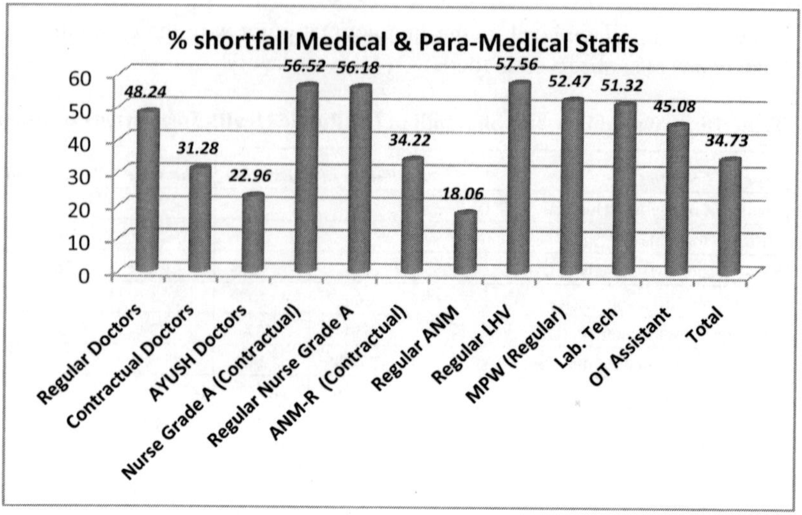

job responsibility. For example, job insecurity, less payment and lack of any proper job description are some of the impending problems of the ad-hoc system.

Table 18.3: Availability and Shortfall of Medical & Para-Medical Staffs in Bihar

Medical & Para-Medical Staffs	*Required*	*Existing*	*Shortfall*	*% shortfall*
Regular Doctors	4867	2519	2348	48.24
Contractual Doctors	2375	1632	743	31.28
AYUSH Doctors	1694	1305	389	22.96
Nurse Grade A (Contractual)	3395	1476	1919	56.52
Regular Nurse Grade A	1004	440	564	56.18
ANM-R (Contractual)	11433	7521	3912	34.22
Regular ANM	11808	9676	2132	18.06
Regular LHV	1171	497	674	57.56
MPW (Regular)	1700	808	892	52.47
Lab. Tech	680	331	349	51.32
OT Assistant	122	67	55	45.08
Total	***40249***	***26272***	***13977***	***34.73***

Source: SPIP-2012-13, State Health Society Bihar, Govt. of Bihar.

Under the National Rural Health Mission (NRHM), Project Management Units have been established at different levels i.e. State, district and blocks. In Bihar, there are 9 additional Regional Project Management Units (RPMUs) at all nine divisions of the state. Since there are a large number of districts in the state and the geographical area is also very large, these RPMUs have been created at the divisional level to function as bridge between the state and districts. The health programs and schemes are brought under one umbrella and these health programs and schemes are managed by the skilled managerial staffs deployed at the project management units. The focus of NRHM is on establishing a fully operational, community owned, and decentralised health care delivery system with inter-sectoral convergence at all levels. The focus is also to ensure action on a wide range of determinants of health such as water, sanitation, education, nutrition, social and gender equality.

If we see the availability and shortfall of the managerial staffs under NRHM in the state at different levels, the situation is satisfactory in most of the categories. Most of the positions are filled except the Junior Child Health Managers (65.79 percent shortfall) and District and Block Community Mobiliser- ASHA (36.84 percent and 22.59 percent respectively) and District Planning Coordinator (23.68 percent). The key positions at the district level such as District Program Manager, District Accounts Manager, and District Monitoring & Evaluation Officer and at block level such as Block Health Manager and Block Accounts Manager are mostly filled.

Table 18.4: Availability and Shortfall of the Managerial Health Personnel in Bihar

Managerial Staffs	*Required*	*Existing*	*Shortfall*	*% Shortfall*
District Program Manager	38	36	2	5.26
District Accounts Manager	38	35	3	7.89
District Monitoring & Evaluation Officer	38	36	2	5.26
District Planning Coordinator	38	29	9	23.68
District Community Mobiliser (*ASHA*)	38	24	14	36.84
District Data Assistant (*ASHA*)	38	31	7	18.42
Junior Child Health Managers	38	13	25	65.79
Hospital Managers	76	63	13	17.11
Block Health Managers	518	459	59	11.39
Block Accounts Manager	518	457	61	11.78
Block Community Mobiliser (*ASHA*)	518	401	117	22.59
Total	***1896***	***1584***	***312***	***16.46***

Source: SPIP-2012-13, State Health Society Bihar, Govt. of Bihar.

The next table 18.5 shows the availability of number of public health facilities in the state and district. It can be seen that the district has only one tertiary level health facility i.e. District Hospitals. Other tertiary level facility is not available in the district while the state has seven Govt. Medical Colleges and Hospitals. There are three Sub-Divisional Hospitals in the district but Community Health Centers is not available. Similarly, there are 534 Primary Health Centers in the state and 17 in the district. Of these, 518 and 16 Primary

Health Centers are fully functional in the state and district respectively. Total Health Sub-Centers in the state is 8858 (9696 as per CRM report, 2011) and total HSC in the district is 335. A large number of these HSCs are without their own building (4875). These are running either in the rented building or some other facilities.

Table 18.5: Availability of health facilities in the state and studied district

Indicators	*Bihar*	*Vaishali*
Govt. Medical Colleges & Hospitals	7	0
District Hospitals	36	1
Sub-Divisional Hospitals	46	3
Community Health Centers	70	0
Primary Health Centers	534	17
Additional Primary Health Centers	1243	30
Health Sub Centers	8858	335

Source: SPIP-2012-13, State Health Society Bihar, Govt. of Bihar.

The state has been trying to catch up with the required health facilities and trying to meet the shortfalls by initiating the constructions of new buildings or renovations of the existing building. The Government has so far been able to complete some projects under NRHM but there is still a huge gap and many more projects are to be completed particularly the buildings for the HSC, APHCs and CHCs. It will take a long time to meet the shortages. There is also a huge gap in the residential quarters at all levels. If the Govt. is serious to improve the quality of health services round the clock it has to ensure the mandatory health staffs should stay at the facility. This cannot be ensured without providing the residential quarters in the premises of the health facilities.

2. Public Health Services Utilisation by Women

Promotion of maternal and child health is one of the important components of the Health and Family Welfare program of the Govt. of India. The Government initiated several programs to strengthen the maternal and child health services right from the first Five Year Plan (1951-56). Under the Minimum Needs Program initiated during the fifth Five Year Plan (1974-79), maternal health, child health and nutrition services were integrated with Family Planning Services, with focus on providing minimum level of health services to the pregnant women and lactating mothers. The next action in this regard was the launch of Child Survival and Safe Motherhood (CSSM) program in 1992-93 (Somayajulu, 2004).

Another initiative in this direction has been taken recently in 2005 under the flagship program of National Rural Health Mission (NRHM) initiated by the Central Government. Some new components have been added to the existing health services under NRHM such as incentives to the mothers and community health workers (ASHA- Accredited Social Health Activist), integration of AYUSH (Ayurveda, Yoga, Unani, Sidhha and Homeopath), mobile medical units, free ambulatory services etc. As mentioned before, NRHM has also erected a huge health team of health officials and workers at all levels of facilities i.e. state region, district and block. To monitor the health programs, a reporting system has been developed in which the concerned health staffs have to report the health services provided to the beneficiaries in the field and at the health facilities. This reporting format has been undergone revisions at different point of time. To process the data collection, compilation, reporting, analysis and finally use of information in improving the public health care services for the purpose of planning, problem solving and decision making in healthcare services, a computerised Health Management Information System (HMIS) has also been developed by the Government.

The following section shows the utilisation of maternal health and Family Planning Services by the women of Vaishali district of Bihar. The health service utilisation data is taken from the official website of State Health Society Bihar (SHSB) for the period of April, 2011 to March, 2012.

2.1 Utilisation of Maternal Health Services

Health services utilisation data on maternal health and family planning services in Vaishali district has been drawn from the Govt. website of State Health Society Bihar for the Financial Year 2011-12. State Health Society Bihar sets a target each year which is called as *'expected level of achievement'* (ELA) for each type of services to be given to the beneficiaries in the area. This expected level of achievement is calculated on the basis of population size. The target or expected level of achievement is given to all the districts of Bihar at the beginning of every Financial Year and percentage achievement is monitored and reviewed throughout the year by the concerned district and state level officials. Table 18.6 shows the utilisation of different maternal health services in Vaishali district in FY 2011-12.

It can be seen that the three-fourth of pregnant women were registered for the Ante-Natal Check-ups in 2011-12. Ideally all the pregnant women should be covered for the ANC services but the district has not been able to cover all the pregnant women. Also these women are to be tracked and registered early with the help of health and community workers (ANM, ASHA) so that they may be registered early during the first trimester (within first three months after pregnancy). The early ANC registration is necessary for timely intervention and also to give all the three mandatory ANC services in due course of pregnancy. If we see the data, only 53 percent pregnant women were registered early for ANC services and 64 percent women have received all the three mandatory ANC Check-ups. After registration, only 43 percent women have been given 100 Iron Folic Acid (IFA) tablets and 63 percent women received TT2/booster dose.

The lowest level of Govt. facility where deliveries are conducted is the Primary Health Center. However the Govt. has been putting efforts to start the delivery at the HSC level as well so that more women may be covered. Beside this, the Govt. has also accredited some private facilities for the delivery services. If we see the data, a good percentage of women have utilised this service i.e. 70 percent deliveries conducted at both public and private accredited facilities. Of this, only 27 percent women have received the incentives under Janani Suraksha Yojana (JSY) after the delivery. The facility of cesarean-section is available in higher facilities such as District Hospital of Vaishali. In the state also the C-section deliveries are either conducted at the Sub-Divisional Hospitals (SDH) or higher level of facilities such as First Referral Units (FRUs) and District Hospitals. The district has performed very poorly in the C-section as only seven percent of targeted women are able to avail this facility.

Table 18.6: Utilisation of Maternal Health Services (ANC&Delivery) in Vaishali district (FY 2011-12)

Type of Services	*Services given*	*Services to be given*	*Percentage Utilisation*
ANC Registration	82723	109576	75.49
Early ANC Registration	40764	76703	53.15
Pregnant women received 3 ANC Check-ups	49386	76703	64.39
Total no. of pregnant women given 100 IFA Tablets	47465	109576	43.32
No. of Pregnant women who received TT2/Booster	68964	109576	62.94
Institutional Deliveries at both public & private facilities	58105	83278	69.77
No. of Institutional deliveries where mothers get the JSY incentives (public & private)	22505	83278	27.02
No. of C-section performed at both public & private facilities	293	4164	7.04

Source: HMIS data (2011-12) taken from DHIS-2 (bihardhis.nhsrc-hmis.org)

2.2 Utilisation of Family Planning Services

Table 18.7 shows the utilisation of selected family planning services viz. FP operations, IUD insertions, and distribution of Oral Contraceptive Pills (OCP) by the women of Vaishali district in the Financial Year 2011-12. It can be seen that all the three selected FP services are less utilised. However a good percentage (81 percent) of women has received the OC pills. Number of FP operations conducted at both Public and Private facilities are 51 percent and Intra-uterine Device (IUD) inserted is 29 percent during the same period.

Table 18.7: Utilisation of Family Planning Services in Vaishali district (FY 2011-12)

Type of Services	*Services given*	*Services to be given*	*Percentage Utilisation*
FP operations conducted at Public & Private facilities	17912	34952	51.25
IUD insertions	10132	34952	28.99
OC Pills distributed	28174	34952	80.61

Source: HMIS data (2011-12) taken from DHIS-2 (bihardhis.nhsrc-hmis.org).

Thus most common method of family planning is OCP which is temporary in nature and usually used for spacing. It is also most preferred and convenient method as it involves less risk. Motivating the women to go for the IUD insertions and FP operations is quite difficult as evident from the data also. Another reason for less utilisation of these two health services may be the lack of awareness and misconceptions among the people and half hearted efforts on the part of the Govt. in motivating them to adopt these services. The facilities at most of the lower level public health institutions is worrisome and women usually hesitate to go for family planning operations.

3. Utilisation of Health Services in PHCs

To understand the utilisation of maternal and family planning services by the women of the studied district two block PHCs namely Rajapakar and Patepur were selected for the study. The purpose was to see whether utilisation level at the district matches with the utilisation of health services by the women of these block PHCs. These PHCs were selected on the basis of proximity from the district headquarter. Rajapakar block PHC is closest to the district headquarter while the other PHC Patepur is farthest. Also the first PHC is better managed in terms of the services provided and the quality of HMIS data and reports than the later. A total of 140 women were interviewed (70 from each PHC) and after editing the filled schedules 130 respondents were found suitable for the meaningful analysis.

3.1 Socio-Economic Profile of the Respondents

All the selected respondents are women as the study is done on the maternal health services. Table 18.8 shows the age profile of the respondents. It may be observed that nearly half of the respondents belong to young age group of below 25 years of age (49 percent) as most of the respondents had come to these PHCs for the ante-natal check-ups and delivery services. The least category of respondents is in the age group of 36-40 years (7.9 percent). Almost one-third respondents belong to the age group of 26-35 years. Most of the respondents (89.0 percent) are married and only a few of them are either unmarried or widow (3 percent each).

Table 18.8: Respondents by age groups and marital status

Age (in years)	*No.*	*%*
15-25	64	49.23
26-35	40	30.77
36-40	10	7.69
41 & above	16	12.31
Total	130	100.0
Marital Status		
Married	116	89.2
Unmarried	4	3.1
Widow	4	3.1
No Response	6	4.6
Total	**130**	**100.0**

It has been observed that women belonging to better socio-economic background have more opportunities to avail the health services as well. They are able to make the decisions about themselves and also have greater stake in the family decision (Kumar and Khandade, 2015). The health facility and physical infrastructure at the public hospitals, educational achievement, economic independence and monthly family income are other important factors which are responsible for availing the health services by the women.

Table 18.9: Respondents by Educational Level, Occupation and monthly family income

Educational achievement	*No.*	*%*
Illiterate	19	14.6
Below 10th Standard	54	41.5
Up to 10th Standard	29	22.3
12th Standard & above	4	3.1
No Response	24	18.5
Total	130	100.0
Monthly family Income (Rs.)		
1000-3000	33	25.38
3001-5000	76	58.46
5000 & above	17	13.08
No Response	4	3.1
Total	**130**	**100.0**

It may be seen from the above table that more than half (56 percent) of the respondents are either illiterate or have education below 10th Class. Only 26.2 percent have education up to 10th class and very few respondents have completed 12th standard or higher degrees. Regarding the type of occupation of the respondents, nearly half of the respondents are housewife (46 percent). After that the respondents are also involved in the agricultural practices (24.6 percent) and involve in daily wages, mostly as landless agricultural labourers (13 percent). If we see the monthly family income of the respondents, the situation is also not very good as most of the respondents having less than Rs. 5000/ income (almost 84 percent). Only 13% respondents said their monthly family income is Rs. 5000/ or more (tables 18.9).

3.2 Knowledge about Government Health Services

As per the Indian Public Health Standard (IPHS), different levels of health facilities such as District Hospital, Sub-Divisional Hospital /Community Health Centre (CHC), Primary Health Centre and Health Sub-Centre are set up to cater the health services to the rural population. Recently the Government has also launched National Rural Health Mission in the year 2005. Due to these efforts the awareness about the government's health services has increased. These are reflected in the data of increased institutional delivery, increased rate of immunisation and more utilisation of public health services in last few years.

The respondents were also asked about knowledge of Govt. Health facilities in the area and source of information for the same. It was also found that more than half of respondents (55.4%) were self aware about the existence of PHC and for other respondents the source of information was ASHA/ANM, neighbors or their family members (table 18.10).

Table 18.10: Respondents by knowledge and source of information of public health facility

Knowledge about the type of health facility	***No.***	***%***
Yes	128	98.5
No	0	0.0
No response	2	1.5
Total	130	100.0
Source of information regarding the Govt. health facility		
Self	72	55.4
ASHA/ANM	30	23.1
Mother/Father/ husband	10	7.69
Neighbours	16	12.3
No Response	2	1.5
Total	**130**	**100.0**

The next table 18.11 shows the respondents experience with the Govt. facilities in the past and reasons for choosing the same. Most of the respondents (85 percent) have also enjoyed Govt. health facilities in the past. The responses reflect the positive attitude of women towards the Govt. health institutions. When it comes to reasons for choosing the Government health facility, majority (90.8 percent) of the respondents chose it because of better health services provided at the Govt. health institutions.

Table 18.11: Respondents by status of availing and reasons of choosing Govt. health facilities

Whether Health services were availed in the past		
Yes	110	84.6
No	20	15.4
Total	130	100.0
Reasons of choosing Govt. Health Facility (Multiple response & N= 130)		
Proximity	82	63.1
Free services	48	36.9
Better health services	118	90.8
Rely more on Govt. facilities	48	36.9
Others	2	1.5

The following table shows type of services availed by the women. As discussed elsewhere in the study, most of the respondents were married and visited these PHCs either for the Ante Natal Check-up services (56%) or the institutional delivery (37.7%). A good number of the respondents were also come for the OPD services (39%) and only a few of them came to avail the FP services (13%).

Table 18.12: Respondents by types of health services availed at Public Health Facilities

Type of Maternal and FP Services	***Service Availed (Multiple response N=130)***	
	No.	***%***
Registering for ANC	73	56.2
Institutional Delivery	49	37.7
48 hrs stay in hospital after delivery	9	6.9
OPD services	51	39.2
Family Planning services	17	13.1
Surgical Services	0	0.0

It may be seen from the above tables that the overall utilisation of any of the health services by the women of the two block PHCs is better than the district. However if we see the particular maternal health services viz. ANC registration, Institutional deliveries and family planning services, the utilisation level is lower in these block PHCs than the district. Besides the awareness about the health facilities, the utilisation of public health services by women also depends upon other important factors such as physical infrastructure, basic amenities at health facility, quality health services, behavior of doctors and other nursing and paramedical staffs towards the patients etc. The utilisation also depends upon socio-economic and cultural background of the respondents.

4. Conclusions and Suggestions

As discussed in the study that women need more health services than men due to obvious biological and other reasons of MCH services. The health care is not only important for the individual woman but also to the baby she is giving birth. A healthy woman can only give birth to a healthy baby. It has often been seen that the due to lack of availability and accessibility of good health facilities and health care services the woman has to suffer long. A lot of women and infants die during the process of child birth itself or they become permanent disable or develop complications for life long. Studies have proved that due to neglect of essential public health care services and proper nutrition to women both maternal mortality and infant and child mortality are high in the state as compared to some other states. This gap is even very higher as compared to the developed countries.

Health is a state subject and it is the utmost responsibility of the state to provide affordable and quality health care services to all especially women. If we ignore the quality health care, then also the State Government is not even able to cover the numbers of women needing basic health services at the public health institutions. The Government is not able to meet the expected level of achievement (target) set by itself. If we are not able to ensure basic minimum health services to the women then we cannot think of a healthy and prosperous society. Health is one of the most important indicators of development along with education and income. It is a well established fact that without ensuring the good health and well being of women, their development and empowerment cannot be achieved.

The Government has been trying hard to provide affordable and quality health services through its network of public health facilities. But it has been found in the study that the State has been lagging far behind in providing the proper health facilities. The shortfall in terms of the physical infrastructure at all the levels (district hospital, sub-divisional hospital, CHC, PHC, APHC and HSC) and health personnel in all the categories of the staffs (medical, Para-medical and nursing staffs) is evident. The state has not been able to increase these with the increase of population in due course of time. Now the state has been trying to meet the needs but the gap is so wide that it will take considerable time to bridge the gap.

Other issue which comes out distinctly is the low utilisation of different maternal health services in the district especially the early registration for ANC (53 percent), distribution of 100 IFA tablets (43 percent), Institutional deliveries (27 percent), C-section (only 7 percent) and family planning services such as FP operations (51 percent), IUD insertion (29 percent). It was found that the district was not able to cover the expected level of beneficiaries for most of the maternal and FP services. Availability and accessibility of health services, physical infrastructure, and skilled human resources are closely linked with the utilisation of health services of women in Vaishali district.

It has also emerged from the study of women respondents of the two PHCs that most of them know about the public health facilities and they have also visited these facilities in the past. They have the information of public health facilities on their own or from the health and community workers. The main reason of choosing the Govt. health facility is better health services, proximity of the facility from their residences etc. It was found that women utilizing any health services in these two studied PHCs are better as compared to the district level utilisation by the women. However the utilisation of particular MCH and family planning services are less.

To increase the utilisation level of maternal health and FP services, it is suggested that the shortfall in infrastructure and human resources should be immediately addressed by the Government. However, these are long time interventions but by prioritizing different activities, the utilisation of health services by the women may be increased considerably. To increase the coverage and utilisation, the Government should focus more on increasing the number of HSCs as these are the first contact point of public health care services especially for the women in rural areas of the state. The second priority should be given to filling of the vacant positions especially of Medical and Nursing staffs. As found in the study, the situation of managerial staffs are satisfactory but the filling up of vacant positions of medical and nursing staffs are more essential and detrimental to the health care services. In addition to meeting the shortfall of physical infrastructure and human resources, a separate strategy such as BCC campaign, large scale FP camps at regular intervals etc. may be more useful for increasing the utilisation of FP services.

References

Basu, S.K. and Mitra, K. 1992. Need for Gender Sensitive Approaches for Improving Women's Reproductive Health care Services http://www.isical.ac.in/~wemp/Papers/PaperSalilBasuAndKoumariMitra1.doc.

Berman, P., Zeitlin, J., Roy, P, and Khumtakar, H. 1997. Does maternal employment augment spending for children's health care? A test from Haryana, India. *Health Transition Review,* 7 (2), 187-204.

Caldwell, J.C. Reddy, P.H. and Caldwell, P. 1983. The social component of mortality decline: an investigation in South India, employing alternative methodologies. *Population Studies, 37 (2), 185-202.*

5th Common Review Mission (CRM) Report- 2011. NRHM, MoHFW, Govt. of India.

Launch of HMIS web portal 2008. NRHM Ministry of Health and Family Welfare, Govt. of India. http://nrhmmis.nic.in/UI/Portal%20Content/Website%20Launch/web_launch.htm

New NRHM monthly reporting format [Internet]. NRHM Ministry of Health and Family Welfare Government of India: http://nrhm-mis.nic.in/UI/User%20Guidelines/HMIS_User_Guidelines.pdf (cited on 2012 January 15)

Kumar, Rajeev. K. and A.K. Kapoor, 2009. Management of a Primitive Tribe: Role of Development Dynamics, Delhi: Academic Excellence.

Kumar, Rajeev K. and T. Khandade, 2015. Ability to Take Health Care Decisions: A Case of Rural Women of Vaishali district of Bihar. In *Relocating Women equal Role in Indian Society*, By P Kumar & S Gupta (eds), pp 32-47, Rawat Publications, Jaipur, ISBN 978-81-316-0742-8.

Rao, A. Prakash and U.V. Somayajulu. 2004. Health Status of Women Living in the Slums of Bangalore. In, *Women, Health & Development*, P.J. Reddy (ed.), 106-121, Tirupati, Dept. of Population Studies, SVU.

Somayajulu, U.V. 2004. Maternal Health Care Practices in Indian States- An Analysis of NFHS Data. In, *Women, Health & Development*, P.J. Reddy (ed.), 63-77, Tirupati, Dept. of Population Studies, SVU.

Salganicoff, A., Ranji. Usha R. and Wyn, R. 2005. Women and Health Care: A National Profile. Kaiser Family Foundation.

Sample Registration System. Vol. 45 (no.1), January, 2011. RGI, New Delhi.

State Project Implementation Plan of Bihar-2012-13, State Health Society, Health Department, Govt. of Bihar.

World Health Organisation. 1946. Constitution of the WHO as adopted by the International Health Conference, New York, 19-22 June, 1946.

Part - V

VOICES OF PROTESTS

19

Women's Organisations and Movements in India: Struggle for Gender Equality

— *Md. Tarique Anwer*

Introduction

A large number of women participate in different movements along with other groups. Nevertheless this does not amount to a women's movement. A women's movement exists merely as gender domination; definite to this assembly is called into query. It implies a move violently to convert social relation of authority which oppresses women. Feminism, the cognizant political movement of women, has been the standard competitor in the struggle for the reformation of sexual divergence and division of labour and poses its objection in terms of women's perceptions of themselves.

On the other hand, there has been substantial amount of discussion on the questions of women's position in class society within this women's movement; women's contribution in terms of wage work and unwaged work, towards the process of capitalist buildup, the definite character of women's exploitation, and the consequential strategies for women's movement. Hitherto, they all reject the 'male domination' and the 'subordination' and 'oppression' of women and plan to offer justice to them. The exponents of justice for women point out that the subordination of women is not basically a matter of unreasonable discrimination based upon sex but more because of male supremacy under which gender differences are made applicable to the sharing of profit to the organised disadvantage of women.

In India there is a women's movement and vibrant movement that is considered a very rich that has been taken diverse forms in different parts of the country. Urvashi Butalia[2] contends that the nonexistence of a single solid movement, rather than being a foundation of weakness, may be one of the strengths of the movement. Even if scattered and disjointed, it may be a physically powerful and plural movement.

It is vital to be familiar for a country like India's size; change in male-female relations and the kinds of issues the women's movement is focusing on determination not come simple. For every step the movement takes forward, there will be a potential counterattack, a possible failure. And it is this that makes for the contradictions, this that makes it promising for present to be women who can seek to, and accomplish, the highest political office in the country, and for women to continue to have to tackle patriarchy within the home, in the headquarters, all the way through their lives. While activists not at all fatigue of repeating, out of the earnest oppression is born the greatest resistance.[3]

The birth of a new awareness that looked at women's rights was seen in the nineteenth century. This was the time to launch first campaign against purdah, women's health, literacy and other subjects. It was led by a combination of well-known women leaders like Annie Besant, Margaret Cousin, Kamladevi Chattopadhay, Sarojini Naidu, Pandita Ramabai and also male leaders like Rammohan Roy and Jyotiba Phule.[4]

The author of book entitled "Women and The New Race" is Margaret Sanger, argues that as the dilemma arises from 'male domination', the feminist justice should not imprison itself to the absence of discrimination flanked by men and women but also focus on the conceding of power to women. Equality should denote not only an equality of opportunity to pursue male clear roles or genderless roles that men and women have an identical interest to fulfill. The consequence of empowerment of women might be very different from the like opportunities to come into male dominated institutions which have come into existence as a consequence of the getting of sex discrimination theories.[5]

Women and Political Parties

When India got her freedom in 1947, it was broadly recognised that the struggle for freedom had been fought as much by women as by men. One of the methods chose by M K Gandhi to weaken the power of the British was for Indians to challenge the law which made it illegal for them to make salt. At the time, salt-making was a monopoly and earned substantial revenues for the British. Gandhi began his movement by going on a march – the salt march – from beginning to end numerous villages, leading finally to the sea, where he and others broke the law by making salt. No woman had been included by Gandhi in his chosen number of marchers. But nationalist women protested, and they enforced him to permit them to take part.[6]

The anti-imperialist movement marked the emergence of women in political arena, at all by the reasons after the mobilisation of Indian Women. The Satyagraha campaigns of 1930 led by Gandhi and Communist led movements are renowned for the huge participation of women. The powerful presence of women was also felt in a variety of peasant and working class movement, which strengthened the place of the Congress vis-à-vis the British Government.

At the global level, a wider popular unrest and women's movements had been seen for the expansion of military among women in the post independent period. This period was characterised by mass movements for peace and human rights and against imperialism, racism, contamination and 'development models' of growth.

The country also saw growing incidents of violence and discrimination against women during the 18 years of reign of women Prime Minister of India. This is no diverse from any additional time: a informal visitor to any Indian city – for example Mumbai – will see hundreds of women, young and old, working in all kinds of professions: doctors, nurses, teachers, engineers, scientists... and so far newspapers in India are full of stories of violent incidents against women, of rape, sexual harassment, sometimes even murder. But to have a woman in the highest office of the State and to concurrently have tremendous violence against women are just the two trimmings of the scale. As always, a more complex reality lies in between.[7]

On one hand, on this background links for women emerged in the early hours in the 20th century, at a standstill initiated by men. Clubs, groups and links that provided training at ground level and right of entry to education for women, but did still also compel customary gender roles and values. When women tried to define their own values and questioned the customary outlook on gender the shortcomings of these links became understandable. These are the three important national women's movements that emerged from the local associations; Women's Indian Association (WIA) in 1917, the National Council of Indian Women (NCIW) in 1925 and the All-India Women's Conference (AIWC) in 1927. The first two associations like WIA and NCIW, which representing all women of India did not successful in their efforts and claim. They were both exclusive organisations with partial class and caste representation and had also limited geographical impact, but they still played a significant role due to their contacts through family relations and social interaction within the upper classes and castes. Nevertheless, the latter of the organisations, through its alliance with the Indian National Congress had more success in representing women nationwide. The crusade for the Child Marriage Bill was strengthened, consolidated and brought consensus to the women's movement. Women were progressively more being mixed up in politics, but chiefly as tokens with modest authentic pressure.[8]

On the other hand, there are three women organisations in India: All India Women's Conference (AIWC), National Federation of Indian Women (NFIW), and All India Democratic Women's Association (AIDWA). Neither of them has direct political affiliations. But the AIWC is known to have close links with the Congress Party, the NFIW with the CPI and AIDWA with the CPI (Marxist). All the three organisations have different views about the role of women as a social group. They also respond differently to issues articulated in the political process.

The AIWA formed in 1927, was very active in the national movement. Now it is primarily concerned with social welfare. It has actively lobbied and pressurised the government to reformed social laws concerning women. Along with other women's organisations, the AIWC applied pressure on the government to enact the Special Marriage Act of 1954, the Hindu Marriage Act and Divorce Act of 1955, Inter-State Succession Act of 1956 and Dowry Act of 1961. Ishwar Chandra Vidyasagar sent a petition signed by 987 persons to Government of India urging it for legislative action. His efforts were rewarded when the Hindu Widows' Remarriage Act (Act XV of 1856) legalised marriage of widows and declared issues from such marriages as legitimate.[9]

During the national movement, some Communist sympathizers wanted the AIWC to transform itself from an elite organisation to a massed-based one. They felt constrained by the scope and functioning of the organisation. They, therefore, formed new organisation NFIW in 1954. The NFIW projects a different view about women's role in Indian society. It claims that the specific oppression of women is only one aspect of a more comprehensive oppressive structure, supported by a system of unequal property rights. So it aims at transforming those social relations of power which oppress not only women but other social groups.

While recognizing the relevance of social welfare activities, the NFIW feels that it is necessary to organize women on political issues along with other groups. This is evident in its commitment to alleviate conditions of other oppressed groups like working class, peasants and tribals. Besides, it has taken up innumerable individual cases of women who have been victims of rape and police tyranny. The NFIW was also active along with other women organisations in the Anti-Price rise movement between 1972 and 1974.

The social reform movement in India also has aimed at uprooting social evils, and inculcating in men and women, the spirit of sacrifice for general good of the society. The first and foremost social problem that attracted enlightened opinion was the need for a better deal for women in society, in the abolition of the cruel rites of sati and infanticide, in the condemnation of child marriage and polygamy and popularisation of widow remarriage, in the abolition of purda, in provision of educational facilities for women and economic openings to make them self-supporting and finally an equal share for women in the political life of the country by enfranchisement.[10]

The fight for equal rights for women has been also taken up by AIDWA which came into existence as national organisation only in 1981. Its mass base is mainly among agricultural workers, peasantry working class and professional groups. It's campaigns have revolved around basic issues like, civic amenities, water supply, regular transport to resettlement colonies and around women's economic and legal oppression. As compared to other organisations, AIDWA has emphasized successfully the social roots of the dowry problem and brought pressure on the government to formulate an d implement anti-dowry legislations.

In the recent past leading women's organisations, were involved in mobilizing public opinion in the Shah Bano case. Shah Bano, is a divorced Muslim women, sued her husband for financial support. Her husband claimed he had done in accordance with obligatory under Muslim law, although the court granted Bano support under a provision in secular criminal law (section 125), which is not match under Islamic law. So this judgment motivated enraged Muslim antagonism and precipitated a national crisis.

Women's organisations intervened to highlight, how gender identity was subsumed in the larger issue of community identity. The campaigned to oppose the exclusion of Muslim women from the purview of the Criminal Procedure Code. Yet the government surrendered to a section of conservative Muslim opinion which was incensed by the Supreme Court verdict granting maintenance to a divorced Muslim woman. Some women groups were unclear as to how to proceed, for the occasion was used by Hindu communalism to attack the Muslim for being backward. The conflict between communalism and women's rights cropped up again in the incident of Sati.[11] Women's groups were successful in getting a bill passed against Sati, but ineffectual in getting their suggestions incorporated into the Bill. This case illustrates the argument that a women's movement must expose women's specific oppression while struggling against general oppressive structures.

Women and Trade Union

The problems of mobilizing women through political parties are that, issues specific to the group get submerged in the concern for large issues. The views of political parties are further reflected in their attitude towards women's participation in trade unions.

As mentioned earlier workers in the Indian manufacturing sector can be broadly divided into two categories, such as organised and unorganised. The census of 1981 showed that of the 63.6 million women employed, 94% are employed in the unorganised sector. Only 6% of the female force is in the organised sector. The unorganised sector is the greatest employer of women. It is an area where there is a flagrant violation of the laws; unions have failed to cover wage earners outside the factory sector in a significant way.

The participation of women in the political and productive sphere is therefore, severely limited. The problem of top-down organisation is that it taps and organizes the force of women to feed its own machinery but does not make it a permanent movement. It would not be wrong to assert that women have in the main, been drawn into work which is low paid, often includes personal service elements, and in general, lacks authority.

In recent years new protest movements have developed outside these structures and sometimes voluntary agencies, research and educational institutions, many of these are focusing the relevant problem areas not covered by women organisations and political parties.

There are two other type organisations of women in the informal sector: one is Self Employed Women's Association (SEWA) and other is Working Women's Forum (WWF), which is based in Ahmadabad and Madras respectively.

Both arose out of the frustration of several women members, working with the Congress and Communist party. They came into being with the realisation that, specific issues could not always be tackled through hierarchical party organisations. From the organisational pattern of SEWA and WWF, it is clear that they are grassroots organisations. Although run by middle class women, they are less hierarchical and more flexible, than most organisations, in responding to new demands of its social group.

Having no problem with the women's groups, to succeed in creating a awareness so much so that more and more corporate entities are coming forward and giving aid and credit incentives to self-help groups like SEWA. It's extremely remarkable. During the last 30-40 years, to improve levels of governance, it was the lack of break down. We have the lowest figures of police per citizen, judges per individual due to not growing police force and so this is the reason we have created a lawless society.

We have found an impact on a wide range of activities owing to women's groups. Women at the political level may not have seen an increase, but today we can see self-help groups run by women; they are organised in trade unions, rape crisis centres, trauma centres, women's shelters; they are running plenty of legal reform and campaign groups and are in panchayats. All the major political parties have their own women's organisations.[12]

At around the same time, as women issues and campaigns began to be more widely taken up, women began to move away from methods of agitation, such as demonstration, public campaigns, street theatre, etc. They felt that these had limited meaning unless they are accompanied by attempts to develop their own structures to aid and support individual woman. Women's centres have been formed in several cities which provide a mixture of legal aid, health care and counseling.

Women's quotas in legislative bodies in India

It was stated by the Committee of the Status of Women in its report from

1974 the seats should be reserved for women in municipalities, and proposed that panchayats[13] should include women to secure a minimum percentage of female participation. The all-women panchayats should be set up in accordance with the suggestion of committee. This was a reply to the fact that Indian women had had very little representation in institutional politics since independence. The matter of representation did not materialize from the women's movements and the deliberate on reservation was equally strong outside of the movement as within, but it was still welcomed cordially by several women's movements.

In local governance, the participation of women in the Panchayat Raj had already been debated in since 1957. The debate surrounding the reservation in the Panchayat Raj has not been tough. The first solution to the demand was to include women, who were interested in working for children and other women, in the panchayats. This followed carefully the traditional patriarchal patterns of the society and posed slight treat to men, and men's position. A breakthrough came in 1983 when women were granted 25% of the seats in local councils by law in Indian state of Karnataka. In 1993 this was adopted nationally when the Constitution Act 1992 (73rd Amendment) and The Constitution Act 1992 (74th Amendment) were passed, relating reservations for women to panchayats and municipalities. One-third of seats in all panchayats and municipalities nationwide, as well as one-third of the position of being chairpersons in the bodies, were reserved for women.[14]

In the midst of simply a minor debate, the reservations acts were passed without any opposition in the Parliament. The men of Parliament, with the passing of the panchayati reservations, left one-third of the seats in the lowest elected bodies to women, a shift that also reached and soothed the grass-root. The reservation for women in the lower elected bodies has by many been regarded as a success. The elected women in the first round did in many cases have little or no political experience, but they did, in the course of their commitment to the positions they have been elected to, expand both the misplaced experience and self confidence to question priorities and front issues of magnitude for them. The experiences have showed that elected female party members have been additional committed to building large alliances among themselves rather than to the party.[15]

The debate on reservations for women in Parliament in examination of the soft process relating to reservations in the lower elected bodies as well as the experiences gained from the process and the consequences. Two tendencies have been present as a result of female reservations in the lower elected bodies. First, a new Bill has been proposed for the reservation of one-third of the seats in Parliament, and, second, the male opposition against women's inclusion in higher elected bodies has toughened. The debate in this time has been much sharper, and has shaped new alliances and tensions, both in the women's movements and across the political lines. A more democratic gender representation in Parliament has been secured by both, but has at the same time been regarded as highly undemocratic as "a citizen of India will be barred from contesting a particular seat on grounds of gender"[16], referring to men being slowed down to stand for election in selected districts. Those representatives who were elected by view of gender are argued will not be representing the district they are elected from when they are elected gravely on the ground of their gender. The women who had full rights of being elected to parliament and the State Assembly since the formation of the Constitution in 1950 argued by Dasgupta. Connected to this it has been raised questions on if men cannot represent women, how can women represent the male population in the districts they are elected from? And supplementary; will women represent the uniform interest of their gender regardless of caste, class and/or religious differences? Sen addresses this opinion and points to the unwillingness of political parties allow women a voice in policy making, as well as opportunities for leading positions.[17]

The introduction of 33% reservation for women in local, village-level elections has the most important development in the last few decades. In the early days, when this progress was introduced, there was considerable disbelief. How will women survive? Are they prepared to be privileged? Will this mean any real change, or will it merely mean that the men will take a backseat and use the women as a front to implement what they want? While all these problems still remain, in a greater or lesser degree, what is also true is that more and more women have shown that a long time ago they have power, they are competent to use it, to the benefit of society in general and women in particular.

Role of Indian Women in Women's Movement

Sarojini Naidu, the first women who became the first woman President of the Indian National Congress in 1925. Her charisma was indication for hundreds of other women to join, and ultimately the salt protest was made successful by the many women who not only made salt, but also sat openly in marketplaces selling, and indeed, buying it.

Today thousands of Indian women have courage of Sarojini Naidu. Some years ago, Rojamma, a poor woman from the southern state of Andhra Pradesh, attended a literacy class. Here, she read a story which described a life very like her own. It was a fairy-tale of about a poor woman to struggle to make both ends meet, who was regularly beaten by her husband. Whatsoever her husband earned, he spent on liquor, and then, drunk and aggressive, he attacked her because she had no food to give him. Unable to stand the continuing violence, the woman went from house to house, to find every other woman who had the same story to tell. Once the woman got in somebody's company, and decided that they would throw their attack where it hurt most; they would picket liquor shops and stop liquor being sold. Their husbands then would have no liquor to drink, and the money they earned would be saved. Inspired by the story, Rojamma collected her friends together, and they began to picket liquor shops. This movement reached like wildfire in the state of Andhra Pradesh. In village after village, women got together, they talked, they went on strike, they beat up liquor shop owners, and they refused to allow their husbands to misuse money on liquor and in the last they succeeded. The sale of liquor was banned in Andhra Pradesh, unwillingly, by the government for liquor brings in huge amounts of money. As a result, savings went up, violence levels dropped, and the lives of poor women began to improve.

Today, in the women's movement, the hundreds of thousands of Rojammas and Sarojini Naidus who are to be found all over India form part of one of the most dynamic and vibrant of political movements in India. The path of this movement is frequently traced from the social reform movements of the 19th century when campaigns for the betterment of the state of affairs of women's lives were taken up, initially by men. By the end of the century women had begun to organize themselves and step by step they took up a number of causes such as education, the conditions of women's work and so on. It was in the early part of the 20th century that women's organisations were set up, and many of the women who were active in these later became involved in the freedom movement.

It has been seen that due to independence, many promises and dreams for women in India – the dream of an egalitarian, just, democratic society in which both men and women would have a voice. The actuality, when it began to sink in was, however, somewhat different. For all that had happened was that, regardless of some improvements in the status of women, patriarchy had simply taken on new and different forms.[18]

Unfulfilled promises

Many of the promises of Independence were at a standstill unfulfilled; it was clear till the end of 1960s. It was thus that the 1960s and 1970s saw a wave of movements in which women took part: campaigns against rising prices, movements for land rights, peasant movements. It has been acknowledged that women from diverse parts of the country came together to form groups both inside and outside political parties. Everywhere, in the different movements that were sweeping the country, women participated in large numbers. Everywhere, their participation resulted in transforming the movements from within.

Indira Gandhi's government declared a State of Emergency in 1975 due to worrying of advancing in political activity, putting a stop to all democratic political activity. Activists, both young and old, women and men, were forced to go underground or to stop all political work. It was only when the Emergency was lifted, some 18 months later that over ground political activity resumed.

It was around this time that many of the contemporary women's groups began to get formed, with their members often being women with a history of involvement in other political movements.

It is the most shameful matter of our society that prevailed all over India, this the first issues to take delivery of countrywide attention from women's groups was violence against women, specifically in the form of rape, and what came to be known in India as 'dowry deaths' – the killing of young married women for the 'dowry' or money goods they brought with them at marriage. This was also the opening of a process of learning for women: most protests were directed at the State. For the reason that women were able to mobilize support, the State responded, seemingly positively, by changing the law on rape and dowry, making both more rigorous. This seemed, at the time, like a great conquest. It was no more than later that the knowledge began to sink in that simple changes in the law meant little, unless there was a determination and a machinery to implement these. And that the root of the problem of discrimination against women lay not only in the law, or with the State, but was much more prevalent.

Groups learnt from day to day that targeting the State in the early hour's campaigns was not enough and that victims also needed support. So additional level of work was needed: awareness raising or conscientisation so that violence against women could be prevented, rather than only dealt with after it had happened. To establish women's shelters as well as counseling centres and also tried to set up legal aid. It was only when groups began to feel sucked into the overwhelming volume of the day-to-day work of such centres that they began to believe that it was not sufficient to do what they now saw as 'reformist' and 'non-campaign' work. Knowledge was documented as a significant need. India is such a vast country; what did activists in Karnataka, a state in southern India, know of what was going on in Garhwal in north India? And hitherto, all over the place you looked, there was women's activity, activity that could not unavoidably be defined as 'feminist', but that was, nonetheless, geared towards improving the conditions of women's lives.

The excitement of the 1970s and early 1980s, symbolised by street-level protests, campaigns in which groups mobilised at a national level in the modern times, the sense of a harmony of experience hurtful across class, caste, region and religion – all this seems to have disappeared, replaced by a more painstaking and complex response to issues. In many parts of India, women are no longer to be seen out on the streets protesting about this or that form of injustice. This noticeable lack of a visible movement has led to the allegation that the women's movement is dead or dying.

Supplementary thrashing firewood have been brought out: little has happened to improve women's lives, so how can the movement be called successful? Activists within the movement are urban, Western, and middle class, so the movement was careful an alien thing, a Western invention. It has modest to do with the lives of thousands of poor, rural, underprivileged women all over India.

These allegations make the classic blunder: they judge a multifaceted authenticity as a result of that part of it that is most noticeable. Since urban, middle-class women are visible and articulate, consequently they must be the only participants in the women's movement.[19]

Challenges for Women

While the participation of urban, middle class women is undeniable in the context of diverse reality, it is not they who make up the stamina of the movement, or of the many, different campaigns that are generally seen as comprising the movement. The anti-alcohol agitation in Andhra Pradesh and similar campaigns in other parts of India were started and continued by poor, low-caste, often working-class women. The movement to save from harm the environment was begun by poor women in a village called Reni in the northern hill regions of India, and only after that did it spread to other parts of the country. There are several facts of such examples.

Women had to face in recent years is the growing influence of the religious right in India is one of the biggest challenges. Right-wing groups have built much of their support on the participation of women: contribution to help them with domestic problems, enabling them to go into the public breathing space in an imperfect way, and all whereas ensuring that on the whole ideology within which they operate remains determinedly patriarchal. For activists too, this has posed main problems. It has required them to tackle the fact that they cannot take for granted harmony as women that cuts across class, religion, caste, ethnic difference. And yet, they must seize fast to such an statement if they are to work with women: for how, as an activist, do you deal with a woman who takes part in a aggressive right wing demonstration one day, and comes to you for help as a victim of domestic violence the next?

The introduction of 33% reservation for women in local, village-level elections has been seen in mainly considerable development in the last few decades. In the early hours, when this progress was introduced, there was considerable doubt. How will women cope? Are they prepared to be leaders? Will this mean any real change, or will it merely mean that the men will take a backseat and use the women as a front to implement what they want? While all these problems still remain, in a greater or lesser degree, what is also true is that more and more women have revealed that on one occasion they have power, they are able to exercise it, to the benefit of society in general and women in particular.

Again it is said that the women's movement in India is a rich and vibrant movement, which has spread to various parts of the country. It is often said that there is no one single unified movement in the country, but a number of disjointed campaigns. Activists see this as one of the strengths of the movement which takes different forms in different parts. While the movement may be scattered all over India, they feel it is however a strong and plural energy.[20]

Gender Equality

Gender equality is also known as various name such as sex equality, gender egalitarianism, sexual equality or equality of the genders that refers to the outlook that men and women should receive equal treatment, and should not be discriminated against based on gender, unless there is a sound biological reason for different treatment. This is the objective of the United Nations Universal Declaration of Human Rights, which seeks to create equality in law and in social situations, such as in democratic activities and securing equal pay for equal work.[21]

While women and men enjoy the same rights and opportunities across all sectors of society is achieved through gender equality, including economic participation and decision-making, and as soon as the different behaviours, aspirations and needs of women and men are equally valued and favoured. Gender equality is measured by looking at the depiction of men and of women in a variety of roles. A number of international comparative gender equality indices have been prepared and these offer a way to compare Ireland's achievements with those of other countries. Each index looks at a separate list of parameters and the choice of parameters affects the outcome for each country. The United Nations Gender Inequality Index is based on the basis that "all too often, women and girls are discriminated against in health, education and the labour market with negative repercussions for their freedom". The UN GII is a measure of inequalities based on these inequalities.[22]

Feminist writers criticized this pro-gender biological evidence as fallacious. They call it gender inequality which is expected in many areas of social life that include culture, ideology and discursive practices. The gender division in the home and in wage labour, the organisation of state, sexuality, the structuring of violence and many aspects of social organisation contribute to the construction of unequal relations between man and women. Though gender relations took different forms in different societies, historical periods, ethnic groups, social classes and generations, yet they have one thing in common- the gender relations are unequal and men are superior to women.[23]

The emergence of gender perspective of power is a significant political development in recent years. Gender usually refers to the masculine and feminine attributes of human species and the social roles each of them plays in society. Gender power refers to the domination of men as a group over women as a group. It is widely believed that due to biological differences, men are superior to women and, therefore, it is natural that they dominate over women.[24]

Gender Equity Issues in India

Inside Indian society, gender discrimination is continued to be a massive problem. Customary patriarchal norms have relegated women to inferior status within the household and workplace. This radically affects women's health, financial status, education, and political involvement. Women are commonly married young age, quickly become mothers, and are afterward loaded by rigorous domestic and financial responsibilities. They are commonly half-starved since women naturally are the last member of a household to eat and the last to receive medical attention. Additionally, only 54 percent of Indian women are literate as compared to 76 percent of men. Women be given slight schooling, and suffer from unjust and prejudiced legacy and divorce laws. These laws prevent women from accumulating extensive financial assets, making it hard for women to create their own security and autonomy.

All of these problems are motivated by towering levels of cyclic relocation in the Indian state of Rajasthan. For many men in Rajasthan, migration is required since rural parts of Rajasthan frequently be short of a sufficient economy to offer income for a family year-round. Women are commonly left behind to care and make available for the entire household. This is gradually more difficult because it is estimated that an average woman's wage is 30 percent lower than a man's wage working in a similar position. While these mothers work, they must also be inclined to domestic responsibilities. This method for sustaining Rajasthani families leaves little resource for the growth and development of women's rights and education levels.

A strong "son preference" exists in the region, as it does throughout the country, and high rates of female infanticide and female feticide epidemic in the area. In 2001, for every 1,000 males living in Rajasthan there were only 922 women (Marthur et. al., 2004). Having sons is economically beneficial to families due to literary institutions; these institutions serve to radically bring down the roles women play in the traditional society. Women continue to struggle to achieve equal status to men, making gender justice an issue of particular importance for Rajasthan.

A number of NGOs that have hosted FSD participants are instrumental in providing opportunities for women in Rajasthan. These organisations assist to put up networks among women to produce financial self-help groups. They introduce ideas about microfinance, allowing women to participate in management activities. Other local NGOs execute projects that export the skills of women abroad to produce major income. In 2006, Olen Crane, an FSD intern, helped nearly 400 women artisans in the Udaipur area by collecting samples of their textile products and transport them abroad to sell to American companies. Similar projects have massive potential to advance the financial and social status of Rajasthani women. Organizing change at a local level and planning participatory achievement will facilitate to eliminate bias and stereotypes, and generate awareness of the significant gender divide that exists within Indian society.[25]

Indians Support Gender Equality but Man is in Priority

This is ashamed to all Indian about the recent gang rape and killing of a young woman in New Delhi – and the subsequent protests – have focused worldwide attention on gender issues in our country. According to a survey of 2010 that Pew Global Attitudes Project examined attitudes about gender around the world sheds a few lights on how public opinion in India compares to the other 21 nations surveyed.

Women should have equal rights with men according to a report of 92% of Indians. But when asked specifically which gender should take priority in the workplace during tough times or in higher education, attitudes in India are less supportive of gender equality than in many other countries around the world.[26] (The survey did not include specific questions about sexual harassment or rape). Women should be able to work outside the home; it is agreed by almost all Indian (95%). But more than eight-in-ten (84%) said that when jobs are insufficient, men "should have more right to a job than women." That response made India stand out – it was among the highest percentages in the nations surveyed; a similar percentage (82%) had been seen in Pakistan.

In the western countries, by comparison, 97% of Americans reported that women should be able to work outside the home, while just 14% reported that when jobs are insufficient, men should have more right to a job. That was among the lowest percentage on this question, comparable to the 12% reported from Britain and Spain.

The analysis that men get more opportunities than women for jobs that reimburse well, even when women are as qualified for the job, was prevalent in most of the countries surveyed. In India, 83% agreed with this statement, among the highest along with Germany (84%) and Poland (83%). In the U.S., roughly two-thirds (68%) agreed.

On a separate issue, more than six-in-ten in India (63%) agreed that a university education is more important for a boy than for a girl, the highest number was reported from the survey. About half in Pakistan (51%), Egypt (50%) and China (48%) also expressed this view. In the U.S., 83% disagreed. Similarly, more than eight-in-ten disagreed in Britain (87%), Brazil (87%), France (87%), Mexico (84%) and Germany (83%). Virtually all of those surveyed in Lebanon (97%) disagreed.

A majority of Indians (60%) reported that a marriage in which both husband and wife have jobs and take care of the house and children is a more satisfying way of life than having the husband provide financially while the wife cares for the household. That's lower than the majorities in many other countries, including 91% in Spain and France, 84% in Brazil and 78% in China. In the U.S., 71% reported a marriage in which both husband and wife have jobs is more satisfying.

Other statistics also shows India as a country with a continuing gender gap. The World Economic Forum ranked India 105th out of 135 countries in its 2012 Global Gender Gap Index. By comparison, several northern European countries – Iceland, Finland and Norway – top the list, meaning men and women are more likely to have equal opportunities. In this year's report, the U.S. ranked 22nd.

The ratings combine four sub-indexes to come up with the overall ranking: economic participation and opportunity; educational attainment; health and survival; and political empowerment.

According to the World Economic Forum, India's ranking gained eight places in 2012 compared to a year ago as a result of improvements in the educational attainment and political empowerment sub-indexes. Still, it is the lowest ranking among emerging BRIC economies of Brazil, Russia, India and China in the index.[27]

Conclusion

To conclude the feminist movements in India are becoming quite strong and are having an impact on the socio-economic and political bearing of the state. They are in the forefront and forceful instruments to highlight the injustices which are inflicted on Indian women. The women's movement in India is a rich and vibrant movement, which has spread to various parts of the country. It is often reported that there is no one single cohesive movement in the country, but a number of fragmented campaigns. Activists see this as one of the strengths of the movement which takes different forms in different parts. While the movement may be scattered all over India, they feel it is nonetheless a strong and plural force. There has always been a connection between the West and India. During the 1920s-30s, the language of the contemporary Indian woman was very similar to her European and American counterparts. The women's movement had a very strong Maoist influence. Some of these Maoist groups were Naxalite affiliates. The Maoist- Dalit movement also made its presence felt in a big way. The women's and social reform movements of the late-19th and early-20th century were all development-focuses, they dealt with women's health and education, eradication of purdah, dowry and sati, working conditions, and by the early-20th century also included political rights such as to franchise and representation.

References

1. R. L. Gupta, *Political Theory New Concept: New Perspective,* Sultan Chand & Sons, New Delhi, 2003, p. 380.
2. Urvashi Butalia is the co-founder of Kali for women, India's first and only feminist publishing house.
3. Third World Resurgence, No. 94, June 1998.
4. file:///C:/Documents%20and%20Settings/Home/Desktop/women%27s%20 movement-5.htm ;

   Dr Radha Kumar, author of a history of the women's movement in India, counters the charge that the women's movement has focused narrowly on dowry and sati and not sufficiently on important development issues such as women's health and education.

   Radha Kumar is Visiting Professor at Jamia Millia University, and trustee of the Delhi Policy Group, where she is directing a programme on 'Durable Peace Processes and Partners' jointly sponsored by the India International Centre. Formerly Senior Fellow in Peace and Conflict Studies at the Council on Foreign Relations in New York, Dr Kumar has also been Executive Director of the Helsinki Citizen's Assembly in Prague and an Associate Fellow at the Institute for War and Peace Studies at Columbia University.
5. Op.Cit.,No.1
6. file:///C:/Documents%20and%20Settings/Home/Desktop/The%20women% 27s%20movement%202.htm
7. *Ibid.*
8. Sen, Samita, *Towards a Feminist Politics? The Indian Women's Movement in Historical Perspective,* in Karen Kapadia (red.) *The Violence of Development. The Politics of Identity, Gender & Social Inequalities in India.* London & New York: Zed Books, 2002.
9. B.L. Grover and S. Grover, *A New Look at Modern Indian History*, S. Chand & Company Ltd., New Delhi, 2006, p. 284.
10. *Ibid.,* pp.282-283.
11. *Ibid.* The term sati literally means a 'pure and virtuous woman'. It was applied in case of a devoted wife who contemplated perpetual and uninterrupted conjugal union with husband life after life and as proof thereof burnt herself with the dead body of her husband.
12. *Rashme Sehgal is a senior journalist and writer based in Delhi.*
13. Op.cit., No. 1.

    Rural local government units, "Panchayat" mean assembly of five wise and respected elders chosen and accepted by the village community. Traditionally, these assemblies settled disputes between individuals and villages.
14. *Ibid.*
15. *Ibid.*
16. Swapan Dasgupta, *Women's quota Bill restricts democracy*, Columnist 7th of March 2010, the Daily Pioneer.

    http://www.dailypioneer.com/240428/Women%E2%80%99s-quota-Bill-restricts-democracy.html

17. Op.Cit., No. 8.
18. The Communique, Nos. 42-43, July-Aug, 1997.
19. *Ibid.*
20. Op.Cit., No. 2.
21. file:///C:/Documents%20and%20Settings/Home/Desktop/Gender%20equality %202.htm
22. file:///C:/Documents%20and%20Settings/Home/Desktop/Gender%20Equality. htm
23. R. C. Vermani, An Introduction to Political Theory & Thought, Gitanjali Publishing House, New Delhi, 2010, p. 412.
24. Op Cit., No. 1, p, 89.
25. file:///C:/Documents%20and%20Settings/Home/Desktop/Gender%20Equity% 20Issues%20in%20India.htm
26. Survey results are based on national samples except in China and India. Results for the survey in India represent roughly 61% of the adult population.
27. *Michael Remez, Senior Writer, Pew Research Center for the People & the Press,* January 4, 2013.

    file:///C:/Documents%20and%20Settings/Home/Desktop/Indians%20Support% 20Gender%20Equality%20But%20Still%20Give%20Men%20Edge%20in%2 0Workplace,%20Higher%20Education%20%20%20Pew%20Research%20Center% 27s%20Global%20Attitudes%20Project.htm

20

Rural Women Folks Unite for Gender Equality (A Case Study of '*Khabar Lahariya*')

— ***Neelu Sharma and Gopal Singh***

Abstract

Women are in need of information that will lead to economic empowerment. Governmental organisations have sought to find ways and means of empowering women in order to assist them to stand up for themselves and achieve economic, social and political independence. This story of women's activism in Chitrakoot seeks to weave together these disconnected strands of feminist conversations by engaging with 'questions of political consciousness and self-identity' which, according to Mohanty (Mohanty, Russo, & Torres, 1991) are crucial in defining 'third world women's engagement with feminism'.

'Bhawra tora pani gajab kar jaye gagri na phoote, chahe khasam mar jaye' *(Can't bear to lose my pitcher of water, even if my man dies) These lines (couplet) are often repeated to caution visitors when they first arrive in Chitrakoot. The picture of a region characterised by a harsh climate, barren land, vanishing forests, and acute water crisis is further complicated by a long tradition of bonded (indentured) labor, an almost ubiquitous presence of bandits and 'daduwas' (powerful men). Ranking near the very bottom of the national and state averages in income, sex-ratio (879 women per 1000 men) and literacy (66.52%), with raping, burning, and battering of women as everyday occurrences, Chitrakoot district is often described as a 'society driven by the rule of the gun'(Nagar, 2000). Evolution of* Khabar Lahariya *(Women lead rural weekly Bundeli Newspaper) is a ray of hope for the women's of this region. It is newspaper written, edited, illustrated, produced and marketed by rural women. It is an eight page weekly local language newspaper. With over 40 members,* Khabar Lahariya *team sells 6000 copies across 600 villages of Uttar Pradesh and Bihar to a readership of 80,000 per week(Lahariya D. K.). This newspaper made a big splash in Indian newspapers when it won the Media Foundation's prestigious 2004 Chameli Devi Award for the 'outstanding media persons'. This paper is based on case study method which examines how rural female journalists of* Khabar Lahariya *strategically use and create social spaces to generate collective dialogue and critical rejection on issues of patriarchy and gendered violence. A related aim is to highlight the ways in which female journalists working at the grass-roots level theorize the interrelationships among their own political actions, their vision(s) of empowerment, and the everyday gendered spaces they seek to transform. Through this paper, researcher explores how efficiently women can run newspaper and how they empower community and women. Problems like: discrimination, Patriarchal society, conservative mindset and problem of recognition, etc. The aim of the present paper entitles 'Rural Women Folks Unite For Gender Equality (a case study* of Khabar Lahariya*) is to provide an insight how these rural women and women of marginalised section successfully run a newspaper.*

"I think a newspaper should be provocative, stir'em up, but you can't do that on television. It's just not on" – **Rupert Murdoch**

Introduction

The struggle of female to achieve parity in the male dominating society is yet to be achieved in this running Century. Not only in India but also in the world, it is a major issue. Many research and project works are running to explore this problem. Media are considered as a greatest source to inform and to educate the masses for the purpose to eradicate the thought of gender discrimination within the mind of individuals. And it is visible that time to time media has raised the questions for women empowerment but when it comes to running a media house completely by women they lack resources funds and they face numerous.

Khabar Lahariya – Grassroots Media Revolution

Khabar Lahariya: Grassroots Media Revolution by Women

*Khabar Lahariya (*Women lead rural weekly Newspaper*)*- Bundeli for 'News Waves'---is a group of newspapers written, edited, illustrated, produced and marketed by rural women in Uttar Pradesh and Bihar. The first edition of *Khabar Lahariya* was launched in May 2002 in Chitrakoot district of Uttar Pradesh. Today, *Khabar Lahariya* has six editions in five local languages: Awadhi, Bundeli, Bajjika, Bhojpuri, and Hindustani. Its online edition at *www.khabarlahariya.in* contains a selection of news from different editions in all edition languages(ketto). This eight page weekly local language newspaper is being brought out by rural women journalist, with approximately 40 members, 6000 copies of *Khabar Lahariya*are being sold across 600 villages of Uttar Pradesh and Bihar to a readership of 80,000 per week. It is the only Bundeli newspaper in India and now has editions in Awadhi, Hindustani, Bhojpuri, and Bajjika. This newspaper connects with its rural audiences through their unique local language content which is rarely seen in printed form. A Delhi based NGO, Nirantar, a Centre for Gender and Education conceptualised *Khabar Lahariya*.

Table 20.1: Editions of Khabar Lahariya

Year	*Place*	*Edition*
2002	Chitrakoot, Uttar Pradesh	First Bundeli Edition
2006	Banda, Uttar Pradesh	Second Bundeli Edition
2010	Sitamarhi, Bihar	First Bajjika Edition
2012	Mahoba, Uttar Pradesh	Third Bundeli Edtion
2012	Lucknow, Faizabad and Ambedkar Nagar	Awadhi and Hindustani edition
2012	Varanasi, Uttar Pradesh	First Bhojpuri Edition
2013	—	Online Edition

Source: http://khabarlahariya.org/khabar-lahariya-is-the-only-bundeli-language-newspaper-published-in-india/

This newspaper *Khabar Lahariya*has originated from Bundelkhand region it's a place with high levels of poverty, low literacy rates, slanted sex ratio, high caste and gender based violence and poor health, sanitation, education and employment. In such kind of place *Khabar Lahariya* is the only space for women journalists.

'Its now a collective of 40 women from 2 states in North India which actually began with 6 women in 1 district,'

– Shalini Joshi,
Director and Team Leader, *Khabar Lahariya*

Khabar Lahariya is run by a collective of rural women journalists, most of them from marginalised communities- in terms of their caste, religion and ethnicity. Many are women who have has no or little access to formal education. This collective report, writes, edits, designs, takes photographs and illustrates for the newspaper and then distributes it far and wide and the end of the week. Like its reporters, *Khabar Lahariya*'s 80,000 readers are also those in media dark areas; daily wage earners, farmers, teachers, activists, Panchayat administration, politicians and students in remote rural areas(Lahariya H. K.).

'Khabar Lahariya is bridging the void where the access to information is scanty'

– Meera Jatav,
Editor, *Khabar Lahariya*

"Thriving under the constant fear of facing the dacoits I ensure that my readers are served with the news that matters."

– Suneeta,
Reporter, *Khabar Lahariya*

*Being a media watchdog Khabar Lahariya*empowers rural community by providing access to right information.Khabar lahariya also imparts skill education to rural women, as it promotes rural women to be the agents of news information creation and distribution.

What make *Khabar Lahariya* unique is not just their journalist- women from Dalit, tribal, Muslim and backward castes - but also its journalism. It's one of the local language newspaper available to readers in the three districts of Uttar Pradesh and Bihar where it is published, it covers local news that mainstream media often ignores. The distinctive voice and popularity of*Khabar Lahariya* comes from the fact that it reports on local issues with a perspective sensitive to structures of power - whether gender, class, caste or religion. As the only newspaper produced by women in districts where gender-development indices are among the poorest in the country, *Khabar Lahariya* reports on issues of violence against women with an astute understanding of gender and caste structures within which this violence is situated. News reports in*Khabar Lahariya* question structures of power and inequity in the personal sphere of the family, as well as in the public realm(Lahariya K.).

The *Khabar Lahariya* team goes through intensive training in all aspects of journalism: news gathering, writing, editing, designing, photography and the use of computers and the internet. "At first, I was afraid of computers, but now I am comfortable dealing with them" says Savita, *Khabar Lahariya journalist*. Since its launch in 2002, *Khabar Lahariya* has changed not just the landscape of media, but also the landscapes of gender, caste, access to information, accountability and democracy. By enabling women from the most marginalised communities to enter the well-guarded male preserve of the media, *Khabar Lahariya* has challenged caste and gender norms in one of India's most casteist and gender-bias regions. As these journalists have struggled for and attained identity, respect, recognition and a renewed sense of self, they have become role models for other women in their communities. In addition to ensuring women's presence as journalists, *Khabar Lahariya* also makes women's news a matter of public concern and brings gender issues centre-stage.

Changing their own lives

Many of the women feel that becoming a journalist has changed their own lives. They now have stronger self-esteem. For Rupali from Chitrakoot district, being a *Khabar Lahariya* journalist has helped to strengthen her self-confidence. "Earlier I used to be hesitant when gathering news. I couldn't speak with confidence when visiting government offices. I used to wonder how I was supposed to speak, what I should and shouldn't do. I used to constantly have a fear inside of me, but I don't have it anymore," says Rupali.

Another journalist, Sunita says, "It was only after I become a journalist that I was able to buy land. Earlier I did not have the belief that I could become a journalist because I am not that educated. Standing on my own two feet, I have done it."

Most feel that they now have the confidence to take charge of their destinies. "Since I started working with *Khabar Lahariya*, I make my own decisions about what I want to do and what's most important in my life," says another *Khabar Lahariya* journalist. In the same context Shanti quoted, "My main identity in every *zilla* (district council), every block and every police station is that of a *Khabar Lahariya* journalist."

Awards

- In 2004 *Khabar Lahariya* received the *Chameli Devi Jain Award* from the Media Foundation for outstanding media persons.
- Members of the group have also received fellowships from the Dalit Foundation, Inclusive Media Foundation and the National Foundation for India, for reporting on issues related to rights of the Dalit community, education and development(Nirantar).
- In 2009 Nirantar won the *UNESCO King Sejong Prize* for *Khabar Lahariya.* The King Sejong prize recognises Nirantar's role in setting up an initiative like *Khabar Lahariya*, as well as its "well-structured method of training newly literate women as journalists and democratizing information production, which provides an easily replicated model of transformative education"(parekh).
- The *Khabar Lahariya* team has also won the *Women's World Summit Foundation Prize for Creativity in Rural Life* (2009).*Khabar Lahariya* has been lauded as an exemplary model for transformative rural media by the Wharton Business School and a CII/KPMG report on ICT in India. The Hindu's comment on *Khabar Lahariya* recognises the important role that the newspaper plays in the Bundelkhand region. It wrote: 'In a region notorious for its feudal mindset, where remnants of erstwhile aristocracy still rule the roost, an eight-page weekly, *Khabar Lahariya* is a ray of hope. In 2013 the newspaper was presented the Kaifi Azmi Award (Ketto).

Some Comments from Readers Received through Interview Schedule

'Khabar Lahariya is my only link with the outside world'

– Raj Kumar Gupta,
a reader in Chitrakoot

'Sometimes when I read an issue related to women in Khabar Lahariya. I feel that the article is representing me and my world'.

– Sheela,
a grassroots activist in Banda, Uttar Pradesh

'Khabar Lahariya is different from all other newspapers. I look forward to receiving, it every time'.

– Moharrimad Haroon,
a journalist in Karvi, Uttar Pradesh.

'I feel that the writers don't impose their views on the readers in Khabar Lahariya. Instead they raise questions that make readers think on their own. Gender issues are dealt with sensitively in Khabar Lahariya. The issues address both female, as well as male readers of the Newspaper'.

– Daddu Prasad
- Politician

Research Problem

In India, media are known as fourth pillar of democracy. Media is a profession which is dominated by males, although globally there are many female journalists and even the scenario is changing in India too. This Research paper discusses and highlights the real situation of a village in India where how women folks despite low levels of literacy and without holding any degree in journalism became journalists.

Chitrakoot, the place where Lord Rama performed penance has a great historical significance. Unfortunately, the womenfolk of this region troubled with sexual and household atrocities face a difficult time. To combat against such situation, the local women used *Khabar Lahariya* as a tool. The research paper aims to find out how those women, despite less literacy and facilities are able to bring out the newspaper? How do they reach it to the masses and the government? It is proposed to hold dialogues with the readers, correspondents, reporters and local officers to find out that if bringing out a newspaper has made any change in the lifestyle of these women? And Has *Khabar Lahariya*becomes an instrument of change in the society?

Objectives

1. To study how these women, despite less literacy and facilities are able to bring out the newspaper.
2. To study how *Khabar Lahariya* became an instrument of change for the marginalised sections of the society including women.

Research Questions

RQ1: Does newspaper like *Khabar Lahariya* benefits society in any manner?

RQ2: Does *Khabar Lahariya* helps in eliminating social evils?

RQ3: Is *Khabar Lahariya* working towards bringing a change in the society?

RQ4: Is *Khabar Lahariya* working towards bringing a change in the society?

RQ5: What problems are faced by you while collecting news for *Khabar Lehariya*?

RQ6: The newspaper is concerned with societal issues. As such does the male dominant society become an obstacle in your endeavor to collect news matter?

RQ7: What kinds of problems are faced by you while collecting news in a male dominant society?

RQ8: Has *Khabar Lahariya* brought out any change in the patriarchal set-up of the society?

Method

This paper is based on Case Study Method.In this paper descriptive study of *Khabar Lahariya* institution is been done. Origin of *Khabar Lahariya*, why it is different from other newspapers and how it enlightens women and rural communities are the factors which are being described in this paper.

Researcher selected two methods of data collection, Census method and sampling.Census method is used to collect data from reporters and founder members of *Khabar Lahariya*. Questionnaire is being used as a tool for data collection from reporters of *Khabar Lahariya*and Interview is being used as a tool for data collection with founder members of *Khabar Lahariya*. Purposive sampling is done amongst readers of *Khabar Lahariya* and interview schedule is being used as a tool for data collection with readers of *Khabar Lahariya*newspaper. Sample size of readers is 100.The data was taken during March, 2014 to April, 2014.

Results

The case study of the institution *Khabar Lahariya* for two months (March, 2014 to April, 2014) was done by the researcher and such results are obtained:

RQ1-Does newspaper like *Khabar Lahariya* benefits society in any manner?

In the survey it is been found out that 96% of the respondents said 'yes' newspaper like '*Khabar Lahariya*' provides benefit to the society whereas 4% of the respondents said 'no' it does not benefit society in any manner.

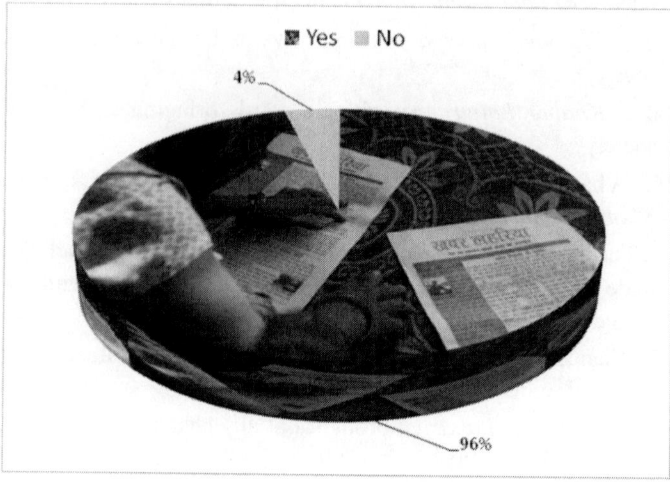

Figure 20.1: Percentage of benefits provided by Khabar Lahariya tosociety

RQ2-Does *Khabar Lahariya* helps in eliminating social evils?

Khabar Lahariya not only imparts news but it also helps in eliminating social evils of the society. In the survey 80% of the respondents said 'yes' *Khabar Lahariya* helps in eliminating the social evils of the society, whereas 11% of the respondents said 'no' *Khabar Lahariya* does not helps in eliminating social evils of society and 9% of the respondents said that they 'cannot say' anything about it.

Figure 20.2: Percentage of role of Khabar Lahariya in eliminating social evils.

RQ3-Is *Khabar Lahariya* working towards bringing a change in the society?

Ninety six percent of the respondents said 'yes', *Khabar Lahariya* is working towards bringing a change in the society whereas in the survey 4% of the respondents said they 'cannot say' anything about the role of *Khabar Lahariya* in bringing a change in the society.

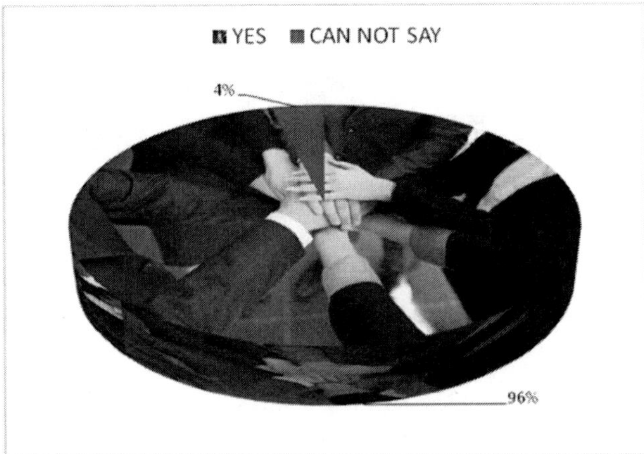

Figure 20.3: Percentage of change brought by newspaper in the society.

RQ4-Does *Khabar Lahariya* in any way help in making illiterates and women of the weaker section of society empowered?

Khabar Lahariya is a newspaper which is totally being run by females in the survey 91% of the respondents said that, 'yes' *Khabar Lahariya* in helps in making illiterates and women of the weaker Section of society empowered, whereas 5% of the respondents are of opinion that 'no' *Khabar Lahariya* does not helps in making illiterates and women of the weaker Section of society empowered and 4% of respondents do 'cannot say' anything about it.

RQ5- What problems are faced by you (Reporters) while collecting news for *Khabar Lahariya*?

Khabar Lahariya Journalists face a lot of problem while collecting news for *Khabar Lahariya*, 30% of the respondents said 'conservative Society' is a problem for gathering news, followed by another 30% who said 'administration does not cooperates' whereas 20% of the respondents said the problem which they face while collecting news is 'people don't up easily' and 20% of the respondents face the 'problem of recognition' while collecting news for *Khabar Lahariya*.

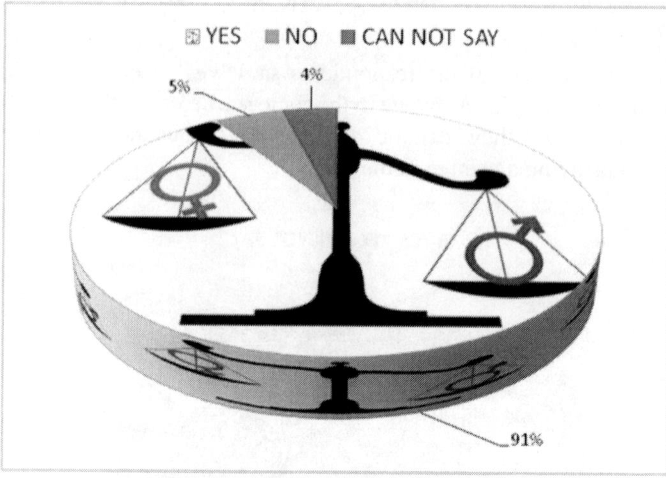

Figure 20.4: Percentage of how Khabar Lahariya is making society empowered.

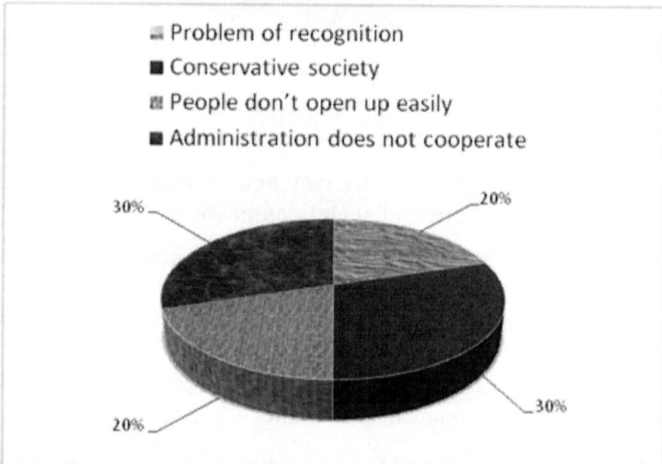

Figure 20.5: Percentage of problems faced by Khabar Lahariya Reporters

RQ6- The newspaper is concerned with societal issues. As such does the male dominant society become an obstacle in your endeavor to collect news matter?

The newspaper is concerned with societal issues. As such does the male dominant society become an obstacle in reporters endeavor to collect news matter, 90% of the respondents said 'yes' where as 10% of the respondents said 'no' the male dominant society does not become an obstacle in reporters endeavor to collect news matter.

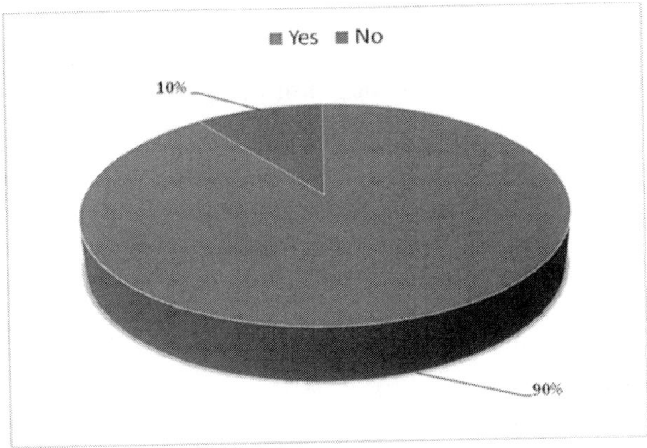

Figure 20.6: Percentage of obstacles faced by Reporters in their endeavor to news collection.

RQ7- What kinds of problems are faced by you while collecting news in a male dominant society?

Journalists of *Khabar Lahariya* face a lot of problems while collecting news in a male dominant society as 50% of the respondents said 'Males ogle and lewd comments' followed by 20%who said 'apathetic administration' is a problem in gathering news whereas another 20% of the respondents said they

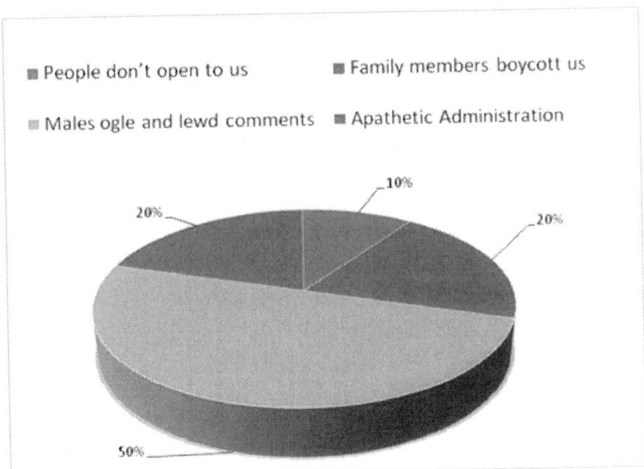

Figure 20.7: Percentage of problems faced by Khabar Lahariya Reporters in a male dominant society.

face a kind of problem in male dominant society where 'family members boycott us' because male members of the family has asked them to do so, and 10% of the respondents said the problem which they face while collecting news is 'people don't up easily'.

RQ8-Has *Khabar Lahariya* brought out any change in the patriarchal set-up of the society?

In the survey 80% of the respondents said 'yes' *Khabar Lahariya* has brought out change in the patriarchal set-up of the society followed by 20% who said 'no' *Khabar Lahariya* has not brought out change in the patriarchal set-up of the society.

Figure 20.8: Percentage of change Khabar Lahariya has brought in the patriarchal set up.

Conclusion

The present study found that the rural folks of *Khabar Lahariya* are running a newspaper successfully despite low levels of literacy and without having any degree in journalism.It is also found in the study that majority of readers feel that *Khabar Lahariya* benefits the society by bringing forth social evils before the society and by eliminating those evils. It is observed from the study that *Khabar Lahariya* in any way helps in making illiterates and women of the weaker section of the society empowered by creating awareness, spreading education and by arousing feeling of being independent among its readers. Majority of reporters said that the problems which they face while collecting news in male dominant society are male ogle & lewd comments, apathetic administration and conservative society. These rural women have taken special training to be a *Khabar Lahariya* journalist.The researcher concludes that*Khabar Lahariya* is enlightening rural communities and women. Rural women folks unite for gender equality using *Khabar Lahariya* as an instrument for change and it was found that a newspaper that has just entered into its teens has certainly made an impact in the patriarchal set up of the society.

References

Lahariya, D. K. (n.d.). *www.khabarlahariya.org*. Retrieved January 25, 2014, from Khabar Lahariya: http://khabarlahariya.org/khabar-lahariya-is-the-only-bundeli-language-newspaper-published-in-india/

ketto, d. (n.d.). *www.ketto.org*. Retrieved January 25, 2014, from ketto: https://www.ketto.org/campaign/campaign_details.php?fmd_id=170

Lahariya, H. K. (n.d.). *www.Khabarlahariya.org*. Retrieved january 25, 2015, from Khabar Lahariya: http://khabarlahariya.org/khabar-lahariya-is-the-only-bundeli-language-newspaper-published-in-india/

Lahariya, K. (n.d.). *www.khabarlahariya.org*. Retrieved february 2, 2014, from khabar lahariya: http://khabarlahariya.org/about-us-%E0%A4%B9%E0%A4%AE%E0%A4%BE%E0%A4%B0%E0%A5%87-%E0%A4%AC%E0%A4%BE%E0%A4%B0%E0%A5%87-%E0%A4%AE%E0%A5%87%E0%A4%82/

Nirantar. (n.d.). *www.nirantar.net*. Retrieved february 5, 2014, from dph: http://base.d-p-h.info/en/fiches/dph/fiche-dph-8901.html

parekh, j. (n.d.). *the better india*. Retrieved february 7, 2014, from www.thebetterindia.com: https://www.thebetterindia.com/882/khabar-lahariya-a-weekly-newspaper-in-bundeli/

Ketto. (n.d.). *Ketto*. Retrieved january 25, 2014, from www.ketto.org: https://www.ketto.org/campaign/campaign_details.php?fmd_id=170

IANS. (n.d.). *Business Standard*. Retrieved january 25, 2014, from www.business-standard.com: http://www.business-standard.com/article/news-ians/khabar-lahariya-making-rural-media-a-force-for-change-media-feature-114030200350_1.html

Mohanty, C. T., Russo, A., & Torres, L. (1991). *Third World women and the politics of feminism*. Bloomington : Indiana University Press.

Nagar, R. (2000). Mujhe Jawab Do! (Answer Me!): Women's grass-roots activism and social spaces in Chitrakoot (India). *Gender,Placeand Culture* .

Bibliography

Lahariya, D. K. (n.d.). *www.khabarlahariya.org*. Retrieved January 25, 2014, from Khabar Lahariya: http://khabarlahariya.org/khabar-lahariya-is-the-only-bundeli-language-newspaper-published-in-india/

ketto, d. (n.d.). *www.ketto.org*. Retrieved January 25, 2014, from ketto: https://www.ketto.org/campaign/campaign_details.php?fmd_id=170

Lahariya, H. K. (n.d.). *www.Khabarlahariya.org*. Retrieved january 25, 2015, from Khabar Lahariya: http://khabarlahariya.org/khabar-lahariya-is-the-only-bundeli-language-newspaper-published-in-india/

Lahariya, K. (n.d.). *www.khabarlahariya.org*. Retrieved february 2, 2014, from khabar lahariya: http://khabarlahariya.org/about-us-%E0%A4%B9%E0%A4%AE%E0%A4%BE%E0%A4%B0%E0%A5%87-%E0%A4%AC%E0%A4%BE%E0%A4%B0%E0%A5%87-%E0%A4%AE%E0%A5%87%E0%A4%82/

Nirantar. (n.d.). *www.nirantar.net*. Retrieved february 5, 2014, from dph: http://base.d-p-h.info/en/fiches/dph/fiche-dph-8901.html

parekh, j. (n.d.). *the better india*. Retrieved february 7, 2014, from www.thebetterindia.com: https://www.thebetterindia.com/882/khabar-lahariya-a-weekly-newspaper-in-bundeli/

Ketto. (n.d.). *Ketto*. Retrieved january 25, 2014, from www.ketto.org: https://www.ketto.org/campaign/campaign_details.php?fmd_id=170

IANS. (n.d.). *Business Standard*. Retrieved january 25, 2014, from www.business-standard.com: http://www.business-standard.com/article/news-ians/khabar-lahariya-making-rural-media-a-force-for-change-media-feature-114030200350_1.html

Mohanty, C. T., Russo, A., & Torres, L. (1991). *Third World women and the politics of feminism.* Bloomington : Indiana University Press.

Nagar, R. (2000). Mujhe Jawab Do! (Answer Me!): Women's grass-roots activism and social spaces in Chitrakoot (India). *Gender,Placeand Culture* .

Index

D

N

O